Damages for Personal Injury and Death

Seventh Edition

By David Kemp,
one of Her Majesty's counsel,
a Bencher of the Inner Temple

Assisted by Peter Mantle
Barrister of the Inner Temple

LUX GENTIUM LEX

Sweet & Maxwell

First edition published by Longman Group UK Ltd 1980
Seventh edition published in 1999 by
Sweet & Maxwell Limited of
100 Avenue Road
London NW3 3PF

Printed by Bell and Bain Ltd., Glasgow

A CIP catalogue record for this book
is available from the British Library

ISBN 075200 4433

Contents

Acknowledgements

This edition includes material from *Kemp & Kemp on the Quantum of Damages*.

"Actuarial Assessment of Damages" by J H Prevett (Chapter 7) includes material from an article by the same author that originally appeared in 35 M.L.R. 140, 257, and we are grateful to the *Modern Law Review* for permission to refer to and reproduce this material.

Extracts from the Rules of the Supreme Court and the County Court Rules are reproduced in Appendices C and D respectively by kind permission of the Controller of Her Majesty's Stationery Office.

Preface to Seventh Edition

Since the last edition, there have been two very important developments in the law. In July this year in *Wells v. Wells* and Associated Appeals [1998] 1 W.L.R. 329 the House of Lords laid down new "Guidelines" for the discount rate to be used when calculating future pecuniary loss. The discount rate is to be 3 per cent per annum, unless and until the Lord Chancellor prescribes a different rate pursuant to Section 1(1) of the Damages Act 1996. Such rate is based on the net rate of return after tax from investment in appropriate Index-Linked Government Stock ("ILGS") The Judicial Committee held that investment in ILGS is a prudent and practical course for injured plaintiffs to adopt, and that it is wrong to impose on them the risk of investing in equities. The extent of that risk is illustrated by the recent collapse of equities, world wide. The new "Guidelines" will result in a significant increase in awards for future pecuniary loss, especially when the loss will extend over a long period. The second important development was the Judicial Committee's approval of acturial evidence in general and the Ogden Tables in particular: *per* Lord Lloyd of Berwick: *ibid*. p. 347D:

> "The tables should now be regarded as the starting point rather than a check. A judge should be slow to depart from the relevant actuarial multiplier on impressionistic grounds, or by reference to 'a spread of multipliers in comparable cases' especially where the multipliers were fixed before actuarial tables were widely used."

The Judicial Committee also decided that a 3 per cent interest rate should be adopted pursuant to *Roberts v. Johnstone*, when assessing damages for the cost of acquiring accommodation suited to a plaintiff's needs. By like reasoning, althought the matter was not in issue before the Judicial Committee, 3 per cent should be the rate of interest awarded on general damages for pain and suffering and loss of amenities. A further important decision was that no discount should be made from the appropriate acturarial multiplier, when assessing the cost of whole-life future care. As this edition was already in page proofs when *Wells* was decided, appropriate amendments had to be made to the existing text, which has resulted in a certain amount of repetition.

We have continued to expand and update this work, in the belief that this edition will now provide a concise and comprehensive introduction to, and account of, the principles and practice applicable to the assessment of damages in personal injury litigation. We have included in Appendix A the full judgment of Rose J. (as he then was) in *Cassel*'s case, to illustrate how the court deals with the assessment of damages in a case of serious disability. We do not attempt in the space available to include awards for various types of injury: other works exist for this purpose. We have, however, included in Chapter 3 some extracts from the revised "Guidelines" issued by the Judicial Studies Board to give a rough idea of the general level of awards currently made for non-pecuniary loss. Readers requiring more detailed knowledge are referred to *Kemp & Kemp on the Quantum of Damages*. Appendices B, C, and D provide a comprehensive summary of statutory material relevant to personal injury litigation. Appendix E contains information needed to ascertain the value of earlier awards in terms of the present "money of the day", to use Lord Diplock's phrase in *Wright*'s case.

So far as more experienced practitioners are concerned, we shall be content if this edition fulfils the prophecy made by a kind reviewer of the first edition that this work that would "become a useful *vade-mecum*" for practitioners".

David Kemp
September 30, 1998.

Table of Cases

All references are to paragraph numbers.

Table of Statutes

All references are to paragraph numbers.

Table of Statutory Instruments

All references are to paragraph numbers.

Table of Rules of Supreme Court

All references are to paragraph numbers.

Table of County Court Rules

All references are to paragraph numbers.

Chapter 1

Pre-Trial Considerations

Peter Mantle, *Barrister*

Contents *Para*

ESTABLISHING LIABILITY

1.1 The emphasis of this work is on quantum but even the biggest case will fail at trial if the plaintiff cannot establish the defendant's liability. In considering pre-litigation inquiries, therefore, a few points about liability and contributory negligence should be remembered. These points generally apply equally whether the action is brought in the High Court or county court.

Oral evidence

1.2 The first point is of general importance to both liability and quantum: namely, that the basic rule relating to evidence contained in RSC, Ord. 38, r.1 (see Appendix C) and CCR, Ord. 20, r.4 provides that questions of fact should be proved at the hearing of any action begun by writ or of any action in a county court by the examination of witnesses orally in open court. Although the Civil Evidence Act 1995 abolishes the rule against hearsay evidence, the best way of proving anything that the other side will not agree to remains to be prepared to call the witness to give evidence about it at trial. Remember that a *subpoena* in the High Court, once issued, is valid only for 12 weeks and must be served not less than four days before the day on which the witness is required to attend before the court unless the court fixes a shorter period. More than one witness can be named in a *subpoena ad test.* but not in a *subpoena duces tecum*. Under section 36 of the Supreme Court Act 1981 a *subpoena* can be issued for service on a witness anywhere in the UK, but the court must give leave to issue a *subpoena* for service in Scotland or Northern Ireland. County court witness summonses can name only one witness, should be applied for not less than seven days before attendance is required and must also be served not less than four days before the day on which the witness is required to attend before the court unless the court otherwise directs.

Now that both the High Court and county courts require exchange of written statements of oral evidence and may direct that any statement stand as the evidence in chief of the witness, particular attention needs to be given to the preparation of witness statements. Accuracy and comprehensiveness are paramount. Witness statements should, so far as possible, be expressed in the witness's own words although there has been judicial comment that what a court needs is as accurate a reproduction of the substance of what the witness has told his solicitor as possible, written comprehensibly, be as concise as the circumstances of the case allow, omitting irrelevant and inadmissible material, simply covering those issues on which the party serving the statement wishes that witness to give evidence in chief. Where a party is unable to obtain a written statement from an intended witness it is good practice to identify the witness and provide a statement of the nature of the evidence intended to be adduced.

Hearsay

1.3 The Civil Evidence Act 1995 (see Appendix B) has fundamentally altered the rules concerning the admissibility of evidence in civil proceedings, including actions for personal injury. The Act provides that evidence shall not be excluded on the ground that it is hearsay and creates provisions on the procedures for adducing hearsay evidence. The High Court and County Court rules relating to the reception of such evidence have also been revised. Hearsay of whatever degree is no longer excluded in cases to which the Act applies. As well as hearsay evidence of fact, hearsay evidence of opinion from expert witnesses is admissible.

Although there is now no obstacle to the receipt of hearsay evidence, such evidence is unlikely to carry the same weight as oral evidence from a witness with personal knowledge of relevant facts. Courts when estimating the weight, if any, to be given to hearsay evidence will have regard to all circumstances from which any inference can reasonably be drawn as to its reliability. The 1995 Act sets out at s. 4 various factors to be taken into account in assessing weight, including, in particular, whether it would have been reasonable and practicable to have produced the maker of the original statement as a witness. Where a witness has died, is unfit to give oral evidence or has disappeared and cannot reasonably be traced, or there is some other substantial reason preventing or militating against the attendance of a particular witness at trial, hearsay evidence is likely to carry greater weight. So too where the original statement was made contemporaneously with relevant events and where no multiple hearsay is involved.

1.4 A party proposing to adduce hearsay evidence must serve a hearsay notice giving particulars of the evidence. A single notice may deal with the evidence of more than one witness. Hearsay notices applying to witness statements should be served at the same time as the witness statement. Otherwise hearsay notices should generally be served, in the High Court, within 28 days after a case is set down for trial and, in county courts, not less than 28 days before the day fixed for hearing, unless specific directions provide otherwise (see RSC, Ord. 38, r.20 and CCR, Ord. 20 r.15). Where a party tenders a hearsay statement but does not propose to call the maker, the other party can, within 28 days of receiving the hearsay notice, apply to call the maker to cross-examine him. Notice should likewise be given by a party who wishes to attack the credibility of the maker of a hearsay statement who is not to be called. Statements in documents which are admissible in evidence can be proved by producing either the original document or a copy.

Recourse to hearsay evidence may be obvious and necessary, for example to put in a statement from a witness to a road traffic accident who has died, or a medical report from a doctor who examined a plaintiff at a vital stage and cannot be called for some reason. Hearsay statements relevant to quantum can be adduced, such as statements from a deceased employer. Where facts relevant to quantum cannot be agreed it will usually remain preferable to call a live witness, and additional costs incurred by unreasonable refusals to make admissions are likely to be visited with adverse costs orders. However, now technical objections to the admissibility of hearsay evidence cannot be raised, there may be circumstances in which it will be proper and acceptable for plaintiffs to rely on hearsay evidence as to matters which cannot seriously disputed such as pre and post accident earnings, particularly in claims of low value. Where a witness is unable to attend trial due to illness it is advisable to obtain and serve on other parties a medical certificate or other suitable evidence of incapacity.

1.5 Whilst the Civil Evidence Act 1995 applies generally to civil proceedings, the Court of Appeal has held that the provisions of that Act only apply to actions commenced on or after January 31, 1997 when the majority of the Act came into force (see *Bairstow v. Queen's Moat Houses Plc* [1997] T.L.R. 520). Thus whilst practitioners will mainly and increasingly be concerned with litigation to which the 1995 Act applies, when dealing with cases commenced before January 31, 1997 it must be borne in mind that hearsay evidence is only admissible pursuant to the Civil Evidence Act 1968 or, in the case of expert opinion evidence, the Civil Evidence Act 1972. Practitioners should still refer to the 1968 Act and, it would appear, to the former rules of court, which governed the giving of notices and other procedures relevant to hearsay evidence under the 1968 Act, before the new rules relevant to the 1995 Act were substituted, when dealing with such cases. The extent of hearsay evidence admissible under the 1968 Act was much more limited than that now admissible, generally limited to first-hand hearsay and statements contained in certain records. Nevertheless, in older cases the ability to put in hearsay evidence contained in witness statements or other documents at trial if a party cannot call the witness may prove of considerable value, particularly where a witness has died, is beyond the seas, unfit by reason of bodily or mental condition to attend as a witness, or where, despite the exercise of reasonable diligence, it has not been possible to identify or find him or he cannot reasonably be expected to have any recollection of matters relevant to the accuracy or otherwise of the statement, specific reasons which entitled a party to adduce hearsay evidence under the 1968 Act. Where the courts retain a discretion as to the admission of hearsay evidence under the 1968 Act, authorities decided under that Act doubtless remain relevant. Given the new regime instituted by the 1995 Act, it may be anticipated that judges will be more readily prepared to admit hearsay evidence, but no doubt will be cautious as to the weight to be given to such evidence.

1.6 Ogden Tables, the actuarial tables for use in personal injury and fatal accident cases issued by the Government Actuary's Department, are generally accepted by the court. Indeed, the draft of the third edition was accepted and acted upon by the House of Lords in *Wells v. Wells* [1998] 1 W.L.R. 329. The tables will be formally admissible when section 10 of the Civil Evidence Act 1995 is brought into force. This will probably have happened by the time this edition is published.

Expert evidence in road traffic accident and other injury cases

1.7 In *Liddell v. Middleton* [1996] P.I.Q.R. P.36, the Court of Appeal expressed the view that there had been a regrettable tendency in personal injury cases, both road traffic and industrial accidents, for parties to enlist the services of experts whether they are necessary or not. Advisers should now be particularly careful to take a critical view as to what, if anything, expert evidence can add to the case. There may be cases where by examination of the scene or running tests on machinery an expert can give telling evidence, but in road traffic accidents non-medical experts must be seen as the exception not the rule. Expert evidence based solely on eyewitness accounts is likely to be held inadmissible.

Plans, photographs and police reports

1.8 Plans and photographs are indispensable in many personal injury cases and are best prepared at an early stage. RSC, Ord. 25, r.8(1)(d) (with which CCR, Ord. 17, r.11 (3)(c) corresponds) deals with plans and photographs in personal injury actions (with the exception of Admiralty actions and most significantly medical negligence actions in the High Court). Photographs, a sketch plan and any police accident report book are receivable in evidence at trial. The parties should attempt to agree them in advance. If the parties agree the reports, plans and photographs no problem arises. However, if either party specifically does not agree them the party wishing to rely on them must prove them by calling the maker or serving a hearsay notice (see *McSorley v. Woodall* [1995] P.I.Q.R. P. 187, C.A.). It is only if the parties neither specifically agree nor disagree that Ord. 25, r.8(1)(d) renders evidence admissible without calling the maker. In practice the onus is on the plaintiff to obtain the police report and it should be borne in mind that the police destroy such reports as a matter of course after a relatively short period.

1.9 High Court medical negligence actions are governed by Ord. 38, r.5 which requires the party intending to produce plans, photographs or models at trial to give the other side the opportunity to inspect them at least ten days before the hearing unless the court for "special reasons" orders otherwise.

Video evidence

1.10 If a party wishes to adduce video evidence, for example video film of a plaintiff taken after the accident in question, the other parties must be given an opportunity to inspect it at least ten days before trial (RSC, Ord. 38, r.5). Whilst the court may order that the video recording should be admissible in evidence even if the opportunity to inspect beforehand has been denied and may do so at trial, it can only do so for special reasons and is only likely to do so in very rare circumstances. In *Khan v. Armguard* [1994] P.I.Q.R. P. 286, the Court of Appeal, recognising that the practice of "cards on the table" has developed very considerably in the Queen's Bench Division, held that even where video evidence is alleged to support malingering and lack of *bonafides*, disclosure of video evidence should normally be ordered. If a defendant wishes to withhold video evidence it is clearly unsafe simply to wait to seek permission to adduce the evidence at trial and an application should be made pursuant to Ord. 38, r.5 at an early stage. Whilst there is no direct equivalent of RSC, Ord. 38, r.5 in the county court rules it can be anticipated that county courts will also require prior production and inspection (see *Crompton v. Lancashire County Council* (1994) *The Times*, 24 November). Where a party seeks to rely on video evidence, an unedited version of the video tape should be disclosed (*Hadler v. Cape Boards* June 30, 1996, unreported, Wandsworth County Court).

Convictions

1.11 Under section 11 of the Civil Evidence Act 1968 (see Appendix B) parties can plead convictions against one another if they are relevant to issues in the civil proceedings. Obvious examples are convictions for driving offences, for defective vehicles under relevant statutory instruments and in prosecutions by H.M. factory inspectors. For an example of a "successful ambush" after an *ex parte* order had been obtained permitting non-disclosure see *Birch v. Hales Containers Ltd* [1996] P.I.Q.R. P. 307, C.A. The fact of the conviction can be proved just by putting in the certificate from the convicting court. As to the certificate generally, see section 18 of the Prevention of Crimes Act 1871. and section 73 of the Police and Criminal Evidence Act 1984.

1.12 There are special rules of pleading in RSC, Ord. 18, r.7A (see Appendix C) that must be observed: the party who is facing a pleaded conviction cannot simply traverse his opponent's pleading otherwise he runs the risk of having his own pleading struck out. He must either deny the fact of the conviction or admit it, and, if he wants to, allege that it was erroneous or irrelevant. If the defendant states he was wrongly convicted, he puts that fact in issue in the civil proceedings. The plaintiff should then consider putting in the notes of evidence from the magistrates' court (or the Crown Court) with a hearsay notice to establish whether the defendant will seek to call witnesses from the criminal court to give evidence in the civil trial. It is important to remember that the effect of pleading a conviction is to transfer the legal as well as the evidential burden on to the convicted party (*Stupple v. Royal Insurance* Co. [1971] 1 Q.B. 50). Where the defendant alleges that his conviction is irrelevant to the issues in the civil trial, which is the usual line counsel takes, the plaintiff will have to prove its relevance. This may mean having to call some or all of the witnesses from the magistrates' court or Crown Court A defendant who pleads that he was erroneously convicted is putting up a positive case and can be asked for particulars. A defendant who admits his conviction but denies its relevance is probably also putting up a positive case and not just relying on a denial of which particulars would not normally be ordered.

In most cases the defendant will be hard put to give convincing particulars and the results of failure to do so, in different circumstances, are vividly illustrated in *Butcher v. Dowlen* [1981] R.T.R. 24.

1.13 If the judge is undecided on the other evidence after he has heard both sides then the conviction is conclusive, but the judge is not precluded from making a finding of contributory negligence against the plaintiff or accepting (in an appropriate case) a defence of *volenti non fit injuria* (*Murphy v. Culhane* [1976] 3 All E.R. 533).

Contributory negligence

1.14 The definition of "contributory negligence" in section 1(1) of the Law Reform (Contributory Negligence) Act 1945 (see Appendix B) refers to "the claimant's share in the responsibility for the damage" (*not* the responsibility for the cause of the damage). This has been highlighted in decisions in road traffic cases where the plaintiffs' damages have been reduced, even though they in no way caused or contributed to the accidents in which they were injured. These are the seat belt cases.

Seat belts

1.15 In every case the onus lies on the defendant to prove that the plaintiff should have been wearing a seat belt and that his injuries would have been avoided or less severe if he had been. This task will be easier if the plaintiff has been convicted of an offence under the Motor Vehicles (Wearing of Seat Belts) Regulations 1982 or the 1991 Regulations making the wearing of seat belts in rear seats by adults compulsory because that conviction will throw the onus on to the plaintiff who will have to show it was erroneous or irrelevant to discharge it. The defendant will still, of course, have to prove that wearing a seat belt would have avoided or reduced the plaintiff's injuries. A good example of this was *Owens v. Brimmell* [1977] Q.B. 859 where the plaintiff sustained catastrophic brain injury. The court accepted that the plaintiff's injury could have been caused by a brain shake without any actual blow to the head. No reduction in damages was made for the plaintiff's failure to wear a seat belt even though he was found after the collision hanging out of the defendant's car and had suffered a severe blow to the head

1.16 Whether there should be a reduction for contributory negligence and the amount of such reduction is a question of fact to be decided in the circumstances of the particular case. The Court of Appeal laid down some rough guidelines in *Froom v. Butcher* [1976] Q.B. 286 when it decided that the defendant who succeeded in establishing that a plaintiff's injuries could have been avoided by wearing a seat belt would have the benefit of a 25 per cent reduction in the plaintiff's damages, even though the plaintiff was otherwise an innocent party. If the injuries would only have been lessened by wearing a seat belt the damages may be reduced by 15 per cent. The decision in *From v. Butcher* was based on "the duty of every driver of a vehicle and every front-seat passenger to take reasonable precautions for his own safety by wearing a seat belt at all times". That it is now compulsory to do so does not seem to increase that duty and, correspondingly, the plaintiff's share in the responsibility for the damage he suffers. However, it seems that the court will not now have to judge whether the plaintiff has taken "reasonable precautions". The exceptions to the regulations are very limited and the question of whether it is medically inadvisable to wear a seat belt, considered in *Froom v. Butcher*, for obese or pregnant plaintiffs, or in *Mackay v. Borthwick* [1982] C.L.Y. 2157 where the plaintiff suffered from a hiatus hernia, is probably pre-empted by para. 5(d) of the regulations. This requires a certificate of exemption signed by a registered medical practitioner, to avoid conviction for not wearing a seat belt otherwise made compulsory by the Regulations.

1.17 In *Roberts v. Sparks* [1977] C.L.Y. 2643, where the plaintiff was thrown out of the defendant's vehicle, the court reduced his damages by 25 per cent because the injuries he suffered would clearly have been avoided by wearing a seat belt; but it added back 5 per cent for the injuries he would have suffered if he had been wearing a seat belt. This point was developed in *Traynor v. Donovan* [1978] C.L.Y. 2612, where the court refused to make any reduction because the plaintiff's injuries would have been just as severe, but of a different nature, if she had been wearing a seat belt. The argument that the court should take account of the fact that the wearing of a seat belt would have caused other injuries of a different nature was rejected as a matter of principle in *Patience v. Andrews* [1983] R.T.R. 447: it is respectfully submitted that this decision is wrong and does not give effect to the provision in section 1 of the Law Reform (Contributory Negligence) Act 1945, that damages should be reduced to such extent as the court thinks just and equitable. It is surely not just and equitable to reduce the damages if the court is satisfied that as severe, or more severe, damage would have been caused if a seat belt had been worn. The decision in *Traynor v. Donovan* [1978] C.L.Y. 2612 is to be preferred.

1.18 The common point about such cases is of course that expert evidence can be called to dispute the allegations about seat belts, and that must always be borne in mind in these cases. Sometimes the expert evidence is given by a medical witness; more often, an expert motor engineer who has studied the effect of crashes on bodies in a car would be a more appropriate witness. If a medical expert is asked to deal with both injuries and seat belts he should be asked to do so in separate reports.

Drink and driving cases

1.19 The leading case where drink is alleged to be a contributory factor is *Owens v. Brimmell* [1977] Q.B. 859. There the plaintiff passenger's damages were reduced by 20 per cent because he had been out drinking with the defendant driver and a lot of beer had been consumed by both the plaintiff and the defendant. The plaintiff's share of the responsibility for the damage he had suffered in the accident arose out of the finding that either he ought to have known that the defendant's ability to drive was impaired or, more likely, that he had drunk so much himself that he was unable to tell that the defendant's ability was in fact impaired. But the latter is not an automatic finding, however high the blood-alcohol level might be, as was demonstrated by *Traynor v. Donovan* [1978] C.L.Y. 2612. There the court accepted forensic evidence called by the plaintiff that, while a blood-alcohol level of 168 milligrams represented an excessive intake of alcohol, it would not necessarily produce symptoms apparent to a lay person, such as the plaintiff, who had met the defendant in a pub only half an hour before the accident. No reduction was made in that case. There was a similar result in *Campbell (decd) v. Jelley* [1984] C.L.Y. 2296 where the defendant and his passenger drank six pints of beer each in one another's company at lunchtime and two further pints each after the defendant had collected his passenger at 9.30 p.m. that day. The passenger was killed when the defendant's car hit an unlit lorry. The court accepted both the widow's evidence and expert evidence that the defendant's demeanour would have appeared reasonably sober despite an alcohol level of 131 milligrams. The passenger had not been negligent in accepting a lift. In *Donelan v. Donelan* [1993] P.I.Q.R. P. 205, the plaintiff and defendant drank a great deal of alcohol together over a long period. The plaintiff who was older and dominant in every way was the cause of the defendant driving when intoxicated in that she only drove at his instigation. The plaintiff's contributory negligence was assessed at 75 per cent. In *Brignall v. Kelly* (unreported May 17, 1994) the Court of Appeal upheld the trial judge's decision to reject expert evidence as to likely appearance of drunkenness based on back-calculation from a blood sample in favour of lay witnesses' evidence that the defendant had been behaving normally. No finding of contributory negligence was made.

1.20 It is not yet clear how courts would treat the combined effects of, say, negligent driving and failing to wear a seat belt. It seems likely from *Gregory v. Kelly* [1978] R.T.R. 426 that they will simply take a global figure, and not aggregate separate percentages for each type of contributory negligence.

1.21 In *Gregory's* case the plaintiff, who was injured in a way that could have been avoided by wearing a seat belt, suffered a 40 per cent total reduction since he was also travelling as a passenger in a car knowing that it had defective brakes. In conclusion, one must remember that in all cases of contributory negligence the burden of proof lies on the party alleging it. Defendants should always plead allegations of contributory negligence (*Fookes v. Slaytor* [1978] 1 W.L.R. 1293).

Latent defects

1.22 Finally on establishing liability, one should bear in mind the need for experts in cases involving latent defects and inexplicable accidents. The balance might well be tipped by forensic evidence. In personal injury cases the damage caused is usually all too painfully obvious even though its cause was a negligent act or omission many years before; and time usually runs from the injury and not from the act or omission causing it. For instance, a workman may be injured by a chip of metal flying off a hammer which had been negligently manufactured a long time before. Time runs from the date of the injury not from the date of the negligent manufacture. Where the damage is insidious and not discovered until later, eg industrial disease, the provisions of section 14 of the Limitation Act 1980 which define "knowledge" may delay the running of limitation even further, until the plaintiff knows not only that he is ill but also the likely cause. See also *Leadbitter v. Hodge Finance Ltd* [1982] 2 All E.R. 167 at para. 1.60 below.

1.23 In latent defect cases the onus of proof is on the party setting up the defect as a defence (see *Henderson v. Henry E. Jenkins & Sons and Evans* [1970] A.C. 282, but also *Ng Chun Poi v. Lee Chuen Tat* [1988] R.T.R. 298, P.C.). The first obstacle is, of course, to show that the defect caused the accident. There is no point in a defendant blaming his defective brakes if he was going so fast that nothing could have stopped him, or in blaming a puncture if he was driving on a tyre that was worn down to the canvas.

1.24 Where a defendant raises the defence of latent defect, and the defect alleged is one arising in the manufacture of the product, as opposed to a defect caused by lack of maintenance, the plaintiff now has another weapon in his armoury. Section 2 of the Consumer Protection Act 1987 imposes strict liability for a defective product on the producer, and in some cases the supplier, of the defective product. "Product" is widely defined in the Act. It extends, for example, to any ship, aircraft or vehicle. In the case envisaged the plaintiff should inform the defendant that he will join the maker of the product as co-defendant and that, in the event of the court finding that the injury was not caused by the latent defect, the plaintiff will seek a *Sanderson* order against the original defendant in respect of the co-defendant's costs. This course should persuade a defendant who has raised a spurious latent defect defence to drop it: on the other hand, if such defence prevails, the plaintiff will have a valid claim against the producer.

1.25 Usually the onus is on the plaintiff to establish the defendant's fault, but the plaintiff will not necessarily fail if he cannot say exactly how an accident happened. Thus if two vehicles collide and neither driver can say what happened after (and there is no corroborative evidence), the judge cannot simply refuse to make any finding. If he cannot deduce that one or other party was to blame he cannot send them both away empty-handed but must find that both contributed (as happened in *Baker v. Market Harborough Industrial Co-operative Society, Wallace v. Richards (Leicester) Ltd* [1953] 1 W.L.R. 1472). Of course, that does not always happen because the judge is entitled to draw a reasonable inference from the evidence that one party was entirely to blame even though he cannot decide on the basis of the evidence exactly how an accident happened. As a last resort a judge may find against the party on whom the burden of proof lies if satisfied that an accident was caused by negligence but no inference can properly be drawn as to who was negligent. This is illustrated in *Knight v. Fellick* [1977] R.T.R. 316 (which is worth reading). Engineering evidence can help the judge to draw that inference. It is clear from *Sullivan v. West Yorkshire Passenger Executive* [1985] 2 All E.R. 134 that motor engineers' evidence cannot now be excluded *per se* at an interlocutory stage, but *Hinds v. London Transport Executive* [1979] R.T.R. 103 is still good law in so far as the trial judge is still likely to disregard such evidence if it just argues out the cause of the accident without dealing with any real engineering matters.

ESTABLISHING DAMAGE

Medical evidence

1.26 The keystone of any personal injury case, apart from the plaintiff's own evidence, is the medical evidence. This can be the keystone of the defence as well, although the defendant might be prepared to accept the plaintiff's evidence if it contains nothing controversial. At this stage it is worth emphasising that we still deal with personal injury litigation under an adversarial system. This means that neither side—plaintiff nor defendant—has an automatic right of access to the other side's medical (or any other) expert reports. Disclosure of a written report is a pre-condition to calling expert evidence, but the basic rules remain the same: expert evidence is privileged and neither party is obliged to disclose a report from an expert who is hostile to his case and on whom he therefore will not wish to rely (see below).

1.27 In any case involving continuing disability both sides should obtain independent medical evidence. The plaintiff will want an independent assessment of the extent of his disability preferably from a doctor who was not involved in treating him and so will not be influenced by the extent of his recovery to date. The defendant will want to check the extent of any permanent disability alleged by the plaintiff, whether any pre-accident condition has been exacerbated and the extent of the functional element. Neither side should be afraid to instruct more than one doctor when the plaintiff suffers multiple injuries giving rise to a variety of symptoms. It is important to remember that automatic directions under RSC, Ord. 25, r.8 and CCR, Ord. 17, r.11 provide for only two medical experts. If either party wants to call more he must ask the other side to agree or apply for directions to do so. Automatic directions, as stated in para 1.8 above, do not apply to Admiralty actions or medical negligence cases in the High Court in which a summons for directions must be taken out. It is essential that the case is tried on the basis of up-to-date medical reports, whether or not medical evidence is agreed. In *Kaiser (An Infant) v. Carlswood Glassworks Ltd* (1965) 109 S.J. 537 it was said that reports should not be more than a year old, but six months is probably safer in any case of ongoing pain or disability.

1.28 The plaintiff's rights in relation to medical examinations by the defendant's doctor have been redefined in two cases. The first was *Starr v. National Coal Board* [1977] 1 W.L.R. 63 which dealt with the plaintiff's right to object to being examined at all by the defendant's doctor. It is clear that he cannot object solely on the ground of the freedom of the individual or because that particular doctor usually examines for insurance companies. The plaintiff must go further and show that the doctor is not suitably qualified or that the examination is not necessary or that he has a reasonable apprehension about the particular doctor which, if realised, might make a fair trial more difficult than if another doctor were to examine him. The plaintiff's solicitor will have to go on affidavit about that, which is not an easy matter. If the plaintiff unreasonably refuses a medical examination his action is not struck out, it is stayed; but if he continues to refuse to be examined the stay continues and, of course, he runs the risk of dismissal for want of prosecution and, additionally, in the county court, of an automatic strike out under Ord. 17, r.11(9).

1.29 The second case was *Hall v. Avon AHA* [1980] 1 All E.R. 516 in which the Court of Appeal held that the plaintiff cannot insist, as of right, upon having his own doctor present when the defendant's doctor examines him. Limited exceptions were envisaged, for instance where the plaintiff is in a nervous state or confused by the effects of a brain injury or if the defendant's doctor is known to have a fierce cross-examining manner. The note at para. 25/6/2 of the *White Book* says "it is a sensible practice for the medical men on both sides to arrange a joint examination", which is clearly a desirable practice and one more likely to lead to agreed medical evidence. Where a plaintiff is nervous about attending to be examined by the defendant's medical expert a mutually acceptable solution may be for the plaintiff to be accompanied by a friend or relative. However that will not always be seen as reasonable or legitimate where a plaintiff refused to be examined by a psychiatrist without a companion present a stay has been granted (see *Whitehead v. Avon C.C.* 1997 P.I.Q.R. P. 148, C.A.)

1.30 Where the medical examination that the defendant's doctor wants to carry out involves tests and the like, going beyond the usual type of physical examination, the plaintiff may not necessarily be entitled to object. In *Aspinall v. Sterling Mansell Ltd* [1981] 3 All E.R. 866 it was said that there is a difference in kind between an ordinary medical examination and one involving experimenting or a diagnostic procedure. Examinations involving the use of a hypodermic syringe, the administration of a drug or exploratory operations were ruled out. In *Prescott v. Bulldog Tools Ltd* [1981] 3 All E.R. 869 the court adopted a more pragmatic approach by saying that if the defendant genuinely felt he needed an examination of the plaintiff which involved the risk of a real but short-term injury, the court could balance the plaintiff's objections against the defendant's request to ensure a fair determination of the issues. However, the defendant would have to agree to compensate the plaintiff for any such short-term injury caused, obviously regardless of the outcome of the litigation as a whole.

In *Laycock v. Layoe* [1997] P.I.Q.R.P. 519 the Court of Appeal proposed a two-stage test. First, do the interests of justice require the proposed test? If yes, then has the plaintiff put forward a substantial, rather than imaginary or illusory, reason for the test not being undertaken? In that case a very slight danger of a psychotic reaction to an MRI scan was held to be a sufficient reason for refusing a stay.

1.31 The automatic directions now provide for mandatory disclosure of the substance of expert evidence which is to be relied upon at trial within ten weeks of close of pleadings. Nevertheless, the mere submission to a medical examination does not entitle the plaintiff to see the report produced to the defendant as a result of that examination. He will only be entitled to see it if the defendant has agreed to disclose it or, of course, if the defendant subsequently decides to reply on the evidence of the examining doctor. The automatic directions confirm that only those reports on which it is intended to rely at trial need be disclosed.

As a general rule it is clear that the court should not require disclosure of a medical report by the defendant as a condition precedent to agreeing to order a stay following a refusal by the plaintiff to submit to medical examination (see *Hookham v. Wiggins Teape* [1995] P.I.Q.R.P. 392). However, there may, on particular facts be justification for imposition of the condition, for example, where there have been previous examinations, past delay by the defendant or the trial is near.

1.32 This can be disadvantageous to the plaintiff if, for instance, the defendant's report paints a gloomier picture than the plaintiff's report. Therefore, the plaintiff's solicitor should, in any case involving substantial injury and continuing disability, attempt to agree to disclose his reports on the basis of mutual exchange for the defendant's reports. Once proceedings are commenced, a plaintiff is now required to serve a medical report with his statement or particulars of claim (see RSC, Ord. 18, r.12(1A) and CCR, Ord. 6, r.1(5)(a)) (see para. 1.81 below). If agreement for mutual exchange is not reached at an early stage, the defendant will have the advantage of first sight of at least one of the plaintiff's medical reports.

1.33 A further danger to avoid is agreeing in advance to disclose a particular medical report, or indeed any other sort of expert's report, before one has actually seen it. The report might contain some nasty shocks, so the formula to be used by both sides is to agree to disclose reports upon which they intend to rely at trial. If they use this formula and then get a report they do not like and on which they do not intend to rely at trial, then they are not committed to disclose it. It is often unwise for the plaintiff's solicitor to disclose the identity of the doctor who will be examining the plaintiff as a failure to disclose a report from a nominated doctor creates the obvious inference that the doctor did not support the plaintiff's alleged injuries.

1.34 As a result of the automatic directions or a direction for reciprocal disclosure of medical evidence, evidence is agreed in the majority of cases. But even if there is agreement it is clear from *Jones v. Griffith* [1969] 1 W.L.R. 795 that the plaintiff should still be prepared to call his doctor in, say, a serious head injury case, so that the court can be guided on such matters as the management of the plaintiff or the epileptic risk. A defendant whose doctor alleges that the plaintiff is malingering must be prepared to call that doctor at trial to make out the allegation and to face cross-examination. He should not, as seems to have happened in *Stojalowski v. Imperial Smelting Corpn* (NSC) (1976) 121 S.J. 118, rely on a written report. In *Joyce v. Yeomans* [1981] 2 All E.R. 21 the Court of Appeal said that although the impression made on the trial judge by expert witnesses is less important than that made by lay witnesses, it will still carry considerable weight.

1.35 Pursuant to the Queen's Bench Masters' Practice Direction of 29 November 1989, in order to save time at trial, copies of disclosed medical or other experts' reports upon which any party intends to rely (whether agreed or not) must be lodged by that party as soon after setting down as is practicable. These reports will then go with the pleadings and form part of the documents for use of the trial judge. The direction specifically requires (in para. 4) that each report should state on the face of it the name of the party on whose behalf the expert has given the report, the date on which it is given (of course that can be avoided by the use of an indexed bundle), and whether or not it is agreed by the other parties.

1.36 Both sides should of course beware of "agreed" medical evidence that is, in fact, not agreed: orthopaedic reports on the one side referring to arthritic change being probable and on the other to its being possible; or neurologists' reports referring respectively to 10 per cent and 2 per cent epileptic risk are not "agreed". The doctors must be called to explain their differences.

1.37 Where a party intends to rely upon the evidence of a particular expert and has disclosed a report from him, he should consider carefully whether any other medical reports or side letters from that expert need to be disclosed. An expert's evidence upon matters on which it is not proposed to call him to give evidence need not be disclosed. However, if it is intended to call a doctor to, say, give evidence on expectation of life and he writes an accompanying letter to the effect that he suspects that the plaintiff is suffering from a life-threatening disease, the letter must clearly be disclosed if the doctor is to be called upon on the question of expectation of life (see *Vernon v. Bosley* [1997] P.I.Q.R. P. 359, C.A.). A very helpful summary of the duties and responsibilities of experts is to be found in *The Ikarian Reefer* [1993] 2 Lloyd's Rep. 68.

Provisional damages

1.38 Some of the risks have been taken out of the system of "once and for all" compensation by section 32A of the Supreme Court Act 1981 (Appendix B) and the corresponding section 51 of the County Courts Act 1984. They deal with awards of provisional damages where the plaintiff proves or the defendant admits that there is a chance that the plaintiff's health will change or will get worse because he may develop a serious disease or suffer a serious deterioration in his mental or physical condition. It does not matter that the plaintiff cannot say when this is likely to happen. The use of the word "chance" in s. 32A(1) suggests that the test is less than the balance of probabilities. However, the anticipated deterioration must be clear, severable and go beyond ordinary or continuing deterioration (*Willson v. Ministry of Defence* [1991] 1 All E.R. 638).

1.39 The court can make an order for provisional damages at trial or on an earlier settlement, but the settlement must be approved even if the plaintiff is not under a disability. The practice is dealt with in RSC, Ord. 37, rr.7 to 10 (see Appendix C) and Practice Direction (QBD) (Provisional Damages: Procedure) (1985) 5 July [1985] 1 W.L.R. 961 amended by Lord Chief Justice, March 23, 1995 (CCR, Ord. 22, r.6A corresponds). There must always be a judgment whether the action is tried or settled and there are detailed provisions for the retention of documents by the court. The important thing to remember is that the court will have no power to order provisional damages unless the plaintiff has pleaded a claim for it (RSC, Ord. 18, r.8(3), Ord. 37, r.8(1)(a) and CCR, Ord. 6, r.1B).

1.40 If an order for provisional damages is made, the court will make an award of immediate damages excluding any for the risk that the plaintiff will develop the specified disease or suffer the specified deterioration. Thus the plaintiff has to gamble either way. He can still settle or ask the court to award damages on the old basis of including something for the future risk. On the other hand, he can ask for provisional damages and get a lesser sum now which may seem unattractive even though he can go back for more later. In *Cowan v. Kitson Insulations Ltd* [1992] P.I.Q.R. Q. 19 it was emphasised that the plaintiff should never be treated disadvantageously by reason of seeking a final award even if a provisional award appears suitable. The court will assess a fair level of award, recognising that if the risk materialises the plaintiff will be under-compensated and if it doesn't, he will be over-compensated.

1.41 In many cases the problem could be solved by seeking an interim payment, which can take much of the urgency out of getting quantum tried. What is certain is that the plaintiff's solicitor must not overlook the provisional damages machinery when advising a client whose medical prognosis is guarded or unclear.

1.42 The Damages Act 1996, s. 3, has removed the bar which had previously been held to prevent dependants bringing an action under the Fatal Accidents Act 1976 where the deceased had been awarded provisional damages and subsequently died as a result of the act or omission which gave rise to the cause of action for which damages were awarded. This should remove a potentially serious disadvantage to an early application for provisional damages in cases such as those arising out of asbestos exposure. The relevant provision also removes a potential injustice as it applies to awards of provisional damages made before as well as after its coming into force.

Accountants, actuaries and employment consultants

1.43 In any case involving serious and lasting injury, the plaintiff's solicitors may have to instruct an accountant to calculate past and future pecuniary loss. As with any other expert's report the accountant's report will have to be disclosed as a condition precedent to calling him: the defendant's solicitor will be entitled to object to the expense of such evidence if it simply deals with calculations the plaintiff's solicitor could make himself. Where the plaintiff was self-employed, in partnership or the director of a small company, the accountant's evidence may be essential to identify and evaluate the plaintiff's losses. An accountant's evidence may help the court to approach the multiplier, as well as the multiplicand, for example in the case of a one-man business where the accountant has been concerned with the accounts over a number of years and is in a position to give an expert opinion as to the future prospects of the business. Actuarial evidence can also be helpful in such cases. The Court of Appeal said in *Sullivan v. West Yorkshire Passenger Transport Executive* [1985] 2 All E.R. 134 that although the court has power to limit the number of medical or other expert witnesses, it has no power to bar a party from calling expert evidence including actuarial evidence provided he has complied with the rules. The plaintiff will be at risk as to costs, if the court regards the actuarial evidence as unnecessary.

1.44 Consideration should also be given, in substanial claims for loss of earnings to obtaining expert-evidence from an employment consultant. This is particularly important if the plaintiff has an ongoing disability which it is suggested will prevent him from returning to his pre-accident occupation but does not make him unfit for all work or if there is a dispute as to whether the plaintiff retains a residual earning capacity, despite his disabilities. As noted at para. 1.6 above, the Ogden Table, are now admissible in evidence.

Architects, surveyors and experts on aids and equipment

1.45 A badly disabled plaintiff might need specially constructed or modified accommodation and a whole range of appliances to make his life more tolerable (see *George v. Pinnock* [1973] 1 W.L.R. 118, *Cunningham v. Harrison* [1973] Q.B. 942 and *Abdul-Hosn v. The Trustees of The Italian Hospital* (1987) *Kemp & Kemp* Vol. 2, para A4–000/3). Architects and surveyors may have to be called to give evidence in support of, or to dispute, claims concerning accommodation. A number of witnesses are now accepted by the courts as having relevant expertise as to aids and equipment for the disabled whether through specific qualifications or long experience of dealing with seriously disabled patients. Reports from such experts are subject to the same rules and privileges as medical reports but would be classed as non-medical experts so that directions will have to be sought in any type of personal injury case if a party wants to call more than one (see RSC, Ord. 25, r.8 below). *Sullivan v. West Yorkshire Passenger Transport Executive* applies to such reports as well. Under section 5 of the Administration of Justice Act 1982 (Appendix B), the saving to a plaintiff of his being maintained wholly or partly at public expense can be offset against his claim for future loss of earnings. No such offset would apply to a plaintiff living in his modified home, but of course savings in board and lodging may be deducted from private nursing home or hospital fees (*Shearman v. Folland* [1950] 2 K.B. 43).

Nursing

1.46 The need for private nursing is chiefly a matter for medical evidence but the extent and likely cost can best be established by reference to expert evidence such as that available from the British Nursing Association or local nursing agencies whose addresses can be found in the *Nursing Times*. Where the plaintiff is paralysed, valuable advice and evidence as to appliances and nursing and other assistance can be obtained by contacting the Spinal Injuries Association of 76 St James Lane, London N10 3DS. Such a report was relied upon by Taylor J in *Brown v. Merton etc Area Health Authority* [1982] 1 All E.R. 650; and is now an almost invariable feature of serious paraplegic cases. The need for qualified nursing, as opposed to help with housework or companionship, will arise only in the most extreme cases of severe disability (see *Connolly v. Camden and Islington AHA* [1981] 3 All E.R. 250; *Croke v. Wiseman* [1981] 3 All E.R. 852). It is a wise precaution for the plaintiff's solicitor to ensure that the plaintiff is receiving this type of help, where necessary, before trial in order to emphasise the need for it. Indeed, in extreme cases, it may be sensible to organise some form of help even before the nursing expert reports to avoid the argument that such help has only been obtained on the expert's advice. In either case, finance can be arranged by interim payments if liability is not an issue. Both sides would be well advised to check what help is actually available from the plaintiff's local authority. The court cannot refuse to award the cost of private necessary nursing or domestic help, even though State help may be available, when assessing special damage (see the Law Reform (Personal Injuries) Act 1948, s. 2 (Appendix B) but may take available State facilities into account when assessing future loss, following *Cunningham v. Harrison*

[1973] Q.B. 942. In *Daly v. General Steam Navigation Co. Ltd* [1981] 1 W.L.R. 120 the plaintiff housewife was awarded damages for the cost of future help as a measure of damages for her crippled arm even though she had no help up to trial and might have struggled on without it. The plaintiff's solicitor should not overlook the value of gratuitous help given by the plaintiff's relatives or even friends for which damages can be included in the plaintiff's claim. There is no need for any contractual agreement. If the relative or friend gives up work to look after the plaintiff, the measure of damages may be calculated by reference to his or her loss of earnings, provided it does not exceed the commercial cost of the help provided. If not the damages will be such that the plaintiff can make reasonable recompense to the relative or friend for "the proper and reasonable" cost of their services.

Recent practice suggests that "Crossroads" rates may be a suitable base rate for calculating awards for unpaid carers. Two-thirds of the Crossroads rate were awarded in *Nash v. Southmead H.A.* [1993] P.I.Q.R. Q. 156 and three-quarters in *Fairhurst v. St Helens & Knowsley H.A.* [1995] P.I.Q.R. P. 1, in which the carer required special skills.

The damages should also take into account the possibility that the relative or friend might become unable to provide the services. The decision in *Housecroft v. Burnett* [1986] 1 All E.R. 332 provides very clear and comprehensive guidance as to what can be claimed in cases of serious injury. Damages cannot be recovered for voluntary help given by the defendant tortfeasor: *Hunt v. Severs* [1994] 2 A.C. 350. Readers should go to *Kemp & Kemp* Vol. 1, chapter 5 for a detailed consideration of the implications of that decision.

Earnings

1.47 In a serious personal injury case or in a fatal case the initial calculations of loss of earnings or dependency may be made very soon after the accident, based on wage rates provided by the employers at that time. Those rates may be completely out of date by the time a statement of the special damages claimed is drawn up, and even more so by the time the action is tried. The plaintiff's solicitors must make regular checks (and it is a good idea for the defendant's insurers and solicitors to do the same) on the wage rates at regular intervals, and not only on the rates for the job that the plaintiff would have been doing but the rate for any job into which he might have been promoted but for the accident. In a big case (perhaps three, four or even five years old) the rates may have increased very substantially between the issue of the writ and the date of trial; and that makes an enormous difference to quantum. Of course the plaintiff's solicitor will have to bring his calculations up to date and if necessary amend the statement of special damages on service of further medical reports or before trial.

Pre-litigation Procedure

Discovery

1.48 Pre-litigation applications for discovery and inspection of particular documents are mainly relevant to liability. They are now made in the High Court under section 33(2)(i) of the Supreme Court Act 1981 and in the county court under section 52(2) of the County Courts Act 1984. The practice is in RSC, Ord. 24, r.7A which also applies in the county courts. The application must be against someone who is likely to be a party to proceedings but this can extend to cases where even the bringing of these proceedings depends on what is in the documents (*Dunning v. United Liverpool Hospitals' Board of Governors* [1973] 2 All E.R. 454). The defendant's documents may be just as relevant and important as the evidence of eye witnesses as indeed can be the lack of such documents (see *Coyle v. Arnham Timber Co. Ltd* (1981) N.L.J. 367). However, the court's power under the Supreme Court Act 1981, s. 34(2) and the County Court Act 1984, s. 53(2) to order discovery by a non-party after proceedings have been commenced can be useful when difficulties arise in obtaining information from witnesses on quantum (for instance, an unco-operative employer). Discovery under s. 33(2) is limited to personal injury cases. In *Shaw v. Vauxhall Motors Ltd* [1974] 1 W.L.R. 1035 the Court of Appeal gave valuable guidance to applicants for pre-litigation discovery of servicing and maintenance records of machinery and vehicles. In that case a fork-lift truck with a fail-safe device failed; the plaintiff was injured and he had no idea what had gone wrong. He would have been fighting blindly if he started proceedings without seeing the maintenance and servicing records of the fork-lift truck to see whether it had gone wrong before and what went wrong on this occasion. In a case like this the applicant must, before issuing an originating summons, write to his opponent setting out the nature of his allegations and his information that the documents are relevant. If he can satisfy the court (and this is the whole crux of the matter) that discovery would be likely to assist in the fair disposal of the case or in saving costs, discovery will be ordered. The court must particularly bear in mind in the case of a legally-aided plaintiff that it is in the public interest to have such an early disclosure, which might affect the bringing or continuance of legal proceedings; if discovery is ordered and it discloses that there is no case, then that is an end to it. On applications for pre-action discovery the court will not take into account limitation defences unless the prospective plaintiff's claim is bound to be time-barred (*Harris v. Newcastle-upon-Tyne Health Authority* [1989] 1 W.L.R. 96). Order 62, r.6(9) states that the general rule is that the costs of pre-litigation discovery will usually be given to the respondent "unless the court otherwise orders". In *Jacob v. Wessex Regional Health Authority* [1984] C.L.Y. 2618 the respondents were ordered to pay the costs in any event where the plaintiff's solicitors had written letters to them referring to the reasonableness of their request for discovery, the relevant authorities and the saving in public expense from voluntary discovery to a legally-aided plaintiff. Similarly, in *Hall v. Wandsworth Health Authority* (1985) 129 S.J. 188 the court said that costs could be awarded when the respondents had been dilatory in answering the plaintiffs' solicitors' requests for discovery with no excuse and that leave to appeal from the master's order as to costs was not necessary. Useful guidance as to the approach in practice to pre-action discovery against a health authority is to be found in *M v. Plymouth H.A.* [1993] P.I.Q.R. P. 223

1.49 Patients now have an entitlement to see their own medical records under the Access to Health Records Act 1990 which applies to records created after 1 November, 1991. This right can prove to be of particular utility in medical negligence claims. The object of orders for discovery under the Supreme Court and County Courts Acts is to bring forward the time for the disclosure of relevant documents in a personal injury action by, to use the wording of RSC, Ord. 24, r.7A, a "likely" party from the stage after action to the stage before action, and to require disclosure after the commencement of proceedings by someone who is not a party to the proceedings at all, eg, a health authority (*Walker v. Eli Lilley & Co.* (1986) *The Times*, 1 May). In both instances earlier discovery might obviously give rise to great savings in costs. Claims to privilege are the same as they would be on ordinary discovery. In *Campbell v.*

Tameside Metropolitan BC [1982] 2 All E.R. 791 the plaintiff was a teacher who had been assaulted by a pupil. She sought discovery of psychiatric reports held by the defendants who were the education authority. The application was defended on the basis that discovery would be contrary to public interest as the reports were highly confidential and the fact that they might be used in litigation would inhibit the doctors preparing such reports in the future. The Court of Appeal said that public interest in non-disclosure for these reasons had to be weighed against public interest in justice being done. The court could actually look at the documents in order to make a decision.

In *Waugh v. British Rail Board* [1980] A.C. 521 the House of Lords decided that where a report, following an inquiry, had been prepared as much to prevent further accidents as to obtain legal advice about potential claims, it was not privileged because its sole or dominant purpose was not submission to a legal adviser in view of litigation. In *Lask v. Gloucester Health Authority* (1985) *The Times*, 13 December there was a similar decision relating to health authority accident reports required by various health circulars. In *McAvan v. London Transport Executive* (1983) 133 N.L.J. 1101 reports prepared by a bus crew and an inspector after an accident were held to be privileged as their dominant purpose was to ascertain blame if a subsequent claim was made. Discovery will not be ordered of evidence prepared by someone who is not a party at the request of someone who is a defendant or potential defendant wanting to obtain legal advice, even though this amounts to the non-party sheltering behind the privilege of the defendant or potential defendant (*Lee v. South West Thames Regional Health Authority* [1985] 2 All E.R. 385).

Inspection etc of property

1.50 Similarly, even before proceedings are commenced application can be made to the court under section 33(1) of the Supreme Court Act 1981 or section 52(1) of the County Courts Act 1984 for an order for the inspection, photographing, custody or detention of property or for the taking of samples. In *Evans v. Lufthansa Airlines* (1981) N.L.J. 1166 the *Shaw v. Vauxhall Motors* guidance was applied to this type of application. The advantage of following it and the fact that costs will not always be awarded to the respondent in any event under Ord. 62, r.6(9) is illustrated by *Jacob v. Wessex*

R.H.A. and *Hall v. Wandsworth H.A.* above. Similar orders can be made after the proceedings have been commenced in respect of property not in the possession of any party to the proceedings under section 34(3) of the Supreme Court Act 1981. These are not restricted to personal injury or fatal accident cases. The procedure on such applications is described in RSC, Ord. 29, r.7A.

LITIGATION

Allocation and commencement of proceedings

1.51 The allocation of personal injury actions between the High Court and county courts is governed by the Courts and Legal Services Act 1990 and the High Court and County Courts Jurisdiction Order 1991 (S.I. No. 724) (see Appendix B). The relevant county court jurisdiction is now unlimited. Any personal injury action may be started in a county court. Proceedings which include a claim for personal injury or death must be commenced in a county court unless the value of the action is £50,000 or more. Before a writ is issued in a personal injury action it must be endorsed with a standard form statement that the value of the action exceeds £50,000 (see Practice Direction (Q.B.D.) (Personal Injuries Action: Endorsement of Writ) [1991] 1 W.L.R. 642). The relevant value of the action is the amount that the plaintiff reasonably expects to recover, or if there is more than one plaintiff, the aggregate amount. In assessing the value of the action no account is to be taken of a possible but unadmitted finding of contributory negligence, costs or interest. However, the value must be taken to include sums relating to state benefits which by virtue of section 6 of the Social Security (Recovery of Benefits) Act 1997 have to be paid to the Secretary of State. In practice no deduction need be made from the value of the claim on account of state benefits received. Any practitioner intending to commence proceedings in the High Court needs to give careful consideration to the value of the claim, be satisfied that the endorsement can fairly be made and ensure that it is included in the writ. Whilst a writ may be issued in a personal injury action without an endorsement it is likely that in its absence the action will be transferred to a county court or at worst struck out. The High Court can strike out a personal injury action if it was required to be commenced in the High Court and the court is satisfied that the person bringing the proceedings knew or ought to have known of that requirement. It is now clear that the court in fact has an unfettered discretion where proceedings are wrongly commenced in the High Court and may either strike out the action or transfer it to a county court (see *Restick v. Crickmore* [1994] 1 W.L.R. 420). The power to strike out is only likely to be exercised in the absence of a *bona fide* mistake and if the plaintiff has been guilty of contumelious conduct or trying to gain some improper advantage. Failure to commence in the county court when required is however likely to be costly as the Court of Appeal did indicate that wasted or reduced costs orders were an appropriate sanction if the action was transferred. Even where it is clear that proceedings should be commenced in a county court, practitioners must concern themselves with quantum at the pleading stages. County court actions will automatically be allocated for trial by a district judge unless the particulars of claim include a statement that the value of the claim exceeds £5,000.

1.52 It should not be assumed that every action with a value in excess of £50,000 will be retained in the High Court. Inevitably occasions will also arise when an initial valuation proves over-optimistic, for example where a plaintiff makes an unexpectedly good recovery. The defendant or the court of its own motion can (under the Practice Direction (Q.B.D.) (Transfer of Proceedings to County Courts) (1991) 26 July [1991] 1 W.L.R. 643) apply to have the action transferred to a county court under the County Courts Act 1984, s. 40 (as amended). The court itself will, under this Practice Direction, continue to scrutinise every action set down to see whether it is suitable for transfer. Cases valued at more than £50,000 may well be transferred if they do not raise any important or complex questions of law or fact. There is jurisdiction for actions valued at less than £50,000 to be transferred up to the High Court under section 41(1) or section 42(2) of the County Courts Act 1984, although such transfers are likely to occur only in exceptional cases raising questions of general public interest.

1.53 There can no longer be any presumption that personal injury claims are inherently unsuitable to be dealt with by way of arbitration under the county court small claims procedure. In *Afzal v. Ford Motor Co. Ltd* [1994] 4 All E.R. 720 the Court of Appeal held that it was wrong to approach employers' liability cases involving amounts of £1,000 or less as a class of case which was in general unsuited to arbitration. Intentional overstatement of the amount involved in a claim to avoid arbitration is an abuse of the process so that a claim should not be made for damages limited to say £3,000 when the true claim is less than £1,000. A defendant who wishes a claim to proceed to arbitration and believes that damages are less than £1,000 should say so in his defence. The mere fact that unliquidated general damages are claimed will not prevent a reference to arbitration so a plaintiff is advised to plead that damages are likely to exceed £1,000 where that can be sustained and there is no desire for an arbitration.

1.54 Prompt commencement of proceedings is of importance for the maximisation of interest. Interest on general damages should now be 3 per cent following the reasoning of the House of Lords in *Wells v. Wells* [1998] 1 W.L.R. 329. This interest is only recoverable from the date on which a writ has been served. Indeed if a plaintiff delays his action unreasonably he may not even get his 3 per cent and may see interest on special damages reduced (see *Nash v. Southmead Health Authority* [1993] P.I.Q.R. Q. 157 where interest on special damages was only awarded for a seven year period, the plaintiff having been injured at birth but the trial only taking place when he was aged 17).

Initial steps in High Court actions

1.55 There is now only one composite form of writ which must bear the Royal Arms. There must be a copy for service on each defendant and all service copies must be sealed as well as the original under Ord. 10, r.1 and accompanied by an acknowledgement of service form. The plaintiff's solicitor has these alternatives to personal service, which no longer requires production of the original writ:

(1) *By ordinary first class post to the defendant's address* (not by recorded delivery which would destroy the presumption of service).

(2) *By insertion through the defendant's letter box.* In both these cases, the presumption is of service seven calendar days after the date of posting or insertion. In *Hodgson v. Hart District Council* [1986] 1 W.L.R. 317 the Court of Appeal said that the presumption is rebuttable by evidence that the defendant actually received the writ sooner or later. If the letter eventually comes back through the dead letter office, the plaintiff's solicitor should make his own application to set aside any interlocutory judgment he has signed.

(3) *By service on the defendant's solicitor.* Order 10, r.1(4) states that this mode of service is effected by the defendant's solicitor endorsing an acceptance on the writ, which means he must be sent the original as well as the service copy. The note to this rule in the 1997 *White Book* suggests that service on the defendant's solicitors in England pursuant to an unqualified oral agreement by them to accept service is good service but points out that this practice of endorsement is potentially unsafe for defendants since by itself it does not give notice of an intention to defend. Duly completing the acknowledgement of service is recommended.

A writ can still be served on a limited company by sending it by first class post to the registered office, but following the Practice Direction (Q.B.D.) (Service of Documents: First and Second Class Mail) (1985) 8 March [1985] 1 W.L.R. 489 the presumption will be of service on the second working day after posting by first class post or the fourth working day after posting by second class post. In either case "working day" means Monday to Friday and excludes bank holidays. If the plaintiff's solicitor has to swear an affidavit of service he must specifically state that first class post was used, otherwise the court will presume it was second class post.

1.56 The first step in the proceedings taken by a defendant is governed by Ords 12 and 13 and has two functions—to acknowledge that he has been served with the writ and to give the plaintiff notice that he intends to defend the proceedings. If he fails to do *both* the plaintiff will be entitled to interlocutory judgment. However, it seems that if the plaintiff claims provisional damages, the defendant's failure to give notice of intention to defend does not entitle the plaintiff to sign judgment (Ord. 37, r.8(5)). In such cases the procedure set out in the Senior Master's Practice Note of 14 April 1988 should be followed. The acknowledgement of service enables the defendant's solicitor to correct any misnomer in the writ unless, of course, it is so fundamental that he might not accept service at all. The time fixed for filing acknowledgement is 14 days from service of writ, including the day of service, an exception to Ord. 3, r.2(2). This was confirmed by the Court of Appeal in *British Oxygen Company v. John H. Pike (Meat Products)* (1984) C.A.T. 288.

Initial steps in county court actions

1.57 In a county court, proceedings are commenced by the plaintiff and entered in the court record by the court itself. The plaintiff must file in the court office a request for the issue of a summons. It must be accompanied by particulars of claim, a medical report and a statement of special damages together with a copy of those documents for each defendant. If the plaintiff so desires and the proper officer so allows, the summons itself may be prepared by the plaintiff in which case a copy must be filed instead of a request. There are prescribed forms of request for summons and of summons. Personal injury actions, being default actions, can be commenced in any county court of the plaintiff's choice under CCR, Ord. 4, r.2(1)(c). The court has full discretion under Ord. 16, r.1 to transfer an action, on the application of either party, to a more convenient county court. The court will automatically serve the defendant by post following receipt of the request for a summons unless the plaintiff otherwise requests. In a personal injury action where the plaintiff prepares the summons it may now be served by the plaintiff's solicitor sending it by first class post to the defendant at the address stated in the summons under Ord. 7, r.10A. Personal service is also permissible.

1.58 If the defendant disputes liability for the whole or part of the plaintiff's claim he must, under Ord. 9, r.6, within 14 days after service of the summons on him, deliver a defence at the court office. If he fails to do so the plaintiff may request an interlocutory judgment for damages to be assessed. Indeed if the defendant admits liability or delivers no defence it is essential that steps are taken to have such a judgment entered against the defendant.

If 12 months are allowed to expire from the date of the summons, no defence is delivered and judgment has not been entered the action will be automatically struck out pursuant to Ord. 9, r.10. In *Webster v. Ellison Circlips Group Ltd* [1995] 1 W.L.R. 1447, the Court of Appeal held that if satisfied on an application made at a later date that no defence has been delivered, no agreement reached extending time for the defence had been made, and no judgment had been entered, the court could only determine that the action had been struck out. That the action had come back to life and might have progressed well along the road to trial was apparently viewed as irrelevant.

Only one of several defendants needs enter a defence to prevent this automatic strike out (see *Limb v. Union Jack Removals Ltd* (1998) *The Times*, February 17, 1998). Ord. 9, r.10 also has no application where a defendant to a claim in the tort of negligence admits negligence but makes no admission as to damage (see *Parrott v. Jackson* [1996] P.I.Q.R. P. 394). Likewise it does not apply where a defendant admits some loss or damage has been caused to the plaintiff, but puts in issue each item of damage actually claimed. Indeed, it now appears that, in practice, Ord. 9, r.10 may have limited application to personal injury actions following *Limb's* case in which the Court of Appeal expressed the view it had no application to an action for an unliquidated sum unless both liability and the whole of the plaintiff's money claim for damages were admitted. A defendant wishing to expose the plaintiff to the risk of strike out should make the admission in appropriate form (form N9) (see *Perrin v. Short* [1997] P.I.Q.R. P. 426).

1.59 Agreement that the time for delivery of a defence should be generally extended has the effect of ousting Ord. 9, r.10 (see *Heer v. Tutton* [1995] 1. W.L.R. 1336, C.A.) at least where that agreement is not terminated within 12 months of the service of the summons. The plaintiff's representatives should bear in mind the dangers posed by the rule, the risks posed if any agreement with the defendant's representatives is not in express contemplation of the rule and the need to keep the court informed. If in any doubt an extension of time for entering judgment should be prospectively sought. This should be contrasted with the inability of parties to extend time under Ord. 17, r.11 by mere agreement.

Periods of limitation

1.60 Limitation in personal injuries actions is governed by the Limitation Act 1980 (see Appendix B) which consolidates previous statutes of limitation. The basic limitation period is three years from the date on which the cause of action accrued or the date of knowledge (if later) of the person injured. By s. 14, the date of knowledge is the date on which that person first had knowledge that his injury was significant; that his injury was attributable to the act or omission which is alleged to constitute negligence, nuisance or breach of duty; the identity of the defendant; and, if it is alleged that the act or omission was that of a person other than the defendant, the identity of that person and the additional facts supporting the bringing of an action against the defendant. By s. 14(3) a person's knowledge includes knowledge which he might reasonably have been expected to acquire from facts observable and ascertainable by him or from facts ascertainable by him with the help of medical or other appropriate expert advice which it is reasonable for him to seek. In *Leadbitter v. Hodge Finance Ltd* [1982] 2 All E.R. 167 the date of knowledge was taken as that when the police report of a motor accident became available. The plaintiff was allowed to sue a second defendant, whose possible liability was revealed in the report more than three years after the accident. In *Parry v. Clwyd H.A.* [1997] P.I.Q.R. P. 1 the Court of Appeal held that whilst a qualified objective test was to be applied for the purpose of ascertaining whether the plaintiff had actual knowledge within s. 14, the question being whether a person of the plaintiff's intelligence knowing of the facts in question would have appreciated that there was a real possibility of the existence of the s. 14(1) facts; for the purpose of applying the reasonableness test under s. 14(3) the test was exclusively objective (see also *Spargo v. North Essex D.H.A.* [1997] P.I.Q.R. P. 235, C.A.). Where the plaintiff is a minor, the court should look exclusively to the actual and constructive knowledge of the plaintiff and should have no regard to the knowledge of a parent.

1.61 The same time limits apply to claims under the Fatal Accidents Act 1976 but knowledge is that of the dependant not the deceased (s. 12). Where there is more than one, limitation is applied to them separately and not as a class (s. 13). However, where the deceased allowed the s. 11 period to expire during his lifetime his defendants will not be able to rely on the s. 12 period. Limitation for plaintiffs under a disability is three years from the end of their disability or death, whichever is first. Knowledge is irrelevant. The effect of this extended limitation is that, even where the next friend has started proceedings during the disability, the court is unlikely to strike them out for want of prosecution, since the minor or patient could start new proceedings when the disability ceases: *Tolley v. Morris* [1979] 1 All E.R. 71. However, all practitioners should be aware of the increasingly rigorous attitude of the courts to the need to progress actions promptly and should beware of delays which could be characterised as an abuse of process, particularly where a timetable has been imposed or applies. Appropriate directions should be sought where it appears that the plaintiff's condition makes it sensible to issue proceedings but delay trial.

1.62 Whilst sections 11 and 14 of the 1980 Act apply to action for negligence, nuisance and analogous breaches of duties of care not to cause personal injury the House of Lords in *Stubbings v. Webb* [1993] 2 W.L.R. 120 held that the six-year limitation period provided by section 2 of the 1980 Act applied where the cause of action was based on rape or indecent assault, and that the court had no discretion to extend that period.

1.63 The court has a discretion under s. 33 to override the s. 11 or s. 12 limitation periods if it would be equitable to allow an action to proceed having regard to the prejudice to the plaintiff of applying the s. 11 or s. 12 periods against the prejudice to the defendant of not doing so. This discretion can now be exercised by masters or district registrars as well as judges (RSC, Ord. 32, r.9A).

1.64 Section 33(3) requires the court to have regard to all the circumstances of the case and in particular to:

(a) the length of, and the reasons for, the delay on the part of the plaintiff;

(b) the extent to which, having regard to the delay, the evidence adduced or likely to be adduced by the plaintiff or the defendant is or is likely to be less cogent than if the action had been brought within the time allowed by s. 11 or (as the case may be) by s. 12;

(c) the conduct of the defendant after the cause of action arose, including the extent (if any) to which he responded to requests reasonably made by the plaintiff for information or inspection for the purpose of ascertaining facts which were or might be relevant to the plaintiff's cause of action against the defendant;

(d) the duration of any disability of the plaintiff arising after the date of the accrual of the cause of action;

(e) the extent to which the plaintiff acted promptly and reasonably once he knew whether or not the act or omission of the defendant, to which the injury was attributable, might be capable at that time of giving rise to an action for damages;

(f) the steps, if any, taken by the plaintiff to obtain medical, legal or other expert advice and the nature of any such advice he may have received.

Paragraphs (a) and (b) deal with matters affecting the extent to which the plaintiff and the defendant will be prejudiced according to whether or not the action is allowed to proceed. Paragraphs (c), (e) and (f) deal with the question of whether a direction would be "equitable".

The delay referred to in paras (a) and (b) is the delay between the expiry of the limitation period and the issue of the writ, and not the period between the beginning of the limitation period and the issue of the writ nor any period after the issue of the writ (*Thompson v. Brown* [1981] 1 W.L.R. 751; *Donovan v. Gwentoys Ltd* [1990] 1 W.L.R. 472).

1.65 Disability in s. 33(3)(d) has the same meaning as in section 28 of the 1980 Act. It is clear from *Thompson v. Brown* [1981] W.L.R. 744 that the s. 33 discretion is unfettered and can include all relevant matters in balancing the prejudice. The court can therefore have regard to the totality of the delay between the date of accrual of the cause of action and the date of issue of the writ, notwithstanding s. 33(3)(b) and (c) and is likely to pay particular heed to the length of any delay in first notifying the defendant of the claim against him, even if such delay occurred before the expiry of the limitation period (*Donovan v. Gwentoys Ltd* [1990] 1 W.L.R. 472). Likewise where the plaintiff is not under a disability but subject to incapacity which affects ability to prove proceedings that too should be taken into account. (see *Thomas v. Plaistow* [1997] P.I.Q.R. P. 540, (A.) and *Pearse v. Barnet H.A.* [1998] P.I.Q.R. P. 39.) The fact that the plaintiff may have a cast-iron claim against his own solicitor for the full damages which he could have recovered against the defendant, is only one and not an overriding factor. In *Davis v. Soltenpur* (1983) *The Times*, 16 February a writ was issued more than three years after the accident. The master ordered the limitation issue to be set down for trial within 28 days, but it was not set down until ten months later. The likely date of trial was seven years from the accident. Section 33 discretion was refused having regard to three factors: the prejudice to the defendant, the unsatisfactory nature of a trial seven years later and the potential claim the plaintiff had against his solicitors.

1.66 It is also clear from *Walkley v. Precision Forgings* [1979] 1 W.L.R. 606 and *Chappell v. Cooper* [1980] 2 All E.R. 463 that where the plaintiff commences an action during the primary s. 11 or s. 12 limitation period but then puts himself in a position where he cannot pursue it, for instance by letting his writ expire without service or delaying so much that his action is struck out for want of prosecution, the court will have no power to exercise s. 33 discretion, since it is the plaintiff's own action or default which has prejudiced him and not the operation of s. 11 or s. 12. If he tries to start a second action, it will be struck out as an abuse of the process of the court. In *Deerness v. John R. Keeble & Son (Brantham) Ltd* (1982) *The Times*, 18 October this rule was applied even though the defendants had made an interim payment after the plaintiff issued a writ which he subsequently failed to serve. Where, however, the first action is a nullity, for instance because the plaintiff sues a limited company in liquidation without leave of the court, discretion may be exercised (*Wilson v. Banner Scaffolding* (1982) *The Times*, 22 June).

1.67 One of the nightmares of personal injury litigation is a defence blaming someone else who is not already a party, served after primary limitation has expired. If there is any substance in the allegation the plaintiff must apply to join him as a defendant. The question is whether the date of the joinder relates back to the date the proceedings were started, which would avoid the limitation argument. The answer is in section 35 of the Limitation Act 1980 under which the new claim dates back to when the original writ was issued but not so as to defeat a limitation. The plaintiff now seems to have the option of applying to join the new defendant in the existing proceedings as happened in *Liff v. Peasley* [1980] 1 All E.R. 623 or starting separate proceedings and relying on *Thompson v. Brown* above. The court can of course exercise its discretion under section 33 of the 1980 Act, and the provision of Ord. 15, r.6(5) may be relevant. In *Kennet v. Brown* [1988] 1 W.L.R. 582 it was held that a new claim was not dependent on a prior application under s. 33 but that s. 35(3) could be raised in a defence. That decision has now been overruled by a full Court of Appeal in *Welsh Development Agency v. Redpath Dorman Long Ltd* [1994] 4 All E.R. 10. Section 35(3) is a mandatory direction to the court dealing with an application to amend to allow a new claim. Unless an application is successfully made under s. 33 or the case falls within an exception provided by the RSC the court should not allow a new claim after the expiry of the limitation period.

1.68 Suppose time has slipped by and the plaintiff's solicitor suddenly discovers that limitation is on him; he may be saved by the fact that the day the cause of action accrues is excluded from the three-year limitation period (*Marren v. Dawson, Bentley & Co. Ltd* [1961] 2 Q.B. 135). Indeed if the three years and a day expire on a

Saturday or a Sunday or a bank holiday, when one cannot issue a writ, the limitation period is extended until the next day on which one can (*Pritam Kaur v. S. Russell & Sons Ltd* [1973] Q.B. 336). Dozing defendants can take comfort from that as well because the same rule applies to filing acknowledgement of service. A plaintiff has only four calendar months (six if leave to serve out of the jurisdiction is required under RSC, Ord. 11), in which to serve the writ and if he does not serve it within that period the fact that the last day is a Sunday, when it cannot be served, does not come to his aid. Time is extended only if the act requires an attendance at the court office.

1.69 It is clear from *Walkley v. Precision Forgings* (see para. 1.66 above) that an unserved writ is worse than no writ at all. It interrupts limitation only temporarily and does not start interest running. The underlying reason for not serving the writ is frequently a fear of upsetting the insurers and of their consequently breaking off negotiations. That is absolute nonsense. The vast majority of insurers would regard it as a perfectly normal step for a plaintiff's solicitor to issue and serve a writ and, after acknowledgement of service by their solicitors, would call for the papers back and continue negotiations. There is no point in leaving a writ unserved: it does not start interest accruing; it does not do anything but temporarily interrupt the limitation period. It simply creates the need to make another diary entry which can easily be overlooked.

Renewal of writ

1.70 What adds additional force to this argument is that under the Rules of the Supreme Court writs can be renewed only for a good or sufficient reason (see *Kleinwort Benson Ltd v. Barbrak Ltd, "The Myrto" (No. 3)* [1987] A.C. 597). Under Ord. 6, r.8, writs are only valid for four months and may only be renewed by the court for a maximum of four months at any one time, unless the court is satisfied that it may not be possible, despite all reasonable efforts, to serve the writ within four months, in which case renewal of up to 12 months may be ordered. In practice that will only occur if there are difficulties in serving the defendant (see, for example, *Gurtner v. Circuit* [1968] 2 Q.B. 587, *Howells v. Jones* (1975) 119 S.J. 577, *Sisknys v. Hanley* (1982) *The Times*, 26 May) or if there has been an express or implied agreement to defer service of the writ or the plaintiff's delay in serving it or renewing it has been induced or contributed to by the defendant's words or conduct (*Heaven v. Road and Rail Wagons Ltd* [1965] 2 Q.B. 655). The agreement must be clear or the inducement strong—not merely the making of an interim payment as happened in *Deerness v. John R Keeble & Son (Brantham) Ltd* (see para. 1.66 above). Delay caused by a failure of the legal aid authorities to act, or act reasonably, may constitute good reason, but delay caused by the failure of the plaintiff or his solicitors to act promptly in applying for legal aid, or for the removal of a legal aid restriction, will not constitute a good reason (*Waddon v. Whitecroft-Scovill Ltd* [1988] 1 W. L. R. 309). A writ will not normally be renewed so as to deprive the defendant of the accrued benefit of a limitation period, and the court does not deal with the question of whether to renew a writ after expiry of the limitation period on the same basis as an application to disapply the limitation period under section 33 of the Limitation Act 1980 (see paras 1.63 *et seq.* above) (*Waddon v. Whitecroft-Scovill Ltd* [1988] 1 W. L. R. 309). Good reason must be shown for non-service (*Kleinwort Benson Ltd v. Barbrak Ltd* [1987] A.C. 597). The mere fact that negotiations are continuing, in the absence of agreement between the parties to defer service, is not a good reason for extending validity (*The Mouna* [1991] 2 Lloyd's Rep. 221). An expired writ which has not been served creates such a fundamental defect in procedure that the court's wide powers under Ord. 2, rr. 1 and 2 to cure non-compliance with the rules will not be exercised to treat it as valid for service or substituted service (*Bernstein v. Jackson* [1982] 2 All E.R. 806). In *Singh v. Duport Harper Foundries Ltd* [1994] 1 W.L.R. 769 it was emphasised that an application for extension of the validity of the writ had to be made during its original validity or during the following four months and only one extension not exceeding four months could be granted on a particular application. Only in exceptional circumstances will a court invoke Ord. 2, r.1 and Ord. 3, r.5 to allow an extension beyond that permitted by Ord. 6, r.8. An application is properly made within four months if the summons is taken out in that period, even if the hearing date is outside the period (see *Husseyin v. Crumplin* [1997] P.I.Q.R. P. 481).

1.71 CCR, Ord. 7, r.20 contains comparable provisions for summonses and the same considerations apply (see *Ward-Lee v. Lineham* [1993] 1 W.L.R. 754), but it is clear that where through no fault of the plaintiff, the county court fails in its duty to effect service, exceptional circumstances exist and the court will, in the interests of justice, extend time under Ord. 13, r.4 (see *Kelliher v.*

E.H. Savill Engineering Ltd [1994] P.I.Q.R. P. 387). In *Lewis v. Harewood* [1997] P.I.Q.R. P. 59, a county court action, the Court of Appeal set out a two-stage approach to the injury. The first stage is to examine whether there is good reason to extend time and the plaintiff's explanation for failure to apply before the validity of proceeding expired. Only if satisfied on these points does the general discretion arise, although the same considerations can be relevant to both stages.

1.72 Even if the writ is renewed the plaintiff's troubles are not over. Where a writ is served after its original period of validity has expired, even though its renewal period has not expired, the defendant may apply to set aside service and the order for renewal, which would of course have been made *ex parte*. He no longer has to enter a conditional appearance, since that practice was abolished when acknowledgements of service were introduced, but must file his acknowledgement and give notice of intention to defend and then issue his application to set aside service and the renewal order within 14 days. It appears that time can be extended under Ord. 3, r.5. Where a plaintiff simply agrees to extend time for service of a defence, that will be taken to include an extension of time for challenging the validity of the writ unless there is an express agreement that it should not have that effect (*Lawson v. Midland Travellers Ltd* [1993] 1 W.L.R. 735). The duration of a county court summons is also four months (six months if leave is required to serve out of the jurisdiction under CCR, Ord. 8).

Split trials in the High Court

1.73 One of the main reasons for delay in personal injury cases is the fact that the plaintiff's solicitor is waiting for a medical prognosis before being able to quantify the claim. This uncertainty need not prevent the action being run up to setting-down provided the liability issue and special damages to date can be reasonably particularised and the plaintiff's injuries described. The plaintiff's solicitor need not wait until it is all neatly tied up before serving a statement of claim (although note the operation of RSC, Ord. 18, r. 12(1A-C)). However, a problem arises if the medical prognosis or prospects of employment are unclear by the time the trial is close. If liability is not in dispute, appropriate direction can be sought. The action can simply be stood out by agreement or an application made to the judge of the lists, or to the judge on circuit, for a standing-out order, or possibly an application made to claim provisional damages; but if liability is still in dispute the action must be tried and ought to be heard as soon as possible, irrespective of the uncertainties on quantum. Application should be made for a split trial under Ord. 33, rr. 3 and 4, under which liability can be tried first and quantum tried when the plaintiff's medical or employment position, or any other doubt on quantum, has been clarified.

The court now has a wide power in personal injury actions to order, of its own motion and at any stage in the proceedings, that issues of liability be tried before quantum (Ord. 33, r.4(2A)) This power has not as yet been used often, but as care management now requires pre-trial reviews in longer cases it is possible that it may take on greater significance.

1.74 It was said in *Coenen v. Payne* [1974] 1 W. L. R. 984 (which was a defendant's application for a split trial) that such a trial will be ordered whenever it is just and convenient, and not only in difficult and unusual cases, and in *Ashworth v. Berkeley Walbrood* (1984) *The Times*, 13 July that the court can be asked to try a preliminary issue whenever there is a real probability that the effect will be to save time and expense and simplify the issues, which need not be limited to questions of law. This procedure can be used by defendants, as happened in *Coenen v. Payne*, to dispose of a plaintiff's claim which is weak on liability but difficult and complicated on quantum, so that substantial costs of investigating and defending it may be thrown away, particularly if the plaintiff is legally aided. Affirmation of the courts' power to order preliminary issues and the unwillingness of appellate courts to interfere is to be found in *Ashmore v. Lloyds* [1992] 1 W.L.R. 447 and is clearly compatible with the increasing tendency towards case management.

1.75 Where the plaintiff obtains such an order, the defendant may not be able to make an effective payment in. He can protect himself under Ord. 33, r.4A by making a written offer to accept liability up to a specified proportion, which can be brought to the attention of the judge after he has decided the liability issue at trial. Although the rule does not specifically say so it seems clear that the plaintiff can treat the offer as an admission of liability and apply to enter judgment on the basis of the offer with damages to be assessed when ready. Clearly, he will be entitled to an interim payment. The judgment given after the trial of a preliminary issue is not interlocutory even though quantum is still to be tried. This means that the parties do not need leave to appeal from it (*White v. Brunton* [1984]

2 All E.R. 606). Costs normally follow the event on the hearing of the preliminary issue so that a plaintiff who gets judgment on a preliminary trial of the liability issue will usually be entitled to his costs up to that point straightaway, which is an advantage over simply getting an interim payment.

Service on insurers etc

1.76 Reference was made earlier to cases in which delay arose because a defendant could not be served and the fact that a writ would not necessarily be renewed in these circumstances. In a running-down case it is quite simple to get round this problem. The answer is in RSC, Ord. 65, r.4, under which the court can, on an ordinary application for substituted service with the usual evidence of attempts, make an order for substituted service on the defendant's insurers or on the Motor Insurers' Bureau (MIB). This has been the case since about 1965 (*Gurtner v. Circuit* [1968] 2 Q.B. 587). This is obviously a safer course than renewing the writ although it was said in *Sisknys v. Hanley* (1982) *The Times*, 26 May that the fact that the plaintiff's solicitor could have but did not use this substituted service procedure was not a good reason for refusing renewal. There seems to be no reason why the attempts to serve the defendant before applying for substituted service on his insurers or MIB should not be by post, but it is probably safer to try personal service.

1.77 A great advantage of using this procedure is that the court can order substituted service on MIB even where the defendant vanishes after the accident and is never found, provided he was properly identified. If he gave a false name and address, substituted service will not be ordered, *Clarke v. Vedel* [1979] R.T.R. 26. Substituted service on the MIB does of course mean that the case can be tried by the court under the adversary system and the plaintiff avoids the disadvantages of an application under the Motor Insurers' Bureau (Compensation of Victims of Untraced Drivers) Agreement. It is now clear from *Cooper v. Motor Insurers' Bureau* [1985] Q.B. 575 that MIB's liability does not extend to a judgment obtained against the owner of a vehicle by the person actually using it who is injured because of its dangerous condition.

Pleadings

1.78 Pleadings in running-down cases are usually in common form and none more so than the defence—often a straight denial of everything the plaintiff claims, although Ord. 18, r.12(1)(c) requires that where a claim for damages is made against a party, a defence must contain particulars of any facts on which the party relies in mitigation of, or otherwise in relation to, the amount of damages. Ord. 18, r.13(4) used to provide that allegations as to the amount of damages were deemed to be traversed unless specifically admitted. The rule has now been revoked. This is an important change in practice and unless denied, damages are now deemed to be admitted. All pleadings must be on A4 paper. Under RSC, Ord. 3, r.3 they may be served during the Long Vacation including the month of August. The advantage of serving a writ with statement of claim endorsed is that it can be served after 4 p.m. on a weekday or all day Saturday.

1.79 Given this formality of pleading it is easy to overlook the basic rule that what one does not plead one will not get at trial. Convictions have to be strictly pleaded, and pleaded to. If the defendant wants to allege contributory negligence (eg in the manner of the plaintiff's driving or his failure to wear a crash helmet or a seat belt, or his drinking) then it must be pleaded. It was emphasised in *Fookes v. Slaytor* [1978] 1 W.L.R. 1293 that the court has no power to make a finding of contributory negligence if it is not pleaded. In a Canadian case, *Ducharme v. Davies* [1984] C.L.Y. 2291, the defendant was denied a finding of contributory negligence against an infant for failing to wear a seat belt because she was too young and against her mother because he had failed to plead contribution or indemnity against her for failing to ensure that her daughter wore a seat belt. Similarly, in *Bowes v. Sedgefield DC* [1981] I.C.R. 234 the defendants were not allowed to rely on a statutory defence at trial which they had not pleaded. The same rule applies to quantum. Under Ord. 18, r.8 the plaintiff must plead both the claim for provisional damages and the facts relied on to support it as specified by section 32A of the Supreme Court Act 1981.

1.80 If the plaintiff is going to see additional damages for loss of earning capacity this, too, should be specifically pleaded in order to give the defendant proper notice (*Chan Wai Tong v. Li Ping Sum* [1985] 2 W.L.R. 396). In *Thorn v. Powergen plc* [1997] P.I.Q.R. Q. 71 the Court of Appeal endorsed the pleading of a claim for a *Smith v. Manchester* award as good practice, failure to do so may not be a bar to an award of such damages at least where the facts pleaded obviously raise the need for consideration of such loss. The plaintiff will not be allowed to give evidence at trial of any special damage not explicitly claimed in his pleadings or particulars (Ord.

18, r.12). Therefore, where the plaintiff claims continuing loss of earnings or loss of dependency and the rate has changed, for instance because of salary increases, the defendant must be given notice either by service of an updated schedule of special damages and/or if necessary notice of intended amendment of the Statement of Claim. In *Owen v. Grimsby Cleethorpes Transport* [1992] P.I.Q.R. Q. 27 the Court of Appeal stated that it is not always necessary for the pleadings in personal injury cases to be amended each time a fresh medical report leads to developments in the case. However, in that case the defendants had been aware of the plaintiff's medical evidence and to avoid possible objections at trial it is good practice to amend to plead any substantial changes to the plaintiff's claim.

1.81 To comply with RSC, Ord. 18, r.12(1A-C) and CCR, Ord. 6, r.1(5), a plaintiff is now obliged to serve with his statement of claim or file with his particulars of claim:

(a) a medical report, substantiating all the personal injuries alleged in the statement of claim which the plaintiff proposes to adduce in evidence as part of his case at trial; and

(b) a statement of the special damages claimed, giving full particulars of the special damages for expenses and losses already incurred and an estimate of any future expenses and losses, including loss of earnings and pension rights.

If the required documents are not so served, the court may specify a time limit for providing them, or make such order as it thinks fit, including dispensing with the requirements or staying proceedings.

1.82 The Lord Chief Justice's Practice Note [1984] 1 W.L.R. 1127 still applies to High Court actions requires the plaintiff to serve a schedule of particulars of any claims for loss of earnings, loss of future earning capacity, medical expenses, the cost of care, attention, accommodation or appliances or loss of pension rights on the defendant. The time limits for doing so are not later than 14 days after the action appears in the Warned List in London, or the lodging of the Certificate of Readiness outside London. The defendant has to reply in writing also within 14 days, confirming which items are agreed and at which figure, which items are not agreed and why, and giving his counter-proposals. The plaintiff's solicitor should draw up the schedule in four columns, for item number, description, amount claimed and the fourth, blank, for the defendant's comments. In complicated cases, the schedule can and should be drafted by counsel. When the defendant has served his comments, the schedule should be lodged with the court, so that the trial judge can, before the hearing starts, get a clear picture of which of the issues raised in the case are agreed and which disputed and why from the pleadings, the experts' reports and the schedule. In many cases of substance it may well be appropriate for the parties to seek further or different directions, from the court, at a considerably earlier stage, as to how claims for damages should be pleaded out. The importance of the use of schedules of damages and counter-schedules in cases of catastrophic injury and, indeed, all substantial claims for damages under several heads cannot be over-emphasised. Properly and constructively used they can be a vital tool both in narrowing issues and clarifying points in dispute.

1.83 The schedule is, of course, not intended to be a means of adding new heads or items of damage to the plaintiff's claim which have not already been pleaded. The plaintiff will still have to make any necessary amendments to his statement of claim and, if he has left it this late to do so, may well find himself in difficulty over costs if the action has to be stood out or adjourned because the defendant has not been given adequate notice.

1.84 Finally, RSC, Ord. 18, r.8(4) and CCR, Ord. 6, r.1A make it clear that the plaintiff must specifically plead a claim for interest even thought it is awarded automatically in personal injury claims unless the defendant can show good reason (see para. 1.107 et seq).

1.85 Where either party gives particulars RSC, Ord. 18, r.12(7) provides that both request and particulars must be incorporated in the same document and go into the bundle of pleadings immediately after the pleading to which they refer. Similar provisions apply in the county courts (see CCR, Ord. 6, r.7 and Ord. 9, r.11). Pleadings close 14 days after service of defence, reply or defence to counter-claim, even though a request for further and better particulars is outstanding. This date is particularly important now, because it fixes the date upon which automatic directions apply in most personal injury actions and the time for discovery in all actions.

Discovery

1.86 Discovery in personal injury cases in the High Court, or at least in running-down cases, is an exception to the general rule for mutual discovery by both parties without order since the defendant in such cases is specifically relieved of any obligation to make discovery unless he is ordered to do so. In relation to running-down cases or cases where liability is admitted automatic discovery is limited to disclosure by the plaintiff of any documents relating to special damages. In the county courts discovery in personal injury cases remains mutual but in running-down cases or cases where liability is admitted, discovery is limited to documents relating to the amount of damages, and so in practice the defendant, unless the employer, is unlikely to have any documents to disclose. In certain running-down cases, however, a defendant should be asked to make discovery (eg latent defect cases, where the plaintiff may want to see all his maintenance and servicing records; accidents alleged to have been caused by sudden and unexpected illness or death, where the plaintiff wants to see the medical records; and of course claims in nuisance against highway authorities and their contractors, where discovery can often reveal breaches of prescribed safety codes and bad accident records). Medical or other expert reports that have been disclosed to the other side should not go in Sched. 1, Pt 1, of the list, even if they have already been disclosed to the other side, but always go in Pt 2, otherwise one will lose the right to claim privilege for such reports. (See generally as to the privilege attaching to medical reports: *Worrall v. Reich* [1955] 1 Q.B. 296, and *Causton v. Mann Egerton (Johnsons) Ltd* [1974] 1 W.L.R. 162.) At a later stage one might, for some reason, want to prevent the other side using reports disclosed to them voluntarily as part of their case, and if they have been put in the wrong part of the list of documents the right to do so will have been lost. In *Earle v. Medhurst* [1985] C.L.Y. 2650 the plaintiff's claim to privilege for medical reports he had disclosed in a previous action against a different defendant claiming damages for similar injuries was not upheld.

1.87 The obligation to give discovery of relevant documents is continuing, so that documents which come into existence or a party's possession after he has made formal discovery must be disclosed to the other side. This was confirmed by the Court of Appeal in *Vernon v. Bosley* [1997] P.I.Q.R. P. 326.

Interrogatories

1.88 The potentially useful role of interrogatories in personal injury actions should not be overlooked by representatives of plaintiffs or defendants. Interrogatories can be served without order (see

RSC, Ord. 26, rr. 1–3 applied to the county court by CCR, Ord. 14, r.11). Interrogatories without order may be served twice. A party can object to answering such interrogatories and should apply to the court within 14 days of service to have them varied or withdrawn. It must be borne in mind that interrogatories should only be served if necessary to dispose fairly of the action or to save costs. Useful guiding principles on the service of interrogatories in personal injury cases were given by the Court of Appeal in *Hall v. Sevalco Ltd* [1996] P.I.Q.R. P. 344. Interrogatories should not be used to obtain information or admissions which were or were likely to be contained in pleadings, medical reports, discoverable documents or witness statements. Suitable times to interrogate are probably after discovery and after exchange of witness statements.

Payment into court

1.89 Payments into court are the defendant's finest weapon and they are not used often or effectively enough. Sometimes insurers might feel that they can get a better deal at the doors of the court in a heavy case, and the identity of the judge allotted to that case can influence corridor negotiations pretty heavily, but an experienced plaintiff's solicitor with nothing much to worry about in court who has gone that far will strike a fairly hard bargain. The payment in can be made at any time after service of the writ or particulars of claim, and should be made at least 21 days before trial if it is to protect the defendant in costs. Under RSC, Ord. 22, r.3 or CCR, Ord. 11, r.3 the plaintiff may accept a payment in as of right within 21 days of receipt of notice of the payment in, provided that the trial has not begun. If a payment in is made less than 21 days before the trial, and is not accepted, the court is entitled to take the fact and amount of the payment in into account in exercising its discretion as to costs (*King v. Weston-Howell* [1989] 2 All E.R. 375). In *Kinvig v. Holland Hannen & Cubbitts* [1977] C.L.Y. 373 an interesting situation arose because the plaintiff failed to beat a payment in but had his damages increased on appeal, although still not so as to beat the amount that the defendant had paid into court. However, the Court of Appeal gave the plaintiff his costs of the appeal because it was unlikely that the defendant would have allowed him to take out from the sum paid into court an amount equal to the increased amount the Court of Appeal eventually awarded him. Acceptance of a payment into court operates only as a stay of the proceedings. In

Buckland v. Palmer [1984] 1 W.L.R. 1109 it was held to be an abuse of the process of the court for a plaintiff's insurance company to start a second action for insured losses when the plaintiff had accepted a payment into court in his action for uninsured losses. The proper course was for the insurance company to apply to remove the stay in the plaintiff's action.

1.90 Once the 21 days for acceptance have passed or the trial has started the plaintiff can take the money in court only with the defendant's consent or by order unless the payment in itself was made or increased after the trial started, when he has two days after receipt of notice in the High Court or 14 days in a county court to accept, but must do so before the judge begins to deliver his judgment (RSC, Ord. 22, r.5; CCR, Ord. 11, r.3). The court will order the money to be paid out only if the risks are the same as they were when it was paid in and on terms protecting the defendant as to costs. If the trial goes so badly that the plaintiff wants to take the money out during it he must, as was decided in *Gaskins v. British Aluminium Co. Ltd* [1976] Q.B. 524, make an application to do so, and he must have the defendant's consent even to make the application. An order for payment out will normally be needed whenever the money in court is accepted if it was paid in by one of two or more defendants. If the plaintiff is under a disability settlement of the action has to be approved by the court under RSC, Ord. 80, r.13 or CCR, Ord. 10, r.10; so too if the claim is under the Fatal Accidents Act 1976 as amended and more than one person is entitled to the damages even though no one is under a disability. Where a plaintiff under a disability fails to beat a payment in at trial, the usual cost consequences will follow unless the next friend has applied for and failed to obtain the approval of the Court (see *Abada v. Gray* [1997] T.L.R. 369). Under RSC, Ord. 22, r.1(8) or CCR, Ord. 11, r.1(8) the defendant can, and should, pay interest into court as well as damages. The notice of payment in should specify whether interest is included but, it seems, need not itemise the amount. At trial the judge will have to decide whether his award of damages and interest exceeds the payment in of damages and interest. Where the plaintiff claims continuing loss the judge has to decide the issue by reference to interest on the loss calculated up to the date of payment in. If the defendant has made an interim payment before he pays in, his notice must specifically refer to the interim payment and aggregate the two amounts if he is to put the plaintiff at risk for the total. He can do this whether the interim payment was voluntary or under order.

When making a payment into court in respect of an accident or injury the defendant should first obtain a current certificate of recoverable benefit from the CRU at the Department of Social Security. (Under previous enactments the recoupment regime introduced by the Social Security Act 1989 applied only to payments in respect of accident, injury or disease on or after January 1, 1989. The 1997 Act now applies to compensation payments made after October 6, 1997 in respect of any accident or injury, even one occurring before that date, or in respect of disease even if the first claim for relevant benefit was before that date.) This will state the amount of relevant recoverable State benefits paid to the plaintiff, for which the plaintiff must give credit and which the compensating defendant must reimburse the Department of Social Security. In accordance with sections 6 and 16 of the Social Security (Recovery of Benefits) Act 1997 (see Appendix B) the defendant should deduct an equal amount from the payment into court, lodge a current certificate of recoverable benefit with the payment into court and, where the payment is calculated under section 8 of the 1997 Act, must give the information under s. 9(1) to the plaintiff. The present regulations (see Appendix B) do not appear to permit the making of a payment in the absence of a certificate. The defendant is not bound to reimburse the Department of Social Security until he is notified that the money in court has been paid out to the plaintiff. The best course is to apply for the relevant certificate at an early stage when a payment in is contemplated. The defendant's position in costs can be protected by making a "Calderbank" offer, which, provided a certificate has been applied for and not received, will be effective for up to seven days after receipt of the certificate, by when it should be superseded by a payment in (RSC, Ord. 69, r.9(2); CCR, Ord. 11, r.10(3)).

1.91 The rules still refer to the earlier legislation but presumably will be applied to payments under the 1997 Act. Money in court belongs to the party who paid it in until it is accepted. It follows that the defendant will be entitled to the interest it has earned on deposit up the point of acceptance. Where the plaintiff is under a disability, he cannot accept a payment into court without approval under RSC, Ord. 80, r.11 or CCR, Ord. 10, r.10 which is likely to take place later than the time limited for accepting the payment in.

1.92 The duty imposed by RSC, Ord. 22, r.7 and CCR, Ord. 11, r.7 not to disclose a payment in to the trial judge until all questions of liability and damages have been decided is extended to the Court of Appeal by Ord. 59, r.12A. It applies not only to the appellant's notice and respondent's counter-notice, but also to the copy documents lodged by the appellant under Ord. 59, r.9 including, of course, the transcript of the proceedings in the court below. The exceptions to this rule are that the plaintiff can disclose the fact that there has been a payment in into court, and how much it is, on the hearing of an application for an interim payment (*Fryer v. London Transport Executive* (1982) *The Times*, 14 December. Another exception is that, under RSC, Ord. 22, r.7(2), any party may bring the attention of the court to the fact that a payment in has or has not been made and the date (but not the amount) of such payment where the question of the costs of the issue of liability falls to be decided, that issue having been tried and an issue of question of quantum remaining to be tried separately. There may also be other interlocutory applications, such as applications to dismiss for want of prosecution where it is legitimate to draw the Court's attention to a payment in.

1.93 As we have seen, defendants can protect themselves by making written offers when they cannot make an effective payment into court because they are faced with a split trial. There is a similar procedure available to a defendant faced with a claim for provisional damages. Under Ord. 37, r.9 the defendant can make a written offer to the plaintiff tendering a sum in satisfaction of the plaintiff's claim on the basis that he will not suffer the disease or deterioration claimed and identifying the disease or deterioration in question *and* agreeing to the court making an award of provisional damages. He can, of course, also make a payment into court, but the difficulties of calculating it are obvious and he would probably have to pay in more than the value of the claim for immediate damages to tempt the plaintiff.

Interim payments

1.94 Interim payments are one of the most important procedural developments in personal injury cases in recent years. The practice is contained in RSC, Ord. 29, rr. 9–18 which apply (with minor amendments) in a county court by virtue of CCR, Ord. 13, r.12. A recent innovation has been introduced by section 2 of the Damages Act 1996. A court can now order that interim payments are wholly or partly to take the form of periodic payments.

1.95 The majority of personal injury action defendants will be in one of three categories. An interim payment can only be ordered against a person who is insured in respect of the plaintiff's claim, a public authority, or a person whose means enable him to make the payment. An interim payment can now also be ordered where a person's liability will be met by an insurer under section 151 of the Road Traffic Act 1988 or an insurer concerned under the MIB agreement (see RSC, Ord. 29, r.11(2). A payment will be ordered, of course, if liability is admitted on the pleadings and the court is satisfied that substantial damages will be recovered.

It seems that the admission need not be an express one and that if, for instance, a plaintiff has pleaded a relevant conviction and the defendant admits it and does not claim that it was erroneous or irrelevant, the plaintiff should get his interim payment. It is yet to be seen whether the courts' narrow approach to relevant admissions for CCR, Ord. 9, r.10 will affect the approach to interim payments, but it is to be hoped that the courts will not be deterred by, and insurers will not attempt to stand on, technicalities. An interlocutory judgment will certainly enable the plaintiff to get an interim payment as will a judgment on liability tried first (ie when a split trial has been ordered).

1.96 Finally, a plaintiff can obtain an interim payment if he can satisfy the court on the balance of probabilities that he will recover substantial damages at trial from the defendant or, where there are two or more defendants, from any given defendant (*Breeze v. McKennon* (1985) 32 Build L.R. 41; *Ricci Burns Ltd v. Toole* [1989] 3 All E.R. 478). If he can show this, then the onus will be on the defendant to prove that the plaintiff's claim will fail or be so reduced by contributory negligence that the damages he is likely to recover will not be substantial. Now that, following *Fryer v. L.T.E.* (see para. 1.92 above), a payment into court can be disclosed on an interim payment application, a defendant who has paid anything more than a small proportion of the value of the plaintiff's claim into court will find it difficult to resist the application on this ground, especially as the court will usually order the interim payment to be paid out of the money in court. Proof of hardship is not a condition precedent as emphasised by the Court of Appeal in *Schott Kem Ltd v. Bentley & Ors* [1990] 3 W.L.R. 397 which disapproved the then current practice of limiting awards to sums for which the plaintiff could show a need (see also *Stringman v. McArdle* [1994] 1 W.L.R. 563). In assessing a just amount the court will obviously take account of the fact that the plaintiff has incurred or will incur specific expenditure, eg private medical treatment. However, there is no need to demonstrate a particular need beyond the general need to be paid damages as soon as reasonably possible.

1.97 An interim payment is, in effect, a payment in advance of the plaintiff's own money to which he is entitled. Obviously he is entitled to it if he has got a good case. Thus an interim payment will be made directly to a legally-aided plaintiff. The only exception to the rule is when the plaintiff is under a disability, when of course the interim payment has to be approved and directions given about how it is to be applied. The time limit for an application for interim payment is any time after the plaintiff has served his writ and the time for acknowledgement of service has expired.

1.98 The summons and supporting affidavit should be served together 10 clear days before the return date (Ord. 29, r.10) (seven days before the hearing of the application in a county court). The form and content of the affidavit are very important. It should be sworn by the plaintiff, his next friend, or solicitor. The affidavit must verify that the defendant falls within the categories in Ord. 29, r.11(2), set out the procedural steps taken and facts of the cause of action briefly, explain the basis on which the application is made, state the amount of the damages to which the application relates and contain enough information to enable the master or district judge to reach a preliminary valuation of the claim (because he has got to order a part of it to be paid to the plaintiff). Thus the medical reports on which the plaintiff intends to rely must be exhibited. Special damages must be calculated to date and verified by exhibiting vouchers (eg employers' letters). The best way to treat special damages is to deal with each item of special damage in a separate paragraph and to have a final paragraph totalling them all up and giving a global figure.

1.99 If it is a fatal accident case, full details of the dependants and the loss of dependency up to the date of the application must be included. This must be calculated just like special damage and must be verified by exhibits in the same way. It is not sufficient for the plaintiff merely to refer to his affidavit to the statement of claim or statement of special damages for the calculations of special damage. Those calculations might be out of date by the time the application is made. Indeed, if he tries to deal with the application on that basis the affidavit may be considered defective and the application may fail. The affidavit is not specifically required to deal with future loss but it is advisable to indicate what items are continuing so that the master or registrar has a global view of the case. The affidavit should explain why the plaintiff needs an interim payment and details should be given of any special needs and hardship. This remains good practice although an affidavit which failed to do so would not be defective. In *Stringman v. McArdle* [1994] 1 W.L.R. 1653 the Court of Appeal emphasised that the court should not concern itself with investigation of how an interim payment would be used once in the plaintiff's hands. A court may be more easily persuaded to order a high interim payment if the plaintiff intends to purchase a capital asset and the plaintiff will undertake to so apply the interim payment and to execute a charge over the asset (see *Harris v. Ellen* unreported December 21, 1994 C.A.)

1.100 There are three grounds for defending the application. The first is that the plaintiff's solicitor has the practice wrong.

1.101 The second is that the plaintiff is unlikely to recover substantial damages. It is not enough for the defendant to argue that he denies liability or denies a conviction in his defence; he must also show that his grounds for doing so are sufficiently strong to put the plaintiff at risk of either complete or substantial failure at trial or that, on the face of it, the plaintiff's claim is not worth very much even on full liability. A defendant who relies on this ground would be wise to file an affidavit in answer to the plaintiff's affidavit and not leave all the argument to the application itself.

1.102 The third ground for defending an application is that the defendant from whom the interim payment is sought is not a person who appears to the court to fall within one of the categories listed in Ord. 29, r.11(2).

1.103 Second or subsequent applications for an interim payment can be made even if the first one failed.

1.104 As we have seen, when the defendant pays into court after making an interim payment, he must ensure that this notice of payment in states that the interim payment has been taken into account (Ord. 29, r.15) if he wants to put the plaintiff on risk for the aggregate of the two payments. If he pays in first and then has to make an interim payment and he wants to make that payment out of the money in court, he must ask specifically for leave to do so and also to amend his notice of payment in so as to refer to the fact that some of the money has been paid out. Where the defendant has made a voluntary interim payment before proceedings, the plaintiff must still plead the whole of his claim including any special damage for expense paid for by the interim payment. If he does not, and the defendant aggregates the interim payment with his payment into court, as he is entitled to, the plaintiff will be doubly put at risk. The court has the power to include interest on an interim payment but will rarely do so. There is no provision for it to order a payment on account of costs but Lord Woolfs, new regime anticipates earlier costs determination.

1.105 The trial judge will deduct the interim payment from the final award for damages. The way this is done can affect the award of interest. If the interim payment was specifically assigned to one head of damage (*e.g.* on account of nursing services or the cost of a specially modified bungalow for a quadraplegic) there is no difficulty, and the note at para. 29/11/5 of the 1997 *White Book* encourages the court to assign the payment to special damages to simplify the calculation of interest at trial.

1.106 By section 50 of the County Courts Act 1984 and CCR, Ord. 13, r.12, the county court has power to order interim payments in cases where the action is not referred to arbitration. As in the High Court the power is not limited to personal injury cases. The procedure in Ord. 13, r.12 is the same as that in the High Court save that the summons and affidavit have to be served not less than seven days before the return date of the application

Interest

1.107 The plaintiff's right to interest on damages in personal injury cases is now conferred by section 35A of the Supreme Court Act 1981 and section 69 of the County Courts Act 1984. It is mandatory for the court to award interest where judgement is given for personal injuries or death which exceed £200 unless the court is satisfied there is a special reason.

1.108 RSC, Ord. 18, r.8(4) provides that the plaintiff must specifically plead his claim for interest in a statement of claim (CCR, Ord. 6, r.1A corresponds). It has been held that a claim for interest under s. 35A is sufficiently pleaded even if it only appears in the prayer and not also in the body of the pleading (*McDonald's Hamburgers Ltd v. Burgerking* (UK) Ltd [1987] F.S.R. 112). It is probably wise to include a prayer for interest in the general endorsement on the writ as well, if it is to be served separately, although there is no requirement for such a writ to include a claim for interest (*Edward Butler Vintners Ltd v. Grange Seymour Internationale Ltd* [1987] 131 S.J. 1188). The wording should be "... and interest to be assessed pursuant to section 35A of the Supreme Court Act 1981".

1.109 The original working rules for courts when awarding interest were laid down by the Court of Appeal in *Jefford v. Gee* [1970] 2 Q.B. 130, but have been modified in *Cookson v. Knowles* [1979] A.C. 556; *Pickett v. British Rail Engineering Ltd* [1980] A.C. 136; *Birkett v. Hayes* [1982] 1 W.L.R. 876 and *Wright v. British Railways Board* [1983] A.C. 773.

1.110 The principle remains the same, however, which is that the trial judge must itemise the award of damages and the appropriate rates and periods for interest. The rules at present are as follows:

(1) *General damages for pain and suffering.* Three per cent from service of writ to judgment following the reasoning of the House of Lords in *Wells v. Wells* [1998] 1 W.L.R. 329.

(2) *Damages for bereavement.* Section 1A of the Fatal Accidents Act 1976 gives claims for bereavement to the deceased's wife or the parents of a legitimate, or mother of an illegitimate, unmarried minor. The sum is presently £7,500. Interest is payable at the full rate from the date of death (*Prior v. Hastie* [1987] C.L.Y. 1219; *Khan v. Duncan* (1989) unreported, Popplewell J.).

(3) *Special damages or past loss of dependency under the Fatal Accidents Act 1976.* The general rule is that interest is awarded at half short-term investment account rate from accident to trial (*Jefford v. Gee* [1970] 2 Q.B. 130). This approach is designed to cover cases where the bulk of the special damages comprises separate items of loss (eg weekly wages) occurring fairly regularly throughout the period from accident to trial. It is not satisfactory where a significant separate item of loss is incurred at a particular time. In *Prokop v. DHSS and Another* [1985] C.L.Y. 1037, May L.J. stated the relevant principle clearly in the following passage:

> "On the facts in *Jefford v. Gee* the relevant loss of earnings continued throughout from accident to trial, and indeed went on thereafter ... it is, I think, quite clear from the judgment, and indeed from the application of arithmetical commonsense, that the half-rate approach there referred to is only applicable to cases where the special damages

comprise more or less regular periodical losses which are continuous from the date of the accident to the date of the trial; these are more often than not lost earnings.

If there is any general view in any quarter that the interest on special damages is in any event to be calculated at half-rate, when the losses do not continue from accident to trial, then I think that this is wrong and should not hereafter be followed."

We submit that this approach is preferable to the subsequent decision of the Court of Appeal in *Dexter v. Courtaulds Ltd* [1984] 1 W.L.R. 372 which was given in ignorance of the earlier decision in *Prokop*.

In any event, practitioners should heed the advice given by Lawton L.J. in *Dexter*'s case. Where a plaintiff contends that his is a case justifying a departure from the general approach that contention, and the facts relied upon to support it, should be pleaded.

(4) *Future loss*. No interest at all, as the plaintiff has not suffered the loss by the date of trial and accordingly been kept out of his money.

(5) Interest is not taxable whether it forms part of a judgment debt or a payment in or a settlement (Income and Corporation Taxes Act 1988, s. 329).

1.111 Under the regime established by section 103 of the Social Security Act 1992 it appeared that when assessing interest the amount of damages awarded was to be treated as reduced by the amount of any payment required to be made to the Department of Social Security. That provision has been repealed by the Social Security (Recovery of Benefits) Act 1997. It would therefore appear that plaintiffs, as from October 6, 1997 are entitled to interest on the whole of their damages.

Automatic directions

1.112 Automatic directions now apply to the interlocutory stages of most personal injury actions in the High Court and personal injury actions in a county court. The automatic directions, as previously stated, do not apply to Admiralty actions and High Court medical negligence actions.

1.113 The automatic directions are to be found at RSC, Ord. 25, r.8 and for the county courts at CCR, Ord. 17, r.11 (see Appendix D). They have the same force as an order of the court although they are not peremptory. They establish a conventional pattern and timescale for basic interlocutory stages in personal injury litigation. In the High Court and county courts express provision is made allowing any party to apply to the court for different directions, a provision which should not be overlooked, particularly given the new provisions for early exchange of witness statements, if there is good reason for departing from the normal rule (see RSC, Ord. 25, r.8(3), CCR, Ord. 17, r.11(4)). Before considering the automatic directions, it is as well to remember that (although they will be sufficient in most instances) they are only the bare bones of the directions the parties may need in a personal injury case, and do not prevent the parties seeking any further directions they may need. A party should always seek the opposite party's consent for further directions, in advance of making an application.

1.114 Examples of such additional directions are for amendment of pleadings, further and better particulars, discovery by a defendant excused from this step under Ord. 25, r.8, more medical or other experts than Ord. 25, r.8 allows, trial out of London or not at the trial centre for the District Registry in which the action is proceeding.

1.115 The automatic directions provided for by RSC, Ord. 25, r.8 come into effect at close of pleadings which is 14 days after service of defence, reply, or defence to counterclaim, and are as follows (material differences in the corresponding CCR, Ord. 17, r.11 are noted):

(1) *Discovery* within 14 days (28 days in a county court) and inspection of documents within seven days after (see para. 1.86 above in relation to actions in which liability is admitted or actions arising out of a road traffic accident).

(2) *Experts' evidence*. The parties have to disclose, within 14 weeks, the substance of the experts' evidence on which they intend to rely, in the form of written reports to be agreed if possible. Where both parties intend to rely on experts there should be mutual exchange, medical for medical and non-medical for non-medical. Unless the reports are agreed, the

parties are at liberty to call experts whose reports have been disclosed, limited to two medical experts and one non-medical expert of any kind. In the county court there is no positive obligation to disclose expert reports but the right to adduce expert evidence is lost unless disclosure is made within ten weeks. Failure to disclose means that the leave of the court or agreement of the other parties must be obtained before expert evidence can be adduced.

(3) *Witness statements*. Each party has to serve within 14 weeks (10 weeks in a county court) written statements of all such oral evidence which they intend to adduce.

(4) *Photographs*, sketch plans and the contents of any police accident report shall be receivable in evidence and must be agreed if possible.

(5) *Setting down* within six months (see below for the equivalent county court provisions). Practice Direction (Action: Setting Down) [1996] 1 W.L.R. 1431 requires leave to set down out of time to be obtained if the automatic direction is not complied with.

(6) *Venue*. Trial in London if the action is proceeding there or trial at the trial centre designated for the District Registry in which the action is proceeding, unless the Crown is a party.

(7) *Mode of trial* will be by judge alone in category B, which is a case of substance or difficulty.

(8) The estimated length of trial must be notified to the court on setting down.

1.116 The rule requiring automatic exchange of witness statements is one of the single most significant changes in the pattern of litigation to have taken place in recent years. Exchange of witness statements is to be the norm in all actions, not just personal injury actions. In the High Court supplementary provisions dealing with witness statements are to be found in RSC, Ord. 38, r.2A(4)–(16) (see Appendix C) and in the county courts in CCR, Ord. 20, r.12(A)(4)–(16). Unless otherwise ordered every witness statement stands as the evidence in chief of the witness concerned in the High

Court Practice Direction (Civil Litigation: Case Management) [1995] 1 W.L.R. 262.

1.117 Evidence will now have to be prepared at a much earlier stage. The normal course of trials is likely to be different as the court will often direct that a witness statement stand as the evidence in chief, or at least part of the evidence in chief, of its maker and, in any event, a witness statement may be put to the maker in cross-examination. Where a party fails to comply with the direction for exchange of witness statements, he will not be entitled to adduce evidence to which the direction related without leave of the court (RSC, Ord. 38, r.2A(10)).

1.118 The practice on extension of time for exchange of evidence, when orders and directions had not been complied with was considered in *Hill v. William Tomkins Ltd* [1997] P.I.Q.R. P. 115 and *Otto v. Keys* [1997] P.I.Q.R. P. 120. Judges will seek explanation for the breach and weigh its nature against prejudice to the opposite party and the administration of justice in general as a result of non-compliance as against prejudice to the plaintiff if time was not extended. The Court of Appeal emphasised that there would be increasing imbalance of breaches of timetables, but recognised the overriding principle that justice must be done. Nevertheless, where evidence is of limited value in the eyes of the court, injustice may not be considered to be done by excluding it.

1.119 The parties may stand or fall by the evidence as disclosed in their witness statements, although a witness will always be free to give evidence in relation to new matters which have arisen since the statement was served on the other party. The direction only applies to evidence which a party "intends to place reliance on" and so cannot apply to new evidence which only comes to light after the time for serving statements has passed. RSC, Ord. 38, r.2A deals with the form of statements. Where a party is unable to obtain a written statement from an intended witness it will probably be necessary to apply to the court for directions. Where the maker of a witness statement served on the other parties is not called at trial, no other party can put the statement in evidence. Although no specific provision is made by the rules it can be anticipated that a practice of serving supplementary or additional witness statements will arise in cases in which the evidence cannot be finally settled at an early stage, a paradigm example being personal injury cases in which there may be a permanent or continuing disability or a slow recovery. Practitioners concerned that the other parties may hold back supplementary evidence unless obliged to serve supplementary witness statements can attempt to agree arrangements for exchange of further statements and apply to the court for appropriate directions in the absence of agreement.

1.120 In a county court, unless a hearing date has already been fixed, the plaintiff should request the court to fix a day for the hearing within six months of the close of pleadings (CCR, Ord. 17, r.11(3)(d)). Although the effect of that direction is not peremptory, the plaintiff must be sure to request a hearing within 15 months of close of pleadings. If he does not the action will be automatically struck out in accordance with CCR, Ord. 17, r.11(9).

1.121 Ord. 17, r.11(9) was designed to impel plaintiffs to bring actions on for trial without undue delay. The purpose of discouraging delay which had bedevilled much county court litigation was laudable. However, the automatic strike out sanction has led to a torrent of new satellite litigation in total conflict with the original purposes of the automatic directions, spawning applications to determine whether an application had been automatically struck out and whether it should be re-instituted, often delaying the progress of actions for many months if not years. The rule has been described judicially as ill-considered and badly drafted. It has hardly been an encouraging precursor to the case management regime, although doubtless lessons have been learned by the new Civil Procedures Rules Committee.

1.122 Several dozen points of general application have now been resolved by the Court of Appeal. In reality the conscientious solicitor representing the plaintiff should not become embroiled with difficulties arising out of Ord. 17, r.11(9). In the first place a reliable and fail-safe system of recording and alerting the practitioner to key timetable dates and monitoring compliance is required. The primary requirement of the rules, it should not be overlooked, is for a request within six months from deemed closed of pleadings. For most county court claims, 15 months from commencement of proceedings, as opposed to the date on which the automatic directions timetable commences, should be adequate time within which to prepare so as to be in a position to request a hearing. Generally, it will only be to the client's advantage to be well prepared well before that date. So long as the request is made before that date no issue should arise as to whether the action has been automatically struck out. In those cases where there is some good objective reason for delaying trial, application should be made to the court for substitute directions with an order that Ord. 17, r.11(3)(d) and 9 be expressly dis-applied. If an automatic strike out sanction is to be re-applied, a specified date by which the request must be made should be included in the order. Should a defendant be unco-operative or even obstructive, appropriate applications should be made well before any danger of automatic strike out arises. If foundation for the application has been properly laid in correspondence there is every reason to anticipate that the plaintiff will be properly protected by appropriate costs orders.

1.123 If an action is automatically struck out it has long been established that the county court has jurisdiction to extend time retrospectively for making the necessary request under Ord. 13, r.4 (see *Rastin v. British Steel* [1994] 1 W.L.R. 733). It is clear that the courts will be slow to exercise their discretion to re-instate. The Court will first wish to be satisfied that, failure to request a hearing date aside, there has been no significant failure to conduct the case with expedition on the part of the plaintiff. Secondly the failure must be excusable, for example the result of an isolated clerical error which has not contributed in a significant way to delay in getting the action heard. Thirdly, the Court must be satisfied that the balance of justice indicates re-instalment. If re-instatement causes significant prejudice to a defendant which would not have been suffered if the plaintiff had applied for a trial date in the due time that will usually be a conclusive reason for refusing reinstatement. These stringent tests will be applied unless the failure to apply has been caused by something external to the plaintiff and his advisors which has genuinely and reasonably misled them.

1.124 For guidance on these matters and on issues relevant to whether an action has been struck out automatically reference should first be made to *Bannister v. SGB plc* [1997] P.I.Q.R. P. 165 and *Greig Middleton & Co. v. Denderowicz* [1997] 4 All E.R. 181 which sought to give comprehensive guidance. It should also be borne in mind that yet further issues have subsequently occurred which are now subject to judicial decision. Among controversial issues now settled are that a defence is delivered when delivered at the court office, not when served on the plaintiff and that an application for extension of time to request a hearing date by implication contains a request to fix a date. Judgment for damages to be assessed takes an action outside the automatic directions regime. An admission of liability in correspondence without entry of interlocutory judgment will not (see *Oakley v. Rawlinson* [1998]

P.I.Q.R. P. 161, but see *Gomes v. Clark* [1997] P.I.Q.R. P. 219 as to admissions under Ord. 9, r.6(3) nor, generally, do appeals on interlocutory matters.

Whilst, in most cases, avoidance of an automatic strike out will ensure that the action can progress to trial, it cannot be taken for granted that compliance with Ord. 17, r.11(9) will guarantee that an action is not struck out for want of prosecution. In an appropriate case it can be (see *Jones v. Bayford Mining Co. Ltd* [1997] T.L.R. 297).

1.125 The following points should be borne in mind. It is still necessary to issue a summons for directions in an admiralty or medical negligence case. It may be necessary in any other type of personal injury case. The important difference is that the party who issues a summons for directions in a case to which automatic directions apply must be prepared to justify his summons or run the risk of losing his costs of doing so. The time limit for setting the action down for trial runs from close of pleadings so that it is possible to set the action down the day after the plaintiff's solicitor sends off his list of documents.

Automatic directions under RSC Ord. 25, r.8 will apply to claims for provisional damages when they are at the immediate damages stage, unless the plaintiff wants to call more than two medical experts. The plaintiff must issue a summons for directions after he has given three months' notice under Ord. 37, r.10 that he intends to apply for further damages.

Experts

1.126 Personal injury cases are unique in that they almost always involve at least one expert: the doctor. As we have seen they may involve other types of expert as well. Under Ord. 38, r.36 (see Appendix C), neither party may adduce expert evidence, whether medical or non-medical, at trial unless one of the conditions imposed by the rule is fulfilled. Hence expert evidence is inadmissible unless: (i) the automatic direction, or a specific direction, relating to expert evidence has been complied with; or (ii) all parties agree to it; or (iii) the court gives leave; or (iv) the evidence can be given by affidavit. Order 38, r.40 has been revoked and the evidence of motor engineers is no longer treated differently from that of other experts.

1.127 When automatic directions apply, the court will not now have the opportunity to consider the admissibility of experts' evidence before the trial. Even when it has that opportunity, because directions have to be sought, it is clear, from *Sullivan v. West Yorkshire Passenger Transport Executive*, that it has no power to exclude such evidence at the interlocutory stage other than to limit the number of witnesses. In *Burton v. Chemical Vessel Services* [1984] C.L.Y. 1527 the defendant was granted leave to call two engineers in an industrial injury case, even though one of them had originally been instructed by the plaintiff. The spirit of Ord. 25 was to save time and costs and there was no evidence that two similar experts would waste either.

1.128 In a medical negligence case, where a summons for directions is necessary an application for a direction in relation to expert evidence should ordinarily be made at the hearing of the summons for directions. If an application is not made the court will consider matters relating to expert evidence of its own motion (RSC, Ord. 25, r.3(1)(*a*)).

1.129 It is now clear from *Ollett v. Bristol Aerojet Ltd* [1979] 1 W.L.R. 1197 that the substance of an expert's report, which the rules require the parties to disclose as a condition precedent to calling him at trial, includes his opinion, which is, after all, the whole reason for calling him.

Although the usual direction relating to expert evidence, where both sides will rely on such evidence at trial, is for mutual exchange (*Aston v. Firth Brown* [1984] C.L.Y. 1520), the court is not precluded from ordering sequential disclosure where it is desirable to do so (*Kirkup v. British Rail Engineering Ltd* [1983] 1 W.L.R. 190).

1.130 Practitioners should bear in mind that progressive county courts now issue local practice directions to cover all or certain types of personal injury actions, such as industrial deafness actions in the Liverpool county court. Such practice directions are likely to become more widespread. No doubt county courts seeking to ensure compliance will notify practitioners of requirements when summonses are issued and served, but plaintiffs and their advisers should make early inquiries to unfamiliar county courts at an early stage to ensure that they are well prepared to meet any deadlines.

CASE MANAGEMENT: THE PRESENT AND THE FUTURE

1.131 In the sixth edition of this work we described Lord Woolf's interim report as heralding radical reforms to the civil justice system. Those reforms, in their final version, are not yet with us. There are, however, increasing signs that the Courts are already keen to pursue the new approach of case management. The Practice Direction (Civil Litigation: Case Management) [1995] 1 W.L.R. 262, which concerns personal injury actions as much as any other High Court action, already directs judges to assert greater control over preparation for and conduct of hearings. Cost sanctions are to be imposed for failure by practitioners to conduct cases economically. The court will exercise its discretion to limit discovery, oral submissions and examination and cross-examination of witnesses. Several county courts already operate practice directions which ensure that personal injury actions come on for trial within short and controlled time-scales. The Court of Appeal has also issued a Practice Direction (Court of Appeal: Skeleton arguments and case management). The indication given in it that directions hearings will not be allowed to develop into satellite litigation is likely to be taken up by lower courts.

1.132 Recent decisions have also indicated the strictures and sanctions which are already being and will, no doubt, increasingly be applied by the Courts. Lord Woolf M.R., giving the judgment of the Court of Appeal in *Arbuthnot Latham Bank v. Trafalgar Holdings Ltd* [1998] All E.R. 181, a dismissal for want of prosecution application, struck out an action where there had been considerable delay and a knowing wholesale disregard of the rules of court as an abuse of process, without requiring prejudice to the defendant to be established. He stated that most of the powers which the courts required for the purpose of case management were already contained in the existing rules of court. He recognised that a gradual change to a managed system was taking place. It is inevitably the case that without training and the introduction of the necessary technological infrastructure the courts will presently be unable to take a very pro-active role. However, the Court of Appeal indicated that the additional burdens imposed upon the courts dictated, in the interests of litigants as a whole, that courts' time was not unnecessarily absorbed in dealing with satellite litigation which was created by non-compliance with the timetables laid down in the rules. The Court referred to a change in culture already taking place with an emphasis on ensuring that existing rules designed to achieve the disposal of litigation within a reasonable timescale are observed. The Court's message is for now and not just for the future. That was emphasised when a differently constituted Court of Appeal rejected as unacceptable a submission that the Court in *Arbuthnot* had only intended to state the law as it would be applied in regard to breaches of the rules or orders committed after that case had been decided (see *Choraria v. Sethia* [1998] T.L.R. 43). In personal injury cases, particularly those involving a prolonged recovery period or uncertain medical prognosis, there may be good reason for postponing trial in relation to quantum, but it cannot be assumed that new approaches will not be applied to personal injury actions. An application for a short extension of time to serve an updated schedule of special damages was refused in *Lownes v. Babcock Power Ltd* (unreported, C.A. February 11, 1998). The Court of Appeal upheld the refusal to extend time, in the absence of good excuse for non-compliance with an order, expressly having regard to prejudice to other litigants and prejudice to the administration of justice in reaching their decision. It refused to make a special case for personal injury plaintiffs let down by the conduct of their solicitors.

1.133 Though at least some, if not all, of the cases in which courts have recently struck out actions in circumstances where they might previously have not, were associated with extremely dilatory progress of actions and conduct well below an acceptable standard of diligence on the part of legal representatives, it is likely that courts will become increasingly intolerant of failure to comply with timetables and specific orders for directions and mindful of the impact of decisions on other litigants. The ultimate sanction of dismissing the action may well be visited much more frequently than it has previously been and, at best, cost sanctions are likely to follow serious non-compliance.

1.134 Practitioners can also expect time limits for interlocutory applications to be more strictly enforced. Applications for lengthy hearings over matters such as requests for particulars of pleadings are likely to be viewed as indicative of unjustifiable requests for particulars and/or unreasonable refusals to address pleading deficiencies and may not be granted until counsel or solicitors have met and attempted to resolve the issues. Persistence in unjustifiable requests or inadequate replies which necessitate a court hearing may well attract indemnity costs orders or even wasted costs orders against legal representatives.

1.135 Lord Woolf's final report on "Access to Justice" was published in July 1996. It contained 303 recommendations. The recommendations will be implemented in large part. New unified rules of civil procedure for both the High Court and county court are to be implemented although the timetable for introduction has already slipped substantially. The Civil Procedure Act 1997 has already been enacted to provide the mechanisms for change and the Civil Procedure Rule Committee has already been established to consider new rules.

1.136 Lord Woolf's recommendations propose that there should be a fundamental switch in the responsibility for management of civil litigation from parties to courts. A three-tier system is proposed with an increased small claims jurisdiction, a new fast track for less valuable cases and a new multi-track for remaining cases. Few special proposals were made for personal injury claims, with the exception of medical negligence actions. A separate High Court list envisaged for such actions and a pilot study was proposed to consider best procedures for low value medical negligence claims, which will be excluded from the fast-track.

1.137 However, the fast track is seen as singularly appropriate for other small personal injury claims. All personal injury cases worth up to £10,000 will, it is proposed, be dealt with in the fast track, without oral expert evidence. There will be provision to put written questions to experts. Expert evidence will normally be restricted to one expert and, in road traffic cases, leave will be needed to call a non-medical expert. The fast track will have a set timetable of 20 to 30 weeks with trials limited to three hours, or if justified, one day. This is clearly designed to foster a fast and relatively cheap procedure, although it is clear that courts will retain discretion as to various matters including, for example, the number of experts. It may well be the proposed fixed costs regime which encourages straightforward presentation of fast track cases. Cases will be allocated to the fast track by a district judge. It is recognised that where oral expert evidence is necessary the case should not be included in the fast track, but it is to be expected that courts will be difficult to persuade that oral medical evidence is necessary in claims for less than £10,000. Whilst increased use is envisaged for the small claims jurisdiction in other areas, the fast track is seen as more appropriate for all but the smallest personal injury claims. More substantial cases, of which there will clearly be a very large number of personal injury actions, will be managed by way of an initial case management conference or the issue of specific directions for preparation of the case including a fixed timetable. Information to assist the Court may be provided by the parties in a questionnaire or called for by the Court. A pre-trial review is intended. Parties will generally be able to agree changes to the dates fixed for the timetable, subject to the Court's overriding power to intervene, but will not be able to change the dates of the case management conference, the pre-trial review or trial without the permission of the Court. A streamlined procedure for more straightforward cases is to be developed with limited disclosure and expert evidence and controled costs. New rules will specify automatic sanctions for non-compliance designed to prevent non-compliance rather than punish it.

1.138 A new ethos of pre-action co-operation on the part of litigants and their legal representatives is to be encouraged as is alternative dispute resolution. In *Burrows v. Vauxhall Motors Ltd* [1997] P.I.Q.R. P. 48 the Court of Appeal has already ordered a plaintiff who had issued successful proceedings prematurely to pay the other party's costs. In that case the plaintiff had denied the defendants the opportunity to consider medical evidence or ascertain the plaintiff's condition so preventing them from making a pre-commencement offer of settlement.

Detailed new rules of court have not been published at the time of writing. In at least some respects procedures will be significantly changed. Nonetheless, particularly outside the fast-track, the basic interlocutory steps will remain largely unchanged. The Woolf recommendations contain specific provisions relevant to a simplified standard form for commencing proceedings, pleadings, service, disclosure of documents, witness statements and experts and there are some specific proposals relating to personal injury claims. For example it is recommended that a potential claimant in proceedings for injury or death should be able to make a pre-action application for disclosure against a person who is not expected to be a defendant. It also appears that one object of the reforms is an attempt to limit the necessity and scope for interlocutory applications. Nevertheless, it seems likely that authorities interpreting the existing rules of court will in many areas remain useful for guidance as to the appropriate approach, particularly outside the fast track. Much will remain familiar, but a new culture is intended. All will have to adapt.

The most adept will soon find opportunity to take advantage of the changes to the benefit of their clients.

[*This chapter, substantially expanded and amended by Peter Mantle, Barrister, was originally written by Mr Alan Hughes, Solicitor, in* 1979]

Chapter 2

Damages on Death

Contents *Para*

GENERAL PRINCIPLES

No cause of action at common law

2.1 The common law allowed no cause of action in respect of a person's death. Thus, where a person was killed in circumstances which would have entitled him to recover damages, if he had suffered non-fatal injuries, neither his dependants nor his estate had any cause of action.

The Fatal Accidents Act 1846 and subsequent amendments

2.2 A deceased's dependants were first provided with a cause of action by the Fatal Accidents Act 1846. That act was amended from time to time, then replaced by a consolidating act, the Fatal Accidents Act 1976. That act in its turn was substantially amended by the Administration of Justice Act 1982. The amended provisions apply in respect of all causes of action arising after the end of 1982. The Fatal Accidents Act 1976, as so amended, is set out in Appendix B.

The Law Commission's Consultation Paper No. 147

2.3 The Law Commission in Consultation Paper 147 has made various provisional recommendations for amending the Fatal Accidents Act and changing the case law established by judges in this field. Some of these recommendations are controversial and unlikely, in our view, to obtain parliamentary approval. In any event, resulting legislation is unlikely to be enacted for a considerable time, as the Government will have more urgent candidates for the parliamentary time available for legislation. We therefore confine this chapter to the existing law.

The dependants

2.4 Section 1(3) of the 1976 Act defines dependant as follows:

"(3) In this Act 'dependant' means—
- (a) the wife or husband or former wife or husband of the deceased;
- (b) any person who—
  - (i) was living with the deceased in the same household immediately before the date of the death; and
  - (ii) had been living with the deceased in the same household for at least two years before that date; and
  - (iii) was living during the whole of that period as the husband or wife of the deceased;
- (c) any parent or other ascendant of the deceased;
- (d) any person who was treated by the deceased as his parent;
- (e) any child or other descendant of the deceased;
- (f) any person (not being a child of the deceased) who, in the case of any marriage to which the deceased was at any time a party, was treated by the deceased as a child of the family in relation to that marriage;

(g) any person who is, or is the issue of, a brother, sister, uncle or aunt of the deceased.

(4) The reference to the former wife or husband of the deceased in subsection (3)(a) above includes a reference to a person whose marriage to the deceased has been annulled or declared void as well as a person whose marriage to the deceased has been dissolved.

(5) In deducing any relationship for the purposes of subsection (3) above—

(a) any relationship by affinity shall be treated as a relationship by consanguinity, any relationship of the half blood as a relationship of the whole blood, and the stepchild of any person as his child, and

(b) an illegitimate person shall be treated as the legitimate child of his mother and reputed father."

In *Shepherd v. Post Office* (1995) *The Times*, 15 June, the Court of Appeal held that a divorced woman who remarried but later returned to live with her first husband was capable of being a dependant of her first husband and did not have to have fulfilled a qualifying period of two years as if she were a "common law" spouse.

The Law Reform (Miscellaneous Provisions) Act 1934 and subsequent amendments

2.5 A deceased's estate had no cause of action until one was provided by section 1 of the Law Reform (Miscellaneous Provisions) Act 1934. That Act was also amended by the Administration of Justice Act 1982. Section 1 of the Act, as so amended, is set out in Appendix B.

The law in Scotland

2.6 The Fatal Accidents Act 1976 does not apply in Scotland. The relevant statute governing claims by certain relatives of a deceased victim is the Damages (Scotland) Act 1976. It is not within the scope of this work to consider Scottish claims, except in so far as Scottish decisions may be of persuasive authority in the courts of England and Wales.

What loss is recoverable

2.7 When damages are assessed under the Fatal Accidents Act 1976, "there is no question of what may be called sentimental damage, bereavement or pain and suffering. It is a hard matter of pounds, shillings and pence": *per* Lord Wright in *Davies v. Powell Duffryn Associated Collieries Ltd* [1942] A.C. 601 at 607. The measure of damage is the pecuniary loss which has been suffered and is likely to be suffered by each dependant.

Recent expansion of concept of pecuniary benefit

2.8 In the case of claims for the death of a wife and/or mother, the courts have recently been prepared to expand the concept of pecuniary benefit.

In *Hay v. Hughes* [1975] Q.B. 790 Lord Edmund-Davies, having stated the rule set out in the preceding paragraph, went on to say:

> "... yet it may some time have to be considered whether Mr McGregor is not right in saying (McGregor on Damages (13th ed., 1972), para. 1232): '... it may be argued that the benefit of a mother's personal attention to a child's upbringing, morals, education and psychology, which the services of a housekeeper, nurse or governess could never provide, has in the long run a financial value for the child, difficult as it is to assess.' "

Sedley J. in *Lewis v. Osborne* (unreported, July 4, 1995) applied the observation made in *McGregor on Damages* (15th ed.), para. 1588, that Lord Edmund-Davies's comments in *Hay v. Hughes* had borne fruit in subsequent cases which have moved away from a commercial quantification of services and have sought to recognise the unquantifiable aspects of the loss of a mother's care.

Per Sedley J.:

> "In sum, what has happened is that the courts, fixed with binding early authority that 'injury' in the legislation means pecuniary loss, have been striving to do justice in terms of contemporary perceptions by expanding the meaning of 'pecuniary' as a surrogate for the now forbidden task of giving a natural meaning to 'injury'. Thus in *Regan v. Williamson* [1976] 1 W.L.R. 305 Watkins J. (as he then was), following Lord Edmund-Davies' dictum, held that 'services' is to be given a generous inter-

pretation, with the consequence that the valuation of such services may be in some measure expanded."

On that basis he assessed at £40,000, the damages for a girl who at the age of one had lost her mother and as a result had suffered a distracted and distressing early childhood.

Other cases where judges have awarded damages to a husband or to a child for loss of services provided over and above those provided by a paid housekeeper or other paid care include:

Topp v. London Country Bus (South West) Ltd [1992] P.I.Q.R. P. 206 where May J. awarded £2,500 to the daughter and £2,000 to the husband;

Johnson v. British Midland Airways Ltd [1996] P.I.Q.R. Q. 8 where Drake J. awarded £3,500 to the son and £2,000 to the husband;

Whitmore v. Malin (unreported, December 15, 1995) where Collins J. awarded £2,000 under this head to the husband.

Claim for bereavement

2.9 There has also been a statutory modification of the principle that only pecuniary loss is recoverable. A claim for bereavement was introduced by section 1A of the Fatal Accidents Act, as amended by the Administration of Justice Act 1982. The section provides:

"1A—(1) An action under this Act may consist of or include a claim for damages for bereavement.

(2) A claim for damages for bereavement shall only be for the benefit—

(a) of the wife or husband of the deceased; and

(b) where the deceased was a minor who was never married—

(i) of his parents, if he was legitimate; and

(ii) of his mother, if he was illegitimate.

(3) Subject to subsection (5) below, the sum to be awarded as damages under this section shall be [£7,500].

(4) Where there is a claim for damages under this section for the benefit of both the parents of the deceased, the sum awarded shall be divided equally between them (subject to any deduction falling to be made in respect of costs not recovered from the defendant).

(5) The Lord Chancellor may be order made by statutory

instrument, subject to annulment in pursuance of a resolution of either House of Parliament, amend this section by varying the sum for the time being specified in subsection (3) above."

The bereavement award was originally fixed at £3,500. That sum still applies in the case of causes of action accruing before April 1, 1991.

The increase to £7,500 was made by the Damages for Bereavement (Variation of Sum) (England and Wales) Order 1990 (S. I. No. 2575).

Where child is a minor when injured and over 18 at date of death

2.10 Where a deceased child was a minor at the date of the injury but was over 18 at the date of death, there is no bereavement claim under section 1A(2)(b): *Doleman v. Deakin*, a decision of the Court of Appeal: reported in (1990) *The Times*, January 30.

One parent responsible for child's death: the other not

2.11 In such a case the whole bereavement payment should, in our view, be awarded to the innocent parent. The tortfeasor parent can have no claim since such claim would be barred by public policy. That leaves the only valid claim as that of the innocent parent, who should be entitled to the whole bereavement award, being the only person with a right to claim it. This topic is considered in more detail in *Kemp & Kemp*, Vol. 1 para. 4–007/2.

Criticism of the bereavement award

2.12 There had been some criticism of the amount of the bereavement award on the ground that it is so small as to be insulting to the relatives of the deceased. The Lord Chancellor's Department issued a Consultation Paper inviting views on whether he should increase the level of the bereavement award. The Lord Chancellor raised three options in his paper. To leave the amount at £3,500; to increase it to £5,000 to take account of inflation since the amount was first fixed in 1982; or to increase it to a larger sum, such as £10,000. The response of both the Bar and the Law Society was to recommend an increase to £10,000. The Bar said that, if the figure was not raised, it was in danger of "becoming derisory" with the result that the law in this area would "fall into disrepute". A spokesman for the Law Society said that an increase to £10,000 was more in line with present thinking. Presumably the new figure of £7,500 was fixed as the appropriate sum in terms of the current real value of the pound. We assume that the Lord Chancellor will not vary the sum specified with every year's decline in the purchasing power of the pound but that the sum will be varied when it becomes clear that there has been a substantial decline in the value of the pound since the time when the sum was fixed.

2.13 A further criticism which has been made of the bereavement award is that the class of person to whom the award is payable is too restricted and, in particular, that a "common law wife", as defined in section 1(3)(b) of the Fatal Accidents Act 1976, should be entitled to this award.

The denial of a bereavement claim to a child for the death of a parent has also been criticised. The Pearson Royal Commission had recommended such a claim. Lord Hailsham, Lord Chancellor, explained, in the debate on the second reading of the Bill, why this recommendation had been rejected:

> "I believe that no monetary compensation can adequately compensate a person for bereavement ... It is for this reason that I think the award should be of a conventional fixed kind available only in limited circumstances. My present view is that it should not be available to an unmarried minor child in respect of the loss of a parent because ... such a child is already likely to receive substantial dependency damages in any event."

No steps have been taken to meet these criticisms. An amending Act would be needed for this purpose rather than a statutory instrument.

Provisional recommendations to meet such criticisms are contained the Law Commission's Consultation Paper No. 147.

Interest on award

2.14 Interest on the statutory sum should be awarded from the date of death at the full investment account rate: *Khan v. Duncan* (unreported, March 9, 1989) a decision of Popplewell J., and *Prior v. Hastie*. (1987) C.L.Y. 1219.

Duplication

2.15 The question may arise as to whether there could be any set-off or reduction of damages on the ground of duplication where, for example, the wife of the deceased, who has a claim for nervous shock when seeing her husband killed, also recovers damages for bereavement. In our view there would be no set-off or reduction of damages. The two claims are separate and distinct and arise from different causes of action. The wife has a common law claim in her own right for the personal injury and a separate statutory claim under the Fatal Accidents Act.

Net pecuniary loss subject to statutory exceptions

2.16 Except where there is express statutory direction to the contrary, the damages to be awarded to a dependant of a deceased person under the Fatal Accidents Acts must take into account any pecuniary benefit accruing to that dependant in consequence of the death of the deceased. It is the net loss on balance which constitutes the measure of damages: *per* Lord Macmillan in *Davies' Case* [1942] A.C. 601 at 609.

However, as will be seen when we consider the incidence of benefits (paras 2.82 *et seq*), the statutory disregard of benefits is now so wide that little, if anything, remains to be deducted from a dependant's loss. For either a benefit does not result from the deceased's death and is therefore irrelevant; or it does result from the death and is to be disregarded in the assessment of damages pursuant to section 4 of the Fatal Accidents Act.

Only one action to be brought

2.17 Only one action can be brought. It must be brought for the benefit of all the dependants. An undivided lump sum may be paid into court to satisfy the claims of all the dependants. Nevertheless, the dependants are entitled individually to separate sums of damages and not jointly to a global sum: *Pym v. Great Northern Ry* (1863) B. & S. 396 at 407.

Pecuniary benefit must arise from the relationship between the dependant and the deceased

2.18 Although the Fatal Accidents Act 1976 speaks, in s. 3(1), of damages proportioned to the injury resulting from the death of the deceased, this wide wording has been restricted by a series of decisions. Their effect is to confine damages to the loss of a benefit arising from the relationship between the dependant and the deceased. They do not allow damages for a loss resulting to the dependant in consequence of the deceased's death but which did not arise out of such relationship.

These decisions were reviewed by Devlin J. in *Burgess v. Florence Nightingale Hospital for Gentlewomen* [1995] 1 Q.B. 349. In this case the plaintiff was claiming damages for the death of his wife. They were professional dancing partners and the plaintiff had suffered and was likely to suffer a pecuniary loss by being deprived of his wife as a dancing partner. Devlin J. held that this head of damages could not be allowed, since the benefit arising to the husband from the dancing partnership could not properly be attributed to the relationship of husband and wife. The learned judge added that, if this claim were allowed, then any partner whose prospects were similarly affected by the death of the other, whatever their relationship was, ought logically to be compensated, too. *Burgess's* case was distinguished in *Malyon v. Plummer* [1964] 1 Q.B. 330, C.A. In this case the dependant wife had been paid a salary by her husband's company in excess of the market value of the work which she performed for the company. It was held that excess was a benefit derived from her relationship to the deceased as his wife and was thus a benefit lost by his death and should be taken into account in assessing her damages under the Fatal Accidents Acts.

Statutory limitation of damages recoverable and imposition of time limits for issuing proceedings.

2.19 When death occurs in circumstances to which the Carriage by Air Act 1961 or the Merchant Shipping Act 1894 applies, the amount of damages recoverable may be limited, and time limits imposed for issuing proceedings. Practitioners are referred to specialist works on marine and aviation law.

Damages are assessed on a logical basis

2.20 Though the assessment of damages under the Fatal Accidents Acts is often difficult and complicated, it is at least a task which can be approached upon a logical basis. Indeed, if the court knew with certainty all the relevant factors, it could assess the damages arithmetically with a high degree of accuracy. In this respect, therefore, the court's task is easier than in the assessment of damages in cases of severe personal injury. For in the latter case there are some important heads of damage which defy arithmetical calculation, such as pain and suffering or the loss of amenities.

In fact, however, in all but the simplest claims under the Fatal Accidents Acts there are so many uncertain and imponderable elements that an accurate arithmetical approach is quite impossible. The court has to do the best it can in the circumstances.

The effect of adoption on a dependant's dependency

2.21 In *Watson v. Willmott* [1991] 1 Q.B. 140, an infant's mother was killed. His father committed suicide shortly afterwards. This death was also due to the defendant's negligence. The infant was adopted two years later by his aunt and uncle.

Dependency on father. As from the date of the adoption, the dependency on the father was reduced by the amount of the dependency on his adoptive parents.

Dependency on mother. As from the date of adoption, the non-pecuniary dependency on the mother ceased.

2.22 It is doubtful whether the decision in this case is correct in the light of the Court of Appeal's decision in *Stanley v. Saddique* [1992] Q.B. 1. It is arguable that either the adoption was a benefit accruing as a result of the deceased's death, in which case it should not have been taken into account by virtue of the Fatal Accidents Act 1976, s. 4 (as amended). Alternatively, that the adoption did not result from the death but from the adopter's benevolence, in which case it should not be taken into account at common law. See our comments on *Hayden v. Hayden* [1992] 1 W.L.R. 986, C.A. in paras 2.86 *et seq*.

Infant's claim not barred by foreign judgment

2.23 An infant's claim cannot be validly extinguished without the court's approval. Consequently such claim is not barred by judgment in a foreign court. But the widow's claim is barred. In *Black v. Yates* [1992] Q.B. 526 Potter J. held that the claim of infant dependants was not barred by their mother, the deceased's widow, settling a claim for compensation brought in a Spanish court on behalf of herself and the infants. The defendant sought to rely upon section 34 of the Civil Jurisdiction and Judgments Act 1982 which provided as follows:

> "No proceedings may be brought by a person in England . . . on a cause of action in respect of which a judgment has been given in his favour in proceedings between the same parties . . . in a court . . . of an overseas country, unless that judgment is not enforceable or entitled to recognition in England . . ."

The defendant's defence succeeded in respect of the claim brought on the widow's behalf but failed in respect of the infant dependants' claim

Dependency arising after the injury which caused deceased's death

2.24 In *Phillips v. Grampian Health Board* [1989] S.L.T. 538 a case in the Outer House of the Court of Session, Lord Sutherland held that, where a dependant had married the deceased after his condition, caused by the defendants' negligence, had become fatal, she could claim damages in respect of the deceased's death.

Although this decision is based on the relevant Scottish legislation, it is submitted that the principle stated applies to claims brought under the Fatal Accidents Act 1976 which applies in England and Wales.

Funeral expenses

2.25 Until the Fatal Accidents Acts were amended by the Law Reform (Miscellaneous Provisions) Act 1934, funeral expenses could not be recovered in a Fatal Accidents Acts claim, nor could they be recovered at common law. The Law Reform Act provided for the recovery of funeral expenses both in claims brought on behalf of the deceased's estate under the Law Reform Act itself and in Fatal Accidents Acts claims. By virtue of section 3(5) of the Fatal Accidents Act 1976, damages may be awarded in an action under the Act in respect of the funeral expenses of the deceased if the dependants have incurred such expenses.

No definition of funeral expenses; examples

2.26 There is no definition of funeral expenses in either the Law Reform Act or the Fatal Accidents Act 1976. It has been held that the cost of mourning clothes does not form part of the funeral expenses, and nor does the cost of a wake. The cost of a headstone finishing off, describing and marking the grave is a funeral expense, while a memorial is not. Otherwise whether an expense incurred in relation to the funeral of the deceased is recoverable would seem to depend upon whether it was reasonably incurred. The cost of embalming a child's body has been held to be reasonably incurred. Where the deceased was not native or ordinarily resident in England, it appears that the cost of transporting the body and relations from England to the deceased's native land may form a proper part of the funeral expenses.

Claim for funeral expenses by a plaintiff on point of death

2.27 In *Bateman v. Hydro Agri (U.K.) Ltd* (September 15, 1995) Mr Anthony Temple Q.C. sitting as deputy High Court judge, held that this was a valid claim. The plaintiff was suffering from mesothelioma and was likely to die within three months of the date of the trial. The parties had agreed £1,500, as the cost of the funeral, if damages could be awarded under the Law Reform Act for such expense. This was a bold decision, but we believe it to be right in principle.

Strictly, there should be some discount for receiving a lump sum in advance of incurring the expense, but with the short time involved the discount would be *de minimis* and was rightly ignored.

THE GENERAL APPROACH IN PRACTICE

Note: This topic is considered in more detail in Kemp & Kemp, Vol 1, Chapter 21.

Damages to be proportioned to the dependant's loss

2.28 Section 3(1) of the Fatal Accidents Act 1976 provides that the damages awarded to each dependant are to be such as are proportioned to the injury resulting from the death of the deceased. The court is perfectly entitled to consider the case of each dependant separately, and occasionally this is the only satisfactory method. But in most cases the court first assesses the dependants' loss as a whole and then apportions the damages between the dependants. The method usually adopted is stated by Lord Wright in *Davies v.*

Powell Duffryn Associated Collieries Ltd [1942] A.C. 601 at 617, in the following passage from his speech:

> "There is no question here of what may be called sentimental damage, bereavement or pain and suffering. It is a hard matter of pounds, shillings and pence, subject to the element of reasonable future probabilities. The starting point is the amount of wages which the deceased was earning, the ascertainment of which to some extent may depend on the regularity of his employment. Then there is an estimate of how much was required or expended for his own personal and living expenses. The balance will give a datum or basic figure which will generally be turned into a lump sum by taking a certain number of years' purchase ..."

The multiplicand

2.29 The basic figure defined by Lord Wright in the passage above is termed "the multiplicand".

The multiplier

2.30 The basic figure referred to by Lord Wright in the passage above is the value of the dependency. It should be possible to assess the value of the dependency at the date of the death of the deceased with reasonable accuracy. To that multiplicand, the court applies a multiplier, calculated as from the date of the deceased's death, and not as from the date of the trial. This is different from the practice in the case of a claim made by a live plaintiff. The reason was stated by Lord Fraser in *Cookson v. Knowles* [1979] A.C. 556 at 575–6:

> "In the present case the deceased was aged 49 at the date of his death and the trial judge and the Court of Appeal used a multiplier of 11. That figure was not seriously criticised by counsel as having been inappropriate as at the date of death, although I think it is probably generous to the appellant. From that figure of 11, the Court of Appeal deducted 2½ in respect of the 2½ years from the date of death to the date of trial, and they used the resulting figure of 8½ as the multiplier for the damages after the date of trial. In so doing they departed from the method that would have been appropriate in a personal injury case and counsel for the appellant criticised the departure as being unfair

to the appellant. The argument was that if the deceased man had had a twin brother who had been injured at the same time as the deceased man was killed, and whose claim for damages for personal injury had come to trial on the same day as the dependant's claim under the Fatal Accidents Acts, the appropriate multiplier for his loss after the date of trial would have been higher than 8½. On the assumption, which is probably correct, that that would have been so, it does not in my opinion follow that the multiplier of 8½ft1 is too low in the present claim under the Fatal Accidents Acts where different considerations apply. In a personal injury case, if the injured person has survived until the date of trial, that is a known fact and the multiplier appropriate to the length of his future working life has to be ascertained as at the date of trial. But in a fatal accident case the multiplier must be selected once and for all as at the date of death, because everything that might have happened to the deceased after that date remains uncertain. Accordingly having taken a multiplier of 11 as at the date of death, and having used 2½ in respect of the period up to the trial, it is in my opinion correct to take 8½ for the period after the date of trial. That is what the Court of Appeal did in this case."

Relevance of events between death and trial

2.31 Although the multiplier has to be taken as from the deceased's death, the court cannot ignore the relevance of the period which has expired between the death and the date of the trial. In the case of a live plaintiff a substantial discount is made because the award gives him a present lump sum as compensation for a stream of future losses or expenses. In a Fatal Accidents Act claim, if a substantial number of years have expired between the death and the trial, only part of the lump sum will represent compensation for future losses or expenses and therefore a smaller discount should be made to take account of the receipt of the lump sum. The purpose of taking the multiplier as from the death is to take account of the contingencies which might have arisen between the death and the trial. But in most cases, certainly in most cases where the deceased is comparatively young, those contingencies count for less than the fact that a considerable part of the lump sum award represents past loss and does not need to be discounted. Thus, one finds that the multipliers in a Fatal Accidents Act claim, taken from the date of death tend to be rather larger in the case of a deceased than the multiplier, taken from the date of trial, in the case of a live plaintiff of the same age. On the other hand, if in both cases the multipliers were taken from the date of trial, the multiplier in the case of a Fatal Accidents Act claim would be rather lower since contingencies affecting two or more lives have to be taken into account. In the case of a live plaintiff, it is only the contingencies affecting him that are relevant. In the case of a Fatal Accidents Act claim, the contingencies affecting the deceased and all the dependants have to be taken into account.

2.32 A recent decision of the Court of Appeal, *Corbett v. Barking, etc Health Authority* [1991] 2 Q.B. 408, illustrates the relevance of such certainty as has been established by the date of the trial. The claim was brought for the benefit of a boy aged eleven and a half at the date of the trial in respect of his mother's death during his birth. The trial judge decided that in the ordinary way a multiplier of 12 would have been appropriate and so awarded special damages to cover the eleven and a half years prior to trial leaving a multiplier of only a half to cover post trial loss. The Court of Appeal increased the multiplier to 15 thereby applying a multiplier of three and a half to the post trial loss. The decision was by a majority, Purchas and Farquharson L.JJ.: Gibson L.J. dissented.

Per Purchas L.J.:

> "His Lordship could see no justification for denying the court the power to adjust the multiplier to be assessed "as at the date of death" in the light of facts established later at the trial.
>
> It was common ground that either 12 or 13 would have been the appropriate multiplier to cover 18 years of dependency in normal circumstances. It would be illogical not to make a meaningful adjustment where eleven and a half of the 18 years of dependency no longer contained the uncertainties as to the dependant's life expectancy and changing needs, upon which discounts would normally be applied.
>
> In such a case, the correct approach must be to calculate the multiplier from the date of death but in so doing account must be taken of the removal of many of the uncertainties surrounding the provision and receipt of the dependency during the period involved.
>
> Accordingly, the discount from the 18-year period to take account of those uncertainties would itself be reduced. Other

uncertainties, such as those concerning the deceased would remain.

The judge having fixed the multiplier too low, it was open to the court to substitute its own decision. It should be adjusted from 12 to 15."

The modern practice

2.33 The modern practice of judges of first instance and of appellate courts is to state in any particular case the value of the dependency and the multiplier adopted. In the older cases often no multiplier is stated, but if a dependency is recorded the multiplier in fact adopted may be ascertained by dividing the final assessment of damages by the value of the dependency found.

Factors affecting the multiplier

2.34 A number of facts are relevant to the assessment of the appropriate multiplier in a particular case. The most important is usually the age and expectation of working life of the deceased. He or she is the source of the dependency, which in any event would not normally have continued beyond the span of his working life. This is not invariably true. In a case where the deceased's income was derived from investments or pension, the relevant period would be his expectation of life. At the same time one must consider the expectation of life of the dependants, and in particular, where a husband is killed, of his widow.

The "Ogden Tables"

2.35 Assistance in fixing a multiplier may be derived from the Government Actuary's Tables of Multipliers which are contained in the report of the working party chaired by Sir Michael Ogden, now in its third edition. These tables are generally known as the "Ogden Tables". Indeed this description now has statutory authority, since it is used in section 16(5) of the Civil Evidence Act 1995. Section 10 of this Act (which at the time of writing has not yet been brought into force) provides as follows:

> "**10.**—(1) The actuarial tables (together with explanatory notes) for use in personal injury and fatal accidents cases issued from time to time by the Government Actuary's Department are

admissible in evidence for the purpose of assessing, in an action for personal injury, the sum to be awarded as general damages for future pecuniary loss.

(2) They may be proved by the production of a copy published by Her Majesty's Stationery Office.

(3) For the purposes of this section—

(a) "personal injury" includes any disease and any impairment of a person's physical or mental condition; and

(b) "action for personal injury" includes an action brought by virtue of the Law Reform (Miscellaneous Provisions) Act 1934 or the Fatal Accidents Act 1976."

The Ogden Tables are set out in *Kemp & Kemp*, Vol. 1, at pages 8015 *et seq*. Although s. 10 is not yet in force, the courts are now willing to take judicial notice of the tables. The explanatory notes indicate how the tables should be used in various circumstances.

2.36 Tables of this nature are based upon the average life. If the deceased's health was better or worse than the average, that is a matter to be taken into account. So, too, perhaps if the deceased came of unusually long-lived or short-lived stock.

The future prospects of the deceased, if he had not been killed, will also affect the multiplier. If the deceased had good prospects of attaining a much greater wage or salary, or of achieving promotion to a much better position, the court will apply a higher multiplier.

On the other hand the court must take account of the uncertainties of life, particularly where the deceased was engaged in some especially hazardous employment.

Remarriage or its prospects not to be taken into account

2.37 Before the coming into force of the Law Reform (Miscellaneous Provisions) Act 1971 an important factor affecting the multiplier in the case of a widow's claim in many cases was remarriage or the prospect of remarriage. That must now be ignored.

Prior to the enactment of section 4 of the Fatal Accidents Act 1976, as substituted by section 3(1) of the Administration of Justice Act 1982, a widower's remarriage or the prospect of remarriage, had to be taken into account. Similarly, when damages were assessed for an infant child's dependency on her father's death, the benefit which the child was likely to receive from its stepfather had to be taken into account. However, the decision of the Court of

Appeal in *Stanley v. Saddique* [1992] Q.B. 1 and the decision in *Topp v. London Country Bus (South West) Ltd* [1993] 3 All E.R. 448 shows that the law has now changed. A widower's remarriage or prospect of remarriage is not to be taken into account nor is a child's benefit from a stepfather.

Prospect of divorce is relevant

2.38 Although a dependant's remarriage or prospect of remarriage is to be disregarded, the court should take account, if the relevant circumstances justify this course, of the prospect that the dependency might have been shortened or reduced by divorce. The Court of Appeal so held in *Owen v. Martin and Another* on April 15, 1992. [1992] P.I.Q.R. Q. 151.

2.39 In this case the trial judge had adopted a multiplier of 15, which would ordinarily have been appropriate with the deceased husband aged 26 and his widow aged 28 at the time of his death. But the Court of Appeal reduced the multiplier to 11 on the ground that the widow's attitude towards marriage vows as shown by her personal history suggested that her dependency on her dead husband might in any event have been shortened or reduced by divorce.

Prospect of deceased child's marriage is relevant

2.40 For similar reasons the prospect of marriage is a relevant factor when assessing the damages to be awarded to parents for the death of an unmarried child who was contributing to their keep. For on marriage the child would be likely to reduce or even discontinue such contribution.

Assumption that damages will be invested

2.41 The assumption which the court makes, whatever the actual intentions of the dependants may be, is that any sum awarded as damages will be invested so as to produce an annuity. The court is thus seeking, in calculating the multiplier in any particular case, to arrive at a capital sum (after the multiplier has been applied to the multiplicand) which could purchase an annuity which is appropriate on the court's assessment of the evidence. At the same time the court recognises that interest earned on damages awarded may be liable to taxation. If the burden of taxation is likely to be significant that is a reason for increasing the multiplier, *per* Lord Fraser in *Cookson v. Knowles* [1979] A.C. 556 at 577: *per* Lord Reid in *Taylor v. O'Connor* [1971]. A.C. 115 at 129. It is submitted that Lord Oliver's speech in *Hodgson v. Trapp* [1989] A.C. 807, to the contrary is based on a factual error and should logically not be followed. See *Kemp & Kemp*, Vol. 1, paragraphs 9–032 to 9–041/4. However, the House of Lords in *Wells v. Wells* [1998] 1 W.L.R. 329 appears to have approved Lord Oliver's approach although this argument was not raised.

Each case depends on its own facts

2.42 The factors identified above in this section are those which are likely to be especially important in the vast majority of cases in determining the appropriate multiplier. However, each case depends upon its own facts and the list of factors identified is not intended to be exhaustive. Where the facts of a case are similar to the facts of other reported cases some assistance can be derived from an analysis of those cases in deciding upon a proper multiplier.

Multiplier to be decided as at date of death

2.43 The multiplier in any particular case must be assessed as at the date of death of the deceased. For the purposes of calculating interest upon damages awarded under the Fatal Accidents Act 1976 the award has to be divided into categories of pre-trial loss and future loss.

Interest

2.44 Interest is awarded on the total pre-trial loss at half the short term interest rates current between the date of death and the date of trial, while no interest is awarded on the future loss.

The multiplicand in the case of a deceased who had income

2.45 The assessment of the multiplicand in a particular case in fact involves at least two calculations. The multiplicand falls to be assessed as at the date of the trial, and therefore based upon the income which the deceased would then have had, had he survived.

2.46 However, it will not be possible, in a case in which the income which he would have had at the date of trial exceeds his actual income at the date of his death, to determine precisely what would have been the value of the dependency based upon the income as at the date of trial. The starting point is, therefore, to calculate the value of the dependency as at the date of death, usually in terms of a percentage of the income of the deceased. The value of the dependency as so assessed is then revised as may seem appropriate in the light of the income which the deceased would have had as at the date of the trial had he survived.

Accurate evidence of dependency

2.47 Providing that the deceased's dependants can give reasonably accurate evidence, the best way in many cases to establish the annual value of the dependency is to build it up item by item, eg:

Housekeeping money	£C per annum	(less £B per annum spent on deceased)
†Mortgage payments	£C per annum	
†Rates	£D per annum	
†Gas	£E per annum	
†Electricity	£F per annum	
†Coal	£G per annum	
Holidays for dependants	£H per annum	
Clothes for dependants	£I per annum	
School fees	£J per annum	
†Insurance	£K per annum	
Gifts, etc. . . .	£L per annum	
Total annual value of dependency £ . . .		

The items marked with † are all items from which the deceased also derived a benefit, but there would be no saving from the deceased's death and so it is right to count the whole value as part of the dependency.

2.48 At this stage it is often helpful to apply a cross-check to the dependants' estimates by ascertaining the deceased's net annual income at the date of his death to see whether it could in fact cover the total estimated dependency and still allow enough for the deceased's keep and his personal expenditure.

Alternative approach to assessing dependency

2.49 Where it is difficult to obtain reliable evidence as to payments made by the deceased to or for the benefit of his dependants, an alternative, although less accurate, approach may be adopted. Start with the deceased's net income at the date of his death: estimate how much of this he spent on himself: then, if his pattern of life justifies the assumption, take the remainder of his net income as being spent for the benefit of his dependants.

2.50 Indeed, nowadays, the court will often apply the conventional rule of thumb described by O'Connor L.J. in the following passage from his judgment in *Harris v. Empress Motors Ltd* [1984] 1 W.L.R. 212 at 216–17:

> "In the course of time the courts have worked out a simple solution to the similar problem of calculating the net dependency under the Fatal Accidents Acts in cases where the dependants are wife and children. In times past the calculation called for a tedious inquiry into how much housekeeping money was paid to the wife, who paid how much for the children's shoes, etc. This has all been swept away and the modern practice is to deduct a percentage from the net income figure to represent what the deceased would have spent exclusively on himself. The percentages have become conventional in the sense that they are used unless there is striking evidence to make the conventional figure inappropriate because there is no departure from the principle that each case must be decided upon its own facts. Where the family unit was husband and wife the conventional figure is 33 per cent and the rationale of this is that broadly speaking the net income was spent as to one-third for the benefit of each and one-third for their joint benefit. Clothing is an example of several benefit, rent an example of joint benefit. No deduction is made in respect of the joint portion because one cannot buy or drive half a motor car. Part of the net income may be spent for the benefit of neither husband nor wife. If the facts be, for example, that out of the net income of £8,000 pa the deceased was paying £2,000 to a charity the percentage would be applied to £6,000 and not £8,000. Where there are children the deduction falls to 25 per cent, as was the agreed figure in the *Harris* case."

2.51 This rule of thumb will only be applied in a normal case with no unusual features. In *Owen v. Martin and Another* [1992]

P.I.Q.R. Q. 151 a decision of the Court of Appeal the trial judge had applied the two-thirds rule where the facts clearly did not warrant this. *Per* Parker L.J.:

> "The first question is whether the judge was right in taking two thirds net earnings as the value of the dependency. In so doing he relied principally on *Harris v. Empress Motors Ltd.* [1984] 1 W.L.R. 212 citing the following passage from the judgment of O'Connor L.J. at page 216/217: [The Lord-Justice then cited the passage set out above, and continued:]
>
> That O'Connor L.J. did not intend to lay down any rule that in the absence of striking evidence to the contrary two thirds of net income must be regarded as the value of the dependency I have no doubt. If he did he would clearly have been wrong.
>
> It is clear that the value of the dependency cannot be taken at such an arbitrary figure and must always depend on facts. See *Shiels v. Cruickshank* [1953] 1 W.L.R. 536 (H.L.), *Mallett v. McMonagle* [1970] A.C. 167 *per* Lord Diplock at 176 D–G, *Taylor v. O'Connor* [1977] A.C. 115 where the figure taken amounted to about 50 per cent and there was no hint of a two thirds rule, and *Coward v. Comex Houlder Diving Ltd.* unreported C.A. transcript 1988/622, where the extent of the normal rule was discussed and the matter dealt with as a question of fact."

2.52 Further, as was pointed out by the Court of Appeal in *Coward v. Comex Houlder Diving Ltd* [1984] 1 W.L.R. 212 this rule of thumb does not necessarily apply where the wife had been earning a substantial sum herself before her husband's death, or presumably when she had a substantial private income. We set out part of the Court of Appeal's judgment below. *Per* Ralph Gibson L.J.

> "O'Connor L.J. stated the rationale of the conventional figure, ie that broadly speaking the net income was spent as to one third for the benefit of each and one third for their joint benefit. As described by O'Connor L.J. it is clear that he was referring to a family unit dependent upon the earnings of the husband only.
>
> Where both are earning and pooling their net earnings, application of the same principle requires that one third of the joint earnings be treated as spent for the benefit of each and one third for their joint benefit; and the justification for that is that a couple

living together as a stable family are likely to divide their common resources fairly and equally. As O'Connor L.J. pointed out, the principle is always capable of being displaced by evidence. If the joint income is low, it is likely that more than one third will be applied to joint benefit. Next, a wife or husband may have special needs, or make special demands, which in fact require a larger share than can also be applied to the sole benefit of the other spouse. Further, when the joint net earnings are substantial, as they are in this case on the judge's findings, part of the one third proportion retained by either spouse for his or her sole benefit may in probability be retained for purposes which will eventually pass to the benefit of the other."

2.53 Another case in which the *Harris* rule of thumb was not applied, following *Coward v. Comex Houlder Diving Ltd*, is *Crabtree v. Wilson* [1993] P.I.Q.R. Q. 24. There the court had to take into account the fact that during part of the period of the dependency the plaintiff wife would be earning money. The trial judge had not taken this period into account. Accordingly, the Court of Appeal varied the award by reducing the multiplicand for that period. The facts and the calculations are complicated and can best be understood by a study of the full judgments of the Court of Appeal.

2.54 By contrast, in *Wheatley v. Cunningham* [1992] P.I.Q.R. Q. 100 Tudor Evans J. (though urged by the defendant not to apply the *Harris* rule of thumb) held that the *Harris* rule was appropriate on the facts of the case before him, except for a short period for which he applied the *Coward v. Comex* approach.

Private means of a dependant

2.55 In order to determine whether, and if so to what extent, a person was dependent upon the deceased it is necessary to consider that person's own income, earned and unearned, past and prospective. A wealthy wife may receive no financial support at all from her husband. The true prospect of support in any particular case is a matter of evidence.

2.56 Thus in *Davies v. Hawes*, reported in *Kemp & Kemp* Vol. 3 para. M2–236, where a widow was her deceased husband's sole dependant, the widow had been earning substantial sums during the marriage and she and her husband had pooled their earnings to form a joint family purse. Sir Michael Ogden Q.C., following the decision of the Court of Appeal in *Coward v. Comex Houlder Diving Ltd*, held that in such case it was inappropriate to apply the rule of thumb expounded by O'Connor L.J. in *Harris v. Empress Motors*, namely, that the widow's dependency be taken as two-thirds of her husband's anticipated net earnings. Instead he assessed the widow's dependency in the following manner. He ascertained the amount from the joint family purse which was spent solely for the benefit of the widow: he ascertained the amount from the joint family purse which was spent for the benefit of the widow and her husband jointly. The sum of these two amounts, say, £X, represented the total value of the widow's dependency derived from the joint family purse. He held that the widow had not lost the benefit of her own income and so subtracted it from the £X to determine the amount of the widow's lost dependency on her husband. On that basis he held that her dependency should be assessed at slightly over 20 per cent of her deceased husband's anticipated earnings. This method of calculating a widow's dependency is based on the assumption that all the wife's earnings are put into a joint family purse. It is not appropriate where the wife keeps some of her earnings for her own exclusive use.

2.57 There is of course no question of expecting a moneyed dependant to bear part of the loss caused by the wrongdoer. The dependant's money is relevant solely for ascertaining what that loss is, and in ascertaining the loss the court may well have to consider the whole financial relationship between the deceased and the dependant. The distinction is well expressed in the Scottish case of *Shiels v. Cruickshank* [1951] S.C. 741. In the Court of Session Lord Patrick said: "The amounts of support in fact afforded [by the dead person] in the past, and likely to be afforded in the future, have in my experience been the factors taken into account . . ." In the House of Lords, Lord Normand said: 1953 S.C. 1 at 5

> "That is in my opinion an accurate statement and obviously warrants inquiry into the actual amount of the husband's contribution. But it does not make it permissible to inquire what the amount of the wife's estate was and whether her own private income which she enjoyed before her husband's death and continued to enjoy after it would enable her to maintain herself in future, or to make out of it a larger contribution to her maintenance than she had done in the past'."

Higgs v. Drinkwater

2.58 The court will probably also have to estimate how the financial relationship between deceased and dependant would have continued in the future. In *Higgs v. Drinkwater* 1956 C.A. No. 1299 husband and wife had been married a year when the husband was killed. The husband was earning £550 a year, the wife £800, and only £150 to £200 of the husband's earnings were expended for his wife's advantage. However, the widow's evidence was that she and her husband hoped to start a family and that she would have given up work in a few months' time, in which case she would have been more dependant on her husband. Because of the death she had stayed at work at £800 a year. Pearson J. based his award to the widow on a figure considerably in excess of £150 to £200, because of the possibility of becoming more dependent on her husband. The Court of Appeal held that Pearson J. was wrong and that the award should be based on the £150 and £200 only.

> "Owing to her husband's death she has lost the joys of motherhood and a family, or at any rate the chance of them; but we cannot award damages for that loss. We can only award damages for financial loss and she has suffered none through not having a family. On the contrary, she has kept at work earning this salary."

2.59 The Court of Appeal are of course right in saying "We can only award damages for financial loss", but with respect we submit they were wrong in going on to say that the widow had not suffered such loss through not having a family. On the widow's evidence she had in fact as a result of the death lost a prospect of increased financial support from her husband.

2.60 To take a contrary example, if after the death and before trial the dependant comes into a long-expected substantial fortune, the court could properly consider whether on the evidence this would have resulted in the deceased giving the dependant less. If changes in a dependant's income would but for the death have affected the amount of financial support, they are relevant, whether they would have increased the support or decreased it.

2.61 In *Malone v. Rowan* [1984] 3 All E.R. 402 Russell J. felt constrained to follow *Higgs v. Drinkwater* on the ground that he could find no factual distinguishing features between that case and the instant case before him. However, it was clear that he was reluctant to take this course. He said of *Higgs'* case:

> "The case was criticised by the editor of *Kemp & Kemp*, and I must confess that, for my part, I find difficulty in understanding why the prospect of having a family, with the increased dependency that that involves, is different (as is suggested by counsel for the defendant) from other exigencies which might well affect the future dependency.
>
> That future prospective losses which have not materialised at the date of trial can properly form the basis of an award under the 1976 Act is beyond dispute: see *Taff Vale Rly Co. v. Jenkins* [1913] AC 1. A widow in any given case may give up work after the death of her husband, and before or after the date of trial, for a variety of reasons. She may decide to go part-time as opposed to full-time. If, for any reason which the widow demonstrates to the satisfaction of the court, an increase in dependency in the years to come is or would have been likely, I would have thought that she would be entitled to have it reflected in the award.
>
> But, having briefly expressed that view, I recognise that it is of no avail in this case, having regard to *Higgs v. Drinkwater* . . . As I observed earlier, the facts of that case are indistinguishable from that with which I am concerned and, accordingly, following the Court of Appeal's judgment, I must assess the damages recoverable in this case on the basis of the dependency which existed at the date of death, not altering the fraction, as earlier, I indicated I would have done if free from authority."

2.62 This question was mentioned in *Coward v. Comex Houlder Diving Ltd* where Rougier J. referred to the criticism of *Higgs v. Drinkwater* and said that he shared the unhappiness about that decision expressed by Russell J. in *Malone*'s case but, being bound by the Court of Appeal's decision, he applied the law as stated in *Higgs*' case. The matter did not arise for decision on appeal in *Coward*'s case, but Gibson L.J. stated *obiter* that he thought that the Court of Appeal's decision was right.

2.63 In *Halvorsen Boats Pty Ltd v. Robinson* (1993) 31 N.S.W.L.R. 1 the New South Wales Court of Appeal refused to follow *Higgs v. Drinkwater* on the ground that it is inconsistent with the decision of the High Court of Australia in *Carroll v. Purcell* (1961) 107 C.L.R. 73. It is submitted that it would be desirable for the House of Lords to consider the decision in *Higgs'* case if the occasion were to arise.

Widow's unused earning capacity is not to be taken into account

2.64 A kind of case likely to arise in practice is the case where a widow who did not work while her husband was alive goes out to work after his death, to help support herself and the children. In *Howitt v. Heads* [1973] 1 Q.B. 64 Cumming-Bruce J. held that a widow's earning capacity was not to be taken into account in reduction of her damages. He followed the decisions in the Australian cases of *Carroll v. Purcell* above, *Goodger v. Knapman* [1924] S.A.S.R. 347 and *Usher v. Williams* (1955) 60 W.A.L.R. 69. The New Zealand Court of Appeal made a similar decision in *Jamieson v. Greene* [1957] N.Z.L.R. 1154.

Benefits not coming out of deceased's income

2.65 So far as items requiring out-of-pocket expenditure are concerned, it is difficult to establish an annual dependency that cannot reasonably be fitted in with the deceased's annual net income. But there are certain items which can properly increase the value of the dependency, but do not have to come from the deceased's net income.

2.66 It is increasingly common for employees, who have to use a motor car in the course of their employment, to be allowed the free use of that car for private purposes, paying only for the petrol and oil consumed during private use. In order to be provided with a comparable car, taxed, insured and maintained, the dependants would have to pay quite considerable sums. Taking into account depreciation, the value to the dependants of a car always available outside working hours may well amount to several hundred pounds a year. Up-to-date figures for all relevant costs can be obtained from one of the motoring organisations.

2.67 Some employees enjoy free accommodation, eg a tied cottage or premises occupied under a service tenancy. Some farm-workers enjoy free milk or eggs. Colliers may have free or cheap coal. Transport employees may enjoy concessionary fares for members of their family. The value of all such benefits properly forms part of the annual value of the dependency.

2.68 Many husbands, who are keen gardeners, provide their families with considerable quantities of fruit and vegetables from their gardens or allotments. This can amount to quite a valuable benefit. Similarly, many husbands do a good deal of work about the house, decorating, carrying out repairs and improvements, etc. Such work can also have quite a considerable annual value.

2.69 Any service rendered by the deceased or any privilege enjoyed by him, which was of value to his dependants, will count as part of the dependency.

A privilege enjoyed by frequent business travellers is the accumulation of "Air Miles". A dependant who enjoyed the use of the deceased's "Air Miles" could claim for the loss of this benefit. According to recent press reports the division of "Air Miles" between divorcing spouses has given rise to litigation.

Savings made by the deceased: how far part of the dependency?

2.70 In *Gavin v. Wilmot Breeden Ltd* [1973] 1 W.L.R. 1117, the deceased and his widow had only been married for three months at the date of his death. He was earning £30 a week net, of which he paid £6 a week to his parents for board and lodging and saved £10 a week to create a capital sum for future use. The trial judge held that the dependency was £18 a week, apparently including the whole £10 savings as part of the dependency. The Court of Appeal held that the whole £10 a week should not be regarded as spent for the widow's benefit, since some part was likely to be used at some future date for the husband's benefit. Accordingly, the Court of Appeal reduced the weekly dependency from £18 to £15.

The multiplicand in the case of a deceased housewife and mother

2.71 In the ordinary way a person cannot be a dependant of another person unless that other person has income out of which he or she provides for the first person. However, that is not the case where the deceased was a housewife or mother or both. If such a deceased had income then the assessment of any financial dependency would be made on the basis already discussed. However, in the nature of things a housewife, and particularly a mother, provides services which have monetary value in that, to the extent that such services can be replaced, it costs money to do so. In *Regan v. Williamson* [1976] 1 W.L.R. 305 Watkins J. expressed the views that the services to be brought into account should not be considered too narrowly and that it should be acknowledged that a housewife and mother was in virtually constant attendance upon her husband and children. Watkins J. was prepared to value the services of the deceased wife which could not be provided by another and to bring them into account in calculating the dependency. In other cases, however, judges have assessed the dependency simply on the basis of the cost of employing a resident housekeeper or, where there was no accommodation for a resident housekeeper, a daily help.

Where widower gives up work

2.72 The question may sometimes arise of the appropriate basis of quantification of the dependency in a case in which a widower and father, instead of engaging a resident or daily help, gives up his own job in order to be able to look after the home and his children. Provided the decision of the father is reasonable in the circumstances the value of the dependency will be taken to be the wages which he has lost by giving up his job, less any income, such as supplementary benefit, which he receives because he has no other source of income.

2.73 One of the considerations going to the reasonableness of the father's decision will obviously be the amount of the income which he has lost by giving up his job. A court would be unlikely to be persuaded that a father acted reasonably in a case in which there were no special circumstances, if his income was significantly higher than the cost of employing help. In *Bailey v. Barking and Havering Area Health Authority* (1978) *The Times*, 22 July, Peter Pain J. in the converse case, declined to assess damages on the basis of the cost of a housekeeper when the father had in fact given up his own job in which his earnings were less than the cost of a housekeeper.

2.74 The value of the personal care and attention of a wife to her husband is an appropriate element to reflect in the dependency, but the danger of overlap with the value of her housekeeping services should be borne in mind.

Value of having a wife

2.75 If a wife has financial value to her husband by virtue of her existence rather than as a result of her income or the value of her services the husband may recover in respect of the loss of that financial value. Thus in *Oldfield v. Mahoney*, 12 July 1968, a schoolmaster whose prospects of obtaining appointment as a housemaster (with an appropriate increase in salary) were otherwise good, suffered a serious diminution in those prospects as a result of the death of his wife, as ordinarily only married men were appointed housemaster at his school.

The multiplier/multiplicand approach in practice

2.76 The multiplier/multiplicand approach is appropriate to deal with continuing losses to the dependants upon which a present value can be placed as at the date of the trial. That is not to say that, if the multiplier/multiplicand approach cannot be applied to a particular loss, that loss is not recoverable. The words of section 3(1) of the Fatal Accidents Act 1976 are wide. The dependants are entitled to recover in respect of any loss which can be proved to flow from the death of the deceased. In *Collins v. Noma Electric Co. Ltd* (1962) 106 S.J. 431 the wife had gone out to work in order to help the family save for a deposit on a house, her intention being to give up work once a deposit had been raised. She was killed on her first day at work. The damages awarded to her dependants included a lump sum in respect of the loss of her contributions to the deposit. In *Davies v. Whiteways Cyder Co. Ltd* [1975] Q.B. 262, the amount of estate duty paid on gifts made by the deceased less than seven years before his death was held to be recoverable. In *Piggot v. Fancy Wood Products Ltd*, reported in *Kemp & Kemp* volume 3 para. M5–012, the evidence was that the deceased, had he survived, would have helped his parents obtain a house and they were held entitled to recover in respect of the loss of that anticipated contribution.

Events subsequent to the date of death

2.77 Reference has already been made to the fact that the multiplicand is assessed as at the date of the trial, not as at the date of death. The general approach to events occurring subsequent to the date of death of the deceased which are relevant to the assessment of the award under the Fatal Accidents Act 1976 is that "courts in assessing damages are entitled to inform their minds of the circumstances which have arisen since the cause of action occurred and throw light upon the reality of the case"; *per* Scott L.J. in *Williamson v. John I Thorneycroft & Co. Ltd* [1940] 2 KB 658 at 659. In *Williamson*'s case the deceased's widow herself died 14 months after her husband and before the case came to court. The trial judge ignored the fact of the widow's death and assessed the widow's damages on the basis of her expectation of life as it was at the date of her husband's death. The Court of Appeal held that the judge was wrong.

Dependant not bound by agreement limiting the damages for which defendant is liable

2.78 In *Nunan v. Southern Ry* [1924] 1 K.B. 223 the Court of Appeal held that where a railway passenger had agreed with the railway that their liability for personal injuries should not exceed a certain sum, and he had been killed by their negligence, the damages recovered by the dependants under the Fatal Accidents Acts were not limited to that agreed sum.

Contributory negligence of deceased

2.79 The Fatal Accidents Act 1976, s. 5 provides:

> "Where any person dies as the result partly of his own fault and partly of the fault of any other person or persons, and accordingly if an action were brought for the benefit of the estate under the Law Reform (Miscellaneous Provisions) Act 1934 the damages recoverable would be reduced under section 1(1) of the Law Reform (Contributory Negligence) Act 1945, any damages recoverable in an action brought for the benefit of the dependants of that person under this Act shall be reduced to a proportionate extent."

2.80 Where the deceased has been unlawfully killed in the course of a criminal affray in which he was taking part his death might, depending upon the circumstances, have been partly the result of his own "fault" within the meaning of the section: *Murphy v. Culhane* [1977] Q.B. 94.

Negligence of dependant

2.81 Where the death of the deceased is caused by the negligence of a dependant the negligence of that dependant prevents him from recovering under the Fatal Accidents Act 1976, but does not affect the claims of other dependants: *Dodds v. Dodds* [1978] Q.B. 543.

INCIDENCE OF BENEFITS

Section 4 of the Fatal Accidents Act 1976

2.82 At common law the general rule, as stated by Lord Macmillan in *Davies v. Powell Duffryn Associated Collieries Ltd* [1942] A.C. 601 at 609, was that the "damages awarded to a dependant of a deceased person under the Fatal Accidents Acts must take into account any pecuniary benefit accruing to that dependant in consequence of the death of the deceased". That rule was made subject to various statutory exceptions over the years and it was totally abrogated as from 1 January 1983 in respect of deaths occurring on or after that date by the Fatal Accidents Act 1976, s. 4 as substituted by the Administration of Justice Act 1982, s. 3(1). Section 4 as substituted provides:

> "In assessing damages in respect of a person's death in an action under this Act, benefits which have accrued or will or may accrue to any person from his estate or otherwise as a result of his death shall be disregarded."

2.83 The effect of this section and in particular the extent of the words "or otherwise" were considered by the Court of Appeal in *Stanley v. Saddique* [1992] 1 Q.B. 1. In that case a claim was brought under the Fatal Accidents Act for the benefit of a boy whose mother had been killed. She was an unsatisfactory and unreliable mother. The father remarried and the boy thus obtained a stepmother who provided him with motherly services of a higher standard than those which had been provided by his own mother. The defendant argued that the stepmother's services to the boy were a benefit to him which should be taken into account in the assessment of his damages on the ground that the statutory disregard in s. 4 was limited to direct pecuniary benefits: the defendant argued for a restricted meaning to be given to the words "or otherwise". The Court of Appeal, Purchas and Gibson L.JJ. and Sir David Croom-Johnson, rejected this argument.

2.84 However, the boy's own mother's services were so unreliable, and the prospect of their continuing, if she had not been killed, so uncertain that the Court of Appeal reduced the award from £32,536 to £15,000.

Implication of *Stanley v. Saddique*

2.85 This decision raises interesting problems which do not appear to have been brought to the court's attention. In *Stanley's* case the boy's dependency on his mother comprised the services and financial support which he could expect to have received from her if she had not been killed. How does such dependency differ from the services and/or financial support which a deceased's wife's husband could expect to have received from her if she had not been killed? It is submitted that there is no material difference. In that case, if the replacement of the deceased mother's services by a stepmother is a benefit to be disregarded by virtue of s. 4 in the assessment of the son's damages, surely the replacement of a deceased wife's services by another wife is likewise to be disregarded in the assessment of the husband's damages. And, if that is so, Parliament appears by s. 4 of have removed the anomalous situation created by section 4 of the Law Reform (Miscellaneous Provisions) Act 1971. The effect of that section was that in the case of a widow's claim for the death of her husband her remarriage or prospects of remarriage were to be disregarded in the assessment of her damages. No statutory provision then required that a husband's remarriage or prospects of remarriage were to be disregarded in the assessment of his damages in a claim for the death of his wife: accordingly the court continued to take a husband's remarriage or prospects of remarriage into account in assessing his damages. As a result the multiplier applied to the annual dependency was usually considerably less in the case of a young husband's Fatal Accidents Act claim for his wife's death than in such a claim by a wife for her husband's death. The decision in *Stanley's* case now requires a husband's remarriage or prospects of remarriage to be disregarded and accordingly to require similar multipliers to be adopted in a husband's claim for his wife's death to those adopted in a wife's claim for her husband's death. May J. so held in *Topp v. Country Bus (South West) Ltd* [1993] 3 All E.R. 448.

Hayden's case

2.86 It has now been held in *Hayden v. Hayden* [1992] 1 W.L.R. 486 by the Court of Appeal (McCowan L.J. and Sir David

Croom-Johnson; Parker L.J. dissenting) that *Stanley v. Saddique* is binding on the Court of Appeal.

2.87 The decision in *Hayden*'s case on the merits raises difficult questions beyond the scope of this work. It is submitted that the dissenting judgment of McCowan L.J. is to be preferred to that of the majority of the court. For a more detailed discussion see *Kemp & Kemp*, Vol I, para. 22–005/3 *et seq*.

Wood v. Bentall Simplex

2.88 In *Wood v. Bentall Simplex Ltd* [1992] P.I.Q.R. P. 332 the Court of Appeal held that in assessing damages under the Fatal Accidents Act 1976 it was irrelevant that there might be established a loss from one source which might be made good from another by using a benefit from the deceased's estate. *Per* Beldam L.J.:

> "During the last 100 years certain benefits accruing as a result of a deceased's death had on the ground of policy gradually been excluded from being taken into account against the expectation of pecuniary benefit, for example, life assurance benefits or state benefits.
>
> In the present case, the dependants enjoyed not only the expectation of pecuniary benefit from the labour and work which the deceased put into the family farm but were also able to rely if necessary on the increasing value, as a result of the deceased's hard work, of the family assets, although tied up in the farming enterprise.
>
> The appellant's assertion was that the dependants received income from assets which in the deceased's lifetime were employed in the farming enterprise and that they had not lost that income as the assets continued to be used after the death.
>
> However, to make good the claim that the dependency on which the award was based already included a sum which represented a return on the assets employed in the enterprise was a difficult task and had never been attempted by the appellant.
>
> The background to the amendments to the 1976 Act included the recommendations of the Royal Commission on Civil Liability and Compensation for Personal Injury (1978 Cmnd 7054–1), *inter alia*, one that all benefits derived from the deceased's estate should be excluded as deductions from the damages received under the Act.

On the facts of the present case, section 4 of the 1976 Act, as amended, required the benefits accruing to the dependants from the deceased's estate to be disregarded, whether at the stage the court first ascertained the extent of the injury to the dependants from the death, or at the stage the damages to be awarded were assessed: *Auty v. National Coal Board* [1985] 1 W.L.R. 784, 805."

2.89 The Law Commission in its Consultation Paper No. 147 expressed the provisional view that section 4 of the Fatal Accidents Act was not intended to have the wide effect that the natural meaning of its words required. We strongly dissent from this view. A consideration of the enacting history of s. 4 and of reports by the Law Commission, the Scottish Law Commission and the Pearson Royal Commission, leading to the enactment of s. 4, show clearly that the section was intended to have the widest possible effect. This matter was dealt with in detail in *Kemp & Kemp*, Vol. 1. Chapter 19A. Chapter 19A also dealt with some *obiter dicta* in *Auty v. National Coal Board* [1985] 1 W.L.R. 784 and in *Wood v. Bentall Simplex Ltd* [1992] P.I.Q.R. P. 332 which are in our view incorrect and stated *per incuriam.*

Pidduck v. Eastern Scottish Omnibuses

2.90 In *Pidduck v. Eastern Scottish Omnibuses Ltd* [1990] 1 W.L.R. 993 the Court of Appeal affirmed the decision of Sheen J., holding that an allowance based on the husband's pension and paid by his former employers to his widow following his death was a benefit which accrued to the widow as a result of his death and was therefore to be disregarded when assessing her damages under the Fatal Accidents Act 1976, as amended by the 1982 Act.

The law prior to January 1, 1983

2.91 There may still be some unresolved cases in which claims are made by a dependant who was an infant at the date of the deceased's death and so protected by section 38 of the Limitation Act, eg *Cresswell v. Eaton* [1991] 1 W.L.R. 1113. To this limited extent the pre-1 January 1983 law is relevant. For an explanation of this law see *Kemp & Kemp*, Vol 1, paras 22–011 *et seq.*

EXAMPLES OF MULTIPLIERS

2.92 Although the size of awards made under the Fatal Accidents Act has increased over the years as a result of inflation and increased earnings, the multiplier adopted in various classes of cases has remained fairly consistent.

In most cases it will be a reasonably straightforward task to assess the multiplicand. That will be a question of fact to be decided on the evidence. The main dispute between the parties will be over the multiplier. There is no room in this book to give summaries of numerous awards. The best we can do is to give some tables of multipliers, dealing with various classes of dependency, with references in the tables to the reported awards in *Kemp & Kemp*, Vol III.

2.93 These multipliers have been adopted under the current conventional practice of assessing a lump sum for future loss by applying a discount rate at 4 to 4.5% per annum. We have consistently contended that this is too high a discount rate and the proper course would be to use a discount rate based on the net return (after tax) to be derived from an index-linked Government security.

Wells v. Wells appeal to House of Lords

2.94 In the combined appeals *Wells v. Wells*, *Thomas v. Brighton Health Authority*, and *Page v. Sheerness Steel plc* [1997] 1 W.L.R. 652 the Court of Appeal reversed the judgments of trial judges who had adopted a lower discount rate based on the net return from investment in an index-linked Government Security and held that the traditional discount rate of 4.5 per cent should be applied. On this basis the Court reduced the multipliers which had been adopted by the trial judges. On appeal the House of Lords reversed the Court of Appeal and held that a discount rate of 3 per cent should be adopted ([1998] 1 W.L.R. 329). Although *Wells* was a claim for personal injury, the application of a 3 per cent discount rate will significantly increase multipliers in Fatal Accidents Act claims.

Note: In considering the following tables, practitioners should bear in mind that the multipliers were fixed under the conventional disount rate of 4 to 5 per cent. Under the new guideline discount rate of 3 per cent the multipliers in most cases would have been considerably higher.

Explanation of tables

2.95 Please note the following:

(a) Name in bold indicates that the award was assessed or affirmed by the Court of Appeal.
Name in ordinary type indicates first instance award.
Name in italics indicates unauthenticated award.

(b) Multiplier is taken from date of death.

(c) Dependency is dependency at date of trial.

(d) The symbol "?" appears where a relevant age is not known.

(e) The penultimate column shows the value of the award in terms of the £ in October 1998.

(f) The reference is to the appropriate paragraph in *Kemp & Kemp*, Vol. 3.

Claims for death of husband

2.96 For an explanation of the table see para: 2.95 above.

Name	*Ref*	*Age* *Deceased*	*Widow*	*Children*	*Occupation*	*Court*	*Damages (£)*	*Damages (£ 1998)*	*Multiplier*
Howitt	M2–011	21	20	one posthumous	Post Office engineer	Cumming-Bruce J.	16,850	123,000	18
Thomas	M2–151	18	17	3	Plumber's mate	Nield J.	9,090	65,000	18
Maxfield	M2–012	28	31	6,3,1, and a stepchild aged 10	Builder's labourer	Stable J. (affirmed by C.A.)	7,200	93,400	17
Thompson	M2–013	24	22	7	—	Boreham J.	8,490	59,450	17
Fox	M2–152	31	35	5	Toy salesman	Melford Stevenson J.	15,900	109,500	17
Nutbrown	M2–014	35	34	19 and 7	Scientist	Myerson Q.C.	204,950	409,900	17
Attree	M2–015	32	?30	? and ?	Professional	Kenneth Jones J.	210,820	368,900	16
Pyne	M2–016	21	—	18 months	Fitter/turner	Thorpe J.	148,000	207,200	16
Robertson	M2–021	29	29	8,4 and 2	Economist	Webster J.	204,790	368,650	16
Wheatley	M2–017	27	25	—	Store manager	Tudor Evans J.	131,582	157,900	16
Malone	M2–018	27	25	—	Security guard	Russell J.	49,180	88,550	16
Neilson	M2–019	24	24	one posthumous	Paper mill worker	Thesiger J.	16,065	120,500	16
Murray	M2–020	36	36	5,4	Businessman	Shaw J.	76,800	476,500	16
Miles	M2–029	38	—	—	Salesman	D. Frank Q.C.	603,210	904,815	15
Wilkinson	M2–027	35	33	13, 9, 7, 4	—	Webster J. (affirmed C.A.)	249,140	348,800	15

		Age							
Name	*Ref*	*Deceased*	*Widow*	*Children*	*Occupation*	*Court*	*Damages (£)*	*Damages (£ 1998)*	*Multiplier*
Skelton	M2–028	34	32	12, 11	Salesman	Griffiths J. (affirmed C.A.)	40,500	121,500	16
Adams	M2–033	39	31	5, 2	Chartered electrical engineer	Lyell J.	15,510	153,100	15
Kay	M2–030	33	29	5, 3	—	Russell J.	200,000	510,000	15
McKenna	M2–157	43	43	18, 15	Sales service manager	Deputy Judge Gibbens Q.C.	36,355	310,924	15
Garner	M2–153	37	28	3	Motor dealer controller	O'Connor J.	21,750	135,000	15
Jones	M2–154	30	40	12, 9, 6, 4	Lorry driver	Mr Commissioner Smith, Q.C.	15,000	112,500	15
Lloyds Bank Ltd.	M2–031	39	39	18, 17, 15	General practitioner	Nield J.	115,000	414,000	15
Davies	M2–032	34	31	—	—	Deputy Judge Ogden Q.C.	50,600	68,500	15
Phillips	M2–034	26	21	—	—	Lord Clyde	22,050	27,250	15
Robert	M2–035	34	28	6, 4, 2	Dairyman	Mais J.	33,700	111,250	15
Gray	M2–142	31	34	11, 8	Farmer	Geoffrey Lane J.	6,000	52,800	15
Cunningham	M2–040	43	?	5 children aged 16 to 1	—	C.A.	5,250	79,000	14½
Lewin	M2–041	40	46	11, 10	Butcher and baker	C.A.	3,750	56,450	14½

Name	*Ref*	*Age*			*Occupation*	*Court*	*Damages (£)*	*Damages (£ 1998)*	*Multiplier*
		Deceased	*Widow*	*Children*					
Jennings	M2–060	43	43	Six children	Third hand on trawler	Payne J.	12,100	140,500	12½
Gilmartin	M2–165	49	40	17, 14, 11, 10, 5	Crane erector	James J.	17,420	130,650	12
Davies	M2–061	25	20	2½	Electrician	C.A.	19,000	222,500	12
Taylor	M2–063	53	52	18	Architect	Lyell J. (affirmed H.L.)	42,000	420,000	16
Prior	M2–062	46	?	—	Lagger	—	66,737	110,116	12
Smart	M2–161	49	—	?	Airline navigator	O'Connor J.	30,000	189,000	12
Butler	M2–068	39	36	Six children	Bricklayer	McNair J. (affirmed C.A.)	10,500	120,750	11
MacKay	M2–069	41	34	8, 6, 4	Consultant radiotherapist, also surgeon	Melford Stevenson J.	23,750	285,000	11
Owen	M2–066	26	28	—		C.A.	150,000	180,000	11
Cookson	M2–067	49	45	16, 13, 12	School cleaner	H.L.	20,040	72,500	10
McGarry	M2–076	41	39	Five children ranging from ?19 to 8	Steel erector	C.A.	6,750	85,050	10
Davies	M2–077	55	45	18	Property developer	O'Connor J.	35,660	220,500	10
Doyle	M2–078	54	—	—	Consultant anaesthetist and General Practitioner	Bristow J.	90,100	208,250	10

Name	Ref	Age: Deceased	Age: Widow	Age: Children	Occupation	Court	Damages (£)	Damages (£ 1998)	Multiplier
Crabtree	M2–078/1	52	—	19, 17	Machinist	C.C.	84,000	94,000	10
Langley	M2–164	49	—		Kiln burner	James J.	15,000	112,000	10
Piper	M2–162	53	62		Building foreman	O'Connor J.	11,360	70,000	10
Mills	M2–075	61	65		Unemployed	C.A.	20,000	24,000	10
Ali	M2–079	51	44		Seaman	Tudor Evans J.	27,000	41,000	10
Allan	M2–046	42	–	Five children	Managing director of textile company	O'Connor J.	181,000	543,000	9½
Gumbrell	M2–085	56	58	18, 14	Brickmaker	Master Diamond (affirmed C.A.)	4,500	56,700	9
Abrams	M2–086	72	?		Retired teacher	C.A.	9,360	32,900	8¾
Duffin	M2–087	63	–		Railway signalman	C.A.	3,000	36,000	8
Newton	M2–088	62	–		Miner	C.A.	1,500	18,000	8
Helsby	M2–089	58	56		Greengrocer	C.A.	2,000	21,000	7½
Benton	M2–167	61	62		Reinsurance underwriter	Lawson J.	7,650	57,500	7
Moss	M2–166	58	62		Canteen assistant	Donaldson J.	3,250	30,500	7
Boreham	M2–168	55	52		Foreman carpenter	Eveleigh J.	7,100	49,700	7
Bartlett	M2–090	71	?		Commercial artist	Howard J. (affirmed C.A.)	3,750	41,540	6½

Name	*Ref*	*Age*			*Occupation*	*Court*	*Damages (£)*	*Damages (£ 1998)*	*Multiplier*
		Deceased	*Widow*	*Children*					
Paramor	M2–092	62	–		Dover Board employee	Donaldson J.	2,700	27,250	6
Lea	M2–093	64	62		Redundant coal miner Pools collector	Bush J.	11,550	31,250	6
Cronin	M2–169	53	47	21, 19, 17 15, 13 & 9	Site foreman	Mocatta J.	17,000	93,500	6
Nightingale	M2–098	63	–		–	C.A.	9,610	36,500	5½
Playford	M2–170	62	64		–	Sachs J.	1,350	14,250	5
Matheson	M2–172	69	73		Company director	Salmon J.	7,550	90,000	4
Jones	M2–101	64	60		–	Diplock J. (affirmed C.A.)	800	11,000	3
Gilbertson	M2–102	71	–		Riveter	Sachs J.	1,250	13,250	2
Cutler	M2–174	63	64		Steelworker	Kenneth Jones J.	2,500	13,750	2

Claims for death of wife

2.97 For an explanation of the table see para. 2.95 above.

Name	*Ref*	*Age*			*Occupation*	*Court*	*Damages (£)*	*Damages (£ 1998)*	*Multiplier*
		Deceased	*Widow*	*Children*					
Grzelak	M3–051	37	43	–	School teacher	Megaw J.	3,000	29,750	15
Topp	M3–052	33	37	5½	–	May J.	–	–	15
Oldfield	M3–055	44	46	?	Housewife	Nield J.	2,270	22,500	14
Mehmet	M3–060	–	–	?	Housewife	Brain Neill Q.C.	14,800	66,500	12 (wife) 8 (family)
Regan	M3–061	37	43	14, 11, 8 & 3	Housewife	Watkins J.	12,300	67,750	11
Jeffrey	M3–065	38	51	9, 6 & 3	Housewife	Melford-Stevenson J. (affirmed C.A.)	5,200	46,750	10
Hurt	M3–066	42	45	22, 21, 16, 14 & 9	Kitchen attendant	Talbot J.	5,150	37,500	9
Collins	M3–067	33	39	12, 10, 9, 8, 7 & 3	?	Paull J.	2,390	28,750	8
Longden	M3–068	28	40	–	Clerk	Caulfield J.	14,680	35,250	8
Morris	M3–070	?	46	15, 12, 10, 7 & 2	Housewife	Cusack J. (affirmed C.A.)	8,000	84,000	7½
Khan	M3–071	45	50	17, 16 & 8	–	Popplewell J.	37,830	54,750	7
Steer	M3–072	?	39	?	Housewife	Caulfield J.	4,880	46,750	6½
Pevec	M3–073	34	38	2	Housekeeper	Megaw J.	2,910	36,500	6
Watkins	M3–075	?	27	5, 3	–	Robert Goff J.	25,620	53,750	–
Jenkins	M3–101	40	?	–	Housewife	Melford Stevenson J.	18,000	61,250	–

Since the decision of the Court of Appeal in *Stanley v. Saddique* [1992] 1 Q.B. 1, the widower's remarriage or prospect of remarriage is to be disregarded: see para. 2.85 above. The multiplier in awards made before this decision should be viewed with care as probably too low if the facts indicate a likelihood of remarriage, eg in the case of a young widower with no children.

Claims for death of adult child

2.98 For an explanation of the table see para. 2.95 above.

Name	*Ref.*	*Age*	*Court*	*Damages*	*Damages (£) 1998*
Dolbey	M5–011	–	C.A.	1,500	22,500
Piggott	M5–012	21	Wrangham J.	1,200	15,750
Appleby	M5–013	19	Hodson J.	750	13,500
Brennan	M5–014	23	C.A.	750	11,750
Lynch	M5–015	18	Brabin J.	750	7,000
Carbery	M5–017	19	Slade J.	500	6,500
Riley	M5–017/1	18	C.C.	1,800	2,250
Doleman	M5–018	17	Potts J. (affirmed by C.A.)	1,500	2,250

Claims for death of infant child

2.99 For an explanation of the table see para. 2.95 above.

Name	*Ref.*	*Age*	*Court*	*Damages*	*Damages (£) 1998*
Wathen	M6–011	17	C.A.	500	4,750
Buckland	M6–012	13	Morris J.	500	9,250
Spitalali	M6–076	14	Norman Richards, Q.C.	800	4,250
Ellis	M6–013	17	Jones J.	110	1,500

2.100 For an explanation of the table see para. 2.95 above.

Name	*Ref*	*Age*		*Occupation*	*Court*	*Damages (£)*	*Damages (£ 1998)*	*Multiplier*
		Deceased Mother/Father	*Children*					
Watson	M4–051	M	3	–	Garland J.	53,320	76,750	11½
Spittle	M4–052	M	3	–	C.A.	25,000	85,000	11
Hayden	M4–053	M	4	Housewife	C.A.	20,000	24,000	11
Muirhead	M4–055	M & F	24, 12	Housewife/ solicitor	C.A.	3,750	64,000	10, 10
Cresswell	M4–055/1	M	7, 6, 4	Housewife	Simon Brown J.	35,400	47,750	10½, 8½, 8
K	M4–056	F	6, 5, 2	Builder's labourer	C.A.	13,700	89,000	10, 8, 7
Hay	M4–057	M & F	4½, 2½	Housewife/ trainee welder	Reeve J. (affirmed by C.A.)	16,400	114,750	9/9
Lindley	M4–058	F	?	Unemployed	C.A.	1,870	14,000	9
Wilson	M4–053	M	3	–	C.I.C.B.	46,060	55,250	8,7
Gee	M4–060	M & F	21, 19, 16 & 14	Canteen assistant/ coalminer	Lawson J.	7,170	26,500	6, 4, 2½
Dodds	M4–065				Balcombe J.	17,170	65,250	5
Turner	M4–066	M	33	Cleaner	Faulks J.	1,040	9,250	5
T, G & J	M4–070	M	5, 3 & 2	Unemployed	C.I.C.B.	76,500	103,250	
Voller	M4–071	F	10, 6	Plumber	Nield J.	4,370	52,250	–
Kassam	M4–072	M/F	?	Shopkeeper	P.C.	3,500	38,500	–
Rawlinson	M4–073	F	14	–	Chapman J.	2,450	25,750	–
Stanley	M4–074	M	1	–	C.A.	15,000	20,000	–
Reincke	M4–075	F	5, 3	–	C.A.	1,000	11,500	–
Betney	M4–076	M/F	23, 22, 20	Part-time	C.C.	32,200	38,500	5–4
C	M4–101	F	8	Schoolteacher	Milmo J.	1,250	13,750	–
White	M4–102	F	4 mths	–	James J.	1,050	10,750	9/1

2.101 Many awards under the head of "claims for loss of husband" will include awards made to the deceased's children, although the major part of the award will usually be to the widow.

APPORTIONMENT BETWEEN DEPENDANTS

Apportionment to be made by the court

2.102 Any sum adjudged or ordered or agreed to be paid in satisfaction of a claim under the Fatal Accidents Act 1976 must be apportioned between the various dependants. The apportionment is effected by the court.

Defendant not concerned with apportionment

2.103 Where the total sum awarded to the dependants as a whole is a proper sum, the defendant is not concerned with the way this sum is apportioned, and cannot attack the award to a particular dependant as being excessive: *Eifert and Another v. Holt's Transport Co. Ltd* [1951] 2 All E.R. 655. In *Eifert*'s case the deceased left two dependants, a widow aged 23 and a child aged one. Barry J. assessed their total damages at £6,750, reduced to £6,400 by a Law Reform Act award. By consent of the widow this sum was apportioned £4,400 to the child and £2,000 to the widow. The Court of Appeal (Singleton and Morris L.JJ. and Roxburgh J.) held that the defendants were not concerned with this apportionment.

Each dependant has a separate judgment debt

2.104 The apportionment between the dependants is an essential part of the verdict and judgment in a Fatal Accidents Act action. Therefore, in a successful action each dependant has a separate judgment debt, equal to the amount of damages apportioned to him, due and owing to him: *Avery v. L.N.E.R.* [1938] A.C. 606. However, if one or more dependants do not join in the action and are not named, the defendant cannot pray in aid of their absence in order to reduce the damages payable to the others, but equally those missing dependants have no right to share in the award or to bring a second action: *Avery*'s case.

Practice

2.105 While the actual apportionment forms part of the judgment of the court the principles upon which the apportionment is made have never really been authoritatively stated. Following early attempts at apportionment of the total sum in amounts proportionate to the loss actually suffered by a particular dependant as a result of the deceased's death, and apportionment in accordance with the Statute of Distribution, the present practice in general "is to award the greater part of the total to the widow, on the reasonable assumption that she will maintain the children so long as they are dependent, and to award comparatively small sums to the children. Usually, though not always, a younger child is awarded more than an older child because the period of expected dependency is greater" (Report of the Committee on Funds in Court (July 1959, Cmnd 818), para. 15).

Of course, if for any reason there is ground for believing that the widow would not maintain the children adequately, the court should assess each child's loss and apportion to that child his assessed share of the total damages.

Criminal Injuries Compensation Board

2.106 *R. v. Criminal Injuries Compensation Board.* A recent decision of Latham J. in proceedings for judicial review in the above case ([1994] P.I.Q.R. Q. 44) has provided a valuable discussion on the current practice adopted by the court in apportioning dependants' damages under the Fatal Accidents Act. The applicants for compensation in respect of a murdered woman were her husband and two children, aged respectively 11 and 8. Under the Criminal Injuries Compensation Scheme a large sum of money, half the proceeds of an insurance policy payable on his wife's death, had to be deducted from the husband's share of the damages. The Board, following the current practice, had apportioned by far the greater part of the total award to the husband. After deduction of the insurance money, too small a sum was left to enable the husband adequately to maintain the children out of his damages. This result was contrary to the rationale upon which the current practice is based, and contrary to the wording of the Fatal Accidents Act which requires the children to recover damages for their loss of support and care. Latham J. accordingly quashed the Board's decision and remitted the claim to the Board for a fresh assessment of the dependants' damages. Latham J. having stated that the claims for compensation had to be assessed in accordance with the principles on which the courts have awarded damages under the Fatal Accidents Act over the years, continued as follows:

> "The basic principle under the Fatal Accidents Act is that the claim, which is a monetary claim, is for the value of that which has been lost by those generally described as the dependants. This is generally described as the 'dependency'. It is the dependency of each of the dependants which has to be determined. Under the Fatal Accidents Act each individual dependant had his own separate claim which he or she is entitled to have assessed separately. However, in procedural terms it is one claim brought usually by the personal representative of the estate of the deceased, which is then apportioned between the dependants.
>
> Over the years the practice has developed in relation to the valuation of the dependency, where there has been the loss of a father or a mother, whereby an overall figure is calculated as representing that which has been lost by reference either, where a father is concerned, to lost earnings, or, where a mother is concerned, to the value of the care which the mother provided. Of course there may be additional circumstances in which, as far as the father is concerned, it may be appropriate to provide further sums representing his care, and the mother, further sums representing lost income. The approach to the apportionment of the overall figure has essentially been pragmatic; the courts have sought to provide as much money in free cash terms for the parent who is caring for the child as is sensible in all the circumstances, so that there can be ready access for that parent to the fund representing the lost dependency. The bulk has therefore been apportioned to the parent. That was and is a fiction, because in most cases, when analysed, it is plain that the children were in fact the parties, or the dependants, for whom the substantial proportion, where care was concerned, of the value of the claim was intended. It was for their benefit. And it is right to say that this has never been reduced to any coherent or sensible principle. It has essentially been an approach which has had the attraction which I have already indicted to the parent who needs the cash; and there is no doubt that it could be said to be founded on good common sense. However, there are dangers. They have been recognised in particular in *McGregor on Damages* (15th ed),

para. 1581, in which the author indicates that there is no real sound basis other than pragmatism for approaching the problems of the apportionment of the amount of money representing the lost dependency in this particular way.

As far as principle is concerned, the principle appears to me to be clear. The principle is that each person who can be described as a dependant is entitled to the value of his or her dependency. The value of that dependency will obviously depend upon, so far as the children are concerned, their age and the financial circumstances in which the family may be at any given time. But the fact remains that when in particular, as in this case, a mother dies, the children have lost her care which has to be replaced; and just as in personal injury actions where one is trying to determine the extent to which care is required for somebody who has been significantly injured, the value or cost of that care is the claim that they have; so the value or cost of the provision of care for a child is the value of the dependency that the child has lost.

When one looks at the Criminal Injuries Compensation Board's Scheme it seems to me to be plain that it was intended that this approach, that is the approach of principle, should be retained because paragraph 15, makes it clear that each dependant has his or her separate claim, and that can only have meaning if one assumes that each dependant has a claim which can be properly valued. In the case of a child that will be, as in the Fatal Accidents Act, a claim for the value of the care he or she was receiving from the parent. In the present case that has been valued by the Criminal Injuries Compensation Board at the value of the grandparents' care to date, or to the date of the award, and the cost of a nanny or live-in help, plus the top-up figure for the mother's special assistance thereafter. These items are prima facie the basis of the claim for each of those children. They are not part of the applicant's claim.

But it is said on behalf of the Criminal Injuries Compensation Board that all that has been done here is to carry out the exercise that the court commonly carries out in terms of quantification on the one hand, and as I have said there is no quarrel with that, but then the distribution or apportionment of it on the other. It is said that what has happened is exactly what would have happened in a Fatal Accidents Act claim in court; and it follows therefore that the award is wholly in accordance with paragraph 12 of the

Scheme and cannot be unreasonable or otherwise challengeable in judicial review proceedings.

In normal circumstances it would clearly not be wrong or unreasonable to follow the normal practice of apportioning damages in the way I have indicated the courts have pragmatically done in the past, even if a strict analysis suggests that this does not give proper effect to the child's separate right to claim the full value of his or her dependency. But that ignores entirely the impact in this case of the insurance provisions. It might be reasonable to give what is rightfully the child's to the parent, in effect for the parent to use it on the child's behalf in normal circumstances, but in the present case the effect of doing that is to reduce the child's compensation by the value of the payments to the applicant under the insurance policy. Neither common law nor the scheme sanction such a deduction. I fully accept that the Criminal Injuries Compensation Board scheme is intended to provide *ex gratia* compensation where there is no other source from which financial loss can be made good, but the children here have their own claim under the scheme, and their position is that they have no insurance money to make up their financial loss. The consequence is that in my judgment this decision was wrong and should be quashed."

Thompson v. Price no longer valid

2.107 The decision in *Thompson v. Price* [1973] Q.B. 838 is no longer good law in the light of the amended section 4 of the Fatal Accidents Act 1976. In *Thompson*'s case, Boreham J. reduced the minor dependants' damages because of their mother's remarriage and their support from their stepfather. Such support would be a benefit accruing from their father's death and should not now be taken into account in assessing the minor dependant's damages: *Stanley v. Saddique* [1992] Q.B. 1.

Table showing apportionments made by the court

2.108 The references are to the appropriate paragraph of *Kemp and Kemp*, Vol III.

Plaintiff's name	*Reference*	*Year*	*Court/ judge*	*Total award*	*Widow's age at death*	*Widow's share*	*Children: age, sex (if known) and share in £*		*Total of children's award*	*Children's % of total award*
Pine	M2–016	1990	Thorpe J.	148,000	young	123,000	F 4½	25,000	25,000	16.9
Murray	M2–020	1975	C.A.	76,800	36	59,600	F 5	8,500	17,000	22.1
							F 4	8,500		
Robertson	M2–021	1984	Webster J.	204,790	29	139,141	F 8½	21,883	65,649	32.0
							M 4	21,883		
							M 2	21,883		
Kay	M2–030	1980	Russell J.	200,000	29	–	5	25,000	50,000	25.0
							3	25,000		
Lloyds	M2–031	1977	Nield J.	115,000	39	100,000	M 18	5,000	15,000	13.0
							M 17	5,000		
							M 15	5,000		
Davies	M2–050	1991	Stocker J.	210,000	38	166,000	F 15	19,000	44,000	20.9
							F 13	25,000		
Metcalf	M2–054	1979	Woolf J.	65,800	32	50,800	16	1,000	13,000	19.8
							14	3,000		
							11	4,000		
							7	5,000		
Jennings	M2–060	1963	Payne J.	12,100	43	10,050	Six children: £200, £200, £200, elder		2,050	16.9
							11	250		
							6	500		
							2	700		

Plaintiff's name	*Reference*	*Year*	*Court/ judge*	*Total award*	*Widow's age at death*	*Widow's share*	*Children: age, sex (if known) and share in £*		*Total of children's award*	*Children's % of total award*
Davies	M2–061	1980	C.A.	19,000	20	13,500	F. 2½		5,500	28.9
Garner	M2–153	1974	O'Connor J.	21,750	28	19,750	F. 3	2,000	2,000	9.2
Jones	M2–154	1971	Commissioner	15,000	40	7,000	F. 12	2,000	8,000	53.3
			Smith				F 9	2,000		
							F 6	2,000		
							M 4	2,000		
Wardell-Yerburgh	M2–155	1973	Brubin J.	36,400	33	35,400	F 3	1,000	1,000	2.7
Pell	M2–158	1972	Mais J.	21,000	40	19,000	F 14	750	2,000	9.5
							M 11	1,250		
Gilmartin	M2–165	1972	James J.	15,000	40	12,000	15*	500	3,000	20.0
							12	500		
							6	1,000		
							5	1,000		
Cronin	M2–169	1975	Mocatta J.	17,000	47	8,000	F 21	500	9,000	52.9
							F 19	750		
							M 17	1,500		
							F 15	1,750		
							F 13	2,000		
							M 9	2,500		
Houghton	M2–171	1991	Macpherson J.	920,000	44	866,000	M 21	3,000	54,000	5.9
						F 18				
						12,000				
							M 9	39,000		

Payment into court

2.109 Under the Fatal Accidents Act only one action can be brought for the benefit of all the dependants and consequently a single undivided sum can be paid into court as proposed compensation for all. This rule may cause embarrassment or even injustice where different dependants have adverse interests. An example would be a case where liability is in dispute and one dependant, a former wife with a small claim, would like to accept a modest amount and bow out of the action, while the current wife has a large claim and wishes to press on with the action.

2.110 An instance was *Hay and Anr v. IBS Cladding*. There District Judge Bullock made an order requiring the defendants to apportion their payment into court between the dependants. The order was clearly a just solution to the facts of the particular case and would have accorded with the principle decided in *Pym v. Great Northern Railway* (1883) 4 B. & S. 396; 122 E.R. 508, namely that the entitlement of a particular dependant is to a separate and individual sum of damages and not merely to a joint interest in a global sum.

2.111 On appeal, however, Potter J. held that the District Judge had no power to make his order: the judgment is set out in *Kemp & Kemp*, Vol I, Chapter 26, App. II. If Potter J.'s order is correct the existing Rules of Court can result in an unjust situation. The *ratio decidendi* of Potter J's decision was that there was only one cause of action and therefore RSC, Ord. 22, r.1(5) did not apply. If there had been more than one cause of action, as in *Walker and Anr v. Turpin and Ors* Ord. 22, r.1(5) would have provided a just solution. For, as the Court of Appeal stated in that case:

> "[. . .] the established approach was that if a defendant wished to have the advantages flowing from a payment into court, he was obliged to make a payment in a form which did not embarrass the plaintiffs.
>
> In the instant case where there were separate plaintiffs, each pursuing his own separate cause of action, the payment should be in a form which enabled each plaintiff to know where he stood, so that he could accept the payment and bow out if he wished.
>
> The defendants were not entitled to insist on making a payment in a form by which they said, in effect, to the plaintiffs: 'You must both accept the payment or the action will have to be continued

by both of you'. The defendant might make a payment which had that effect, but that was always subject to the overriding power of the court under r.1(5)."

2.112 It is arguable, however, that each dependant has a separate cause of action even though only one action may be brought under the Fatal Accidents Act for the benefit of all the dependants. Such a contention would be based on the decision in *Pym*'s case that each dependant is entitled to a separate and individual sum of damages. If the Act were construed in this way, RSC, Ord. 22, r.1(5) would provide a just solution where dependants with conflicting interests are embarrassed by a single payment into court.

2.113 If the Act cannot be so construed, the remedy may lie in Ord. 18, r.19. A payment into court has been well described in *The Supreme Court Practice* 1993 as "a secret plea". Until 1933 a payment into court had to be pleaded, although the plea was not communicated to the jury. A pleading which may embarrass or prejudice the fair trial of the action may be struck out under Ord. 18, r.19, or even under the court's inherent jurisdiction. The threat of such action could persuade the defendant to apportion the payment in so as not to embarrass or prejudice the action.

2.114 If neither of these suggested solutions is acceptable to the court, the situation warrants the attention of the Rules Committee with a view to amending RSC, Ord. 22.

The implications of settlement by one party or a personal representative

2.115 The remedy provided by the Fatal Accidents Act is given to the dependants personally and a personal representative who brings a claim does not act in his normal capacity as a personal representative, but rather on behalf of the dependants directly.

2.116 If there is no personal representative or if he has not brought an action within six months of the death of the deceased the dependants themselves may bring an action.

2.117 A personal representative who is also interested in an action as a dependant may validly settle his own claim under the Fatal Accidents Act by agreeing to accept a sum for himself alone, but he has no power or authority to compromise the action on behalf of the other dependants without the express authority of each dependant who is *sui juris* and the approval of the court on behalf of minor dependants.

2.118 No compromise of an action on behalf of a minor is valid unless the sanction of the court is obtained, and in a Fatal Accidents Act claim such attempted compromise is not only ineffective as against the minor but vitiates the entire agreement: *Jeffrey v. Kent County Council* [1958] 1. W.L.R. 927. Thus although a widow can agree to accept a separate sum for herself provided she does not attempt a global settlement relating to both her own claim and that of any children, the defendants must realise that such an agreement may result in the court giving considerably greater sums to the infants than those provisionally agreed if the court concludes that the amount taken by the widow is not as large as the court thinks proper and that, therefore, the children's chance of being adequately supported during childhood by the widow has been affected. RSC Ord. 80, r. 10 only applies where the Fatal Accidents Act claim is made "in any proceedings". It is not, therefore, a bar of itself to settlement of a claim without proceedings. However, any such settlement on behalf of a minor would be subject to the ordinary rules relating to contracts made with minors and hence made at the defendant's peril. To avoid such perilous settlements and obviate the need to begin proceedings in every case there is procedure for obtaining the approval of the court for a settlement made before proceedings have been commenced.

LAW REFORM ACT CLAIMS

2.119 The Law Reform (Miscellaneous Provisions) Act 1934 lays down the general rule that on the death of any person all causes of action vested in him survive for the benefit of his estate: see Appendix B for the text of the Act, as amended.

2.120 Prior to 1 January 1982 claims under the Act included a claim for loss of expectation of life and a claim for pecuniary loss during "the lost years", ie the period during which the deceased would have lived and earned had he not been prematurely killed. Both these claims have now been abolished. Those interested in the law before 1 January 1982 will find it dealt with:

(a) In the case of loss of expectation of life in *Kemp & Kemp*, Vol. 1, Chapter 4.

(b) In the case of pecuniary loss during the lost years *ibid*, Chapter 6, para. 6–062 to 6–139 and 6–500 to 6–523.

2.121 The claims are in respect of the period between the injury causing death and the date of death. If that period is short, the claims will be small. But if the period is a long one, such claims can be substantial. They fall into the following categories:

(a) Claims for pain and suffering and loss of amenities.

(b) Claims for pecuniary loss.

(c) Funeral expenses.

Claims for pain and suffering

2.122 No such claim will lie if the deceased was unconscious throughout this period. But substantial damages can be awarded when the period of pain and suffering is prolonged and/or where the pain and suffering was severe.

2.123 For example, in *Simpkins v. BREL* (reported in *Kemp & Kemp*, Vol. II, para. F2–018/3) the deceased, a man aged 50 at death, first manifested signs of mesothelioma in June 1988. He died in April 1990. During this period of 20 months he endured severe pain and suffering. In a claim under the Law Reform Act Judge de Cunha awarded £32,000 for this pain and suffering. In *Stratford v. BREL* (*Kemp & Kemp*, Vol. I, para. F2–028/3) the deceased a man aged 74 at death developed mesothelioma in 1988. On 21 September 1988, he died. Judge Fallon in a claim under the Law Reform Act awarded £18,000 for his pain and suffering over this period. But there must be evidence on which the court can find that a claim of this nature has been established: mere speculation will not suffice.

Instances of this type of award will be found in *Kemp & Kemp*, Vol. III, Section L7.

Claims for loss of amenities

2.124 The court does not usually distinguish between such claims and claims for pain and suffering, but makes a single assessment of damages to cover both heads of claim. But, if there is a prolonged period of loss of amenities while the victim was unconscious and suffered nothing, an award under this head can be made. See also Chapter 2 of *Kemp & Kemp*, Vol. 1, para. 2–069 *et seq.*

Claim for pecuniary loss

2.125 This claim is made on the same basis as a similar claim made by a living plaintiff, except that in a Law Reform Act claim there is no claim for pecuniary loss in the lost years.

Chapter 3

Damages for Non-Pecuniary Loss

David Kemp Q.C.

Contents — *Para*

Introduction

3.1 The only mechanism by which a court can seek to compensate a person who has suffered damage or loss in consequence of a wrong done to him is to award him monetary compensation, whatever the nature of the damage which he has in fact sustained. In personal injury cases that element of damage which is common to all physical injury, cannot as such be eliminated or ameliorated by an award of money. Nonetheless, the objective of the courts in the assessment of compensation in a personal injury case is the same as in any other case. The principle was stated by Lord Blackburn in *Livingstone v. Rawyards Coal Company* (1880) 5 App. Cas. 25, an appeal to the House of Lords from Scotland, thus:

> "I do not think there is any difference of opinion as to its being a general rule that, where any injury is to be compensated by damages, in settling the sum of money to be given for reparation of damages you should as nearly as possible get at that sum of money which will put the party who has been injured, or who has suffered, in the same position as he would have been in if he had not sustained the wrong for which he is now getting his compensation or reparation."

The principle applies just as much in English law as in Scots law. Viscount Dunedin expressed it in the following words:

> "... the common law says that the damages due either for breach of contract or for tort are damages which, so far as money can compensate will give the injured party reparation for the wrongful act (*Admiralty Commissioners v. SS Susquehanna* [1926] AC 655 at 661)."

The application of the rule in the case of financial loss presents no conceptual difficulty, although in practice the exercise may prove to be complicated. "A money award can be calculated so as to make a good financial loss": *per* Lord Morris in *West v. Shephard* [1964] A.C. 326 at 345.

3.2 The problems in applying the rule arise when the damage which has been suffered is not financial. In such cases the judge cannot simply replace an amount of money lost or an asset having an ascertainable money value with an equivalent amount of money. The problem was recognised by the Earl of Halsbury L.C. in *The Mediana* [1900] A.C. 113 at 116:

> "You very often cannot even lay down any principle upon which you can give damages ... Take the most familiar and ordinary case: how is anybody to measure pain and suffering in moneys counted? Nobody can suggest that you can by any arithmetical calculation establish what is the exact sum of money which would represent such a thing as the pain and suffering which a

> person has undergone by reason of an accident ... But nevertheless the law recognises that as a topic upon which damages may be given."

What then is the court to do? It recognises that the injured person is entitled to compensation, but can find no logical basis upon which to evaluate that compensation. The answer reached by the court is that it awards a sum which is in the nature of a conventional award. Megaw L.J. described the process, in his judgment in *Fuhri v. Jones*, Court of Appeal, March 30, 1979:

> "It will be appreciated, of course, though it is not always fully understood by persons who are not directly concerned with the law, that the law cannot attempt to attribute any particular figure of damages to any particular physical injury, serious or trivial. There is no way in which it can be said that such-and-such an injury is worth so much in terms of money. Indeed, in most cases for most injuries, anybody would say 'I would rather have avoided this injury than have any amount of money whatever in compensation'. But the court has to do the best it can by way of what are really conventional figures in relation to injuries, the court assessing, of course, on the individual facts of the case, what is sometimes called the tariff, making adjustments for particular facts of the particular case."

3.3 How are the amounts to be awarded as "conventional" amounts arrived at? As the award is conventional in its nature and cannot in fact compensate for the injury suffered there is no logical reason to take one figure rather than another. However, it is recognised that awards for comparable injuries should be comparable and in practice in an individual case the amount of the award is much influenced by the amounts of awards in previous cases in which the injuries appear to have been comparable, adjusted as appropriate in the light of the fall in the value of money since such awards were made. Diplock L.J. in *Every v. Miles*, Court of Appeal, in 1964 explained the process by which a decision as to the amount of the appropriate award in a particular case was made as follows:

> "Any such decision involves an attempt to equate the incommensurable. Such an equation is insoluble, and in the logical sense there is no answer which is right. But since justice is not justice

> unless even-handed, so that one man gets roughly the same treatment from the courts as another in comparable circumstances, and since the law requires that compensation be awarded for physical injuries, and the only kind of compensation which the courts can award is money, the courts are compelled to make a pragmatic solution. They have done so by fixing arbitrary standards of monetary compensation which . . . are not susceptible of analysis. These standards have been evolved from such current consensus of damage-awarding tribunals as is manifested by the amounts they have in fact awarded in broadly similar cases."

Again, in *Wright v. British Railways Board* [1983] 2 A.C. 733 Lord Diplock said of non-pecuniary loss:

> "Such loss is not susceptible of *measurement* in money. Any figure at which the assessor of damages arrives cannot be other than artificial and, if the aim is that justice meted out to all litigants should be even-handed instead of depending on idiosyncracies of the assessor, whether jury or judge, the figure must be 'basically a conventional figure derived from experience and from awards in comparable cases'."

3.4 It may be sufficient, in practical terms, to know that the assessment of damages for pain and suffering or other non-primary loss, is, in any particular case, going to depend largely upon the amounts awarded in previous cases which are perceived to be similar, or at least, where there are no such cases, upon the generality of awards of compensation for injury of that general type. That is, however, unsatisfactory as a conceptual basis of compensation. The approach also provides no explanation or key to an explanation as to why, for example, awards of damages in the United States of America tend to be dramatically higher in personal injuries cases than in England.

3.5 Although it has rarely been the subject of judicial pronouncement the conceptual basis of the "conventional" sums awarded by the courts in respect of non-pecuniary losses appears to be that such sums are what are considered fair and reasonable compensation in the social, economic and industrial conditions which prevail in England and Wales. That the appropriate award for non-pecuniary loss may vary in differing social and economic conditions in different parts of the world has been stated by the Privy

Council in *Jag Singh v. Toong Fong Omnibus Co.* [1964] 1 W.L.R. 1382, *per* Lord Morris:

> "to the extent to which regard should be had to the range of awards in other cases which are comparable such cases should as a rule be those which have been determined in the same jurisdiction or in a neighbouring locality where similar social, economic and industrial conditions exist."

It would seem to follow that awards in England and Wales have been and are to be made by reference to social, economic and industrial conditions there.

3.6 To say that awards of damages in respect of non-pecuniary losses should be of amounts that are fair and reasonable having regard to the social, economic and industrial conditions in England and Wales merely raises the question what, in any particular case, is fair and reasonable. That brings one back to previous awards, for in the absence of any other yardstick the principle of fairness requires that awards in comparable cases should be comparable. The result is that, however unsatisfactory it may be, the court in any particular case is constrained to assess damages for non-pecuniary losses by reference to previous awards in comparable cases or, at least, by reference to the general level of awards where there are no cases which are really comparable. There is no scope in this book for detailed references to decided cases. Readers are referred to *Kemp & Kemp*, Vols II and III and to the Personal Injuries and Quantum Reports (P.I.Q.R.).

3.7 It is clear that the general level of awards must be increased to take account of the decline in the value of money, *per* Lord Diplock in *Wright v. British Railways Board* [1983] 2 A.C. 773 at 785:

> "If judges carry out their duty of assessing damages for non-economic loss in the money of the day at the date of the trial—*and this is a rule of practice that judges are required to follow, not a guideline from which they have a discretion to depart* if there are special circumstances that justify their doing so—there are two routes by which the judge's task of arriving at the appropriate conventional rate of interest to be applied to the damages so assessed can be approached. *The starting point for each of them is to ascertain from the appropriate table of retail price indices*

> *covering the period between service of writ and trial what would have been the equivalent of those damages in the money of the day at the date of service of writ, reckoned in pounds sterling at the higher value that they then stood at at the very beginning of the period for which simple interest is to be given.* That figure represents both the real value, and what was then the nominal value also, of the sum of money for the loss of use of which the plaintiff is to be compensated by interest. Such interest, *like the damages on which it is to be given, is to be calculated in the money of the day at the date of trial*, the real value of which has been depreciated by the full amount of the inflation that has taken place since the date of service of the writ" [Emphasis added].

The logic of this passage from Lord Diplock's speech clearly requires that judges, when having regard to previous comparable awards, should ascertain from the appropriate table of retail indices what has been the decrease in the value of money since the date of a particular comparable award in order that their award "in the money of the day" may be truly comparable in real terms with the earlier award. (A table of retail indices together with a table showing the value of the £ at various dates will be found in Appendix E.)

3.8 But what of the general level of awards itself, ignoring inflation? How is that to be adjusted, whether up or down? That is a function of the Court of Appeal, as Lord Diplock stated in *Wright v. British Railways Board:*

> "The Court of Appeal, with its considerable case-load of appeals in personal injury actions and the relatively recent experience of many of its members in trying such cases themselves is, generally speaking, the tribunal best qualified to set the guide-lines for judges currently trying such actions."

That court certainly exercised such function in *Housecroft v. Burnett* [1986] 1 All E.R. 332. The court in effect decided that certain types of award made in the 1970s, uplifted as they must be to take account of the subsequent decline in the value of money, were too high. A new standard was set. As at April 1985 the guideline figure for damages for pain and suffering and loss of amenities in an average case of tetraplegia was set at £75,000. Current awards now have to fall in line with that figure, always, of course, taking into account any subsequent decline in the value of money. The figure of £75,000 updated to January 1995 is roughly £124,000.

3.9 The deliberate adjustment of the general level of awards, or of any particular category established within that general level, is, however, the sole prerogative of the Court of Appeal, or conceivably of the House of Lords. It is not the function of a trial judge, as the Court of Appeal stated in *Alsford v. British Telecommunications PLC*, October 30, 1986. In that case the trial judge had regarded the general level of awards in the class of case with which he was dealing as "unacceptably low", and had made an award above the generally accepted bracket. The Court of Appeal held that in so doing the judge fell into error, *per* Lloyd L.J.

> "... £15,000 for pain and suffering in this case is out of line with ... awards upheld by this court ... The judge himself recognised as much. He said that he regarded the awards in those cases as being 'unacceptably low' ... But that would be to introduce into this branch of the law an element of uncertainty which I, for one, would regard as undesirable. Apart from any sense of injustice which it might create between one plaintiff and another, it would make it even more difficult for counsel to advise on the correct figure for settlement.
>
> Everybody accepts that awards of damages in this field are necessarily conventional, and that they are based on a scale of comparative seriousness which is also conventional. I do not suggest that the scale is immutable. It may change gradually over time, as indeed may the level of damages generally. If judges consistently award damages for a particular type of injury at the top of the range, then that type of injury may gradually move up the scale of relative seriousness. But in my judgment it should not be open to a judge to award damages outside range because he regards the range as being too low. That is what, as I read his judgment, the judge has done here."

Balcombe L.J. agreed.

3.10 Having quoted from Lord Diplock's speech in *Wright*'s case that the figure must be "basically a conventional figure derived from experience and from awards in comparable cases", Balcombe L.J. continued:

> "As Lord Justice Lloyd has said, if that were not the rule, no one would safely be able to advise litigants in personal injury cases to settle claims, or know what to pay into court. There is also, it

seems to me, a need to maintain the balance between these conventional awards for damages for pain, suffering and loss of amenity for different types of injury. If one judge at first instance decides to increase the level in one type of case, that balance will be disturbed."

TIME AS AT WHICH DAMAGES ARE TO BE ASSESSED

3.11 In the case of a claim for damages for personal injury damage is suffered by the plaintiff, and the injury is actionable, at the time the physical harm is done. When the court comes to assess damages for an injury, however, it will look at the position as it is at the date of the trial. This is a convenient practice as it avoids the need, for example, for speculation as to how the injured person's condition will develop from the time of the initial injury or for speculation as to what his financial loss up to the date of trial at least will be. In a slightly different context, that of the attitude to be adopted by an appellate court where there has been a change in the circumstances of the plaintiff since the trial at first instance, Harman L.J. enunciated the principle that, 'the court should never speculate where it knows": *Curwen v. James* [1963] 1 W.L.R. 748 at 753. That principle is the guiding principle in the assessment of damages in personal injuries cases.

3.12 Failure of the court in making its assessment of damages to take into account all the information available at the time of the trial could lead to illogical and unjust results. In *Jobling v. Associated Dairies Ltd* [1982] A.C. 794 the plaintiff was injured at work in 1973 in consequence of a breach of statutory duty on the part of his employers, the defendants. He sustained injuries to his back and was thereafter only able to undertake light work. In 1976 he was found to be suffering from a spinal disease which was unrelated to the accident but which rendered him totally unfit for work. At the trial of the action in 1979 Reeve J. declined to take into account the supervening spinal disease and awarded damages on the basis that the plaintiff had been capable of light work, not on the basis that he had been incapable of work since 1976 in consequence of a disease for which his employers were in no way responsible. Both the Court of Appeal and the House of Lords held that damages should have been assessed on the basis of the known fact that the plaintiff would in any event have been totally incapable of work as a result of spinal disease from 1976.

3.13 The making of the assessment of damages in the light of all facts known at the date of the trial enables the court to take into account, if it be the case, the fact that the consequences of the plaintiff's injuries were more serious than at first thought; the fact that the expenses to which the plaintiff would be put in consequence of his injuries were higher than was first thought; the fact that the plaintiff has died; or the fact that the plaintiff has, since the accident, volunteered to be made redundant. This list of examples is not intended to be exhaustive.

THE PRINCIPAL HEADS OF NON-PECUNIARY DAMAGE

Pain and suffering

3.14 The expression "pain and suffering" is almost a term of art in so far as the expression embraces different concepts. "Pain", it is suggested, is used to describe the physical pain caused by or consequent upon the injury, while "suffering" relates to the mental element of anxiety, fear, embarrassment and the like. Suffering is used in this sense in section 1 of the Administration of Justice Act 1982 which provides that where a plaintiff's expectation of life has been reduced the court in awarding damages for pain and suffering shall take into account the suffering caused or likely to be caused by awareness that his expectation of life has been so reduced. Similarly, suffering would include the social embarrassment felt by a woman with a disfiguring facial scar.

3.15 An award under the head of pain and suffering depends as Lord Scarman said in *Lim Poh Choo v. Camden and Islington Area Health Authority* [1980] A.C. 174 at 188, upon the plaintiff's personal awareness of pain and her capacity for suffering. Accordingly, no award can be made under this head where the plaintiff has been rendered permanently unconscious. As will be seen below, the position is different with regard to loss of amenities: in such a case damages are awarded for the lost amenity even if the plaintiff is not aware of the loss.

3.16 In practice judges tend to use the expression "pain and suffering" without distinguishing clearly between the two elements. Usually when assessing damages in respect of non-pecuniary loss a court will award one lump sum in respect of "pain and suffering and loss of amenities" and in such cases it is generally impossible to say how much relates to "pain and suffering" and how much to "loss of amenities".

3.17 There must be some evidence on which the court can find as a matter of probability that the injured person has established a claim for pain and suffering: here speculation is not enough. A practical example of this situation was provided in *Hicks and Others v. Chief Constable of the South Yorkshire Police* [1992] P.I.Q.R. P. 433, and [1992] 2 All E.R. 65, H.L. In that case the personal representatives of persons who were crushed to death at the Hillsborough Stadium claimed damages under the Law Reform (Miscellaneous Provisions) Act 1934 for pain and suffering alleged to have been sustained prior to their death. The trial judge rejected this claim. His decision was upheld by the Court of Appeal and the House of Lords. The period of consciousness, while the victims were being crushed prior to their death, lasted some 30 minutes at most. Lord Bridge said:

> "It is perfectly clear law that fear by itself, of whatever degree, is a normal human emotion for which no damages can be awarded. Those trapped in the crush at Hillsborough who were fortunate enough to escape without injury have no claim in respect of the distress they suffered in what must have been a truly terrifying experience. It follows that fear of impending death felt by the victim of a fatal injury before that injury is inflicted cannot by itself give rise to a cause of action which survives for the benefit of the victim's estate."

3.18 The Court of Appeal applied this passage in *Nicholls v. Rushton* (1992) *The Times*, 19 June, C.A. In that case the plaintiff had been involved in a car accident. She had been badly shaken up and obviously distressed by the experience. But she had suffered no physical damage or identifiable psychological illness. The circuit judge awarded £175 for "severe shock and shaking up". The Court of Appeal held that "unless there is a physical injury, no question of damages for mental suffering, fear, anxiety and the like arises", and disallowed the damages awarded for the shock and shaking up.

3.19 It has of course long been recognised that a person who suffers an identifiable psychiatric illness or psychological condition, often referred to as nervous shock, can be awarded damages without the necessity of showing direct impact or fear of immediate physical injuries for himself where another dies or suffers personal injury. Leading cases considering the circumstances in which such awards can be made are *McLoughlin v. O'Brian* [1983] A.C. 411 and *Alcock v. Chief Constable of South Yorkshire Police* [1992] 1 A.C. 310 (another series of claims arising out of the Hillsborough disaster). For a case in which a plaintiff sustained relatively trivial physical injuries, but a severe mental illness reference can be made to *Brice v. Brown* [1984] 1 All E.R. 997 which also illustrates that once causation is established a tortfeasor must take his victim as he finds him. An award of damages will no more be denied to a person vulnerable and predisposed to mental illness than it would to the victim of physical injury with an eggshell skull. Courts now accept that accident victims, particularly those involved in disaster incidents, may suffer "post traumatic stress disorder" and the syndrome is recognised as a psychiatric illness.

3.20 Although the law recognises pain and suffering as a separate head of damages from loss of amenities, the general practice is to award a global sum for "pain and suffering and loss of amenities". This makes it difficult to form a view as to how much has been awarded for pain and suffering *simpliciter*, except in cases where a complete, or almost complete, recovery has been made. In such cases virtually the whole award would have been for pain and suffering.

3.21 The court must take into account, in making its assessment in the case of any particular plaintiff, of the pain which he has actually suffered and will suffer and the suffering which he has undergone and will undergo. Pain and suffering are not measurable by any absolute standard and it is not easy, if indeed possible other than in the most general way, to compare the degree of pain and suffering experienced by different people. However, the individual circumstances of particular plaintiffs clearly have a significant effect upon the assessment of damages. For example, in cases of scarring some plaintiffs are much distressed by their scars, while others are largely unperturbed. The question of the attitude of the particular plaintiff, a woman aged 37 years, to a scar on her forehead arose in *Dimmock v. Miles*, a decision of the Court of Appeal on December 12, 1969. In that case Phillimore L.J. said:

"... the real difficulty here is that she was not asked about her

> own feeling with regard to the scar and that is a much more serious matter in this sort of case. After all, some may treat a scar on the forehead as comparatively trivial, but to another it would be a source of serious worry."

Again, the age of the plaintiff and his expectation of life are of critical importance in all cases in which pain and suffering will continue for life, for they determine the length of time for which he is likely to suffer pain or experience suffering. In cases in which pain and suffering is not expected to continue for life the court has to form a view as to how long it is likely to continue.

3.22 When there is some particular feature in a case which aggravates the degree of suffering it need not arise from the plaintiff's concern about himself. In *Rourke v. Barton* (1982) *The Times*, 23 June the plaintiff was a woman whose husband was suffering from terminal cancer. She sustained an injury to her hip which prevented her from caring for her husband when he was at home. That disability distressed her and McCullough J took such distress into account in assessing damages for her injuries.

Similarly, in *Jefferson v. Cape Insulation Ltd* (December 3, 1981) Farquharson J. awarded substantial damages to a woman who knew she must soon die of mesothelioma for her evident distress in being parted from her family: *per* Farquharson J.:

> "I have also to bear in mind . . . that the major misery this woman is going to sustain is not the pain, serious and terrible as that is, but the prospect which must be continually in her mind of being parted from her family, and particularly her youngest child."

3.23 In considering pain and suffering shock should be taken into account. *Per* Sachs L.J. in *Kaufman v. Ocean Steamship Co.* (a decision of the Court of Appeal in 1969):

> ". . . it can sometimes be overlooked that reasonable damages should always be assessed in respect of that initial period of shock and suffering. In this case the reports show clearly that this was fully of the degree to be expected when somebody has a really severe blow from a heavy block swinging against the face."

3.24 By virtue of the Congenital Disabilities (Civil Liability) Act 1976 a child who is born disabled as a result of injuries suffered *en* *ventre sa mère* has a cause of action *inter alia* in respect of pain and suffering. This Act only applied to births which took place after July 22, 1976. However, the Court of Appeal decided in *Burton v. Islington Health Authority* [1992] 3 W.L.R. 617 that at common law a child *en ventre sa mère* and unborn at the time of the defendant's negligence has a cause of action for injuries caused by that negligence.

3.25 However, there is no cause of action in a child for pain and suffering consequent upon being born disabled on account of any negligent failure to abort the foetus before birth: *McKay v. Essex Area Health Authority* [1982] Q.B. 1166. On the other hand, where a woman undergoes an operation for sterilisation which is negligently performed and she subsequently becomes pregnant she can recover damages in respect of the pain and suffering endured in carrying and giving birth to the child: *Udale v. Bloomsbury Area Health Authority* [1983] 1 W.L.R. 1098.

3.26 The best way to form a view on the current level of damages for pain and suffering *simpliciter* is to study recent awards for minor injuries, where there has been a complete or almost complete recovery. The reader is referred to Section K of Vol. III of *Kemp & Kemp*, where a large number of such awards will be found. Another class of case in which one can isolate the award for pain and suffering is where death follows shortly after the injury and where the award is largely for pain and suffering in the period up to death: see Section L7 in *Kemp & Kemp*, Vol. 3.

Loss of amenities

3.27 There is a head of damage which is sometimes called the loss of amenities; the man made blind by the accident will no longer be able to see the familiar things he has seen all his life; the man who has had both legs removed and will never again go upon his walking excursions—things of that kind—loss of amenities (*per* Birkett L.J. in *Manley v. Rugby Portland Cement Co. Ltd*, a decision of the Court of Appeal in 1951).

3.28 This head embraces everything which reduces the plaintiff's enjoyment of life considered apart from pain and suffering and from any material or pecuniary loss which may be attendant upon the loss of amenity. What matters is the fact of deprivation of an amenity or amenities, not whether the injured person is aware of such deprivation. A plaintiff who is rendered permanently unconscious or whose awareness of his loss of amenities is otherwise impaired is thus entitled to a full award under this head.

3.29 In *Lim Poh Choo v. Camden and Islington Health Authority* [1984] A.C. 174 the defendants sought to persuade the House of Lords to exercise their freedom under the Practice Statement [1966] 1 W.L.R. 1234, to reverse two rules that had been laid down by the majority of the House of Lords in *West & Son Ltd v. Shephard* [1964] A.C. 326, namely:

(1) that the fact of unconsciousness does not eliminate the actuality of the deprivation of the ordinary experiences and amenities of life (see the formulation used by Lord Morris of Borth-y-Gest at p. 349); and

(2) that, if damages are awarded upon a correct basis, it is of no concern to the court to consider any question as to the use that will thereafter be made of the money awarded.

In *West*'s case [1964] A.C. 326 it was pointed out that there is a clear distinction between damages for pain and suffering on the one hand and damages for loss of amenities on the other hand. The former depend upon the plaintiff's awareness of his condition and his capacity to feel pain. The latter are awarded for the fact of deprivation—a substantial loss in itself, whether the plaintiff is aware of it or not.

The House of Lords upheld the law laid down in *West*'s case, Lord Scarman stating at p. 189:

> "If the law is to be changed by the reversal of *West*'s case, it should be done not judicially but legislatively within the context of a comprehensive enactment dealing with all aspects of damages for personal injury."

3.30 Loss of amenities will extend to loss of the pleasure and pride of a craftsman in his work: *Morris v. Johnson Matthey & Co.* (1967) 112 S.J. 32. Similarly, damages will be awarded for the loss of congenial employment: see *Kemp & Kemp*, Vol. 1, Chapter 5, App I. Loss of, or reduction in, the prospects of marriage would come at least partly under this head; in such case there may also be a pecuniary loss; see paras 5–114 *et seq* in Vol. 1 of *Kemp & Kemp* for a more detailed consideration of this topic. Loss or impairment of the enjoyment of a holiday as a result of personal injuries is compensated under this head: *Ichard v. Frangoulis* [1977] 1 W.L.R. 556.

3.31 As in the case of an award for pain and suffering, the assessment of damages for loss of amenities is based upon the level of awards in previous cases which appear to be comparable or, failing such awards, upon "impression based of necessity in large measure on the combination of intuition and experience": *per* Bridge L.J. in *Hughes v. Goodall*, a decision of the Court of Appeal reported in *Kemp & Kemp*, Volume 2 para. F5–100.

3.32 Whatever the nature of the amenities lost the court has to assess the effect of the deprivation of those amenities upon the particular plaintiff. In assessing the appropriate award of damages for loss of amenities an important consideration is how long the plaintiff will be deprived of those amenities.

3.33 In *Bayley v. Bloomsbury Health Authority*. Henry J. said, in making an award to a student nurse who had suffered a prolapsed lumbar disc at the age of 20, that there was a world of difference between such an injury happening to a victim at that age as opposed to the age of 33, the age of a plaintiff who had suffered a comparable injury in a case to which he had been referred.

3.34 If loss of amenities is for the rest of the plaintiff's life the court will need to take into account in assessing damages his age and his expectation of life. That applies as much in the case of an unconscious plaintiff as in the case of one who is sentient: compare, for example, *Wise v. Kay* [1962] 1 Q.B. 638 with *Andrews v. Freeborough* (1966) 110 S.J. 407. However, it is not necessarily the case that the shorter the period during which the plaintiff is likely to be deprived of amenities the lower the award of damages under this head. The loss of amenities caused to an elderly person as a result of his injuries can be more severe precisely because he is old and has already suffered some impairment of his activities on that account. In *Frank v. Cox* (1967) 111 S.J. 670, the plaintiff was aged 77 years. The principal injury which he had suffered was to his hip. In his judgment Sachs L.J. said:

> "It is perhaps as well to remember at the outset that the main injury in this particular case was a hip injury which, if it had occurred to a younger man, would have produced an arthrodesis operation. In other words, the injury was such that the degree of pain which it produces from day to day throughout the years is at any rate sufficient for experienced medical men to say that the

rather drastic operation of arthrodesis would normally be the best thing in the circumstances. Owing to the plaintiff's age, however, medical experience shows that that operation is not advisable in this case—so the pain continues.

The trial judge later went on to deal with other and more serious injury: amongst other things he mentioned the question of arthritic changes. The important passage that I would quote in regard to this injury is as follows: "Undoubtedly, this is a very severe deterrent on his" (the plaintiff's) "movements and activities". I take the view myself that when one has a person in advancing years, in some respects an impairment of movement may perhaps be more serious than it is with a younger person. It is true, as Mr Chedlow has stressed, that he has not got as many years before him through which he has to live with this discomfort, pain and impairment of movement. But it is important to bear in mind that as one advances in life one's pleasures and activities particularly do become more limited, and any substantial impairment in the limited amount of activity and movement which a person can undertake, in my view, becomes all the more serious on that account. It seems to me that this is a very substantial and serious impairment of Mr Frank's movements. He came into the witness-box today, and I gather it is his normal mode of locomotion, using two elbow crutches in order to get about, and from the reports it is quite plain that the pain is more or less continuous—I do not say without any intermission at all, but there is constant pain in his hip. It is a very serious and crippling injury which, in his later years, Mr Frank has had imposed upon him. I think he is entitled to substantial damages for an injury of that kind."

3.35 The consideration that loss of amenities may be more serious for someone already disabled than for someone who is not does not only apply to the elderly. In *Mustard v. Morris*, a decision of the Court of Appeal on July 21, 1981 (see C.A. transcript No. 374) it was argued that the award of damages for loss of amenities to a man who was already quite seriously disabled should be less than that to a previously fit person who had suffered equivalent injuries. Watkins L.J. dealt with that argument thus:

"With respect, I think that argument is misconceived. If a man who is a diabetic and who has arterial disease to the extent that this plaintiff had, is severely injured so that life is much more difficult to bear than otherwise it would have been, a defendant is in my view, quite unable, with justification, to say that a reduction in damages should thereby be brought about. Indeed, an argument to the contrary might well be made. To impose upon a man who, through natural causes, has been made ill to a certain extent, very grave injuries such as were sustained by this plaintiff and which reduces his capacity to bear natural ill health, is in my judgment more likely to increase than reduce damages. That I take to be the situation here. It is a consideration which I should have applied myself to the assessment of general damages to favour this plaintiff."

THE CURRENT LEVEL OF AWARDS FOR NON-PECUNIARY LOSS

3.36 As already stated, the tribunal best qualified to set the guidelines for judges trying personal injury actions is the Court of Appeal. The decision of that court in *Housecroft v. Burnett* [1986] 1 All E.R. 332 has had the effect of substantially reducing the damages for non-pecuniary loss in the most serious cases. Updating the court's guideline figure of £75,000 for an average case of tetraplegia set for April 1985 produces a figure of about £133,000 for 1998. If one has a case of tetraplegia aggravated by exceptional features such as an exceptional degree of pain, the guideline figure will be increased. In *Brightman v. Johnson* an award made in December 1985, Tudor Price J. increased this figure to £95,000 to take account of the circumstances which made the plaintiff's injuries more serious than the average case of tetraplegia (see Report in para A2–001 of Vol. II of *Kemp & Kemp*). Updated, that award would come to about £160,000 in terms of the £ in January 1998.

As well as putting a ceiling on cases of average tetraplegia, the effect of the decision in *Housecroft*'s case has meant that awards in less serious cases have to bear a proportional relationship to the guideline figure for tetraplegia.

Guidelines for the assessment of general damages in personal injury cases

3.37 An interesting and important development in the assessment of general damages for pain and suffering and loss of amenities was the publication in 1992 of "Guidelines for the Assessment of General Damages in Personal Injury Cases". This is the report of a Working Party set up by the Judicial Studies Board with the objective of "Facilitating a more uniform approach to the assessment" of such damages.

The Guidelines had the blessing of Lord Donaldson, the former Master of the Rolls. The revised Guidelines published in 1994 have a similar foreword by Sir Thomas Bingham M.R. As he says "The book does not seek to deprive the judge of the power to decide, after all the evidence has been heard, what is the right sum to award in a given case. But it does mark out the target area". The third edition, published in 1996, has a similar foreword by Lord Woolf M.R.. He said, among other things: "This book, of course, is not in itself exhaustive on the subject of quantum in the areas with which it deals. Usually it will be the starting off point rather than the last word on the appropriate award in any particular case".

3.38 The brackets given in the Guidelines should be of value to practitioners and judges by indicating the area within which an award is likely to be upheld on appeal. But to decide where a proper award lies within a given bracket will still, we believe, require consideration of previous awards in similar cases. We are confirmed in this belief by a passage contained in a Judicial Studies Board paper issued to Circuit Judges and Recorders in June 1991 where the Honourable Mr Justice Wright stated:

> "It is impossible to over-rate the contribution made by *Kemp & Kemp: The Quantum of Damages* to this branch of the law and every Judge who has to deal with personal injury litigation will undoubtedly have to have access to it."

Status of the Judicial Studies Board Guidelines

3.39 In *Arafa v. Potter* (July 8, 1994) the Court of Appeal stated the proper status and function of the Guidelines. *Per* Staughton L.J.

> "We have been referred to the guidelines of the Judicial Studies Board. They are not in themselves law; they form a slim and handy volume which anyone can slip into their briefcase on the way to the County Court or travelling on circuit. But the law is to be found elsewhere in rather greater bulk. In this Court we ought

to look to the sources rather than the summary produced by the Judicial Studies Board."

Similarly, in *Smith v. Vine* (Court of Appeal, December 14, 1993) Hoffman L.J. stated that, although some guidance could be obtained from the Guidelines, "in the end the award must be tailor-made to what the judge regards as the particular facts before him".

3.40 The Working Party's Guidelines are expressed to be based upon an analysis of cases reported up to June 1994. As time passes, they should be updated by practitioners to take account of subsequent inflation.

The Guidelines are reproduced at the beginning of comparable sections of Vols 2 and 3 of *Kemp & Kemp* both in their original form and also suitably updated. The nature of the Guidelines suitably updated to 1998 values can be illustrated by taking some examples:

Quadriplegia	£117,000 to £138,000
Paraplegia	£90,000 to £106,000
Very Severe Brain Damage	£111,000 to £138,000
Moderately Severe Brain Damage	£64,000 to £90,000
Total Blindness and Deafness	£138,000
Total Blindness	£103,000
Loss of Sight in One Eye	£23,000 to £26,000
Total Deafness and Loss of Speech	£48,000 to £60,000
Total Deafness	£40,000 to £48,000
Total Loss of Taste and Smell	£18,000
Loss of Smell	£12,000 to £15,000
Loss of Taste	£9,000 to £12,000
Total Impotence (young man)	£63,500
Infertility (female)	£50,000 to £69,000
Loss of Both Arms	£95,000 to £111,000
Arm Amputation at Shoulder	£61,000
Below Elbow Amputation	£49,000 to £53,000
Total Effective Loss of Both Hands	£58,000 to £79,000
Total Effective Loss of One Hand	£42,500 to £49,000
Above Knee Amputation of Both Legs	£100,000 to £111,000
Below Knee Amputation of Both Legs	£85,000 to £106,000
Above Knee Amputation of One Leg	£42,000 to £57,000

The Guidelines also set out various features intended to indicate the position which a particular injury should take within the suggested brackets. It is here that reference will be required to particular previous awards and especially to those assessed or affirmed by the Court of Appeal.

EXEMPLARY AND AGGRAVATED DAMAGES

3.41 In practice, the distinction between these two kinds of damages is not altogether clear, although in theory exemplary damages are to punish a defendant whose conduct has been outrageous or scandalous, and aggravated damages are to compensate the plaintiff for any aggravated harm done to him, such as injury to his feelings, as a result of the special circumstances of the case.

Exemplary damages

3.42 Exemplary damages will now only be awarded if the claim passes two tests:

(1) it is in respect of a cause of action for which prior to 1964 such an award had been made; and

(2) it has to fall within one of the two categories identified by Lord Devlin in *Rookes v. Barnard* [1964] A.C. 1129 namely,
   (a) where there has been oppressive, arbitrary or unconstitutional action by the servants of the Government, or
   (b) where the defendant's conduct has been calculated by him to make a profit for himself which might exceed the compensation otherwise payable.

The Court of Appeal laid down the law in these terms in *Gibbons and Others v. South West Water Services Ltd* [1992] P.I.Q.R. P. 224. The Court of Appeal held that the first test had been stated, albeit *obiter*, in the speeches of four of their Lordships in *Broome v. Cassell & Co. Ltd* [1972] A.C. 1027.

3.43 In *Gibbons* the cause of action was founded on public nuisance. The allegation was that the defendants had supplied contaminated water to the plaintiffs thereby causing them personal injury. The exemplary damages were claimed on the footing that the defendants had acted in an arrogant and high-handed manner by asserting that the water was fit to drink. The Court of Appeal held that there was no case prior to 1964 in which exemplary damages had been awarded to a plaintiff who proved particular damage resulting from public nuisance, and on that ground struck out the claim for exemplary damages. The court also held that the claim did not fall within Lord Devlin's two categories.

3.44 The author knows of no case prior to 1964 in which exemplary damages were awarded in a personal injuries claim. If that is the position, it would follow that no such award can be made. However, if the incident in which the personal injuries were sustained also involved, for example, wrongful arrest by government servants who had acted unconstitutionally and oppressively, a claim for exemplary damages could be included in the action.

3.45 In *Thompson v. Commissioner of Police* [1997] 3 W.L.R. 403 the Court of Appeal gave guidelines for the award of exemplary and aggravated damages against the police (see *Kemp & Kemp* Vol. 1, para. 1–008/7A).

3.46 A claim for exemplary damages now has to be expressly pleaded, reversing the rule stated in *Broome v. Cassell & Co. Ltd* (RSC, Ord. 18, r.8(3)).

Aggravated damages

3.47 A case in which aggravated damages were awarded in a personal injuries claim was *Westwood v. Hardy* (1964) *The Times*, 24 June. The defendant was guilty of malicious and unjustifiable conduct in the course of which he unintentionally struck the plaintiff with an autoscythe. Havers J.'s award of £550 (1998 value £6,400) for comparatively minor injuries included an unspecified amount in respect of aggravated damages. Provocation on the part of the plaintiff may disentitle him to aggravated damages. But such provocation cannot reduce the plaintiff's damages below the real amount due for the injury done (*Lane v. Holloway* [1968] 1 Q.B. 379, C.A.).

3.48 In *Kralj v. McGrath* [1986] 1 All E.R. 54 which concerned a particularly unacceptable case of medical negligence at a childbirth, Woolf J. reviewed the authorities and concluded that "it would be wholly inappropriate to introduce into claims of this sort, for breach of contract and negligence, the concept of aggravated damages".

3.49 In *Fisher v. Chief Constable of the Cumbria Constabulary* (1997) the Court of Appeal awarded £500 aggravated damages against the police for failing promptly to produce a copy of the search warrant to an interested party: (see *Kemp & Kemp* Vol. 1, para. 1–008/7B).

3.50 Although there is no rule requiring a claim for aggravated damages to be expressly pleaded, the facts relied upon for the claim should be pleaded and it would be wise to plead expressly that aggravated damages are claimed.

3.51 In *Gibbons v. South West Water Services Ltd* (1992) the Court of Appeal struck out the claim for aggravated damages, stating that, if the nuisance continued for longer than it should have done, the plaintiffs would be compensated by normal damages for having drunk more contaminated water.

3.52 The Law Commission in Law. Com. No. 147 made various recommendations on the topic of exemplary, aggravated and restitutionary damages. Practitioners should study this interesting report. It is beyond the scope of this book to consider these detailed recommendations.

CHAPTER 4

Damages for Past Pecuniary Loss

David Kemp QC

Contents	*Para*

INTRODUCTION

4.1 There is no difference in principle between the damages awarded for past pecuniary loss and the damages awarded for future pecuniary loss. In each case the court seeks to assess and award damages that are equivalent to the loss sustained by the plaintiff—in each case the same heads of damage are recoverable and in each case similar deductions have to be made.

4.2 Past loss comprises special damage and is separately assessed. It had always been customary to assess the special damage separately for convenience. Now, since the decision of the Court of Appeal in *Jefford v. Gee* [1970] 2 Q.B. 130, separate assessment is mandatory in order that interest can be awarded on the special damage. Future loss, on the other hand, comprises part of general damages. It, too, must now be separately assessed in order to distinguish it from that part of general damages that bears interest—namely, damages for pain and suffering and loss of amenities (*Pickett v. British Rail Engineering Limited* [1980] A.C. 136). Obviously, damages for future loss bear no interest; on the contrary, their assessment involves a discount for the early receipt of a lump sum representing successive future losses.

4.3 The real difference between the two categories of damage is that past loss is certain, or largely certain, whereas future loss is, by its very nature, uncertain. This difference results in a different approach by the courts to the assessment of the two categories of damage. The assessment of past loss is relatively simple whereas the assessment of future loss involves varying degrees of difficulty. That is why the two categories of damage are dealt with separately. (For future pecuniary loss, see Chapter 5.)

4.4 As has been stated, the principles of assessment are the same for both categories. The principles of assessment, the heads of damage and the deductions that have to be made are dealt with in this chapter.

SCHEDULE OF SPECIAL DAMAGE AND COUNTER SCHEDULE

4.5 These are two of the most important pleadings in a case of severe personal injury. The initial stage is for the plaintiff to comply with RSC, Ord. 18, r.12(1A)(b), which requires that a statement of special damage shall be served with the statement of claim.

4.6 At this stage such statement is usually in fairly general terms, though it should be sufficient to give the defendant a fair idea of the case which he has to meet. But many items of past and future financial loss and past and future expense will not by then have been fully investigated. Such items probably cannot be sensibly assessed until after the exchange of medical and other expert reports. The parties must then comply with the *Practice Direction (Damages: Personal Injuries)* issued by Lord Lane C.J. on August 1, 1984. The plaintiff's schedule requires careful consideration. Care must be taken to include all relevant items. It is desirable that the defendant's counter schedule should plead to the plaintiff's schedule in some detail, rather than by bare denial. Proper pleading should narrow the ambit of dispute and shorten the trial. Useful precedents for a schedule and counter schedule will be found in *Kemp & Kemp*, Vol. I, Chapter 5, Appendix VI.

BASIC PRINCIPLES OF ASSESSMENT OF PECUNIARY LOSS

4.7 In *Lim Poh Choo v. Camden and Islington Area Health Authority* [1980] A.C. 174 (*per* Lord Scarman giving the main speech with which the rest of their Lordships agreed) the House of Lords re-affirmed what Lord Blackburn had said over 100 years ago: 'the principle of the law is that compensation should as nearly as possible put the party who has suffered in the same position as he would have been if he had not sustained the wrong' (*Livingstone v. Rawyards Coal Co* (1880) 5 App. Cas. 25 at 39).

4.8 In relation to past loss the court will usually know all the factors relevant to the assessment of the loss. If it is a loss of earnings the court has only to ascertain and add up the net earnings lost, and if it is loss caused by out-of-pocket expenditure the court has only to ascertain and add up the total expenditure. But even here there may be elements of uncertainty. The plaintiff might claim that during the period between the accident and the trial he would have been promoted and received earnings higher than his pre-accident earnings. The plaintiff might be an author who is prevented by his injuries from writing or completing a book or there might have been high unemployment in the area and large redundancies in the company that had employed the plaintiff. In all such cases the court must estimate as best it can what would have happened if the plaintiff had not been injured and on that basis must assess his loss. Usually, however, there is little difficulty in assessing past pecuniary loss—indeed, in most cases it will have been agreed as special damage before the trial. Accordingly, the way in which past pecuniary loss is calculated will not be dealt with here. The sections below are concerned with heads of recoverable damage commonly encountered. Deductions which have to be made in some cases are considered in Chapter 6, "The Incidence of Benefits".

EXPENSES

4.9 There is a general rule applicable to expenses of all kinds; only reasonable expenses can be recovered. This is a question of fact in every case and two examples may be taken. In *Cunningham v. Harrison* [1973] Q.B. 942 the plaintiff claimed that he required the services of a living-in housekeeper and two nurses at a total cost of almost £6,000 a year (about £39,500 a year in terms of the pound sterling in 1992). The court rejected this claim. Similarly, in *Cassel v. Riverside Health Authority* [1995] P.I.Q.R. Q. 168 the Court of Appeal disallowed the cost of a small swimming pool, which had been allowed by Rose J., the trial judge, in the sum of £30,000.

4.10 A different situation arose in *Willett v. North Bedfordshire Health Authority* [1992] P.I.Q.R. Q. 166. The claim was for the purchase of a house required to enable the plaintiff to be looked after by his parents with helpers. The house bought happened already to have a swimming pool. The defendant sought to reduce the capital cost of the house (for the purpose of a *Roberts v. Johnstone* calculation: see para. 4.21) by the increased value of the house attributable to the swimming pool. Although the medical evidence did not establish a need for a swimming pool, Hobhouse J. refused to make such reduction. A house of this nature was needed and it fell within the reasonable price range for such a house. The fact that it had a swimming pool was irrelevant.

4.11 Provided that it is reasonable to incur the particular expense, it is immaterial that the expense may be very large. Some particular heads of expense commonly encountered will now be considered individually.

Medical expenses

4.12 Section 2(4) of the Law Reform (Personal Injuries) Act 1948 (see Appendix B) provides that in an action for damages for personal injuries there shall be disregarded, in determining the reasonableness of any expenses, the possibility of avoiding those expenses or part of them by taking advantage of facilities available in the National Health Service. In so far as past medical expenses are concerned, the application of this subsection gives rise to no difficulty. While on this topic, it is convenient to anticipate part of the next chapter where future pecuniary loss is considered. The question sometimes arises whether in fact the plaintiff will be able for the rest of his life to obtain outside the National Health Service the facilities that he requires. If the court concludes that a plaintiff will take advantage of National Health Service facilities because no other suitable facilities will be available, it will not award him damages for the cost of notional private facilities that he will not in fact use. In *Lim*'s case [1980] A.C. 174, at 187F–188D the House of Lords affirmed a ruling of the Court of Appeal to this effect given in *Cunningham*'s case [1973] Q.B. 942 at 957 *per* Lawton L.J. However, on the facts of *Lim*'s case the House of Lords upheld the decision of the lower courts that it would be possible to obtain the required facilities outside the National Health Service and that it was reasonable to incur that expense. For an instance where the medical expenses claimed were held to be unreasonably high, see *Roberts v. Roberts* (1960) *The Times*, 11 March; for cases where very high medical expenses were held to have been reasonably incurred, see *Winkworth v. Hubbard* [1960] 1 Lloyd's Rep. 150 and *Hamp v. Sisters of St Joseph's Mount Carmel Convent School* Bar Library Transcript No 305B of 1973 (*Kemp & Kemp*, Vol. 2, paras D2–011 and D2–100). If the medical expenses are incurred in a foreign currency, a sum in respect of those expenses may be awarded in that foreign currency (see *Hoffman v. Sofaer* [1982] 1 W.L.R. 1350 and see para. 4.27 below).

4.13 Provided the medical expense was reasonably incurred, it is immaterial that the particular treatment should transpire to have been unnecessary, or even mistaken: *per* Lord Collins in *Clippens Oil Co. Ltd v. Edinburgh & District Water Trustees* 1907 SC(HL) 9 at p. 14:

> "The wrong doer is not entitled to criticise the course honestly taken by the injured person on the advice of his experts, even though it should appear by the light of after-events that another course might have saved loss. The loss he has to pay for is that which has actually followed under such circumstances upon his wrong."

Lord Patrick followed this *dictum* in *Rubens v. Walker* 1946 S.C. 215 at 216. And Lord Dunedin said much the same in *SS Baron Vernon v. SS Metagama* 1928 SC(HL) 21 at 28:

> "The pursuer is entitled to act on the advice of his experts, and the defender must pay the costs of that acting ... It is a reasonable and probable consequence of a wrongdoer's breach of duty that a person hurt will incur expenses in following the treatment pre-

scribed by reputable experts employed by him to cure him. Each case must be decided upon its own merits. The result might be very different if the injured person acted on the advice of a quack, or if, considering all the advice he had received no reasonable person would have taken the course he did."

Although the two cases mentioned above are both Scottish cases, the law of England is the same on this point.

4.14 Medical expenses may be reasonably incurred even though a less expensive alternative was available to the plaintiff. In *Rialas v. Mitchell* (1984) 128 S.J. 704; the Court of Appeal upheld an award for the continuing cost of caring for an infant plaintiff at home, although care in an institutional home would have cost less.

4.15 Medical expenses cover any form of service, treatment, medicine or appliance reasonably required. The services need not be only professional medical or nursing services. Attendance or help by paid lay persons can also properly be the subject of a claim for expenses. Moreover, it is now well established that an injured plaintiff can recover for the unpaid services of a friend or relative. The Court of Appeal has decided in *Roberts v. Johnstone* [1988] 3 W.L.R. 1247, that where a plaintiff requires care and attendance as a result of his injuries, the cost of persons providing that care up to the date of trial is special damage, even if no one is in fact employed, and that interest is payable on the notional cost at the rate appropriate to special damages (see paras 1.109 *et seq.* above). Whether the appropriate measure will be nearer to a full commercial rate or to a nil rate (as with NHS services) will depend on the facts of each case (see *Housecroft v. Burnett* [1986] 1 All E.R. 332). Numerous instances of awards for unpaid help will be found in Vol 2 of *Kemp & Kemp*. However, if such unpaid help is given by the defendant, damages cannot be awarded in respect of it: *Hunt v. Severs* [1994] 2 W.L.R. 602. For a discussion of this decision and its implications see *Kemp & Kemp*, Vol 1, paras 5–024 *et seq.*

4.16 There are many advanced and expensive appliances now available to assist the disabled and an injured plaintiff's advisers should consult medical experts to ascertain whether any such appliance should be acquired to mitigate the plaintiff's particular disability. Not only the capital cost of such an appliance, but also its running expenses are recoverable. For example, the cost and keep of a guide dog would be recoverable by a blind or partially sighted plaintiff.

4.17 It should be noted that section 5 of the Administration of Justice Act 1982 provides that:

"In an action under the law of England and Wales or the law of Northern Ireland for damages for personal injuries (including any such action arising out of a contract) any saving to the injured person which is attributable to his maintenance wholly or partly at public expense in a hospital, nursing home or other institution shall be set off against any income lost by him as a result of his injuries."

Special living accommodation or other capital asset

4.18 Normally, the measure of damage will be the sum expended to obtain the appliance or facility required plus its current running expenses. But sometimes the expenditure will result in the plaintiff acquiring an asset of a type that he would have required even if he had not been disabled, although he would not have required one with the special attributes of the asset in question. For example, a disabled plaintiff may require a motor car equipped with special devices to enable him to get in and out of it or to control it on the road. In such a case the plaintiff could recover the extra cost of the special equipment, but could not recover the basic cost of the car if he would have needed one in any event.

4.19 In *Povey v. Governors of Rydal School* [1970] 1 All E.R. 841 the plaintiff was awarded £8,400 (1998 value £80,000) to cover the cost of renewing over a period of 25 years the special hydraulic lifting appliance required to lift his wheel-chair in and out of a motor car. This example really falls within the scope of the next chapter, being an award for future pecuniary loss.

4.20 Similarly, a disabled plaintiff often requires special living accommodation (eg a bungalow equipped with doors suitable for the passage of a wheel-chair) or requires special appliances to be installed in his existing accommodation. In the latter case the special appliances are unlikely to have increased the value of his property, and so he can recover their cost in full. But in the former case the plaintiff will have a capital asset in his hands, and he is only entitled to recover damages to compensate him for the additional expenditure involved. There had been various ways of assessing the damages recoverable for such expenditure. In the past the court would approach the problem by awarding damages to cover the extra mortgage which would be paid on the new accommodation, as in

Fowler v. Grace (1970) 114 S.J. 193. For another instance of the courts' approach to this problem see *George v. Pinnock* [1973] 1 W.L.R. 118 at 124–5. (These cases also are examples of future pecuniary loss and are considered in this chapter as a matter of convenience.) But this approach proved unsatisfactory. The resulting sum was much the same as the capital value of the house. The Court was reduced to plucking a figure from the air. But the Court of Appeal's decision considered in the next paragraph has now produced a satisfactory and elegant solution to the problem.

4.21 In *Roberts v. Johnstone* [1988] 3 W.L.R. 1247 the Court of Appeal laid down a general rule for assessing damages where a plaintiff has to purchase special accommodation. The annual additional cost of such accommodation should be taken as 3 per cent of the difference between the capital cost of the special accommodation, and the net proceeds of sale of the property in which the plaintiff had previously lived. To this annual cost a multiplier appropriate to other forms of continuing future expense should be applied. This general rule should solve most of the problems raised by this subject-matter. The increase from 2 to 3 per cent was laid down by the House of Lords in *Wells v. Wells* [1998] 3 W.L.R. 329 at 348E-F.

4.22 The calculation will, of course, vary, depending upon the plaintiff's circumstances and the nature of the new accommodation. Certain expenditure may result in no capital benefit. For example, the cost of ramps and other modifications to enable a paraplegic to get about the house may even reduce the capital value of the house. Such expenditure should be regarded as special damages and recovered in full.

4.23 A calculation of this sort may be illustrated by the following hypothetical example. The plaintiff is aged 30 and has a normal expectation of life. A suitable multiplier to apply in such case to expenses continuing for life would, following the House of Lords' decision in *Wells*, be 23.

Sale price of previous property	£60,000
Purchase price of new property	£100,000
Cost of modifications to accommodate plaintiff's disability, reduction in height of kitchen appliances and all wash basins to allow use from wheel-chair, widening of doors, install ramps and hoist to allow access by wheel-chair:	Cost £10,000

These modifications in fact reduce the value of the new property on the open market to £95,000. The plaintiff has incurred "wasted" capital expenditure of £15,000. This is recoverable in full as special damages.

The plaintiff has a capital asset worth £95,000. Subtract value of previous capital asset, £60,000. Difference = £35,000. 3 per cent of this is £1,050 Apply multiplier of 23. Damages should be:

£1,050 × 23	£24,150
Wasted expenditure	£15,000
Legal costs of sale and purchase	£X
Removal costs	£Y
	£39,150 + £X + £Y.

4.24 In the case of a young man, living at home or in rented accommodation when injured, the court may find that he would in any case have bought a house at some time. The court would adjust the multiplier to take account of its finding.

Extra expenditure of a normal nature

4.25 Often a disabled plaintiff will have to incur extra expenditure on normal items. For example, a paraplegic might require extra laundry or extra clothing. In *Povey's* case [1970] 1 All E.R. 841 at 844h and 846b Crichton J. awarded the plaintiff £1,900 (1998 value £17,100) to cover the extra cost of clothing and £4,200 (1998 value £37,750) to cover the extra cost of laundry and bedding (again, these are instances of awards for future pecuniary loss). A disabled person might have to pay more for his holidays because he has to go to places where there are additional facilities available. In *Povey's* case at p. 846b Crichton J. awarded £900 (1998 value £8,100) under this head (again an instance of an award for future pecuniary loss). No useful purpose would be served by attempting to set out here an exhaustive list of items that have been held to be an admissible claim for damages. In every case the court must decide whether it was reasonable to incur the expense in question, and that will depend upon the facts of the particular case. It is usual in serious cases to call expert evidence as to the plaintiff's needs and the cost of meeting them. Perusal of such cases in *Kemp & Kemp*, Vol. 2, will indicate the type of evidence adduced and the sort of expert called to give it: see also the valuable reports in P.I.Q.R. eg *Routledge v. Mackenzie* [1994] P.I.Q.R. Q. 49 *Fairhurst v. St. Helen's and Knowsley Health Authority* [1995] P.I.Q.R., Q. 1.

4.26 It is important to remember that all items of special damage must be specifically pleaded.

4.27 In most cases expenditure will have been incurred in pounds sterling, but sometimes the expenditure may have been incurred in a foreign currency. In such cases the English court now has power to make an award in that currency if such an award would most fairly compensate the plaintiff for his loss (*The Despina R* [1978] 3 W.L.R. 804, H.L.). In *Hoffman v. Sofaer* [1982] 1 W.L.R. 1350 Talbot J. held that where a foreign plaintiff suffered his injuries in Britain, his damages should be assessed in the currency most closely linked with the loss, namely the currency in which the loss was suffered or the expense incurred, with the exception of damages for pain, suffering and loss of amenity which should be assessed in sterling.

4.28 Where a plaintiff's injuries have rendered him incapable of managing his affairs, Court of Protection fees are recoverable as an expense caused by the injuries (see *Kemp & Kemp*, Vol 1, para. 5/008/11).

4.29 Where a plaintiff's injuries prevent him doing DIY work, which he had previously done, the extra cost of such work is recoverable as damages.

LOSS OF EARNINGS OR PROFITS

4.30 This is the second main head of past pecuniary loss. In the ordinary case of a man earning a regular wage or salary, there is little difficulty in assessing damages under this head. One takes his net loss from the date of the accident up to the date of the trial and awards him that sum. If the net loss was incurred in a currency other than pounds sterling and if an award in the currency would most fairly compensate the plaintiff for his loss, the court will award the damages in that currency (*The Despina R*) [1978] 3 W.L.R. 804, H.L.). In *Hoffman's* case [1982] 1 W.L.R. 1350 Talbot J. awarded the American plaintiff his lost earnings in U.S. dollars. It is important, particularly when a considerable time has elapsed between the accident and the trial, to "update" the plaintiff's wage or salary. With current inflation most wage-earners or salaried employees have regular increases in basic remuneration. The plaintiff's advisers should be sure that the particulars of his special damage take note of all increases in remuneration which the plaintiff would have enjoyed if he had remained in his preaccident employment. If the plaintiff has been unable to work at all up to the date of the trial, his loss will be the entire net remuneration which he would have earned; if for a period he has been able to earn something, but not as much as he would have earned had he not been injured, his loss for that period will be the net difference between what he has earned and what he would otherwise have earned.

4.31 So much for the straightforward case. There can be varying degrees of complication. The plaintiff's remuneration may have been based partly or even wholly on commission on orders obtained, or in the case of more senior employees upon the turnover of the business or some part of the business. In such cases the court will have to estimate what the net commission would have been and award damages accordingly. The plaintiff might be self-employed in some business or profession and the court's task in assessing his net loss might then be more difficult. Even in the case of a regular wage-earner or salaried employee, there might be complications; for example, the plaintiff might claim that he would have been promoted to a more remunerative post (in which case the court must assess his prospects of promotion and award damages accordingly) or the defendant may claim that the plaintiff's employer had suffered severe business setbacks that necessitated redundancies and that the plaintiff would have lost his employment (in which case the court must consider all the circumstances and award as damages what it estimates to have been the plaintiff's net loss). These complications must be mentioned in order to avoid over-simplifying the position. But in the vast majority of cases the assessment of past pecuniary loss is in fact simple and usually special damages under this head are agreed without difficulty. past loss of earnings or profits must be specifically pleaded as special damage.

4.32 The lost earnings must be a real loss. Thus, a plaintiff who receives "sick pay" equivalent to his ordinary pay has suffered no loss and cannot recover damages (*Turner v. Ministry of Defence* (1969) 113 S.J. 585). Likewise, a plaintiff whose contract entitles him to his wages during incapacity has suffered no loss of wages and so cannot recover damages for lost wages. The position is different where the employer advances to a plaintiff who is incapacitated from work a sum equivalent to his usual earnings upon the understanding that such sum should be repaid to the employer in the event of the plaintiff successfully suing the author of his injuries. (This topic is dealt with at greater length in *Kemp & Kemp*, Vol. 1, para.

5–009 *et seq.*) In such a case the plaintiff has lost his earnings and is entitled to damages. A further illustration of the principle that only a real loss of earnings is recoverable is provided by the decision of the House of Lords in *Dews v. National Coal Board* [1988] A.C. 1. The plaintiff was obliged under his contract of employment to contribute a percentage of his weekly wage to a pension scheme. His employer was obliged to match that contribution. As a result of injury he was off work for 31 weeks. He claimed for his loss of earnings during this period and contended that damages should be based on his entire wages, ie including his pension contribution. (A claim to recover his employer's contribution was dismissed by the Court of Appeal.) The fact that no contribution was made to the pension fund during the 31 weeks by the plaintiff would not result in a diminution of his pension. For that reason the House of Lords held that he could not recover. Lord Griffiths, at pp. 14–15, stated:

> "In my view the key to the solution of the present problem is to be found by recognising that in present day society people generally work with two principal aims in view; the first is to provide themselves with an income available for current spending and the second is to provide money that will be put into a pension scheme to provide them with an income after their retirement. When a plaintiff is injured and as a result is paid no wages his immediate real loss is that part of his net earnings that were available for current expenditure. In respect of this part of his earnings the object of which is to provide income available for current expenditure the tortfeasor is, subject to sums necessarily spent to earn the income, entitled to no credit for expenditure saved as a result of the injury; the principle that it is no concern of the tortfeasor how the plaintiff chooses to spend his income applies.
>
> Different considerations, however, apply to the contributions to a retirement pension. This money is not intended to provide any immediate benefit and the plaintiff suffers no immediate loss as a result of the loss of his wages. He may, of course, as a result of a failure to pay contributions to the pension scheme suffer a future loss of pension. This loss he is entitled to recover. The measure of the loss will depend upon the terms of the particular scheme to which the plaintiff is contributing."

LOSS OF OTHER MATERIAL BENEFITS

4.33 Sometimes employments or occupations carry with them the enjoyment of material benefits other than monetary remuneration—for example, free board and lodging in the case of a domestic servant (*Liffen v. Watson* [1940] 1 K.B. 556), free coal for a miner, free or concessionary travel facilities for railway or airline employees, free farm produce for agricultural workers or the free use of a car for travelling salesmen, etc. In all such cases the plaintiff is entitled to damages to compensate him for the lost benefit. In *Ashley v. Esso Transportation Co. Ltd* (1956) *The Times*, 8 February the plaintiff claimed as part of his damages for injury suffered whilst working in a ship the extra expense incurred since the accident in having to buy his cigarettes ashore instead of on board free of duty. The claim was dismissed on liability and so the question of damages was not dealt with; in principle, however, the claim seems to have been well founded.

4.34 Other types of loss under this head are the following:

(1) Loss of opportunity of grammar school education (*Jones v. Lawrence* [1969] 3 All E.R. 267).

(2) Loss of status through inability to complete an apprenticeship (*Dunk v. George Waller & Son Ltd* [1970] 2 Q.B. 163).

(3) Loss of an opportunity to make or enhance one's reputation. For example, the case of an actor (*Marbé v. Edwardes (George) Daly's Theatre* [1929] 1 K.B. 269; *Herbert Clayton and Jack Waller Ltd v. Oliver* [1930] A.C. 209; the claims in these cases were for breach of contract but the same principle applies in tort) and the case of a professional golfer who had been prevented from taking part in competitions by his injury (*Mulvaine v. Joseph* (1968) 112 S.J. 927).

(4) Loss of a craftsman's joy and pride in his work (*Morris v. Johnson Matthey & Co.* (1967) 112 S.J. 32).

(5) Loss of congenial employment (see *Kemp & Kemp*, Vol 1, para. 5–251.

TAX

4.35 It is not possible to deal fully with the question of tax. For a more detailed consideration, see *Kemp & Kemp*, Vol 1, Chapter 9.

4.36 In calculating a plaintiff's loss of earnings or profits the incidence of income tax must be taken into account. This is the rule established by the House of Lords in *British Transport Commission v. Gourley* [1956] A.C. 185.

4.37 Liability to pay national insurance contributions must also be taken into account (*Cooper v. Firth Brown* [1963] 1 W.L.R. 418).

4.38 Only the cases where the relevant tax is UK tax will be considered. The incidence of foreign tax, however, is no more remote a factor in assessing the damages of a plaintiff whose earnings are subject to foreign tax than is the incidence of UK tax where that is relevant. Foreign tax must be proved by expert evidence, if the relevant rates etc cannot be agreed. It is the plaintiff's duty to plead his net loss of earnings, and accordingly the incidence of all relevant taxes (*Phipps v. Orthodox Unit Trusts Ltd* [1958] 1 Q.B. 314).

4.39 When dealing with past loss there is no problem as to the rate of tax to be applied. The lost earnings should be calculated tax year by tax year and the appropriate rates of tax adopted. For each tax year the net earnings after tax that would have been received by the plaintiff if he had not been injured should be calculated, and from this net figure should be deducted the net earnings that the plaintiff has in fact received: the difference is the plaintiff's loss during the tax year.

4.40 It is convenient here to anticipate part of the chapter on future pecuniary loss (see Chapter 5). One of the uncertainties of the assessment of future loss of earnings is the future rate of tax. The courts approach this problem broadly, following the guidance given by Lord Goddard in *Gourley*'s case [1956] A.C. 185 at 209 in his model direction to the jury: "No one can foresee whether tax will go up or down and I advise you not to speculate but to deal with matters as at present". The same approach is adopted with regard to other statutory provisions affecting the calculation of tax (eg allowances and reliefs in respect of tax). The courts make their calculations on the basis of the current provisions and do not speculate on future changes.

4.41 If a plaintiff's loss of wages has resulted in his getting an income tax rebate, the amount of the rebate must be taken into account against his loss of wages (*Hartley v. Sandholme Iron Co.* [1975] Q.B. 600).

4.42 Similarly, when lost earnings have meant that on return to work the plaintiff is free of tax for a period, having fallen below the level of earnings on which tax is payable, the tax that he has escaped during that period is a compensatory gain that must be taken into account in the assessment of his lost earnings (*Brayson v. Wilmot-Breedon* [1976] C.L.Y. 682).

4.43 Where a plaintiff loses only part of his earnings, this part will always be "the top slice" for the purposes of taking tax into account (*Lyndale Fashion Manufacturers v. Rich* [1973] 1 All E.R. 33 at p. 37g-h). It is submitted that in so far as Wynn-Parry J. decided the contrary in *Re Houghton Main Colliery Co. Ltd* [1956] 1 W.L.R. 1219 at 1224–5 he was wrong.

4.44 When calculating future loss of earnings and the incidence of tax upon them, it is proper to take into account steps which the plaintiff could and would have taken to minimise his tax liability (*Beach v. Reed Corrugated Cases Ltd* [1956] 1 W.L.R. 807 at 814). This action was for wrongful dismissal but the same principle applies in a claim for damages for personal injury. As Pilcher J. said in *Beach*'s case at p. 809: "I have to approach the assessment of damages in this case in the light of . . . *British Transport Commission v. Gourley*".

4.45 It is the plaintiff's duty to plead his net loss of earnings. Accordingly, he will be required to give particulars of the factors affecting his tax liability (*Phipps v. Orthodox Unit Trust Ltd* [1958] 1 Q.B. 314).

Chapter 5

Damages for Future Pecuniary Loss

David Kemp Q.C.

Contents	*Para*

THE IMPORTANCE OF THIS HEAD OF DAMAGE

5.1 As will be appreciated from Chapter 3, the Courts in England and Wales, compared with those in some other countries, are not generous in their awards of general damages for pain and suffering and loss of amenities. Lay members of the public, who have read in newspapers of large awards, tend to have exaggerated expectations of the likely award in their particular case if their injury has not resulted in much future pecuniary loss. Some recent examples illustrate the respective importance of non-pecuniary and pecuniary loss, in particular future pecuniary loss which will now be even more important as a result of the decision of the House of Lords in *Wells v. Wells* [1998] 3 W.L.R. 329 (see paras *5.9 et seq.—infra*).

Plaintiff	*Non-pecuniary loss*	*Pecuniary loss:*			
		Past loss of earnings	*Future loss of earnings*	*Past care etc.*	*Future care etc*
Whiteside	£130,000	£8,000	£236,700	£257,939	£1,267,451
Bould	£110,000	–	£149,530	£584,178	£718,750
Cassel	£110,000	–	£350,000	£78,803	£635,625
Almond	£105,000	–	£190,000	£72,700	£515,600
Brittain	£100,000	£50,307	£456,550	£58,500	£283,720
Stephens	£120,000	–	£22,500	£58,250	£976,739
Smith	£110,000	–	£278,800	£108,885	£256,279
Brightman	£96,375	£9,216	£63,000	£96,758	£354,900
Tan	£79,750	£21,000	£136,400	£69,600	£233,700
Francis	£78,700	–	£85,000	£69,000	£167,900

(Details of these awards will be found in *Kemp & Kemp*, Vol. 2.)

It is therefore apparent that the assessment of damages for future pecuniary loss is a matter of great importance.

There are two classes of future loss caused by personal injury.

The victim may have been deprived of some future financial benefit

5.2 This will usually be the loss, in whole or in part, of future earnings. It may, however, include the loss of other pecuniary benefits. For example a woman, who was engaged to a very wealthy man, may lose the prospect of marrying him: *Aloni v. National Westminster Bank* (1982) (see *Kemp & Kemp*, para. A3–007), where the plaintiff was awarded £75,000 (1998 value £151,000) on this basis. A plaintiff may have been deprived of the use of a company car or some other valuable perquisite of his employment, eg free coal for a miner, free milk and other produce for an agricultural worker, regular access to duty free purchases for a travel courier, etc. Sometimes the court may have to make a rough guess at the value of such loss; sometimes it can put an annual value on the loss and treat it in the same way as loss of future earnings, a type of claim which we now consider. The court will take the plaintiff's loss of earnings at the time of the trial and calculate that on an annual basis. That will give the multiplicand. Although, with inflation as a fact of life, earnings would certainly have increased over the years, no account is to be taken of future inflation in determining the multiplicand. If the earnings would have increased for other reasons, promotion, experience or further qualifications etc, such increase is to be taken into account.

Important factors in the assessment of the loss of future earnings are when the loss will start and how long it will continue.

The victim may have to incur future expenditure as a result of the injuries

5.3 Examples of such expenditure are continuing care, continuing medical expenses, the maintenance and renewal of aids and appliances, domestic assistance, etc. The court will assess the annual sum of such expenditure, thereby reaching a multiplicand. As with loss of future earnings, any increase of expenditure caused by inflation is to be ignored, but any increases for other reasons, eg the increased need for nursing care at some future date, will be taken into account in the same way as with a relevant increase in loss of future earnings. In assessing damages under this head an important factor is how long the expenditure will continue.

The court must award a lump sum as compensation for a stream of future losses

5.4 In both classes of case the court's task is to assess the present value of the future loss. The lump sum award should be calculated to compensate for a stream of future lost earnings or a stream of future expenses.

The discount for early receipt

5.5 One element in the calculation of the appropriate lump sum is to discount each future payment so as to allow for its receipt at a time earlier than the loss or expense will occur. The recipient of the lump sum will have the interest on that sum, as well as the capital of the sum itself, out of which to cover the stream of future lost earnings or future expenses. The target to be aimed at is that the total of capital and interest will have been exhausted at the moment when the last earnings have been lost and the last expense incurred.

The multiplier/multiplicand approach

5.6 The way in which the court calculates the appropriate lump sum is by applying a suitable multiplier to the multiplicand. The selection of a multiplier was an arbitrary process in the sense that the multiplier was not calculated in a precise or logical manner. Mustill L.J. in *Cunningham v. Camberwell Health Authority* [1990] 2 Med. L.R. 49 at 52 described the process as follows:

> "... the process seem to have no clear intellectual basis ... What happens in practice is that the judge adopts an intuitive process buttressed by reference to previously decided cases. These cases partly operate as reference points whose features are compared with those of the case under consideration and partly from the basis of a general climate of opinion on the proper multiplier in a particular class of case with which a judge of long experience in the field will be entirely familiar. But it must be observed that these previous cases themselves must ultimately be intuitive in origin. Now this may be a rough and ready approach but it operates in an economical way and it enables the court to achieve a consistency of award which is at least the start of a just system for computing damages."

The old guidelines on discount rate

5.7 The range of multipliers until now chosen by the court corresponded approximately to a choice based on the assumption that a plaintiff who invests his money in the UK will receive a rate of return on the investment of 4.5 per cent a year, after the effects of tax and inflation have been taken into account: para. 648 of the Pearson Royal Commission. The same paragraph points out that this assumption is no longer realistic. It is for this reason, in our submission, that the previous conventional practice of the court was wrong.

5.8 We have long contended that the only logical basis on which to make the required discount is to choose a discount rate which represents the real rate of return on risk-free investments after taking into account inflation and tax. Before the introduction of Index-Linked Government Stock ("ILGS") the assessment of such a rate would have involved the court in undesirable speculation. Now, however, the introduction of such stock has presented the court with a simple and logical solution. The Joint Working Party of Actuaries and Lawyers, chaired by Sir Michael Ogden, produced three Reports pointing out that the net return from time to time payable on such stock accurately reflected the real rate of return on risk-free investments. For much of the time that this stock has been available the rate of return lay in a bracket between 2.5 to 3.5 per cent per annum. Nevertheless, until the decision of the House of Lords in *Wells*, the courts had persisted in applying a discount rate of between 4 and 5 per cent, thereby reaching far too low an assessment of the appropriate lump sum.

This practice was based on "Guidelines" promulgated at a time when ILGS was not available for investors. The Guidelines had been widely criticised by the Law Commission, other official bodies, the Inter-professional Working Party chaired by Sir Michael Ogden Q.C. and textbook writers.

The new guidelines

5.9 Nevertheless, the courts persisted in following the old Guidelines, until in three cases trial judges had the courage to follow their own judgment and apply a discount rate based on the net return after tax from investment in ILGS. The Judges were Dyson J. in *Page v. Sheerness Steel plc.*, [1996] P.I.Q.R. Q. 26, Collins J. in *Thomas v. Brighton Health Authority* [1996] P.I.Q.R. Q. 44 and H.H. Judge Wilcox in *Wells v. Wells* [1996] P.I.Q.R. Q. 62. All three cases went to appeal. The appeals were allowed; [1997] 1 W.L.R. 652. The Court of Appeal held that the old Guidelines should still be followed. The decision was much criticised: see, for example, *Kemp & Kemp*, Volume 1, Release 66, paragraphs 6–003/8 to 6–003/12/3; and (1997] L.Q.R. 195. The House of Lords accepted these criticisms and allowed the appeals, laying down new "Guidelines" [1998] 1 W.L.R. 329. The discount rate should now be 3 per cent per annum net, unless and until the Lord Chancellor prescribes a different rate rate pursuant to Section 1 (1) of the Damages Act, 1996. Their Lordships' speeches ran to many pages and should be studied carefully by practitioners. The main speech (with which the other members of the Judicial Committee agreed) was given by Lord Lloyd of Berwick.

5.10 The essence of decision and the *ratio decidendi* are set out in the following extracts from his speech: at p. 341E to 342E:

"*Conclusion*

My conclusion is that the judges in these three cases were right to assume for the purpose of their calculations that the plaintiffs would invest their damages in I.L.G.S. for the following reasons.

(1) Investment in I.L.G.S. is the most accurate way of calculating the present value of the loss which the plaintiffs will actually suffer in real terms.

(2) Although this will result in a heavier burden on these defendants. and, if the principle is applied across the board, on the insurance industry in general. I can see nothing unjust. It is true that insurance premiums may have been fixed on the basis of the 4 to 5 per cent, discount rate indicated in *Cookson v. Knowles* [1979] A.C. 556 and the earlier authorities. But this was only because there was then no better way of allowing for future inflation. The objective was always the same. No doubt insurance premiums will have to increase in order to take account of the new lower rate of discount. Whether this is something which the country can afford is not a subject on which your Lordships were addressed. So we are not in a position to, form any view as to the wider consequences.

(3) The search for a prudent investment will always depend on the circumstances of the particular investor. Some are able to take a measure of risk, others are not. For a plaintiff who is not in a position to take risks, and who wishes to protect himself against inflation in the short term of up to 10 years, it is clearly prudent to invest in I.L.G.S. It cannot therefore be assumed that he will invest in equities and gilts. Still less is it his duty to invest in equities and gilts in order to mitigate his loss.

(4) Logically the same applies to a plaintiff investing for the long term. In any event it is desirable to have a single rate applying across the board, in order to facilitate settlements and to save the expense of expert evidence at the trial. I take this view even though it is open to the Lord Chancellor under section 1(3) of the Act of 1996 to prescribe different rates of return for different classes of case. Mr. Leighton Williams conceded that it is not desirable in practice to distinguish between different classes of plaintiff when assessing the multiplier.

(5) the plaintiff, or the majority of plaintiffs, in fact invest their money is irrelevant. The research carried out by the Law Commission does not suggest that the majority of plaintiffs in fact

invest in equities and gilts, but rather in a building society or a bank deposit.

(6) There was no agreement between the parties as to how much greater, if at all, the return on equities is likely to be in the short or long term. But it is at least clear that an investment in I.L.G.S. will save up to 1 per cent. per annum by obviating the need for continuing investment advice.

(7) The practice of the Court of Protection when investing for the long term affords little guidance. In any event the policy may change when lump sums are calculated at a lower rate of return.

(8) The views of the Ogden Working Party, the Law Commission and the author of *Kemp & Kemp, The Quantum of Damages* in favour of an investment in I.L.G.S. are entitled to great weight.

(9) There is nothing in the previous decisions of the House which inhibits a new approach. It is therefore unnecessary to have resort to the *Practice Statement (Judicial Precedent)* [1966] 1 W.L.R. 1234.

Consequences

Once it is accepted that the lump sum should be calculated on the basis of the rate of return available on I.L.G.S. then an assessment of the average rate of return at the relevant date presents no problem. The rates are published daily in the 'Financial Times.' A table of average rates for the period June 1990 to December 1994 ("Gross Return on Index-Linked Government Securities") is included in *Kemp & Kemp, The Quantum of Damages*, vol. 1. para. 8–068. No doubt the table will be brought up to date from time to time."

5.11 and at p. 343D to 344C

"*Guidelines*

Section 1 of the Act of 1996 provides:

"(1) In determining the return to be expected from the investment of a sum awarded as damages for future pecuniary loss in an action for personal injury the court shall, subject to and in accordance with rules of court made for the purposes of this section, take into account such rate of return (if any) as may from time to time be prescribed by an order made by the Lord Chancellor."

The section came into force on September 24, 1996, but no rate has yet been prescribed. Lord Mackay of Clashfern, the previous Lord Chancellor, was said to be awaiting the decision of the Court of Appeal in the instant cases. It goes without saying that the sooner the Lord Chancellor sets the rate the better. The present uncertainty does not make the settling of claims any easier.

In the meantime it is for your Lordships to set guidelines to replace the old 4 to 5 per cent, bracket. There is something to be said for a bracket, since it allows some flexibility in exceptional cases, as where, for example, the impact of higher-rate tax would result in substantial undercompensation. Thus on an award of £2 m. higher-rate tax payable over the first half of a 20-year period would alone amount to nearly £75,000. But the majority of your Lordships prefer a single figure. I do not disagree provided it is subject to the same flexibility as is to be found in section 1(2) of the Act of 1996.

What then should the figure be? The average gross redemption yield on I.L.G.S. has fallen steadily over the last year. In May 1997 it was 3.68 per cent., by May 1998 it was only 2.8 per cent. Less tax at, say, 15 per cent., this would give a net return of 2.38 per cent. Logically, therefore, we should take 2.5 per cent, as the guideline figure, since the assumption is that the plaintiff will purchase in the market at that price. The higher-yielding stock is no longer available. If therefore the calculation is done at 3 per cent. instead of 2.5 per cent., he would be substantially undercompensated.

But since it is undesirable that the guidelines should be changed too often, it may be better that the average gross return should be ascertained over a period of months rather than on a particular day; and since, as I have said, the average return has been falling over the last year, one would expect the average return over that period to be higher than the current return. Such proves to be the case. Over the last six months and 12 months to March 1998 the average return has been 3.02 per cent, and 3.28 per cent, respectively. These figures justify a guideline rate of return of 3 per cent, net rather than 2.5 per cent, and this is the rate, which I would propose for general use until the Lord Chancellor has specified a new rate under section 1 of the Act of 1996.

I would not, however, accept that the average should be taken over as long a period as three years. For if the rate of return had been falling steadily over the whole period (in fact this has not been the case) it would work very unfavourably to the plaintiffs; and vice versa if it had been rising steadily over three years. A year would seem to be the best compromise period. Once the net return has been established to the nearest 0.5 per cent., it is a simple enough matter to find the correct multiplier from the Ogden Tables."

5.12 Their Lordships also dealt with another problem of general importance. They held that, as 3 per cent was now the "going rate" for discounting future loss, the same rate should be adopted in a *Roberts v. Johnstone* calculation. *Per* Lord Lloyd at p. 347F to 348F.:

"I can deal with the second of the two miscellaneous points in *Thomas v. Brighton Health Authority* quite shortly. In October 1990, 15 months after the plaintiff's birth, and five years before the trial, the plaintiff's parents moved into a larger house. They needed more space, because of his disability. The additional cost was some £60,000 which they raised by way of a mortgage. The question is how the additional cost should be reflected in the award of damages.

Obviously the plaintiff is not entitled to the additional capital cost, since the larger house is a permanent addition to the family's assets. It will be there, and could be realised, at the end of the period covered by the award. How then should this head of damages be calculated? Should it be the interest on the mortgage? or interest calculated in some other way?

The answer to this question, described in *Kemp & Kemp, The Quantum of Damages*, vol. 1, para. 5–044 as "a satisfactory and elegant solution," was provided by the Court of Appeal in *Roberts v. Johnstone* [1989] Q.B. 878. It is to be assumed that the plaintiff will pay for the additional accommodation out of his own capital. It is further to be assumed that the capital input will be risk-free over the period of the award, and protected against inflation, by a corresponding increase in the value of the house. What the plaintiff has therefore lost is the income which the capital would have earned over the period of the award after deduction of tax.

But the lost income is not to be calculated by reference to a normal commercial rate of interest. For interest, as Lord Diplock explained in *Wright v. British Railways Board* [1983] 2 A.C. 773, 781, normally includes two elements, "a reward for taking a risk of loss or reduction of capital," and "a reward for forgoing the use of the capital sum for the time being." Since the capital input in the new accommodation is free of risk, or virtually free of risk, it is only the second of the two elements of interest that the plaintiff has lost, namely, the "going rate" for forgoing the use of money. The Court of Appeal in *Roberts v. Johnstone* took 2 per cent. as the "going rate." This was the figure originally chosen by Lord Denning M.R. in *Birkett v. Hayes* [1982] 1 W.L.R. 816, and accepted by Lord Diplock in *Wright v. British Railways Board. Birkett v. Hayes and Wright v. British Railways Board* were both cases of non-pecuniary loss, but the point is the same.

Both sides accept that the correct approach is that adopted by the Court of Appeal in *Roberts v. Johnstone.* The only question is how that approach should be applied. Collins J. arrived at the "going rate" by taking the average return on I.L.G.S. as the best possible indicator of the real return on a risk-free investment over the period of the award. In other words, he took the same discount of 3 per cent. net of tax as he had taken for the calculation of future loss. The Court of Appeal disagreed. They took the "conventional rate" of 2 per cent., pointing out that Stocker L.J. had not tied his 2 per cent. to the return on any particular form of investment.

It is true that there is no reference to I.L.G.S. in *Roberts v. Johnstone.* But in *Wright v. British Railways Board* Lord Diplock chose the return on I.L.G.S. as the first (and in my view simpler) of the two routes by which courts can arrive at the appropriate or "conventional" rate of interest for forgoing the use of capital. At that time the net return on 15-year and 25-year index-linked stocks was 2 per cent. I can see no reason for regarding 2 per cent. as sacrosanct now that the average net return on I.L.G.S. has changed. The current rate is 3 per cent. This therefore is the rate which should now be taken for calculating the cost of additional accommodation. It has two advantages. In the first place it is the same as the rate for calculating future loss. Secondly it will be kept up to date by the Lord Chancellor when exercising his powers under section 1 of the Act of 1996. On this point I would restore the order of Collins J."

5.13 The *ratio decidendi* of the *Roberts v. Johnstone* issue has implications in respect of a more important issue, namely, the rate to be used when calculating interest on general damages for pain and suffering and loss of amenities. This question was not in issue before their Lordships, but their reasoning should surely result in this rate becoming three per cent rather than the hitherto conventional rate of 2 per cent, since 3 per cent is now the "going rate". At the date of revising this Chapter, there has been no reported decision on this point.

5.14 Their Lordships also dealt with the so-called "Judicial Discount". They held that, while there may be grounds for a discount when assessing damages for future loss of earnings there is (apart from special cases) no ground for any discount when assessing life-long future cost of care. *Per.* Lord Lloyd at p. 345G to 347F.

"*Thomas v. Brighton Health Authority*

The agreed medical evidence was that the plaintiff has a life expectancy to the age of 60. Collins J. [1996] P.I.Q.R. Q44, 57 held, however, that he ought to reduce the arithmetical multiplier by about 20 per cent. "to cater for the hazards of life in such cases." In the result he took a multiplier of 23. The Court of Appeal agreed with the judge's approach but started from a different starting-point. With a 4.5 per cent. discount rate the arithmetical multiplier came to 20. Reduced by 15 per cent., rather than 20 per cent., they arrived at a multiplier of 17.

Was it correct for the judge and the Court of Appeal to reduce the arithmetical multiplier, and therefore, in effect, override the expectation of life agreed by the doctors? Mr. Owen submitted that there could be no rational basis for applying a further discount for "contingencies," since the doctors had already taken account of all the contingencies that might affect the plaintiff, such as the increased risk of accident, chest infection, and so on. The only reason given by the judge was that the courts had "tended to reduce multipliers by about 20 per cent." The Court of Appeal took the same line.

I can see no answer to Mr. Owen's argument. The inevitable result of reducing the multiplier to 17, as Mr. Havers pointed out, will be that the plaintiff's damages will run out when he is 39. He will have nothing to cover his needs for the remaining 21 years of his life.

Mr. Havers conceded that there is room for a judicial discount when calculating the loss of future earnings. When contingencies may indeed affect the result. But there is no room for any discount in the case of a whole life multiplier with an agreed expectation of life. In the case of loss of earnings the contingencies can work in only one direction in favour of the defendant. But in the case of life expectancy, the contingency can work in either direction. The plaintiff may exceed his normal expectation of life, or he may fall short of it.

There is no purpose in the courts making as accurate a prediction as they can of the plaintiff's future needs if the resulting sum is arbitrarily reduced for no better reason than that the prediction might be wrong. A prediction remains a prediction. Contingencies should be taken into account where they work in one direction, but not where they cancel out. There is no more logic or justice in reducing the whole life multiplier by 15 per cent. or 20 per cent. on an agreed expectation of life than there would be in increasing it by the same amount.

It follows from what I have said that I do not agree with the discount which McCullough J. allowed in *Janardan v. East Berkshire Health Authority* [1990] 2 Med.L.R. I. In that case the plaintiff, aged five at the time of trial, had a life expectancy to 55. This indicated a multiplier of just under 20 by reference to a 4.5 per cent. discount rate (p. 8). McCullough J. held, at p. 7, that a discount was required to allow for the possibility that the plaintiff might not survive to 55. I do not accept this; and it may be that McCullough J. would not have accepted it either, if he had not felt constrained by previous authority. Left to himself, he said, at p. 9, he would have taken a whole life multiplier of 17.5 to 18. But the multiplier chosen by the Court of Appeal in *Croke v. Wiseman* [1982] 1 W.L.R. 71 and by the House in *Lim Poh Choo v. Camden and Islington Area Health Authority* [1980] A.C. 174 required him to choose 17 instead. But this meant, as Mr. Havers pointed out, that the plaintiff in *Janardan's* case would have run out of damages at the age of 33. although he was expected to live to 55.

In *Hunt v. Severs* [1994] 2 A.C. 350 the plaintiff had a life expectancy of 25 years. The appropriate multiplier by reference to a 4.5 per cent. discount rate was [4.82]. But the judge reduced this figure to 14 because 14 seemed more in line with the multiplier applied in other comparable cases. The Court of Appeal [1993] Q.B. 815, correctly in my view, substituted a multiplier of

15, as being the nearest round figure to 14.821. Sir Thomas Bingham M.R. observed, at p. 841, that an allowance for contingencies may sometimes be appropriate. But he continued: "Such an allowance is not appropriate in the present case, where the agreed life expectancy of the plaintiff is 25 years. That is a fact, or rather an agreed assumption, upon which the damages payable for future care must be based."

But the House disagreed. Lord Bridge of Harwich said, at p. 365:

> "The passage I have cited from the judgment of the Court of Appeal appears to show the court as treating the circumstance that both doctors in evidence estimated the plaintiff's expectation of life at 25 years as establishing the 'fact' or 'assumption' that she would live for 25 years and thus converting the process of assessing future loss into 'a simple arithmetical calculation.' I cannot think that this was the correct approach to the evidence. A man or woman in normal health, at a given age, no doubt has an ascertainable statistical life expectancy. But in using such a figure as the basis for assessment of damages with respect to future losses, some discount in respect of life's manifold contingencies is invariably made."

I have some difficulty with this passage. The plaintiff's life expectancy was not derived from any tables. It was the agreed life expectancy of this particular plaintiff, taking her individual characteristics into account. I cannot for my part see what further room there was for "life's manifold contingencies." The whole point of agreeing a life expectancy, if it can be done, is to exclude any further speculation. With respect therefore I prefer the approach of Sir Thomas Bingham M.R. and the Court of Appeal.

The explanation for the different approach of the House in *Hunt v. Severs* may be a continuing hesitation to embrace the actuarial tables. I do not suggest that the judge should be a slave to the tables. There may well be special factors in particular cases. But the tables should now be regarded as the starting-point, rather than a check. A judge should be slow to depart from the relevant actuarial multiplier on impressionistic grounds, or by reference to "a spread of multipliers in comparable cases" especially when the multipliers were fixed before actuarial tables were widely used. This may be the explanation for the relatively low multiplier chosen by the House in *Lim Poh Choo*'s case.

For the reasons I have given, I consider that the Court of Appeal in the present case were wrong to substitute a multiplier of 17 for the judge's 23. But the judge himself was also too low. The appropriate multiplier derived from the tables on the agreed life expectancy was 26.58."

5.15 The decision in *Wells* will result in significantly higher damages for future loss, particularly where whole-life care is involved. Various aspects of the practical impact of *Wells* are considered in a special edition of "Quantum" published in September 1998. It will no longer be appropriate to have regard to multipliers adopted when the old Guidelines applied. Indeed, in cases of whole-life future expenses the Court should find the multiplier by going straight to the actuarial table issued to the Government actuaries' department.

5.16 There may be a need for a new table of multipliers for loss of *future earnings*, where contingencies have to be taken into account. It could be useful to see what discount the court has made for contingencies in comparable cases.

DEALING WITH FLUCTUATING FUTURE LOSS USING THE MULTIPLIER/MULTIPLICAND APPROACH

Future loss of earnings

5.17 Take the case of a professional or business man incapacitated early in his career, when he was still earning comparatively little, but who had good prospects of greatly increased earnings as his career advanced. Suppose, too, that his age and pre-accident health were such that a multiplier of 15 would be appropriate in the case of a man with steady earnings, where the net annual loss at the date of the trial would be the appropriate multiplicand. The court can approach this problem in two ways, both arbitrary as compared with a reasoned actuarial approach, but both a reasonable way of applying the multiplier/multiplicand method.

The first way would be to estimate the plaintiff's average net annual earnings (ignoring the effect of inflation) over the whole of his future working life and to apply the multiplier of 15 to that sum.

The second way would be to take a low multiplicand for the first part of the multiplier, a rather higher multiplicand for the next part and a still higher multiplicand for the final part.

5.18 We illustrate these methods by taking purely hypothetical figures. If the average net annual earnings were £2X, the multiplier of 15 would result in an award of £30X. If the average initial salary were £X, rising by stages through £2X to a final average net annual figure of £3X, the court could calculate the total award by splitting the multiplier into three parts and award £X × 5, £2X × 5 and £3X × 5, which would give the same total of £30X.

5.19 Examples of the former method are *Brightman v. Johnson* (1985) *The Times*, 17 December (14 × £4,500), *Housecroft v. Burnett* [1986] 1 All E.R. 332 (10 × £5,600), and *Bowden v. Lane* (1990) (see *Kemp & Kemp*, para. A2–104) (14 × £11,000). Examples of the latter method are *Brittain v. Gardner* (4 × £27,462 and 10 × £34,671 and *Burke v. Tower Hamlets H.A.* (1989) *The Times*, 10 August (7½ × £3,865 and 7½ × £2,972). These cases are reported in *Kemp & Kemp*, Vol 2.

Fluctuating future cost of care

5.20 The same methods can be used where the cost of future care will fluctuate, for example where parents who have been looking after a child at home will become too old to continue such intensive care and will have to transfer the child to a residential establishment, or where an elderly plaintiff who is currently able to look after himself with help at his home will likewise have to be cared for in an establishment.

Sometimes the basis of calculating the average annual cost will be stated in the judgement: often, however, it is agreed by the parties or determined by the court without such explanation.

5.21 An example of the split multiplier method is *Francis v. Bostock* (1985) (see *Kemp & Kemp*, para. A2–102) where a multiplier of 13 was applied in the following way: 2 × £6,616 to cover the plaintiff's time at college and 11 × £11,360 to cover residential assistance in her home thereafter. A further example is *Rialas v. Mitchell* (1984) 128 S.J. 704 where a multiplier of 14 was split: as to 5½ × £8,544 for the period when the plaintiff would be at school and as to 8½ × £11,360 for the rest of his life.

5.22 A slightly different method was adopted by Judge J. in *Eastman v. South West Thames Health Authority* [1991] 2 Med.

L.R. 297. He held that the appropriate multiplier to assess the cost of future care for a woman almost 70 years old was 8. The current cost of care was £440 a year, but it was likely to rise to about £5,200 a year. He applied a multiplier of 8 to £440 and took twice £5,200 to cover the increase in cost over the whole period, thereby reaching a total figure of £13,728. (These cases are reported in *Kemp & Kemp*, Vol 2.)

PERIOD OF LOSS

5.23 In the case of both future expense and future loss of earnings the most important contingencies will usually be when the loss will start and how long it will continue.

In cases involving a child

5.24 Take, for example the case of a very young child who is seriously disabled, needs constant care and attention, will never be gainfully employed, but whose expectation of life is not materially reduced. A very different approach is required for the calculation of such plaintiff's future expenses on the one hand and loss of future earnings on the other hand.

5.25 The future expenses will commence at once and will continue throughout the plaintiff's life: indeed, they may increase during the latter part of that life span, since parents, for as long as their age and health permit, will often look after a child at less cost than the cost of outside help, but there will come a time when more expensive outside help has to be obtained. Furthermore, whereas future loss of earnings are subject to contingencies other than mortality, the future expenses will continue subject only to mortality.

5.26 The future loss of earnings, however, will not commence till the child would have been gainfully employed and will continue only from then for the plaintiff's working life. The future earnings would also be subject to contingencies other than mortality, eg unemployment, redundancy, time off work for illness, etc. It follows that the multiplier to be used in such case for the calculation of future expenses should be considerably larger than the multiplier used for the calculation of future loss of earnings.

5.27 The leading case dealing with future loss of earnings in the case of a child is *Cassel v. Riverside Health Authority*: see Appendix A *infra*. Other cases on this aspect of damages are to be found in *Kemp & Kemp*, Vol. 1, para. 6–058 and 6–059.

In cases involving an adult

5.28 Even in the case of adult plaintiffs there may be a considerable difference in the period for which these two different kinds of future loss will be likely to continue.

Take two contrasting cases. Consider first the case of a male manual worker aged 50, who needs constant care and attention and who will never be gainfully employed. He would probably have retired at 65. Accordingly, the span of his loss of future earnings will be 15 years and the calculation of such loss must take account of the receipt of a lump sum in advance of the losses, the risk of mortality and the risk of contingencies other than mortality. Assuming that it has not been reduced by his injuries, his expectation of life would be 23 years. His need for care and attention would continue throughout that period subject to no contingency other than mortality. Accordingly, the multiplier to be used in the calculation of compensation for the future expenses should be considerably larger than that used in the calculation of compensation for his future loss of earnings. The disparity in the respective multipliers should be even greater if we take the case of a female typist of the same age in similar circumstances. She would probably have retired at 60. The span of her future lost earnings would be 10 years, again subject to mortality and other contingencies. But her expectation of life, assuming it not to have been reduced by her injuries, would be 28, and her future expenses would continue throughout this period, subject only to mortality.

5.29 Consider next the case of a male manual worker aged 20, who needs constant care and attention, will never be gainfully employed, but whose expectation of life has been reduced to about three years. The span of his future expenses is three years. But his loss of earnings would cover the three years remaining of his life plus a further loss over 42 "lost years". The calculation of the future loss of earnings may not be easy in such a case, but the multiplier to be used would be much greater than that used for his future expenses.

5.30 If the Tables of Multipliers in *Kemp & Kemp* are analysed, it will be found that sometimes there is surprisingly little difference between the multipliers used for the calculation of future expenses and those used for the calculation of future loss of earnings in factual situations where a significant difference should logically be expected. The calculation of whole-life continuing expense is considered in para. 5.14 *supra*.

PROSPECTIVE LOSS OF EARNINGS

The period of the loss

5.31 As we have already stated, the most important contingency is the period of the loss, when it will start and how long it will continue. An important element in this contingency is the plaintiff's mortality. What are the chances that he would have died before the end of his normal working life? It is here that actuarial evidence can be of great value.

Other contingencies

5.32 The contingencies to be considered in the case of an employed manual worker are likely to include the following: How secure was his job? Did he have periods off work in the past when he was laid off by his employer? Would that probably have happened in the future if he had not been injured? Did he have prospects of promotion? What increase or increases in earnings could he expect if he had been promoted? Even if he could not expect promotion, could he expect better pay as his skills and experience improved? If so, when and at what earnings? If he was in a dangerous and demanding job such as a steel erector, up to what age could he have continued this work? What would the chances of his suffering an injury which would have ended that career in any event? What would he have done and what would he have earned, when he gave up steel erecting? If he was employed in a declining industry, how long would his employment have been likely to continue and what were his prospects of employment outside that industry? Many other contingencies may have to be considered in the circumstances of particular cases.

5.33 In the case of an employed business executive or employed professional, the plaintiff's pre-accident anticipated career will have to be considered. What were his prospects before he was injured?

What are they now? Even if he is not permanently incapacitated from work, the interruption to his career due to injury may have had serious consequences, going far beyond his past loss of earnings during the period of incapacity. A rising business executive may have lost the opportunity of a posting abroad, an important step up the ladder of promotion: the posting may even have gone to a younger person who thereafter remained above him in the company hierarchy, blighting the plaintiff's prospects. A schoolteacher may have lost the opportunity to become head of a teaching department or headteacher. A very promising young professional—actuary, doctor, lawyer or accountant—may have been permanently incapacitated very early in his career: in such a case the court must seek to determine the likely course of his career, if he had not been injured, and his probable earnings at various stages of his working life. In this class of claim, the relevant contingencies can vary so much that little purpose is served in postulating particular contingencies except by way of example. The case of *Cassel v. Hammersmith and Fulham Health Authority* [1992] P.I.Q.R. Q. 1 (see Appendix A) provide a good instance of how the court may approach this problem.

5.34 In the case of a self-employed plaintiff, where the pre-accident earnings of such a plaintiff show a fairly steady trend, the court is likely to assume that the trend would have continued, unless there is some good reason to reach a contrary conclusion. Much will depend upon the nature of the self-employment. The earnings of a window-cleaner or jobbing gardener are not likely to have varied greatly. But if the plaintiff is self-employed in his own business, there may be many imponderable contingencies. He may be in a declining industry, struggling to keep going, in which case his pre-accident earnings will be too favourable a basis on which to assess his future loss of earnings. On the other hand the plaintiff may have invested all his capital and time in a new venture, which was just about to bear fruit and would have been very profitable in years to come.

5.35 The court must in such case assess the plaintiff's financial prospects, on the basis of the probably conflicting evidence of the plaintiff and his accountant on the one hand and the defendant's accountant on the other hand. In some cases, the court may be reduced almost to guesswork. Would an actor have got a certain part, and, if so, what difference would that have made to his career? Would a university lecturer have published his *magnum opus*, the product of years of study, which in the end were wasted and, if so, how would that have affected his academic career? In the field of self-employment there is no limit to the various contingencies that may have to be considered in particular cases.

Loss of or reduction in pension

5.36 In many cases where an injured plaintiff has had to give up work or take less well-paid work this will result in his losing his right to a pension or being entitled only to a lower pension on reaching pensionable age. The calculation of the present value of such loss will depend upon a number of uncertainties, in particular what would have been the pension if the plaintiff had not been injured. If the plaintiff was unlikely to have received promotion, it should be possible to ascertain from the trustees of the pension fund what his pension would probably have been if he had remained in his pre-accident work up to a pensionable age. It should certainly be possible to ascertain what the pension will now in fact be. Given these two pieces of information, there are at least two practicable ways of assessing the present value of the loss. By way of example, take the following postulated facts. The injured plaintiff is aged 36 at the date of the trial. If he had continued in his pre-accident work he would have expected to receive a pension of £4,500 at the age of 60. In his present work he can only expect to receive a pension of £2,000 at the age of 60. One way of ascertaining the present value of this loss would be to seek quotations on the insurance market for a pension of £2,500 for this plaintiff from the age of 60. Another way would be to get an actuary to assess the present value of payments for life of £2,500 per annum commencing at the age of 60. The latter way should produce the fairer result for the defendant since the price charged on the insurance market would include an element of profit for the person providing the pension.

5.37 Tables 7, 8, 9 and 10 and 17, 18, 19 and 20 of the Third Edition of the Ogden Tables should assist practitioners in calculating damages for future pension loss. Dyson J. in *Phipps v. Brooks Dry Cleaning Service Ltd* [1996] P.I.Q.R. Q. 100 used Table 9 to assess damages for loss of future pension. The Court of Appeal approved the use of the Tables.

Handicap in the labour market (commonly known as *Smith v. Manchester* damages)

5.38 In a case where the plaintiff can be shown at the date of the trial to be suffering a loss of earnings, he is obviously "handicapped in the labour market". The phrase "handicap in the labour market" is however not used here to embrace that type of case. The phrase has become almost a term of art to describe the class of case where a disabled plaintiff is not suffering a current loss of earnings at the date of the trial but his injuries have placed him at a disadvantage as compared with his competitors in the labour market (so that he may lose his job more readily than his able-bodied competitors and, if he loses his job, he may find it harder than his able-bodied competitors to obtain another job). The following remarks equally cover the case where the plaintiff is suffering a limited current loss of earnings at the date of the trial but where his handicap in the labour market might well result in a further and greater loss at some future date (the occurrence, timing and amount of such loss being an unknown factor).

5.39 In this class of case the multiplier/multiplicand approach cannot be used. For since the plaintiff is not suffering a current loss there is no relevant multiplicand to be ascertained. The court has to assess the probability and gravity of the plaintiff's future loss owing to his handicap in the labour market. For some sort of guidance given by the Court of Appeal as to the rough scale of damages appropriate to particular classes of cases, see, for example, *Smith v. Manchester Corporation* (1974) 17 K.I.R. 1; *Roberts v. Heavy Transport* (ECC) Ltd Bar Library Transcript No 213 of 1975; *Herod v. Birdseye Foods Bar* Library Transcript No 506 of 1975; *Nicholls v. National Coal Board* [1976] I.C.R. 266; *Moeliker v. A Reyrolle & Co. Ltd* [1977] 1 W.L.R. 132; *Cook v. Consolidated Fisheries Ltd* [1977] I.C.R. 635.

5.40 The best guidance is contained in a passage from the judgment of Stephenson L.J. in *Moeliker's* case [1977] 1 W.L.R. 132 at 144:

> "In assessing damages under this head the judge has to engage in a double speculation, to measure, first, the plaintiff's chances of losing his job, and then his chances, if he loses it, of getting other employment . . . [The judge] has to turn his assessment of the two risks into . . . a suitable number of pounds sterling 'plucked from the air'. The extent of each risk varies with the circumstances of every case. If, as will be rare, both are negligible or fanciful (I avoid 'speculative' because this head of damages can really be nothing else), no award should be made: *Browne v James Broadley Ltd* (unreported) July 16, 1975; a decision of Crichton J. If

one or both are real or substantial, but neither is serious, the award should not be a token or derisory award, but should generally be in hundreds of pounds: *Roberts v Heavy Transport (ECC) Ltd*, May 14, 1975, Bar Library Transcript No 213, a decision of this court . . . The risk of the plaintiff falling out of his present job may be serious or slight, and so may be the risk of his losing much or little if he does fall out of it, because he may be expected to have little or much difficulty in getting equally or less well-paid work. If both risks are serious, the compensation should generally be in thousands of pounds."

(The principles stated in the passage still apply, but the sums should be increased to reflect inflation since 1977. See the Table of awards in *Kemp & Kemp*, Volume 1 paragraph 6–601.

Structured settlements

5.41 The court has no power to order that damages be paid by way of a structured settlement except with the consent of the parties. But, where the award is likely to be a large sum, say, £200,000 or more, there may be such significant advantages for both parties that we expect this practice increasingly to find favour with both plaintiffs and defendants.

5.42 A structured settlement is the facility for a defendant to pay damages in the form of a stream of future annual payments rather than in the traditional lump sum. If the form of such a settlement abides by the agreement made between the Inland Revenue and the Association of British Insurers ("ABI"), then such future payments will be non-taxable. As a result of these arrangements, plaintiffs have the opportunity to save tax and costs that would otherwise have arisen on the investment of the traditional lump sum. They also have the option of receiving their damages in a manner which is linked to their own life expectancy and can also have the certainty of an index-linked income guaranteed for their life. Accordingly, these additional options will provide insurance companies with the possibility of settling the large personal injury and fatal accident cases at sums appreciably lower than might otherwise have been the case. Experience from North America has shown that insurers have benefited to a significant extent by being able to utilise structures. The underwriting market in Canada has shown a noticeable improvement in profits over the years in which structures have become commonplace.

5.43 Structured settlements have been a feature of claims awards in the USA for around 20 years. While such forms of settlement are now extremely popular there, they still rely heavily on agreement between the parties. In only a handful of states does the judiciary have the power formally to award a structured settlement. Specialist companies have been established there in order to advise insurers on the question of structured settlements. The market size of money going into structured settlement annuities is apparently in the order of US$30 billion per annum.

5.44 In Canada, the structured settlement market has been in existence for around 20 years. It was only recently that a formal statute was passed which has simplified the mechanics of paying structures and has provided a clear framework to be followed by those involved in structures. The judiciary does not have the power to award a structured settlement but it is anticipated that this will be a development that will take place shortly. The market for structures in Canada is estimated at over Canadian $150 million per annum.

5.45 The concept of structured settlements allows plaintiffs to receive whatever proportion of their damages they so wish in the form of a series of future annual payments. The balance of the damages would be paid in the manner of the traditional lump sum.

5.46 The general philosophy behind the structure is that once a plaintiff in a large personal injury or fatal accident case had been provided with his/her set-up costs, eg home, equipment and car, and also has a reasonable contingency fund, then the balance of the lump sum is only required as a means to provide an annual income. What happens in fact is that the amount of money that is used to provide a structure is applied by the general insurer to purchase an annuity in order to fund the regular payments that it has to make to the plaintiff as damages by instalments. Effectively the arrangements are back-to-back but there are two very distinct contractual relationships. Thus first, the insurer has an obligation to pay damages to the plaintiff and secondly, by the purchase of an annuity the insurer has a right to receive a series of future payments which are linked to the life of the plaintiff. While there is maximum flexibility in how the annuity can be established at the outset, it should be pointed out that once the structure is established, it cannot be varied. Hence the need for an adequate contingency fund. The types of annuity that are typically of interest to a plaintiff are as follows:

(a) index-linked;

(b) guaranteed for a minimum number of years or for the duration of the plaintiff's life, whichever is longer;

(c) can allow for streamed lump-sum payments in the future, in addition to the regular sums, in anticipation of the changing needs of the plaintiff.

The mechanics are that the general insurer will pay out to the plaintiff damages by instalments which may be index-linked and last for the life of the plaintiff or for a specified number of years, if longer. In turn, the general insurer purchases an annuity from a Life Office in order to fund the series of payments as determined above.

5.47 The first structured settlement in a personal injuries claim in England took place in July 1989. Potter J. approved it in a claim by Catherine Kelly, a plaintiff under a disability. The judge was satisfied that the form in which the plaintiff's case was settled was advantageous to the plaintiff. The defendant's insurers clearly regarded this arrangement as satisfactory from their view-point: they would not otherwise have agreed to it.

An important recent development was the agreement in 1991 of a structured settlement in an English medical negligence action against a health authority. The plaintiff was Rebecca Field. Following a change in 1990 in the rule regarding Crown indemnity, such settlements are now possible in cases involving health authorities and it is hoped and expected that many more such settlements will follow.

5.48 Details of the mechanism required to gain the tax advantages provided by the Inland Revenue's agreement are complex and beyond the scope of this book. Readers who wish to know more about this interesting and important development in personal injuries litigation are referred to Chapter 6A of *Kemp & Kemp*, Vol 1. This Chapter was kindly contributed by Peter Andrews Q.C. the joint author of "Catastrophic Injuries"

Where the Plaintiff's Expectation of Life is Reduced

5.49 We conclude this chapter with a consideration of pecuniary loss in "the lost years". We are directly concerned only with claims made by a living plaintiff, whose life has been shortened by injuries and who seeks damages as compensation for the pecuniary benefit which he would have received during the span of life of which he has been deprived—'the lost years'. This was held to be a valid claim by the House of Lords in *Pickett v. British Rail Engineering* [1980] A.C. 136 reversing *Oliver and Ashman* [1962] 2 Q.B. 210.

5.50 We shall nevertheless have to consider and discuss claims made on behalf of the estate of a deceased victim under the Law Reform (Miscellaneous Provisions) Act 1934 for damages in respect of pecuniary benefit which the deceased would have received during the span of life of which he has been deprived. Such claims were held by the House of Lords to be valid in *Gammell v. Wilson* [1982] A.C. 27, a necessary logical consequence of the decision in *Pickett*'s case but one which could cause injustice to a defendant, who might have to pay damages twice over where the beneficiaries entitled to share in the deceased's estate do not coincide with the dependants entitled to claim under the Fatal Accidents Act 1976. This injustice was removed by section 4(2) of the Administration of Justice Act 1982, which abolished such claims in the case of deaths after December 31, 1982.

5.51 The reason why "*Gammell* claims" must be considered here is that the principles governing the practical assessment of "*Pickett* claims" have to a large extent been worked out in *Gammell* claims. There is, indeed, a danger that in the court's understandable desire to reduce the undeserved windfall in some *Gammell* claims, assessments at the lowest margin of any reasonable bracket may become the rule, and so may rub off on and adversely affect meritorious *Pickett* claims.

5.52 Pecuniary benefits which may form the subject of a "lost years" claim are not confined to lost earnings. Nevertheless, that is the most usual class of "lost years" claim, and our observations are largely confined to that class of claim.

5.53 With a living plaintiff the size and significance of a *Pickett* claim will largely depend upon his age and his expectation of life at the date of the trial. If, for example, he is a labourer aged 20 with a normal expectation of life of about 51 years, which has been reduced by his injuries to an actual anticipated life of 36 years, the loss in the "lost years" is so far away that little value will be attributed to it. A multiplier of 16 or 17 would probably be used to calculate the damages over the period of his actual anticipated life of

36 years and nothing would be added to cover the span of years from 56 to 71 of which he has been deprived.

5.54 On the other hand if the plaintiff is a high earning professional or business man aged 55, with a normal expectation of life of 19 years, which has been reduced by his injuries to two years, the *Pickett* claim would be substantial.

5.55 We have taken these two extremes to illustrate our point. Each case will depend on its particular facts.

General principles

5.56 Before considering the practical approach adopted by the court, one should bear in mind the general principles to be applied in the assessment of damages in "lost years" claims, as stated by Lord Scarman in *Gammell*'s case at p. 78:

> "The correct approach in law to the assessment of damages in these cases presents, my Lords, no difficulty, though the assessment itself often will. The principle must be that the damages should be fair compensation for the loss suffered by the deceased in his lifetime. The appellant in *Gammell*'s case was disposed to argue by analogy with damages for loss of expectation of life, that, in the absence of cogent evidence of loss, the award should be a modest conventional sum. There is no room for a 'conventional' award in a case of alleged loss of earnings of the lost years. The loss is pecuniary. As such, it must be shown, on the facts found, to be at least capable of being estimated. If sufficient facts are established to enable the court to avoid the fancies of speculation, even though not enabling it to reach mathematical certainty, the court must make the best estimate it can. In civil litigation it is the balance of probabilities which matters. In the case of a young child, the lost years of earning capacity will ordinarily be so distant that assessment is mere speculation. No estimate being possible, no award—not even a 'conventional' award—should ordinarily be made. Even so, there will be exceptions: a child television star, cut short in her prime at the age of five, might have a claim: it would depend on the evidence. A teenage boy or girl, however, as in *Gammell*'s case may well be able to show either actual employment or real prospects, in either of which situations there will be an assessable claim. In the case of a young man, already in employment (as was young Mr Furness), one would

expect to find evidence upon which a fair estimate of loss can be made. A man, well established in life, like Mr Pickett, will have no difficulty. But in all cases it is a matter of evidence and a reasonable estimate based upon on it."

The practical approach

5.57 Until the decision of the Court of Appeal in the combined appeals, *Harris v. Empress Motors Ltd* and *Cole v. Crown Poultry Packers Ltd* [1984] 1 W.L.R. 212, different judges at first instance had adopted varying methods to assess damages for lost income during the lost years. The House of Lords in *Pickett*'s case and *Gammell*'s case had laid down the principle that the amount to be recovered in this type of claim should be assessed after deduction of an estimated sum to represent the victim's probable living expenses during the lost years, but gave little assistance as to how such living expenses should be ascertained. In the appeal in *Harris*'s and *Cole*'s cases O'Connor LJ, giving the man judgment of the court, sought to give practical guidance on this aspect of the problem. Prior to this decision of the Court of Appeal there had been conflicting decisions.

5.58 As already stated, for the purpose of deducting an estimated sum for the victim's living expenses during the lost years, there is no difference in principle between the court's approach to a *Pickett* claim and its approach to a *Gammell* claim.

5.59 The effect of the Court of Appeal's decision in *Harris*'s and in *Cole*'s cases can best be explained by citing passages from O'Connor L.J.'s judgment, with which Stephenson and Goff L.J. agreed.

5.60 In each case the judge at first instance had adopted the Fatal Accidents Act dependency approach and had deducted 25 per cent from the net earnings in assessing damages for the lost earnings during the lost years.

5.61 O'Connor L.J. analysed the speeches of their Lordships in *Pickett*'s and *Gammell*'s cases. He then continued at p. 228 as follows:

> "I return to the two decisions in the House of Lords. In my judgment three principles emerge: (1) the ingredients that go to make up 'living expenses' are the same whether the victim be young or old, single or married, with or without dependants;

(2) the sum to be deducted as living expenses is the proportion of the victim's net earnings that he spends to maintain himself at the standard of life appropriate to his case; (3) any sums expended to maintain or benefit others do not form part of the victim's living expenses and are not to be deducted from the net earnings.

The second and third principles, apparently straightforward enough, in fact contain a hidden difficulty. The difficulty is well exemplified by the example given by Mr Ogden in argument. A bachelor is living in a flat which is costing him £2,000 per annum rent, rates, light and heat. This expenditure undoubtedly forms part of his living expenses. He marries a wife who moves in to live in the flat, and for this example is not herself earning or providing money to the family fund. Her presence makes no difference whatsoever to the cost of the flat. I find it quite impossible to say that this expenditure has suddenly ceased to be part of the husband's living expenses, yet the Fatal Accidents Act solution would lead inexorably to that result, for if one is considering the wife's dependency she is dependent to the value of the whole cost of the flat. In contrast I can see the attraction of asserting that the full cost of the flat remains part of the husband's living expenses, but I do not think that that result is compatible with the third principle.

The cost of the flat which had been expenditure solely for the benefit of the husband has now become expenditure for the joint benefit of husband and wife: this presents a simple compromise, namely that half the cost should be looked upon as referable to each of them. I recognise that it may be argued that it is no more logical to assert that this head of living expense has been halved by marriage, rather than altogether extinguished, but I do not think that this is right because to consider it extinguished involves a change in principle, namely that the cost of housing does not form part of a person's living expenses, whereas to consider it halved does not involve such a change but only an alteration in the amount of money allocated to it. It also confirms the old adage that 'two can live cheaper than one'.

The items of living expenses which are shared in practice will be found to be limited to the cost of housing, that is to say rent or mortgage interest, rates, heating, electricity and gas; the cost of running a motor car, the telephone and I suppose the television licence. Further, it seems to me that as the numbers of persons provided for out of the victim's net earnings increase, so must the amount to be allocated as being his share of those items fall. Therefore, in the present case, where the households consisted of four persons, one-quarter of the cost of the joint items should be deducted. In practice this may result in the total deduction not being very much greater than that made for the purposes of the Fatal Accidents Act 1976.

I think one can say in relation to a man's net earnings that any proportion thereof that he saves or spends exclusively for the maintenance or benefit of others does not form part of his living expenses. Any proportion that he spends exclusively upon himself does. In cases where there is a proportion of the earnings expended on what may conveniently be called shared living expenses, a pro rata part of that proportion should be allocated for deduction. In rejecting the straight Fatal Accidents Act solution I realise that I am differing from a considerable body of judicial opinion in the Queen's Bench Division, including the two judges in the present cases. I also reject the 'savings only' solution because I do not think it possible to say that money spent on others should be reckoned as part of a man's living expenses in the sense required by the House of Lords."

5.62 O'Connor L.J. then went on to consider the "available surplus" propounded by Webster J. in *White v. London Transport Executive* [1982] Q.B. 489, concluding that it was an acceptable approach in cases of young persons. He then considered whether the court should, as requested, lay down guidelines on the proportion of net earnings in the lost years which should be deducted in Law Reform Act claims. He continued:

"Regretfully, I find it impossible to do this because so much depends upon the amount of the joint expenditure and the number of persons among whom it is to be divided; but in general, according to the circumstances it seems to me that the proportion will be greater than the percentage used for calculating the dependency under the Fatal Accidents Act.

What is to be done in the present two cases? As I am clear that the judges have made the Law Reform assessment on an erroneous principle, the appeals must be allowed. We have no material upon which we can make the assessment ourselves; therefore the cases will have to go back for reassessment unless, as

I hope, the parties can agree what the figures should be in these two cases. As I have said earlier in this judgment, it may well be that the result will not have any drastic effect on the double recovery that has occurred in the *Harris* case, and nor will there be any great reduction in the amount of the award in the *Cole* case."

5.63 Although the Court of Appeal felt unable to give any more precise guidance as to what proportion of the net earnings should be deducted as being the estimated living expenses of the injured victim, an attempt is made below to apply the three principles laid down by O'Connor L.J. to certain hypothetical cases.

The basic principle is that sums spent to maintain the victim at the standard of life appropriate to his case should be deducted. This is subject to the qualification that sums expended for the joint benefit of the victim and others should only be regarded as the victim's living expenses to the extent of his share of the joint expenditure.

Married man with no children

5.64 Take the case of a married man with no children and apply the conventional basis of calculating the dependency, described by O'Connor L.J. The Fatal Accidents Act dependency would be about 66 per cent of net earnings, including therein about 33 per cent for joint expenditure. Deduct half the value of the joint expenditure, and the resulting deduction for estimated living expenses is about 50 per cent.

5.65 But in making such an assessment in the case of a young, newly married victim it would not be right to assume that this childless state would necessarily continue. Accordingly, after the expiry of part of the lost years, it might be right to assess his deductible living expenses on the basis of a married man with, say, two children. On the other hand a middle-aged couple, who have been married some time and have no children, may reasonably be deemed to remain childless. Much must depend upon the facts of the particular case.

Married man with two children

5.66 On the same conventional basis take the case of a married man with two children. The Fatal Accidents Act dependency would be about 75 per cent of net earnings. The items of joint expenditure, namely, rent or mortgage interest, rates, heating, gas, electricity, telephone, motor car, television etc, would not significantly increase with the increased family unit, and so would remain at about 33 per cent of net earnings. One-quarter of this joint expenditure is to be added to living expenses solely attributable to the victim, say, 8 per cent. The resulting deduction for living expenses would be 25 per cent plus 8 per cent, ie 33 per cent.

Married man with four children

5.67 Add two more children: the victim's share of the joint expenses comes down to 33/6 per cent = 5.5 per cent. The resulting deduction for the victim's living expenses would thus be about 30 per cent. This, as O'Connor L.J. remarked, is not much greater than the conventional deduction from net earnings in calculating the Fatal Accidents Act dependency in like circumstances.

Young single man

5.68 How are the three principles to be applied to a young single man? Webster J.'s approach in *White v. London Transport Executive* (see para. 5.62 above) gives some guidance. A young man living at home with his parents may be regarded as having an available surplus of 33 per cent of his net earnings. When he gets a flat of his own, the available surplus may fall to 25 per cent. But when he marries, the available surplus may rise to 50 per cent since one-half of the joint expenditure will not count as part of his living expenses. And, as his family increases, the available surplus will increase as indicated in the examples already considered.

5.69 And it must be remembered that a young victim, unmarried at the date of the trial or his death, as the case may be, is not normally to be treated as an eternally single man.

Other categories of victim

5.70 The word "victim" is used to include the deceased in a *Gammell* type claim and a living plaintiff in a *Pickett* type claim. There may well be other types of victim. Young single girls, middle-aged or elderly single women, with or without dependent relatives. It would serve no useful purpose to speculate how the court will deal with such cases. No doubt the court will seek to apply the principles laid down in *Harris*'s case, as best it can.

5.71 When one is dealing with a very young victim, whether alive or dead, the loss of earnings in the lost years is so far distant and so speculative that no award under this head is likely to be made, except perhaps in such cases as that of a child film star cut off in her prime, a possibility envisaged by Lord Scarman in *Gammell*'s case.

Pecuniary loss is not confined to lost earnings

5.72 Although most of the reported cases are concerned with lost earnings during the "lost years", the principle laid down by the House of Lords goes wider and extends to all pecuniary loss. Lord Scarman dealt with the point at p. 169 in *Pickett*'s case: "If damages are recoverable for the loss of the prospect of earnings during the lost years, must it not follow that they are also recoverable for loss of other reasonable expectations, eg a life interest or an inheritance?" He continued at p. 170:

> "I agree with the Law Commission, where in paragraph 90 of Law Case No 56 they say:
>
> 'There seems to be no justification in principle for discrimination between deprivation of earning capacity and deprivation of the capacity otherwise to receive economic benefits. The loss must be regarded as a loss of the plaintiff; and it is a loss caused by the tort even though it relates to moneys which the injured person will not receive because of his premature death. No question of the remoteness of damage arises other than the application of the ordinary forseeability test.'
>
> For myself, as at present advised (for the point does not arise for decision and has not been argued), I would allow a plaintiff to recover damages for the loss of his financial expectations during the lost years provided always the loss was not too remote."

5.73 This question in fact arose for decision in *Adsett v. West* [1983] Q.B. 826 and in *Marley v. Ministry of Defence* (1984) (unreported); *Kemp & Kemp*, Vol. 1. In both cases damages for loss other than loss of earnings were awarded. For a fuller discussion of the decision in *Adsett v. West* see *Kemp & Kemp*, Vol. 1, para. 6.113.

Exceptional cases, where scope of loss may be wide and only minimal living expenses would be deducted

5.74 It has already been emphasised that the heading to this topic is pecuniary loss and not merely lost *earnings* in the lost years. As Lord Scarman indicated in the passages already cited from his speech in *Pickett's* case, the victim should also be entitled to recover damages for the lost expectation of a capital sum, eg the vesting of a reversionary interest within the lost years or the receipt of a legacy or inheritance, or some other specific sum which would have come to him during the lost years. An example of this last category might be the sum due upon the completion of an entire contract most of which had already been carried out prior to his injury and which would certainly have been completed by some early period—within the lost years. There is a further feature of this type of lost financial expectation. Where a substantial capital sum would have been due early in the lost years, there is no reason to make any deduction for living expenses except for the period of the lost years expiring before the sum would have fallen due.

5.75 The following hypothetical cases will illustrate this point: suppose that, in consideration of A marrying B, C covenants to pay A £50,000, if A attains the age of 25. Suppose further that A's life expectation is held to have been reduced to one year at the date when his claim comes to trial and when he is aged 22. In a *Pickett* type claim, A should be awarded substantial damages for loss of the almost certain expectation of £50,000 in three years' time and at most only three years' living expenses should be deducted when assessing those damages.

Loss of pension rights

5.75 In appropriate cases loss of pension rights, whether under a State scheme or under a private scheme, could also found a claim for pecuniary loss in the lost years. Its assessment would no doubt present difficulties in many cases. An instance of a successful claim for loss of pension rights is *Marley v Ministry of Defence*. Loss of pension rights is considered in more detail in *Kemp & Kemp* Vol. 1 paras 6.121 6.134.

Chapter 6

The Incidence of Benefits

David Kemp Q.C.

Contents *Para*

PERSONAL INJURY CLAIMS

THE INCIDENCE OF BENEFITS OTHER THAN SOCIAL SECURITY BENEFITS

The general rule

6.1 The rule is well stated in the following extract from the speech of Lord Bridge in *Hodgson v. Trapp* [1989] A.C. 807 at 819E:

"My Lords, it cannot be emphasised too often when considering the assessment of damages for negligence that they are intended to be purely compensatory. Where the damages claimed are essentially financial in character, being the measure on the one hand of the injured plaintiff's consequential loss of earnings, profits or other gains which he would have made if not injured, or on the other hand, of consequential expenses to which he had been and will be put which, if not injured, he would not have needed to incur, the basic rule is that it is the net consequential loss and expense which the court must measure. If, in consequence of the injuries sustained, the plaintiff has enjoyed receipts to which he would not otherwise have been entitled, *prima facie*, those receipts are to be set against the aggregate of the plaintiff's losses and expenses in arriving at the measure of his damages. All this is elementary and has been said over and over again. To this basic rule there are, of course, certain well established, though not always precisely defined and delineated exceptions. But the courts are, I think, sometimes in danger, in seeking to explore the rationale of the exceptions, of forgetting that they are exceptions. It is the rule which is fundamental and axiomatic and the exceptions to it which are only to be admitted on grounds which clearly justify their treatment as such."

The established exceptions

6.2 *Insurance money. Bradburn v. Great Western Railway* Co. (1874) L.R. 10 Ex. 1: the rationale of this exception is twofold. First, the plaintiff does not receive the money because of the injury but because he has made a contract providing for payment in the event of injury. Secondly, it would be unjust to allow the tortfeasor to take the benefit of the premium paid by the plaintiff.

6.3 *Private pensions:* The law on this subject was established by the House of Lords in *Parry v. Cleaver* [1970] A.C. 1, overruling the decision of the Court of Appeal in *Browning v. War Office* [1963] 1 Q.B. 750. Private pensions are disregarded when assessing damages for lost earnings. On the other hand, they are taken into account in assessing damages for loss of pension rights. This is an instance of the general rule that only benefits of a like nature are deducted against a particular head of damage. Thus, the House of Lords held in *Longden v. British Coal Corporation* [1997] 3 W.L.R. 1336 that against loss of retirement pension there are to be set off only sums received by way of incapacity pension arising *in the same period.*

6.4 The present position can be summarised as follows:

A. Sums received by way of pension (whether retirement pension or incapacity pension) cannot be set off against loss of earnings.

B. This principle applies even if the defendant has paid for or contributed to the pension: *Smoker v. London Fire and Civil Defence Authority* [1991] 2 A.C. 502, *per* Lord Templeman:

> "In the present case counsel for the defendants sought to distinguish the decision of this House in *Parry v. Cleaver* [1970] A.C. 1 on the ground that the defendants are in the triple position of employers, tortfeasors and insurers. In my opinion this makes no difference to the principle that the plaintiff has bought his pension which is, in the words of Lord Reid, at p. 16 'the fruit, through insurance, of all the money which was set aside in the past in respect of his past work'. The fruit cannot be appropriated by the tortfeasor."

C. Only incapacity pension to which a plaintiff is, or would be, entitled during retirement is to be set off against loss of retirement pension: (see *Longden's* case).

D. Where incapacity benefit is paid wholly or partly by a lump sum, only such proportion of the lump sum should be set off against loss of retirement pension as is attributable to the period when a plaintiff is, or would be, entitled to retirement pension: (see *Longden's* case).

6.5 *An hypothetical example*: The plaintiff is a man injured at age 30, who thereby suffers loss of earnings; his expectation of life is then 45 years; he would be entitled to a retirement pension at age 65.

If he had not been injured, the present value of the future retirement pension would have been £X: as the result of his injury it is now only £Y. Accordingly, his loss of pension before setting off any relevant benefit is £X − £Y.

Result:

No part of the incapacity benefit is set off against loss of earnings.

The present value of the pension payable for the first 35 years (up to retirement) is disregarded in the assessment of pension loss.

£P, the present value of the pension payable for the remaining 10 years of life is set off against pension loss.

The proportion of the lump sum attributable to the first 35 years is disregarded in the assessment of pension loss.

£L, the proportion of the lump sum attributable to the remaining 10 years of life is set off against pension loss.

The pension loss is, therefore, (£X − £Y)–(£P + £L).

6.6 In *West v. Versil Ltd* (Court of Appeal, July 2, 1996) the plaintiff, because of his injuries, had retired early and chose to draw his pension at 60 rather than 65. He claimed loss of earnings from his retirement date up to age 65, when he would have retired if he had not been injured. The court held that his pension should not be taken into account against his loss of earnings.

6.7 The plaintiff, because of his reduced expectation of life, had chosen to take a surviving wife pension, rather than a single life pension. The court held that his widow's entitlement to a pension after his death should not be taken into account against his claim for loss of his own pension during his "lost years". He had bought his wife's pension by taking a lower pension himself. The defendants could not take credit for this benefit which the plaintiff had paid for.

6.8 *Ex gratia pension*: An *ex gratia* pension paid by the injured plaintiff's employer is not taken into account: (see *Cunningham v. Harrison* [1973] Q.B. 942.

This is really an instance of a charitable donation rather than a pension. It should be noted, however, that the employer was not the defendant. If he had been, the court might well have taken the *ex gratia* pension into account, depending on the circumstances of the donation.

6.9 *Charitable donations*. Charitable donations are not deducted from a plaintiff's damages, except perhaps where the donor is the defendant himself. In such a case much would depend upon the circumstances of the donation and in particular whether it was intended to be taken into account in assessing any sum for which the defendant might be liable to the plaintiff.

The rationale of the charitable exception is that the injured plaintiff does not receive the money because of the injury but because of the bounty or benevolence of third parties motivated by sympathy for his misfortune. It would be unjust to allow the tortfeasor to take the benefit of this benevolence. In *Parry v. Cleaver* (see para. 6.3 above) Lord Reid said:

> "It would be revolting to the ordinary man's sense of justice, and therefore contrary to public policy, that the sufferer should have his damage reduced so that he would gain nothing from the benevolence of his friends or relations or of the public at large, and that the only gainer would be the wrongdoer."

6.10 *Other charitable assistance.* Benevolent payment of proceeds from an accident insurance policy taken out by the defendant-employer: *McCamley v. Cammell Laird Ltd* [1990] 1 All E.R. 854:

> "The reason why the judge came to the correct decision on this matter is that the payment to the plaintiff was a payment by way of benevolence, even though the mechanics required the use of an insurance policy. The payment was not an ex gratia act where the accident had already happened, but the whole idea of the policy, covering all the many employees of British Shipbuilders and its subsidiary companies, was clearly to make the benefit payable as an act of benevolence whenever a qualifying injury took place."

6.11 Assistance by parent's provision of board and lodging: in *Liffen v. Watson* [1940] 1 K.B. 556, C.A., the plaintiff was a domestic servant and as the result of her personal injuries she was unable for a period to continue in her employment in which she received, in addition to her wages, free board and lodging by her father. Stable J. refused to award the plaintiff any damages in respect of the loss of board and lodging. The Court of Appeal reversed the decision of Stable J. on this point. *Per* Goddard L.J.:

> "The question whether the plaintiff was entitled to recover damages under that head from the defendant does not depend on whether or not she had made a contract for board and lodging with someone else. The plaintiff lost her right to the board and

lodging provided by her employer because she was rendered by the accident unfit for work. The only consideration is what the plaintiff lost."

THE INCIDENCE OF OTHER BENEFITS

Statutory sick pay

6.12 This should be deducted: *Palfrey v. G.L.C.* [1985] I.C.R. 437. Nor does it make any difference if the employers, who paid the plaintiff sick pay, are reimbursed for such payment by reason of an insurance policy taken out by the employers (see *Hussain v. New Taplow Paper Mills Ltd* [1988] A.C. 514). The sums were payable under a term of the employee's contract to the employee *qua* employee as a partial substitute for earnings. *Per* Lord Bridge:

> "It positively offended his Lordship's sense of justice that a plaintiff who had certainly paid no insurance premiums as such, should receive full wages during a period of incapacity from two different sources the employer and the tortfeasor. It would seem still more unjust and anomalous where, as in the present case, the employer and the tortfeasor were one and the same." (See para. 6. below.)

Redundancy payments

6.13 A redundancy payment is made because the recipient has been dismissed by reason of redundancy. Normally the payment has nothing to do with the recipient's injury or incapacity and, in principle, should not therefore be taken into account in the assessment of damages for personal injuries. *Mills v. Hassal* [1983] I.L.R. 330 is a decision of Heilbron J. to this effect. The decision of the Court of Appeal in *Cheeseman v. Bowaters U.K. Paper Mills* [1971] 1 W.L.R. 1773 should not be regarded as authority for the contrary proposition. In that case it was conceded at first instance that a redundancy payment should be taken into account in reduction of the plaintiff's damages. On appeal the plaintiff sought to resile from this concession but was not allowed to do so.

6.14 Whilst the decision of Heilbron J. in *Mills v. Hassel* represents the normal position, there may be exceptional circumstances where the redundancy payments should be deducted. In *Wilson v. National Coal Board* [1981] S.L.T. 67, a decision of the House of Lords, the plaintiff, a miner, was injured in an accident at work. He was kept on the workforce, although unable to resume his duties, until the colliery closed about a year after his accident, whereupon he was dismissed for redundancy. But for his incapacity the plaintiff would not have been made redundant but would have accepted alternative employment at a neighbouring colliery, as did his workmates. The House of Lords held that it would be unjust and unreasonable to assess the damages on the basis that but for the accident the plaintiff would have remained in his employment and yet to refrain from taking into account a redundancy payment made because he was not going to continue because of his injuries. The redundancy payment was therefore deducted from the loss of earnings claim. The position in law is that if the plaintiff would not have been made redundant if he had not been injured, the redundancy payment is to be deducted from his pecuniary damages: if he would have been made redundant even if he had not been injured, the redundancy payment is not to be deducted. The issue will be a question of fact to be determined on the circumstances of the particular case.

Conditional loan by employer

6.15 Sometimes, though the plaintiff has been incapacitated from work because of his injuries, his employer has paid him a sum equivalent to the wages which he would have earned during the period of incapacity, upon the understanding that such sum should be repaid to the employer in the event of the plaintiff successfully suing the author of his injuries. In such case the plaintiff is entitled to recover damages in respect of the loss of wages.

6.16 The position is different if the plaintiff had not in fact lost his wages because, for instance, his employer is obliged by statutory regulations to pay him his wages whether he is fit for duty or not. In such a case the plaintiff has suffered no loss and can recover no damages.

Free maintenance in a public institution

6.17 Section 5 of the Administration of Justice Act 1982 provides that any saving to the plaintiff which is attributable to his maintenance wholly or partly at public expense shall be set off against any income lost by him as the result of his injuries. The effect of this provision is to reverse the decision of the Court of Appeal in *Daigh v. Wauton* [1972] 2 Q.B. 262.

Savings on living expenses in other respects

6.18 The general principle to be applied in decided what living expenses should be deducted from pecuniary damages can be derived from the decision of the Court of Appeal in *Shearman v. Follard* [1950] 1 Q.B. 43, and the decision of the House of Lords in *Lim Poh Choo*'s case [1980] A.C. 174. In *Lim*'s case the plaintiff, who had sustained extensive and irremediable brain damage, was totally dependent upon others. The claim included claims for both loss of earnings and cost of care. The House of Lords held that the "domestic elements" of the plaintiff's care should be deducted from the cost of care claim and that, by the same token, the expenses that she would have incurred in earning her living should be deducted from the loss of earnings claim.

6.19 A further case of saving in living expenses would be where an injured plaintiff had commuted, say from Brighton to London, regularly in order to earn in the City the lost earnings in respect of which he claims damages. As a matter of principle the expense of such travel to work should be deducted as being an expense required in order to earn the lost earnings. This topic arose for discussion but not decision by the House of Lords in *Dews v. National Coal Board* [1988] 1 A.C. 1. *Per* Lord Griffiths:

> "... wherever a man lives he is likely to incur *some* travelling expenses to work which will be saved during his period of incapacity, and they are strictly expenses necessarily incurred for the purpose of earning his living. It would, however, be intolerable in every personal injury action to have an inquiry into travelling expenses to determine that part necessarily attributable to a chosen life-style. I know of no case in which travelling expenses to work have been deducted from a weekly wage, and although the point does not fall for decision, I do not encourage any insurer or employer to seek to do so. I can, however, envisage a case where travelling expenses loom as so large an element in the damage that further consideration of the question would be justified as, for example, in the case of a wealthy man who

commuted daily by helicopter from the Channel Islands to London."

Tax rebate due to period off work

6.20 If as the result of the plaintiff's absence from work due to his injuries, he receives a tax rebate, the tax rebate is to be deducted from his lost earnings: *Hartley v. Sandholme Iron Co. Ltd* [1975] Q.B. 600.

Payment under a job release scheme

6.21 Where consequent upon his injuries the plaintiff availed himself of a job release scheme, the payments received under the scheme were deducted from his lost earnings: *Crawley v. Mercer* (1984) *The Times*, 9 March.

Student maintenance grant

6.22 In *Sully v. Doggett*, Court of Appeal, Transcript 1984 No. 463, the plaintiff, who suffered injuries in a road accident, employed the time during which, because of her intermittent spells in hospital, she was unable to take remunerative employment, in taking a university degree course. To enable her to pursue the course she obtained a local authority student maintenance grant under the Education (Mandatory Awards) Regulations 1981. The Court of Appeal held that the plaintiff would not have been able, apart from the accident, to attend the course unless she had given up her job and the wages attached to it. Taking the course and receiving the grant were therefore directly related to the accident and her loss of wages, and the maintenance payments under the grant could not properly be treated as collateral benefits. Accordingly the award fell to be deducted from the plaintiff's damages.

Foreign welfare benefit: repayable by plaintiff if he is awarded damages: not deductible

6.23 In *Berriello v. Felixstowe Dock & Railway Co* [1989] 1 W.L.R. 695, the plaintiff was an Italian seaman who was injured when the vessel on which he was employed was being loaded by the defendants, a firm of stevedores, at Felixstowe docks. As a result of his disabilities the plaintiff received 11,875,480 lire as indemnification for temporary disability and was notified that he would receive a further capital payment of 121,965,619 lire in respect of future income from a seaman's fund administered by the Italian State. Under Italian law those sums could be recovered from the plaintiff by the fund if he was awarded damages in respect of losses for which the payments were made.

6.24 The Court of Appeal held that, in assessing damages, the two sums paid and payable to the plaintiff to compensate him for his loss of earnings should not be deducted.

THE INCIDENCE OF SOCIAL SECURITY BENEFITS

The Social Security (Recovery of Benefits) Act 1997

6.25 The Social Security Act 1989 introduced the new concept of recoupment of benefits from damages. We refer to this concept as "the new law". The new law has from time to time been contained in various statutory provisions. Now, however, all its relevant statutory provisions are contained on the Social Security (Recovery of Benefits) Act 1997 ("the Act") and the Regulations made thereunder. The Act came into force on October 6, 1997. The text of the Act is set out in full in Appendix B. The pattern of the law continues as before, but there are important changes as detailed below.

Changes from previous law

6.26 The following important changes were made by s. 8 read with Schedule 2:

(i) Recoupment is no longer to be made from general damages for pain and suffering and loss of amenities.

(ii) Recoupment from damages for loss of earnings is to be made only in respect of specified benefits, which go to compensate for loss of earnings.

(iii) Recoupment from damages for cost of care is to be made only in respect of specified benefits, which go towards the cost of care.

(iv) Recoupment from damages for loss of mobility is to be made only in respect of specified benefits, which go towards the cost of mobility.

In short, there is deduction only of like from like.

6.27 The previous "small payments exemption" of £2,500 no longer exists, but the Secretary of State has power under s. 24 read with Schedule 1 to provide by regulation for "small payments" as defined in the regulation to be exempt.

6.28 Section 8 has one surprising and unfortunate effect. It provides:

> "This Act applies in relation to compensation payments made on or after the day on which this section comes into effect, unless they are made in pursuance of a court order or agreement made before that date."

The section came into effect on October 6, 1997. Thus, compensation payments made after that date in respect of an accident or injury occurring *before January 1, 1989*, or in respect of a disease if the victim's first claim for a relevant benefit in consequence of the disease was made *before January 1, 1989*, now fall retrospectively into the jaws of the recoupment scheme. Such compensation payments were not affected by the Social Security Act 1989, since that Act did not come into force until September 3, 1990. Such payments were later expressly excluded from the recoupment scheme by s. 81(7) of the Social Security Administration Act 1992. Section 81(7) was repealed by the 1997 Act, which included no comparable exclusion.

Interest

6.29 Section 103 of the 1992 Act had provided as follows:

> "In assessing the amount of interest payable in respect of an award of damages, the amount of the award shall be treated as reduced by a sum equal to the amount of the relevant payment (if any) required to be made in connection with the payment of the damages and:
>
> (a) in England and Wales, if both special and general damages are awarded, any such reduction shall be treated as made first against the special damages and then, as respects any remaining balance, against the general damages; and
>
> (b) in Scotland, if damages are awarded both for patrimonial loss and for solatium, any such reduction shall be treated as made first against the damages for patrimonial

loss and then, as respects any remaining balance, against the damages for solatium."

Section 103 (which was contained in Part IV of the 1992 Act) was repealed by the 1997 Act. The repeal appears to have been effected twice!—both by section 33(1) read with Schedule 3 to the Act and also by section 33(2) read with Schedule 4 to the Act. There is no provision in the 1997 Act comparable to section 103 of the 1992 Act. It would, therefore, appear that plaintiffs, as from October 6, 1997, are entitled to interest on the whole of their damages. (See the article by Nicholas Davies in *Quantum*, Issue 5/6 of 1997.)

Contributory negligence

6.30 The position remains the same as under previous legislation. There is no provision in the Act for reducing recoupment to take account of contributory negligence. The practical consequences are considered in an article by Julian Horne in *Quantum* Issue 5/6 of 1997. For example, a defendant held liable for only 20 per cent of the damages will have, by virtue of section 6 of the Act, to pay to the Secretary of State 100 per cent of the certified recoverable benefits.

Main provisions of the Act

6.31 There are set out below the main provisions of the Act. The Act is complex and detailed. Practitioners should study the full text of the Act to gain a proper understanding of its provisions.

Compensation payments to which the Act applies

6.32 Section 2 provides:

"This Act applies in relation to compensation payments made on or after the day on which this section comes into force, unless they are made in pursuance of a court order or agreement made before that day."

Cases in which the Act applies

6.33 Section 1 provides:

"(1) This Act applies in cases where—

(a) a person makes a payment (whether on his own behalf or

not) to or in respect of any other person in consequence of any accident, injury or disease suffered by the other, and

(b) any listed benefits have been, or are likely to be, paid to or for the other during the relevant period in respect of the accident, injury or disease.

(2) The reference above to a payment in consequence of any accident, injury or disease is to a payment made—

(a) by or on behalf of a person who is, or is alleged to be, liable to any extent in respect of the accident, injury or disease, or

(b) in pursuance of a compensation scheme for motor accidents; but does not include a payment mentioned in Part I of Schedule 1.

(3) Subsection (1)(a) applies to a payment made—

(a) voluntarily, or in pursuance of a court order or an agreement, or otherwise, and

(b) in the United Kingdom or elsewhere.

(4) In a case where this Act applies—

(a) the 'injured person' is the person who suffered the accident, injury or disease.

(b) the 'compensation payment' is the payment within subsection (1)(a), and

(c) 'recoverable benefit' is any listed benefit which has been or is likely to be paid as mentioned in subsection (1)(b)."

[NOTE:

(1) A "listed benefit" is defined in section 29 as a benefit listed in column (2) of Schedule 2.

(2) Payments mentioned in Part I of Schedule 1 are certain unusual payments.]

Definition of "the relevant period"

6.34 Section 3 provides:

"(1) In relation to a person ('the claimant') who has suffered any accident, injury or disease, 'the relevant period' has the meaning given by the following subsections.

(2) Subject to subsection (4), if it is a case of accident or injury, the relevant period is the period of five years immediately

following the day on which the accident or injury in question occurred.

(3) Subject to subsection (4), if it is a case of disease, the relevant period is the period of five years beginning with the date on which the claimant first claims a listed benefit in consequence of the disease.

(4) If at any time before the end of the period referred to in subsection (2) or (3)—

(a) a person makes a compensation payment in final discharge of any claim made by or in respect of the claimant and arising out of the accident, injury or disease, or

(b) an agreement is made under which an earlier compensation payment is treated as having been made in final discharge of any such claim.

the relevant period ends at that time."

Certificates of recoverable benefits

6.35 Section 4 provides:

"(1) Before a person ('the compensator') makes a compensation payment he must apply to the Secretary of State for a certificate of recoverable benefits.

(2) Where the compensator applies for a certificate of recoverable benefits the Secretary of State must—

(a) send to him a written acknowledgement of receipt of his application, and

(b) subject to subsection (7), issue the certificate before the end of the following period.

(3) The period is—

(a) the prescribed period, or

(b) if there is no prescribed period, the period of four weeks, which begins with the day following the day on which the application is received.

(4) The certificate is to remain in force until the date specified in it for that purpose.

(5) The compensator may apply for fresh certificates from time to time.

(6) Where a certificate of recoverable benefits ceases to be in force, the Secretary of State may issue a fresh certificate without an application for one being made.

(7) Where the compensator applies for a fresh certificate while a certificate ('the existing certificate') remains in force, the Secretary of State must issue the fresh certificate before the end of the following period.

(8) The period is—

(a) the prescribed period, or

(b) if there is no prescribed period, the period of four weeks, which begins with the day following the day on which the existing certificate ceases to be in force.

(9) For the purposes of this Act, regulations may provide for the day on which an application for a certificate of recoverable benefits is to be treated as received."

6.36 Section 5 provides:

"(1) A certificate of recoverable benefits must specify, for each recoverable benefit—

(a) the amount which has been or is likely to have been paid on or before a specified date, and

(b) if the benefit is paid or likely to be paid after the specified date, the rate and period for which, and the intervals at which, it is or is likely to be so paid.

(2) In a case where the relevant period has ended before the day on which the Secretary of State receives the application for the certificate, the date specified in the certificate for the purposes of subsection (1) must be the day on which the relevant period ended.

(3) In any other case, the date specified for those purposes must not be earlier than the day on which the Secretary of State received the application.

(4) The Secretary of State may estimate, in such manner as he thinks fit, any of the amounts, rates or periods specified in the certificate.

(5) Where the Secretary of State issues a certificate of recoverable benefits, he must provide the information contained in the certificate to—

(a) the person who appears to him to be the injured person, or

(b) any person who he thinks will receive a compensation payment in respect of the injured person.

(6) A person to whom a certificate of recoverable benefits is

issued or who is provided with information under subsection (5) is entitled to particulars of the manner in which any amount, rate or period specified in the certificate has been determined, if he applies to the Secretary of State for those particulars."

Liability of compensator

6.37 Section 6 provides:

"(1) A person who makes a compensation payment in any case is liable to pay to the Secretary of State an amount equal to the total amount of the recoverable benefits.

(2) The liability referred to in subsection (1) arises immediately before the compensation payment or, if there is more than one, the first of them is made.

(3) No amount becomes payable under this section before the end of the period of 14 days following the day on which the liability arises.

(4) Subject to subsection (3), an amount becomes payable under this section at the end of the period of 14 days beginning with the day on which a certificate of recoverable benefits is first issued showing that the amount of recoverable benefit to which it relates has been or is likely to have been paid before a specified date."

Compensation payments made by more than one person

6.38 Where compensation payments are made by more than one person. the position is covered by regulations made under section 19 of the Act.

Wide scope of section 6

6.39 Before making any compensation payment, practitioners should remember the all-embracing scope of section 6. Where a defendant regards the plaintiff's claim as weak or misconceived, it was often the practice to make a token offer or payment into court to be rid of the nuisance value of the claim. It could now be expensive to act in that way. By making a small compensation payment, a defendant would render himself liable to pay to the Secretary of State the whole of the certified recoverable benefits.

Liability of insurers

6.40 Section 22 provides:

"(1) If a compensation payment is made in a case where—

(a) a person is liable to any extent in respect of the accident, injury or disease, and

(b) the liability is covered to any extent by a policy of insurance, the policy is also to be treated as covering any liability of that person under section 6.

(2) Liability imposed on the insurer by subsection (1) cannot be excluded or restricted.

(3) For that purpose excluding or restricting liability includes—

(a) making the liability or its enforcement subject to restrictive or onerous conditions.

(b) excluding or restricting any right or remedy in respect of the liability, or subjecting a person to any prejudice in consequence of his pursuing any such right or remedy, or

(c) excluding or restricting rules of evidence or procedure.

(4) Regulations may in prescribed cases limit the amount of the liability imposed on the insurer by subsection (1).

(5) This section applies to policies of insurance issued before (as well as those issued after) its coming into force.

(6) References in this section to policies of insurance and their issue include references to contracts of insurance and their making."

Recovery of payments

6.41 Section 7 provides:

"(1) This section applies where a person has made a compensation payment but—

(a) has not applied for a certificate of recoverable benefits, or

(b) has not made a payment to the Secretary of State under section 6 before the end of the period allowed under that section.

(2) The Secretary of State may—

(a) issue the person who made the compensation payment

with a certificate of recoverable benefits, if none has been issued, or

(b) issue him with a copy of the certificate of recoverable benefits or (if more than one has been issued) the most recent one and (in either case) issue him with a demand that payment of any amount due under section 6 be made immediately.

(3) The Secretary of State may, in accordance with subsections (4) and (5), recover the amount for which a demand for payment is made under subsection (2) from the person who made the compensation payment.

(4) If the person who made the compensation payment resides or carries on business in England and Wales and a county court so orders, any amount recoverable under subsection (3) is recoverable by execution issued from the county court or otherwise as if it were payable under an order of that court.

(5) If the person who made the payment resides or carries on business in Scotland, any amount recoverable under subsection (3) may be enforced in like manner as an extract registered decree arbitral bearing a warrant for execution issued by the sheriff court of any sheriffdom in Scotland.

(6) A document bearing a certificate which—

(a) is signed by a person authorised to do so by the Secretary of State. and

(b) states that the document, apart from the certificate, is a record of the amount recoverable under subsection (3), is conclusive evidence that that amount is so recoverable.

(7) A certificate, under subsection (6) purporting to be signed by a person authorised to do so by the Secretary of State is to be treated as so signed unless the contrary is proved."

Deduction of recoverable benefits

6.42 Section 8 provides:

"(1) This section applies in a case where, in relation to any head of compensation listed in column 1 of Schedule 2—

(a) any of the compensation payment is attributable to that head, and

(b) any recoverable benefit is shown against that head in column 2 of the Schedule.

(2) In such a case, any claim of a person to receive the compensation payment is to be treated for all purposes as discharged if—

(a) he is paid the amount (if any) of the compensation payment calculated in accordance with this section, and

(b) if the amount of the compensation payment so calculated is nil, he is given a statement saying so by the person who (apart from this section) would have paid the gross amount of the compensation payment.

(3) For each head of compensation listed in column 1 of the Schedule for which paragraphs (a) and (b) of subsection (1) are met, so much of the gross amount of the compensation payment as is attributable to that head is to be reduced (to nil, if necessary) by deducting the amount of the recoverable benefit or, as the case may be, the aggregate amount of the recoverable benefits shown against it.

(4) Subsection (3) is to have effect as if a requirement to reduce a payment by deducting an amount which exceeds that payment were a requirement to reduce that payment to nil.

(5) The amount of the compensation payment calculated in accordance with this section is—

(a) the gross amount of the compensation payment less

(b) the sum of the reductions made under subsection (3), (and; accordingly, the amount may be nil)."

6.43 Section 9 provides:

"(1) A person who makes a compensation payment calculated in accordance with section 8 must inform the person to whom the payment is made—

(a) that the payment has been so calculated, and

(b) of the date for payment by reference to which the calculation has been made.

(2) If the amount of a compensation payment calculated in accordance with section 8 is nil, a person giving a statement saying so is to be treated for the purposes of this Act as making a payment within section 1(1)(a) on the day on which he gives the statement.

(3) Where a person—

(a) makes a compensation payment calculated in accordance with section 8, and
(b) if the amount of the compensation payment so calculated is nil, gives a statement saying so, he is to be treated, for the purpose of determining any rights and liabilities in respect of contribution or indemnity, as having paid the gross amount of the compensation payment.

(4) For the purposes of this Act—
(a) the gross amount of the compensation payment is the amount of the compensation payment apart from section 8, and
(b) the amount of any recoverable benefit is the amount determined in accordance with the certificate of recoverable benefits."

Schedule 2 to the Act

6.44 "Section 8 SCHEDULE 2

CALCULATION OF COMPENSATION PAYMENT

(1) *Head of compensation*	(2) *Benefit*
1. Compensation for earnings lost during the relevant period	Disability working allowance Disablement pension payable under section 103 of the 1992 Act Incapacity benefit Income support Invalidity pension and allowance Jobseeker's allowance Reduced earnings allowance Severe disablement allowance Sickness benefit Statutory sick pay Unemployability supplement Unemployment benefit
2. Compensation for cost of care incurred during the relevant period	Attendance allowance Care component of disability living allowance Disablement pension increase payable under section 104 or 105 of the 1992 Act
3. Compensation for loss of mobility during the relevant period	Mobility allowance Mobility component of disability living allowance

NOTES

1.—(1) References to incapacity benefit, invalidity pension and allowance, severe disablement allowance, sickness benefit and unemployment benefit also include any income support paid with each of those benefits on the same instrument of payment or paid concurrently with each of those benefits by means of an instrument for benefit payment.

(2) For the purpose of this Note, income support includes personal expenses addition, special transitional additions and transitional addition as defined in the Income Support (Transitional) Regulations 1987.

2. Any reference to statutory sick pay—

(a) includes only 80 per cent of payments made between April 6, 1991 and April 5, 1994, and

(b) does not include payments made on or after April 6, 1994.

3. In this Schedule "the 1992 Act" means the Social Security Contributions and Benefits Act 1992."

6.45 Sections 8 and 9 read with Schedule 2 provide the mechanism by which benefits are to be deducted from compensation. No benefits are to be deducted from compensation for pain and suffering and loss of amenities, since there is nothing in Schedule 2 requiring recoupment in respect of that head of compensation.

6.46 Similarly, no recoupment is to be made from compensation paid in Fatal Accidents Act claims, since there is no relevant head of compensation listed in column (1) of Schedule 2 from which reduction of compensation could be made. A Fatal Accidents Act award is for loss of dependency and/or bereavement. Loss of dependency may be founded on the deceased's inability to spend money on the dependants, but the award is not for loss of earnings, nor for the costs of care, nor for loss of mobility. Nor are there any relevant benefits listed in column (2). It was unnecessary, therefore, to include in the 1997 Act provisions corresponding to those in sections 81(1) and 83(1)(c) of the Social Security Administration Act 1992, which excluded Fatal Accidents Act claims from the recoupment provisions in the 1992 Act. Those provisions were repealed, together with the whole of Part IV of the 1992 Act, by Schedule 3 of the 1997 Act. No corresponding provision is included in the 1997 Act.

6.47 In respect of pecuniary loss, like is to be deducted only from like. Thus mobility allowance is not to be deducted from compensation for loss of earnings. Also, income support is not to be deducted from compensation for the cost of care.

6.48 One can foresee negotiations between the injured person and the compensator as to the way in which damages are to be attributed to particular heads of compensation, with a view to minimising the recoupment to be made overall. For example, where an overall sum of compensation has been agreed in principle, the injured person might seek to have the greater part of that compensation attributed to general damages for pain, suffering and loss of amenities, in respect of which no recoupment is made. There is often room for flexibility in negotiations. For example, a lower multiplier might be agreed for future loss of earnings in exchange for higher damages for pain, suffering and loss of amenities.

Disregard of listed benefits

6.49 Section 17 provides:

"In assessing damages in respect of any accident, injury or disease, the amount of any listed benefits paid or likely to be paid is to be disregarded."

Definitions

6.50 Section 29 provides:

"In this Act—

'benefit' means any benefit under the Social Security Contributions and Benefits Act 1992, a jobseeker's allowance or mobility allowance,

'compensation scheme for motor accidents' means any scheme or arrangement under which funds are available for the payment of compensation in respect of motor accidents caused, or alleged to have been caused, by uninsured or unidentified persons,

'listed benefit' means a benefit listed in column 2 of Schedule 2,

'payment' means payment in money or money's worth, and related expressions are to be interpreted accordingly,

'prescribed' means prescribed by regulations, and

'regulations' means regulations made by the Secretary of State."

6.51 We have set out in full the principal sections of the Act. We see no point in setting out the other provisions in such detail. The reader is referred to the text of the Act in Appendix B.

There follows a general description of certain other provisions:

Section 10 empowers the Secretary of State to review certificates of recoverable benefits.

Section 11 provides for appeals against certificates of recoverable benefits.
Section 12 provides for reference of questions to a medical appeal tribunal.
Section 13 provides for appeals from a medical tribunal.
Section 14 is supplementary to the review of certificates of recoverable benefit.
Section 16 deals with payments into court.
Section 18 deals with lump sum and periodical payments.
Section 19 deals with payments by more than one person.
Section 20 deals with amounts overpaid under section 6.
Section 21 provides for compensation payments to be disregarded in certain circumstances when the Secretary of State has failed to send a certificate of recoverable benefit within the prescribed time.
Section 23 deals with the provision of information to the Secretary of State.
Section 24 empowers the Secretary of State (subject to the approval of Parliament) to amend by regulations Schedule 2 of the Act.
Section 25, 26 and 27 deal with Northern Ireland.
Section 28 provides that the Act applies to the Crown.
Schedule 3, paragraph 2, repeals Part IV of the Social Security Administration Act 1992.

6.52 "*The relevant period*": Recoupment to be made is limited to the amount of any relevant listed benefits paid or likely to be paid during the limited period as defined in section 3. This is the effect of section 1(1)(b). The Act does not apply to benefits paid outside the relevant period.

6.53 Recoupment is not made where the listed benefit would have been received even if the injured person had not been injured Under section 7 only listed benefits paid in consequence of the accident, injury or disease in respect of which the compensation payment is made are deducted. Thus, if the injured person would have been entitled to the benefit, even if he had not suffered the accident, injury or disease, no deduction will be required.

Hassall and Pether's case

6.54 In *Hassall and Pether v. Secretary of State for Social Security* [1995] P.I.Q.R, P. 292 the appellants appealed on the basis that post-accident benefits received by them had been wrongly recouped and deducted from the sum agreed as compensation for their non-pecuniary damages. They had both been unemployed and actively seeking work before the accident in which they were injured. As such, Hassall was then receiving unemployment benefit and income support and Pether, who had exhausted his unemployment benefit, was in receipt only of income support. After the accident both received the same amount of benefit, but of a different nature because they could not work and so no longer qualified for unemployment benefit or income support as unemployed persons seeking work. The appellants contended:

(1) That as the same amount of benefit was paid before as after the accident, one should look at the substance and not to the "re-labelling" of the benefits, and conclude that the post-accident benefits were not paid as a consequence of the accident, because the same quantum of benefit would have been paid had the accident not happened.

(2) That the income support element of the post-accident benefits was in reality still being paid because the recipients were still unemployed with no income, and not because of the accident.

(3) That the recouped benefit certified was in any event too large because it sought to recover the totality of the benefits received by the appellants, including that part of the "claimant's weekly applicable amount" which is increased by the fact that he is "part of a couple" and has a child or young person "who is a member of his family."

(4) That the result in the particular cases was unfair.

The Court of Appeal rejected all these submissions, holding that all the post-accident benefits had been paid in consequence of the accident, and that the unfairness could have been avoided by recovering special damages for loss of the non-recoupable pre-accident benefits. This aspect of the Court's reasoning is dealt with in *Kemp & Kemp*, Vo. 1 at paragraph 5–087/1.

Hodgson v. Trapp excluded

6.55 Section 81(5) provides that:

"In assessing damages in respect of any accident, injury or disease the amount of any listed benefit paid or likely to be paid is to be disregarded."

Section 17 thus excludes listed benefits from the application of the common law principle as enunciated by the House of Lords in *Hodgson v. Trapp* [1989] A.C. 807 whereby the benefits received as a consequence of injury sustained are taken into account in the initial assessment of damages.

Section 17 is not limited to the relevant period. It therefore operates to the advantage of a victim who is likely to continue to receive any relevant benefit previously fully offset at common law after the relevant period has expired, as no deduction is required under the new regime in respect of benefits to be received outside the relevant period.

6.56 The effect of this section is that listed benefits received or likely to be received after the said five years' period, or after the date when a compensation payment is made in final discharge of the claim, are not to be deducted. With benefits such as unemployment benefit, which is soon exhausted, the section's effect may be of little significance. The same is likely to be true of income support, since injuries with a long-term adverse pecuniary effect are likely to have resulted in a large award the income from which would disentitle the plaintiff from income support. But the position is different with mobility allowance and attendance allowance. These allowances are substantial and are paid regardless of a plaintiff's financial position. In *Hodgson v. Trapp* a four-and-a-half of the five years' period had expired by the date of the trial. A multiplier of 13 was adopted by the House of Lords to apply to the multiplicand for the cost of future care. From this multiplicand the House of Lords deducted £2,792, the agreed annual aggregate of mobility and attendance allowances currently paid to the plaintiff, and thereby reduced the award by £36,296 (calculated as £2,792 × 13). If the new law had then been in force, its effect would have been to increase the award by £36,296, the amount by which the House of Lords had reduced this head of damage. In this postulated situation the plaintiff would appear to be over-compensated by an award which covered the cost of future care but which disregarded a substantial part of the statutory benefit intended to mitigate the cost of such care.

Rees v. West Glamorgan C.C.

6.57 In *Rees v. West Glamorgan* C.C. [1994] P.I.Q.R. P. 37 the Court of Appeal (Ralph Gibson L.J. and Sir Michael Kerr) held that, where the plaintiff had agreed to accept £33,000 in settlement of his claim, the defendants were entitled, indeed required, to deduct the amount stated in the certificate of deduction, namely, £10,121.50, and to pay the plaintiff the balance, namely, £22,878.50.

The moral is that if a plaintiff intends to receive the whole sum named in a settlement he should first have stipulated that the sum is the actual sum to be paid to him, having taken into account any sum stated or to be stated in a certificate of total benefit.

McCaffery v. Datta

6.58 In *McCaffery v. Datta and Others* [1997] P.I.Q.R. Q. 64 the defendants paid £2,500 into court. The notice of payment into court made no reference to any sum payable to the Compensation Recovery Unit. The plaintiff recovered judgment for £22,373. But £25,419 had to be paid to the Compensation Recovery Unit. The trial judge awarded the defendants the costs of the action. The Court of Appeal (Stuart-Smith, Aldous and Ward L.JJ.) allowed the plaintiff's appeal and awarded the plaintiff the costs of the action. The Court held that the trial judge was wrong to regard the payment into court of £2,500 as akin to £25,419. It was not. The defendants could not be said to have been successful when they had incurred a liability as a result of the judgment to pay £22,373.

Oldham v. Sharples

6.59 The Court of Appeal (Roch, Henry and Ward L.JJ.) so held in *Oldham v. Sharples*. [1997] P.I.Q.R. Q. 82 following the reasoning in *McCaffery v. Datta*. The plaintiff was awarded a total of £886.76 damages. He had already received an award from the Criminal Injuries Compensation Board of £3,000. The trial judge, H.H. Judge Holman refused to allow the plaintiff his costs on the ground that he had not benefited from the court's award of damages. The Court of Appeal allowed the plaintiff's appeal and awarded him his costs.

Per Roch L.J.:

"The first question is whether this was a case where an order for costs should have been made. The answer to that, in my judgment, must be 'yes'. The judge was departing from the usual practice as regard costs in personal injury cases, namely, that absent a payment in, or a written offer of settlement, or misconduct, the plaintiff who recovers damages is awarded costs. This was a claim for damages for personal damages for personal injury; liability and causation were in dispute; there were issues on contributory negligence and quantum. The plaintiff was entitled to bring his action. The fact that he had an award from the Criminal Injuries Compensation Board did not disentitle him from bringing his claim against his employer in a court.

From the point of view of the fund operated by the Criminal Injuries Compensation Board, and the public interest in the call on such a fund being minimised by those injured seeking compensation in the courts, persons injured by criminal conduct are to be encouraged, rather than discouraged, from bringing actions. The judge's opinion that there should be no costs order because the plaintiff had recovered a higher award of compensation from the Criminal Injuries Compensation Board than the damages the judge had awarded him, was not, in my judgment, a valid reason for saying that this was a case where it was appropriate to refuse to make a costs order."

Changes in Rules of Court

6.60 Rule changes have been made in both the High Court and in the county court. The two main points arising are as follows:

First, in the case of a payment into court after the deduction of benefits the notice of payment should state:

"The defendant has withheld from this payment into court the sum of £X in accordance with section 93(2)(a)(i) of the Social Security Administration Act 1992."

Secondly, having applied for a certificate of total benefit, and while awaiting its receipt, the defendant may make an offer without prejudice save as to costs (*Calderbank* offer) stating that the amount offered is subject to whatever deduction is ultimately required. This offer holds good in respect of costs until seven days after the certificate is received. In the county court a copy of the offer should be lodged with the court in a sealed envelope (see RSC (Amendment

No. 2) 1990; County Court Rules, Ord. 11, r.10(2) amended by County Court (Amendment No. 3) Rules 1990).

Contributory negligence disregarded

6.61 There is no provision in the statutory scheme for a *pro tanto* reduction of recoupment where the victim's damages have been reduced on the ground of contributory negligence. Accordingly, regardless of the amount of contributory negligence on the plaintiff's part, 100 per cent of the relevant benefits received over the relevant period will always be recouped.

Documentation required

6.62 A further practical consequence of the new law is that practitioners will need to enter into correspondence with the Compensation Recovery Unit of the Department of Social Security.

The Law Reform (Personal Injuries) Act 1948

6.63 From January 1, 1989, under the new law, this Act became irrelevant in assessing damages, since for the relevant period all relevant benefits were deducted in full. The same is true under the 1997 Act, since for the relevant period all listed benefits are deducted in full to the extent that recoupment is made against a particular head of compensation. This state of affairs is recognised in the 1997 Act. Paragraph 1 of Schedule 3 to the Act provides that:

> "In section 2 of the Law Reform (Personal Injuries) Act 1948 (assessment of damages in personal injuries actions) subsections (1), (1A), (3) and (6) are omitted."

6.64 This leaves as the only surviving provision section 2(4) which provides:

> "In an action for damages for personal injuries (including any such action arising out of a contract), there shall be disregarded, in determining the reasonableness of any expenses, the possibility of avoiding those expenses or part of them by taking advantage of facilities available under the National Health Service Act 1977, or the National Health Service (Scotland) Act 1978, or any corresponding facilities in Northern Ireland."

The Old Law

6.65 As explained in para. 6.28, the old law no longer applies where compensation payments are made on or after October 6, 1997. The old law would only be relevant in the case of an appeal from an award made before October 6, 1997.

Fatal Accidents Act Claims

6.66 The new law does not affect claims under the Fatal Accidents Act since there is no relevant head of compensation from which reduction of compensation can be made: see para. 6.44 *ante*. However, recoupment still applies to claims for lost earnings between injury and death made under the Law Reform Act.

The General Rule at Common Law

6.67 At common law the general rule, as stated by Lord Macmillan in *Davies v. Powell Duffryn Associated Collieries Ltd* [1940] AC 601, was that "damages awarded to a dependant of a deceased person under the Fatal Accidents Acts must take into account any pecuniary benefit accruing to that dependant in consequence of the death of the deceased.

Statutory Exceptions

6.68 That rule was made subject to various statutory exceptions over the years and it was totally abrogated as from January 1, 1983 in respect of deaths occurring on or after that date by the Fatal Accidents Act 1976, s 4 as substituted by the Administration of Justice Act 1982, s 3(1).

Section 4 as substituted provides:

> "In assessing damages in respect of a person's death in an action under this Act, benefits which have accrued or will or may accrue to any person from his estate or otherwise as a result of his death shall be disregarded."

The effect of this section and in particular the extent of the words "or otherwise" was considered by the Court of Appeal in *Stanley v. Saddique* [1992] 1 Q.B. 1. In that case a claim was brought under the Fatal Accidents Act for the benefit of a boy whose mother had been killed. She was an unsatisfactory and unreliable mother. The father remarried and the boy thus obtained a stepmother who provided him with motherly services of a higher standard than those which had been provided by his own mother. The defendant argued that the stepmother's services to the boy were a benefit to him which should be taken into account in the assessment of his damages on the ground that the statutory disregard in s. 4 was limited to direct pecuniary benefits: the defendant argued for a restricted meaning to be given to the words "or otherwise". The Court of Appeal, Purchas and Gibson L.JJ. and Sir David Croom-Johnson rejected this argument. Their reasoning is set out in the following extract from the judgment, *per* Purchas L.J.

> "The problem is to decide whether in construing the new section 4 there is any justification for construing the words 'benefits which have accrued or will or may accrue to any person from his estate or otherwise as a result of his death shall be disregarded' as in any way being restricted or whether they should be given the full ambit of the word 'otherwise'.
>
> Mr Clegg submitted that the specific exclusion of a widow's remarriage or prospects of remarriage from the assessment of damages provided in s 3(3) indicated that 'otherwise' must be restricted in some way, otherwise s 3(3) was otiose. He suggested that the exclusion should be restricted to direct pecuniary benefits. However, if this course is taken the word 'otherwise' would not be sufficiently wide to reinstate the various rights to benefits which had been progressively introduced since the Act of 1908 culminating in the sections of the Act of 1976 which were wholly replaced by s 3(1) of the Act of 1982. As a result of the passage of this Act none of the pre-existing statutory exemptions from the deductions of benefits from Fatal Accidents Act damage survived unless it is through the medium of the word 'otherwise'. It seems inconceivable that Parliament would have effected a wholesale repeal of all the long-standing previous statutory exceptions from the deduction of benefits by a side wind of this sort with the exception of the exclusion of the prospects of remarriage on the part of the widow (semble but not the widower). In my judgment, the preferable construction is that advanced by Mr Ashworth,

namely, that s 3(3) was left in as being a particularly significant question of policy, but that by s 4 Parliament intended to further the departure from ordinary common law assessment of damages for personal injuries by the artificial concept which has for many decades been the basis of damages recoverable under the Fatal Accidents Acts.

For the reasons I have just given I have come to the conclusion that the judge was correct in his decision that the benefits accruing to the plaintiff as a result of his absorption into the family unit consisting of his father and stepmother and siblings should be wholly disregarded for the purposes of assessing damages."

Per Ralph Gibson L.J.

As to the point of law, based upon the construction of s 4 and of s 3(3) of the Act of 1976 as amended, I was at first inclined to the view that the concept of "benefits which have accrued or will or may accrue to any person from his estate or otherwise as a result of his death" must be held not to extend to the effects of remarriage which are covered specifically by s 3(3) to the extent there provided. I have, however, with no great confidence that we have correctly understood the intention of Parliament as expressed in these provisions, reached the conclusion that the preferable construction is that expressed by Purchas LJ for the reasons given by him.

6.69 Sir David Croom-Johnson agreed with both the previous judgments. However, the boy's own mother's services were so unreliable, and the prospect of their continuing, if she had not been killed, so uncertain that the Court of Appeal reduced the award from £32,536 to £15,000.

6.70 That construction, however, is itself open to criticism made by Mr Clegg based on the rule of statutory construction that militates against construing one part of an Act in a way that renders another part of the Act otiose.

6.71 The provisions of section 4 of the Law Reform (Miscellaneous Provisions) Act 1971 have been re-enacted in s. 3(3) of the Fatal Accidents Act 1976. This sub-section would be completely otiose if the effect of section 4 of the same Act has been that remarriage and prospects of remarriage are to be disregarded in the assessment of both a husband's and a wife's claim for damages under the Act. Parliament may sometimes include in the same Act an otiose provision and the provision which makes it otiose, but not usually in such close proximity.

6.72 However, as was held by the majority of the Court of Appeal in *Hayden v. Hayden*, a decision given on March 24, 1992, *Stanley*'s case (see para. 6.68 above) is binding on the Court of Appeal. Indeed, in *Tapp v. Country Bus (South West) Ltd*, a decision given on November 5, 1991, May J. held that he was bound by the reasoning in *Stanley's* case to ignore the plaintiff widower's prospects of remarriage in assessing damages for his wife's death.

Hayden v. Hayden

6.73 *Hayden v. Hayden* (see para. 6.72 above) was a case under the Fatal Accidents Act where a dependent child's damages had to be assessed to compensate her for the death of her mother. The defendant was the child's father, whose negligent driving had caused her mother's death. It was common ground that the deceased was an excellent mother, a good housekeeper and cook and devoted to her children. The father had given up his job six months after the accident and had himself looked after the dependent child, a girl aged four at the time of her mother's death and aged 13 at the trial. The defendant was not insured and the defence was conducted by Counsel instructed by the Motor Insurers' Bureau. The defence contention was that the dependent child had suffered no damage since her mother's services had been replaced by her father's services. It was contended that if the plaintiff could recover damages for loss of her mother's services, the defendant would have been required to compensate her twice over, he having already compensated her in kind by replacing the mother's services with his own.

6.74 The Court of Appeal's judgments in *Stanley*'s case (see para. 6.68 above) were handed down on May 18, 1990. By then Buckley J., the trial judge in *Hayden*'s case, had already reserved his judgment. In September 1990, when he was about to deliver judgment, he became aware of a newspaper report of *Stanley*'s case. He took the view that he would not hear further argument, as it did not seem to him that *Stanley*'s case would be likely to affect his overall conclusion. There had been evidence before Buckley J. of the cost which would have been and would continue to be incurred if a "nanny" had been employed to replace the mother's services. It was clear, however, that there was no likelihood that a nanny would in fact have been employed, even had this been within the family's means.

6.75 Buckley J stated in the course of his judgment:

> "I hold that Danielle is entitled to recover the lost services of her mother. The fact that the defendant has provided substitute services does not defeat the claim in principle."

Later in the judgment he continued:

> "I also bear in mind the fundamental principle that damages are compensatory and that in this case Danielle has, in the event, been looked after by her father to the date of the trial. This benefit is something which is to be disregarded at common law in the sense that it is not to be set off against any quantifiable loss as on the authorities it is not a benefit which resulted from the death. It is, however, a factor in determining the existence or extent of any loss at least to the date of trial, as it was by then a fact."

[We interpose here that, if the judge had studied a full report of *Stanley*'s case, he should have held that the benefit of her father's services did result from her mother's death and would have reached the same conclusion, namely that this benefit was to be disregarded, but for a different reason, *viz*, that this was the effect of section 4 of the Act, as substituted by the Administration of Justice Act 1982.]

6.76 It is submitted that the judge was wrong in the view stated in the final sentence of the passage cited above.

6.77 The child's loss was the loss of the services provided by her mother. Section 4 required that the father's services are to be disregarded. By treating such services as a factor in determining the existence or extent of the child's loss, the judge was clearly not disregarding them. The judge's error in that respect no doubt explained the basis on which he awarded £20,000 for the child's dependency, a figure not otherwise explicable on the basis of the evidence addressed at the trial. The defendant appealed on the ground that the award was too high. The plaintiff cross-appealed on the ground that it was too low.

6.78 The short report of this case in (1992) *The Times*, 8 April was inaccurate and positively misleading. It implied that the majority of the court (Parker L.J. and Sir David Croom-Johnson) were of the view that *Hay v. Hughes* [1975] Q.B. 790 was to be preferred to

Stanley's case (see para. 6.68 above). In fact, Sir David Croom-Johnson expressly stated: "*Stanley v. Saddique* is binding on this court and it remains to be seen what is its effect on the instant case." *Hayden*'s case is now reported in [1992] P.I.Q.R. Q. 111.

6.79 McCowan L.J. in his dissenting judgment, would have increased the award to £30,000. He said:

> "The principle which emerged from the decision in *Stanley v. Saddique* is that there is to be no reduction in the amount of damages which would otherwise be awarded to take account of care voluntarily provided in substitution for the deceased's motherly services. That principle cannot, in my judgment, be affected by whether or not the person providing the care was the tortfeasor . . .
>
> I would hold, therefore, that the judge was wrong in law to take into account to any extent the care provided by the defendant for the plaintiff in substitution for her mother's care since the latter's death. It follows that the amount he must be taken to have awarded under element (i), [loss of the mother's services] which is put by counsel at either £11,500 or £13,500, is too small. Taking account of the quality and continuity of the services which this mother was likely to have provided, of Mr Brent's mathematical calculations, and of awards made in other similar cases, and in the end making a jury assessment as the judge did, I take the view that the correct overall figure for Fatal Accidents damages is £30,000."

It is submitted that McCowan L.J. was clearly right. It may be a question of fact, depending on the circumstances of the particular case, whether substitute services result from the deceased's death. But in any case, the services are to be disregarded in the assessment of damages. If they do not result from the deceased's death, they are to be disregarded by virtue of previous decisions at common law: if they do result from the death they are to be disregarded by virtue of section 4 of the Fatal Accidents Act in its amended form.

6.80 How was it that the majority of the Court of Appeal reached a different conclusion? As already stated, Sir David Croom-Johnson held that *Stanley*'s case (see para. 6.68 above) was binding on the Court of Appeal, ie that if the father's services resulted from the mother's death, they were to be disregarded. He held that as a matter of fact, the father's services did not result from the mother's death. But, if that was his conclusion of fact, he should as a matter of law have followed the common law authorities which held that a benefit was to be disregarded unless it resulted from the deceased's death. Instead he dealt with the matter in the way set out in the following extract from his judgment:

> "If the result of making an allowance for the fact that the defendant has himself continued to act as a loving father means that his ultimate financial liability to Danielle is smaller, there is nothing wrong or objectionable in that. Emotive phrases like allowing the defendant 'to profit from his wrongdoing' are beside the point. It is preferable to say that what he has done has had, as one result, the reduction of his liability."

It is submitted that Sir David Croom-Johnson fell into the same error as the trial judge. He did take Danielle's continuing benefit from her father's services into account, *pro tanto* setting this off against the admitted loss of her mother's excellent motherly services. We venture to criticise this approach in more detail when we come to deal with Parker L.J.'s judgment.

6.81 Parker L.J followed *Hay v. Hughes* (see para. 6.91 above) rather than *Stanley*'s case and held that the provision of the father's services did *not* result from her mother's death. He recognised that this was not in itself an answer to the plaintiff's claims. He said:

> "Section 4 does not apply. This however does not dispose of the matter because in *Hay v. Hughes* the benefit of such gratuitous services was excluded, quite apart from any relevant statutory exclusion, on the ground that they did not result from the death. That decision was considered to be the result of s. 2 and the common law."

6.82 However, in spite of this correct statement of the common law position, Parker L.J. reached what is submitted to be an erroneous conclusion, on the basis set out in the following extract from his judgment:

> "In my judgment before one gets to s. 4 it must first be established what injury has been suffered by the child. What it has *prima facie* lost, is the services provided by the mother but the fact that they were provided by the mother is irrelevant. If in fact those

services were replaced without interval of time up to the date of the trial by as good or better services it is in my view at least open to a judge or jury to conclude that the child has lost nothing up to that date. But if the replacement services can be discontinued it is of course exposed to the risk that such services may be discontinued and that risk must be quantified."

[We interpose that this was the same approach as Buckley J. had made in the passage from his judgment cited above.]

6.83 Parker L.J.'s conclusion is set out in the following passage from his judgment:

"What then has [Buckley J.] done in this case? He had before him a figure of £48,000 as being the full cost of a nanny until Danielle was 11 and a half such cost from 11–15. He then, without giving specific reasons, concluded that an appropriate figure would be £20,000 apportioned £15,000 to date of trial and £5,000 thereafter. I do not consider that we have before us material to enable us to interfere with this award, which if I am right as to the approach, appears to me to be an entirely reasonable award and to do justice between the parties. I would therefore, like Sir David Croom-Johnson, dismiss both appeal and cross-appeal."

6.84 It is submitted that Parker L.J.'s approach is fallacious. The child undoubtedly lost *her mother's services*. That is a loss. The loss can only be extinguished or diminished by taking into account, or having regard to, the substituted services. That is what the common law prohibits, if the substitute services do not result from the death; it is also what s. 4 prohibits, if the substitute services do result from the death.

It is for these reasons that we submit that McCowan L.J.'s dissenting judgment should be preferred.

Wood v. Bentall Simplex Ltd

6.85 In *Wood v. Bentall Simplex Ltd* (1992) *The Times*, 3 March, C.A. the Court of Appeal held that in assessing damages under the Fatal Accidents Act 1976 it was irrelevant that a loss from one source might be made good from another by using a benefit from the deceased's estate. *Per* Beldam L.J.:

"During the last 100 years certain benefits accruing as a result of a deceased's death had on the ground of policy gradually been excluded from being taken into account against the expectation of pecuniary benefit, for example, life assurance benefits or state benefits.

In the present case, the dependants enjoyed not only the expectation of pecuniary benefit from the labour and work which the deceased put into the family farm but were also able to rely if necessary on the increasing value, as a result of the deceased's hard work, of the family assets, although tied up in the farming enterprise.

The appellant's assertion was that the dependants received income from assets which in the deceased's lifetime were employed in the farming enterprise and that they had not lost that income as the assets continued to be used after the death.

However, to make good the claim that the dependency on which the award was based already included a sum which represented a return on the assets employed in the enterprise was a difficult task and had never been attempted by the appellant.

The background to the amendments to the 1976 Act included the recommendations of the Royal Commission on Civil Liability and Compensation for Personal Injury (1978) Cmnd 7054–1, *interalia*, one that all benefits derived from the deceased's estate should be excluded as deductions from the damages received under the Act.

On the facts of the present case, s. 4 of the 1976 Act, as amended, required the benefits accruing to the dependants from the deceased's estate to be disregarded, whether at the stage the court first ascertained the extent of the injury to the dependants from the death, or at the stage the damages to be awarded were assessed: *Auty v. National Coal Board* [1985] 1 WLR 784, 805."

Fox L.J. agreed. *Per* Staughton L.J.:

"No doubt the law, to some extent, allowed greater damages to be awarded under the 1976 Act than a strict view of the dependants' loss would justify: *Stanley v. Saddique* [1992] 1 Q.B. 1, 10.

However, before one considered deductions under s 4, the court had to determine what loss the dependants had suffered and, if they had inherited the source of the income on which they were dependent, they had not lost it.

In the case where the income was in part derived from labour and in part from capital, the court again had to determine the loss and how much of the deceased's income was derived solely from capital which the dependants had inherited.

In the present case there was no adequate answer. If there had been evidence as to what the deceased was capable of earning without capital and if that had been less than his actual income from the farm his Lordship would have been prepared to ascribe the difference to a return on capital which the dependants inherited and the award would have been so reduced but there was no such evidence.

The sums which the widow and sons were receiving did not show how much of the deceased's estimated income would have been derived otherwise than from his ability to work. There was probably some element of return on capital but a very small amount."

It is respectfully submitted that this decision is clearly correct. We venture to doubt whether the result should be different even if there had been evidence of the nature postulated by Staughton L.J.

6.86 It is submitted that the two-stage approach to the assessment of damages introduced by Oliver J. in *Auty*'s case is wrong and so, too, are *dicta* in *Wood*'s case. See *Kemp & Kemp*, Vol. 1, Chapter 19A.

Pidduck v. Eastern Scottish Omnibus Ltd

6.87 In *Pidduck*'s case [1989] 1 W.L.R. 317; [1990] 1 W.L.R. 993, C.A. the defendants argued that the change of wording effected by the 1982 amendment had reduced rather than increased the scope of the statutory disregard. The previous wording of section 4 of the 1976 Act had been as follows:

"(1) In assessing damages in respect of a person's death in an action under this Act there shall not be taken into account any insurance money, pension benefit or gratuity which has been or will be paid as a result of the death.

(2) In this section—'benefit' means benefits under the enactments relating to social security including enactments in

Northern Ireland and any payment by a friendly society or trade union for the relief of maintenance of a member's dependants.

'Insurance money' includes a return of premiums, and 'pension' includes a return of contributions and any payment of a lump sum in respect of a person's employment."

The defendants contended that "benefits" no longer included a pension. Sheen J. rejected this argument, saying:

"The wording of s. 4 of the Fatal Accidents Act 1976 was changed by the Administration of Justice Act 1982. Benefits which have accrued to a person as the result of the death are to be disregarded. There is no definition of 'benefits'. It seems to me that the word 'benefits' is apt to include a pension. If Parliament had intended to make such a fundamental change in the law relating to the assessment of damages in fatal accident cases as would be involved if the word 'benefits' in s. 4 does not include a pension, I would have expected that change in the law to be made clear beyond doubt."

6.88 The practical effect of the decision in *Pidduck*'s case was that, whereas before his death the widow had been dependent on the pension which her husband had from his employers as the source of her dependency on him, as the result of his death she was awarded damages for loss of that dependency and in addition was drawing a widow's allowance paid by the employers. She thus gained financially from her husband's death. A similar financial gain had resulted in the case of *Lea v. Owen*, a decision of Bush J. on the previous wording of s. 4. Bush J. held that this gain was to be disregarded.

Sheen J.'s decision was affirmed by the Court of Appeal.

The law prior to s. 4

6.89 The previous law had involved narrow distinctions between various types of benefit accruing to a dependant, but as it will only apply in the case of deaths occurring before January 1, 1983, and as claims founded on such deaths will ordinarily have been statute-barred unless commenced before January 1, 1986, the previous law does not warrant detailed consideration here. It is dealt with in more detail in *Kemp & Kemp*, Vol. 1, Chapter 22, paras 22–011 *et seq.*.

Watson v. Willmott

6.90 See *Watson and Others v. Willmott* [1991] 1 Q.B. 140, a decision of Garland J. Garland J.'s decision was given before the Court of Appeal's decision in *Stanley*'s case (see para. 6.68 above). The plaintiff in *Watson*'s case was an infant claiming under the Fatal Accidents Act for the death of both his parents. Not long after both parents had died, the plaintiff was adopted. Garland J. held that the plaintiff's dependency on his mother for non-pecuniary benefits ended on adoption when similar motherly services were rendered by his adoptive mother. The judge also held that the value of the pecuniary dependency on his father was reduced, as from the date of adoption, by the value of the new pecuniary dependency on his adoptive father. It is submitted that the *ratio decidendi* of *Stanley*'s case would require both the non-pecuniary benefit rendered by the adoptive mother and the pecuniary benefit provided by the adoptive father to be disregarded in the assessment of the infant plaintiff's damages.

CHAPTER 7
Actuarial Assessment of Damages

J H Prevett OBE, FIA, FAE

Contents *Para*

INTRODUCTION: *WELLS V. WELLS*

7.1 The important decision of the House of Lords in *Wells v. Wells* [1998] 3 W.L.R. 329 has revolutionised the courts' attitude to actuarial evidence.

THE ASSESSMENT PROBLEM

7.2 The basic principle underlying the assessment of the quantum of damages is *restitutio in integrum*. This principle has been defined in various *dicta* of the courts that will be familiar to legal readers and it is not proposed to reproduce them here.

7.3 This chapter is concerned with the assessment of damages as a capital sum for continuing pecuniary loss flowing from personal injury or death. In a personal injuries case the pecuniary loss may include partial or total loss of earnings and loss of pension rights. It may also include the cost of special care and attention. In a fatal accident case the pecuniary loss will normally be the net loss of "dependency" to the widow and/or children and other dependants.

7.4 The law accepts as relevant to the assessment of damages a concept of value, such that the capital sum awarded should represent the present value as at the date of the trial of the loss of income or of the future expenditure incurred as a result of the tort. It is apparent that the nature of the valuation problem is such as to make this a proper and natural field for the application of actuarial science.

THE THEORY OF PROBABILITIES

7.5 The author's article in the *Modern Law Review* (1972) included the following explanation of the application of the theory of probabilities to the problem of the assessment of damages. This was based on a memorandum prepared for the Law Commission by a Working Party of the Institute and Faculty of Actuaries of which the author was a member.

> "Actuarial calculations are based on the validity attaching to the theory of probabilities or the probabilistic approach and it may be of assistance to give an explanation of the significance and working of that theory. It is an essential element in the proper

understanding of how actuarial evidence can assist the assessment of damages in any particular case.

The association of a survival probability and a rate of discount lies at the root of the actuary's technique of arriving at a 'present value'. Ideally, the actuary turns to statistics of the experience of a class of lives identical in material character to the individual for whom a lump-sum payment equal in value to a series of annual payments falls to be assessed. He then determines from these statistics the probability that the individual will survive to receive each future annual payment, multiplies this by the appropriate amount of the payment and discounts to allow for the rate of interest to the present time. By applying this technique to each future payment and summing the results he produces an overall total which gives the amount of the assessment. The probability of survival can be calculated to allow not only for mortality, but also for early retirement for reasons of ill-health, sickness and other 'incidentals'.

It matters not that only *one* individual is to receive the amount of the assessment or that he may die the next day, or for that matter live to be a centenarian. So far as that individual is concerned, at the date of assessment, he is awarded fair compensation in the sense that *if* there had been a very large number of similar individuals of the same age all receiving the same amount, then overall they would have equated to the stated payments, allowing for the operation in due time of compound interest and mortality. Another way of expressing this concept is to say that if this very large number of individuals made a pool investment of the total of the identical amounts awarded to each at an investment yield equal to the interest rate assumed by the actuary for discount purposes, and if each received from the pool for the remainder of his lifetime the annual loss for which he had been compensated by recourse to both interest and (to the extent necessary) capital, then the total investment would be exhausted on the death of the last survivor provided that the mortality of the group followed the assumed pattern.

Nor are the theories of probability and present value invalidated by the situation—very common in practice—that statistics for an identical group of lives do not exist. In practice it is necessary, more often than not, to proceed from the known to the unknown, to the determination of probabilities suitable to a *particular* risk, using material that is the best available to do the job. The whole of the actuary's training and experience is devoted to bridging this gap—to the choice of the most suitable statistics and, above all, to their application and adjustment to the circumstances of a particular situation, as they are seen to be at a particular moment of time. His opinion of the assessment in an individual case is therefore that of a professional expert skilled in this very art. Moreover, to discard his opinion on the grounds that precisely relevant statistics are not available would be to deny the usefulness of a technique that lies at the root of innumerable commercial transactions that are taking place daily.

The difficulties which judges and lawyers generally have experienced in interpreting actuarial evidence and appreciating the assistance which it can give no doubt largely explain the reluctance of those advising litigants to instruct an actuary."

INTER-PROFESSIONAL WORKING PARTY

7.6 A formal joint working group of the Institute of Actuaries and Faculty of Advocates was established and this group participated in an inter-professional working party with five nominees of the Senate of the Inns of Court and the Bar, three nominees of the Law Society and two Scottish lawyers. The Chairman of this inter-professional working group was Sir Michael Ogden, QC, and its terms of reference were:

"To consider and report on—

1 the feasibility and desirability of issuing authoritative tables for the assistance of the court in assessing an award of damages for continuing pecuniary loss arising out of personal injury or fatal accident litigation;

2 the number and nature of such tables which would, in such circumstances, be required;

3 the explanatory notes that would be required to assist in selecting the appropriate table to be applied to suit the individual case;

4 whether additional guidance is required on the limitations of such tables, or whether there are circumstances in which they would need to be attested by calling an actuary as an expert witness;

5 whether there are any recommendations that could be

> made jointly by the two professions to the Lord Chancellor."

The working party tables (1984)

7.7 The inter-professional working party completed its work in November 1983 and the outcome was the publication by HMSO for the Government Actuary's Department in May 1984 of a booklet entitled "Actuarial Tables with Explanatory Notes for use in Personal Injury and Fatal Accident Cases". The introduction to the tables emphasised that they incorporated a new factor which it was hoped would overcome the problem of how to deal with the uncertainties of future inflation. The proposed solution is to presume that plaintiffs will invest their damages awards in index-linked Government Stocks and therefore to assess damages by using multipliers based on the rate of discount corresponding to the yield on such stocks at the date of assessment. If the courts follow this route, there will be no need to speculate as to the future rate of inflation. The introduction included these words:

> "The Working Party concluded that the following arguments could not be faulted. The courts seek to put the wage earner, or, if he had been killed, his dependant, into the same financial position as if the accident had not happened. Investment policy, however prudent, involves risks and it is not difficult to draw up a list of blue chip equities or reliable unit trusts which have performed poorly and, in some cases, disastrously. Index-Linked Government Stocks eliminate the risk. Whereas, in the past, a plaintiff has had to speculate in the form of prudent investment by buying equities or a 'basket' of equities and gilts or a selection of unit trusts, he need speculate no longer if he buys Index-Linked Government Stocks."

The working party's proposals seek to guide the courts in determining a real rate of return for the purpose of assessing damages without the necessity to consider the opinions of an actuary or other expert as to appropriate assumptions with regard to future rates of investment earnings and inflation.

The working party tables (1994 and 1998)

7.8 The second edition of the "Ogden Tables" published in 1994, incorporates suggested deductions from multipliers for contingencies other than mortality, of which the most significant are unemployment and sickness. A table of deductions is given which is considered appropriate if economic activity in future is expected to correspond to that over the past five years, together with suggested adjustments to reflect the higher expectation of illness and injury in certain occupations and the effect of variations by geographic region. In general, the suggested deductions are lower than those which have been used by the courts.

A third edition was published in June 1998. Whereas all the tables in the previous editions were based on past mortality statistics, the third edition also contains tables based on projecting future mortality trends, to take account of the increasing life expectancy of the general population. The Government already uses such tables when calculating the cost of future pensions etc.. It seems appropriate to have regard to such tables when assessing the capital value of a stream of future income losses extending over a long period. Now that the court has held that actuarial tables should be the starting point in assessing damages for future loss, the tables will now be universally adopted.

THE ROLE OF THE ACTUARY

7.9 It is necessary at this stage to reflect on the role of the actuary as an expert witness in the courts. It is presumed for the purpose of this discussion that the actuary is instructed to value pecuniary loss on behalf of either the plaintiff or the defendant and that there is no question of his evidence being agreed or being submitted by him as a servant of the court, rather than on behalf of one of the litigants. The author is of the opinion, nevertheless, that the actuary's valuation should, within the constraints of the case presented by counsel, be impartial, fair and reasonable. The actuary may be required to make his valuation on the basis of facts selected by counsel as most favourable to his client's case. He should not, however, in arriving at his decision on the elements of the valuation basis, have any regard to the fact that he has been instructed on behalf of either the plaintiff or the defendant.

7.10 Perhaps the greatest problem facing the actuary employed as expert witness is that of communication. It is clearly desirable that legal practitioners should gain some knowledge of the basic principles of actuarial science, but it is also necessary for actuaries to play their part in developing the broad and full understanding between the professions which is essential if actuarial evidence under present circumstances is to be of value. Many of the difficulties that arise in practice could be avoided if all aspects of the evidence given were to be discussed fully in advance of the court hearing. In the author's experience it is almost always desirable for there to be at least two conferences with counsel attended by the actuary, one before and one after he has made his calculations and produced a written draft as proof of evidence. The witness box is perhaps the severest practical test of an actuary's ability to explain and justify concisely and clearly to the layman the valuations he has made and the professional opinion he has formed.

ELEMENTS OF THE VALUATION BASIS

7.11 We now come to consider the principal elements of the basis to be selected by the actuary in undertaking the valuation of pecuniary loss. It will be assumed for the purpose of this discussion that we are concerned with the valuation of loss of earnings and pension rights in respect of an injured plaintiff. The valuation of a dependency loss in a fatal accident case or of the cost of special care and other expenses will involve the same general principles. As a result of the judgment of the House of Lords in *Cookson v. Knowles* [1979] A.C. 556 it has now been established that in fatal accident cases as well as in personal injury actions loss of earnings up to the date of trial should constitute a head of special damage. The date of valuation for future pecuniary loss should therefore be the date of trial in all cases.

The principal elements in the actuarial basis are discussed briefly under separate headings below.

Mortality

7.12 The actuary would have sufficient information to be able to take into account in selecting a mortality table the sex, race, occupation, social status, residential area and state of health of the plaintiff. If, however, he is to employ a table for which monetary functions are readily available (without recourse to a computer) his choice will be effectively limited to a population table or a table of mortality of assured lives or annuitants. He may further have access to tables based on the experience of, and employed for the valuation of, occupational pension schemes. In the author's view a population table, although open to the objection that it is based on lives including the unemployable, would be more appropriate in the majority of cases than a table based on lives selected for insurance or self-selected for annuities. If the pre-accident state of health of the plaintiff were sub-normal or if the actuary were instructed that the valuation must take account of the fact that the accident had reduced the plaintiff's expectation of life, a rating-up could be made in the age. In order to assess such a rating-up the actuary would need to be supplied with a doctor's opinion as to the plaintiff's reduced expectation of life or as to his percentage additional mortality. (Since the decision in *Pickett v. British Rail Engineering Ltd* [1980] A.C. 136 it has been established that an injured plaintiff is entitled to recover damages on a limited basis for the so-called "lost years". His reduced expectation of life is, however, still relevant to the assessment of damages for cost of care.) For occupations which experience particularly heavy mortality an out-of-date population table may be appropriate or a rating-up in age on the normal table. For occupations which experience particularly light mortality the choice is between an assured lives' or annuitants' table or a rating-down in age.

Contingencies

7.13 It is the practice of the courts to make a percentage deduction for contingencies resulting in a temporary loss of earnings, and the author accepts that this is reasonable. The percentage deduction will clearly depend on the facts of the individual case, but substantial guidance is now given in the third edition of the "Ogden Tables".

Earnings progression and inflation

7.14 The valuation of loss of earnings and of pensions based thereon may take account of future increases in earnings as a result of (i) normal age progression and promotion, and (ii) general increases in the level of earnings attributable to increasing national productivity.

Evidence as to future inflation inadmissible

7.15 The court will not accept evidence as to the likelihood or extent of future inflation: (see *Mitchell v. Mulholland* [1972] 1 Q.B. 65. Protection against inflation is to be secured by prudent investment.

Taxation

7.16 We now consider the allowance to be made for taxation in the assessment of damages. No tax is payable on an award of damages for personal injury or death. Acordingly, the principle laid down by the House of Lords in *British Transport Commission v. Gourley* [1956] A.C. 185 applies, so that it is necessary to assess damages on the basis of the net loss after tax. In the author's view, it is clearly correct that the rate of interest used in making a discount, when assessing future loss, should also be the net rate after tax. It may be necessary to take account of the estimated amount to be received under other heads of damage which, if substantial, would increase the plaintiff's post-trial tax liability. Such a case was described by Lord Reid in *Taylor v. O'Connor* [1971] A.C. 115 in the following passage from his speech:

> "This case is in a sense *British Transport Commission v. Gourley* [1956] AC 185 in reverse, for that case instructs us that we must see damages had to be reduced if taxation was taken into account. Here they have to be increased."

This position was fully accepted by the inter-professional working party who, in their explanatory notes to the "Ogden Tables", explained how to take account of tax on the income from investment of a lump-sum award.

THE DISCOUNT RATE: HISTORY AND PRESENT POSITION

7.17 We now come to the most contentious element of an actuarial valuation. In the assessment of damages for future loss, a discount must be made to take account of the receipt of an immediate lump sum as compensation for the future loss. The rate of such discount will depend upon the net return from the investment which it is assumed would be made with the damages awarded. Until the decision in *Wells*, the court's conventional approach has been to assume that the award will be invested in equities, yielding a return of four to five per cent. This was based upon a passage from Lord Diplock's speech in *Mallet v. McMonagle* [1970] A.C. 166. Lord Diplock said:

> "In my view the only practicable course for courts to adopt in assessing damages awarded under the Fatal Accidents Acts is to leave out of account the risk of further inflation, on the one hand, and the high interest rates which reflect the fear of it, on the other hand. In estimating the amount of the annual dependency in the future, had the deceased not been killed, money should be treated as retaining its value at the date of the judgment and in calculating the present value of annual payments which would have been received in future years, interest rates appropriate to times of stable currency such as 4 per cent to 5 per cent should be adopted."

In *Cookson v. Knowles* [1979] A.C. 556 Lord Diplock said that inflation was "taken care of in a rough and ready way by the higher rates of interest obtainable as one of the consequences of it and *no other practicable basis of calculation has been suggested that is capable of dealing with so conjectural a factor with greater precision*". [Emphasis added.]

7.18 There is now, however, a perfectly practicable basis of calculation that is capable of dealing with inflation with absolute precision. As indicated earlier in this chapter in the discussion on the working party tables, the position has been dramatically changed by the advent of index-linked Government stocks. These stocks, of which there are now a number with varying coupons and maturity dates, provide a guaranteed real rate of return above the rate of inflation. The real return will of course depend upon the price at which the stocks are bought, which will in turn reflect the market's assessment of the likely future rate of inflation. At the time of writing, they can be bought to give a real rate of return of about three per cent which is significantly less than Lord Diplock's recommended rate. It would therefore be in the interest of plaintiffs to submit to the court assessments of damages based on the presumption that awards would be invested in these stocks. Such a presumption does not involve any necessity to speculate as to the future rate of inflation, but it is based on the certainty of a modest real rate of return rather than the optimistic and uncertain real rate of return of 4 per cent to 5 per cent postulated by Lord Diplock. This approach would be in line with Lord Diplock's general reasoning in *Wright v. British Railways Board* [1983] A.C. 773

The Law Commission's Consultation Paper

7.19 This approach received powerful support from the Law Commission.

In 1992 the Law Commission issued Consultation Paper No. 125 in which it sought views and information on the assessment of lump sum damages for future loss. At the same time, the Commission carried out empirical research into the problem. One question on which the Commission sought the views of consultees was whether it would be reasonable to use the return on I.L.G.S. as a guide to the appropriate discount rate. Two-thirds of those who responded to this question supported the use of I.L.G.S. rates to determine more accurate discounts and agreed that the assumption of a four to five per cent rate of return over time is crude and inflexible and can lead to over- or under-compensation, and hence to injustice.

The Law Commission's Report No. 224

7.20 In September 1994, the Law Commission published its Report Law Com. No. 224. Paragraph 2.28. of the Report stated:

> "We share the views of those who responded to us that a practice of discounting by reference to returns on I.L.G.S. would be preferable to the present arbitrary presumption. The four to five per cent discount rate which emerged from the case law was established at a time when I.L.G.S. did not exist. I.L.G.S. now constitute the best evidence of a real return on any investment where the risk element is minimal, because they take account of inflation, rather than attempt to predict it as conventional investments do. Capital is redeemed under I.L.G.S. at par and index-linked to the change in the Retail Prices Index (R.P.I.) since issue. Income remains constant in real terms with increases in the R.P.I.. There is no premium available for risk because there is no risk."

7.21 Paragraph 2.31 of the Report stated:

"We are also convinced that I.L.G.S. can be used in a practical way to achieve a discount rate which is more realistic. We believe that I.L.G.S. should always be looked at, but that the parties should have the opportunity to adduce evidence as to alternatives they consider more appropriate if they so wish ... We therefore recommend that there should be legislative provision requiring courts when determining the return to be expected from the investment of the sum awarded in any proceedings for damages for personal injury (including proceedings under the Fatal Accidents Act and the Law Reform (Miscellaneous Provisions) Act 1934) to take account of the net return to any plaintiff on an index-linked Government security ..."

7.22 Paragraph 2.32 of the Report stated:

"... If, as we and most of our consultees believe, index-linked securities represent the best indicator of real rates of return on low-risk investments, it follows that I.L.G.S. should always be taken into account in the first instance. That is why we recommend that the legislation should only permit departure from the I.L.G.S. rates when it can be shown that an alternative rate would be better in the individual case."

7.23 The Law Commission also recommended in paragraph 6.1 of Part VI of their Report that the Ogden Tables should be admissible in evidence in any proceedings for damages for personal injury, when it is desired to establish the capital value of the sum to be awarded as general damages for future pecuniary loss.

7.24 This recommendation resulted in section 10 of the Civil Evidence Act 1995, which provides that the Ogden Tables should be admissible in evidence and may be proved by production of a copy published by Her Majesty's Stationery Office (see para. 2.35 above). The section has not yet been brought into force, but courts have for some time looked at the Ogden Tables as a matter of course. Since the decision in *Wells* the courts will, as already stated, always use the Tables whenever they have to assess damages for future pecuniary loss.

The Damages Act, 1996: Section 1

7.25 The Damages Act, 1996 received the Royal Assent on July 24, 1996. It was enacted in virtually the same terms as the Damages Bill.

Section 1 of the Act provides:

> "1—(1) In determining the return to be expected from the investment of a sum awarded as damages for future pecuniary loss in an action for personal injury the court shall, subject to and in accordance with rules of court made for the purposes of this section, take into account such rate of return (if any) as may from time to time be prescribed by an order made by the Lord Chancellor.
>
> (2) Subsection (1) above shall not however prevent the court taking a different rate of return into account if any party to the proceedings shows that it is more appropriate in the case in question.
>
> (3) An order under subsection (1) above may prescribe different rates of return for different classes of case.
>
> (4) Before making an order under subsection (1) above the Lord Chancellor shall consult the Government Actuary and the Treasury; and any order under that subsection shall be made by statutory instrument subject to annulment in pursuance of a resolution of either House of Parliament.
>
> (5) In the application of this section to Scotland for references to the Lord Chancellor there shall be substituted references to the Secretary of State."

The Lord Chancellor's *volte face*

7.26 It would have been reasonable to assume that the rate to be prescribed by the Lord Chancellor would be based on the current return form appropriate I.L.G.S.. But in the debates during the passage of the Damages Bill through the House of Lords, there was a complete *volte face* by the Lord Chancellor. He stated that he would wait to see what the Court of Appeal decided in the combined appeals, *Page v. Sheerness Steel plc* [1996] P.I.Q.R. Q. 26, *Thomas v. Brighton Health Authority* [1996] P.I.Q.R. Q. 44 and *Wells v. Wells* [1996] P.I.Q.R. Q. 62, before exercising his powers under section 1 of the Act. He gave no explanation why he had changed his mind. He made no criticism of the recommendations or reasoning of the Law Commission, which had previously received his express approval.

THE DECISION OF THE COURT OF APPEAL IN *WELLS*

7.27 On October 23, 1996, the Court of Appeal gave its judgment in the combined appeals. The judges at first instance in these cases had based the discount rate on the return from I.L.G.S.—in the case of *Wells*, 2.5 per cent and in the cases of *Page* and *Thomas*, 3 per cent. The Court of Appeal held that in each case the discount rate should have been 4.5 per cent, based on the return from investing in equities. On this basis, the Court substantially reduced the first instance awards.

THE DECISION OF THE HOUSE OF LORDS IN *WELLS*

7.28 The Court of Appeal's decision was widely criticised. See for example *Kemp & Kemp*, Vol. 1, Release 66, paras 6–003/8 to 6–003/12/3. The House of Lords accepted these criticisms and allowed the appeals, laying down new "Guidelines". The discount rate should now be 3 per cent per annum net, unless and until the Lord Chancellor prescribes a different rate pursuant to section 1(1) of the Damages Act, 1996. The main speech (with which the other members of the Judicial Committee agreed) was given by Lord Lloyd of Berwick. The essence of decision and the *ratio decidendi* are set out in the following extracts from his speech: at pp. 341E to 342E:

"*Conclusion*

My conclusion is that the judges in these three cases were right to assume for the purpose of their calculations that the plaintiffs would invest their damages in I.L.G.S. for the following reasons.

(1) Investment in I.L.G.S. is the most accurate way of calculating the present value of the loss which the plaintiffs will actually suffer in real terms.

(2) Although this will result in a heavier burden on these defendants, and, if the principle is applied across the board, on

the insurance industry in general, I can see nothing unjust. It is true that insurance premiums may have been fixed on the basis of the 4 to 5 per cent discount rate indicated in *Cookson v. Knowles*.

[1979] A.C. 556 and the earlier authorities. But this was only because there was then no better way of allowing for future inflation. The objective was always the same. No doubt insurance premiums will have to increase in order to take account of the new lower rate of discount. Whether this is something which the country can afford is not a subject on which your Lordships were addressed. So we are not in a position to form any view as to the wider consequences.

(3) The search for a prudent investment will always depend on the circumstances of the particular investor. Some are able to take a measure of risk, others are not. For a plaintiff who is not in a position to take risks, and who wishes to protect himself against inflation in the short term of up to 10 years, it is clearly prudent to invest in I.L.G.S. It cannot therefore be assumed that he will invest in equities and gilts. Still less is it his duty to invest in equities and gilts in order to mitigate his loss.

(4) Logically the same applies to a plaintiff investing for the long term. In any event it is desirable to have a single rate applying across the board, in order to facilitate settlements and to save the expense of expert evidence at the trial. I take this view even though it is open to the Lord Chancellor under section 1(3) of the Act of 1996 to prescribe different rates of return for different classes of case. Mr Leighton Williams conceded that it is not desirable in practice to distinguish between different classes of plaintiff when assessing the multiplier.

(5) How the plaintiff, or the majority of plaintiffs, in fact invest their money is irrelevant. The research carried out by the Law Commission does not suggest that the majority of plaintiffs in fact invest in equities and gilts, but rather in a building society or a bank deposit.

(6) There was no agreement between the parties as to how much greater, if at all, the return on equities is likely to be in the short or long term. But it is at least clear that an investment in I.L.G.S. will save up to 1 per cent per annum by obviating the need for continuing investment advice.

(7) The practice of the Court of Protection when investing for the long term affords little guidance. In any event the policy may

change when lump sums are calculated at a lower rate of return.

(8) The views of the Ogden Working Party, the Law Commission and the author of *Kemp & Kemp* in favour of an investment in I.L.G.S. are entitled to great weight.

(9) There is nothing in the previous decisions of the House which inhibits a new approach. It is therefore unnecessary to have resort to the *Practice Statement (Judicial Precedent)* [1966] 1 W.L.R. 1234).

Consequences

Once it is accepted that the lump sum should be calculated on the basis of the rate of return available on I.L.G.S. then an assessment of the average rate of return at the relevant date presents no problem. The rates are published daily in the "Financial Times." A table of average rates for the period June 1990 to December 1994 ('Gross Return on Index-Linked Government Securities') is included in *Kemp & Kemp, The Quantum of Damages* vol 1, para. 8–068. No doubt the table will be brought up to date from time to time."

And at pp. 343D to 344C.

"*Guidelines*

Section 1 of the Act of 1996 provides:

> '(1) In determining the return to be expected from the investment of a sum awarded as damages for future pecuniary loss in an action for personal injury the court shall, subject to and in accordance with rules of court made for the purposes of this section, take into account such rate of return (if any) as may from time to time be prescribed by an order made by the Lord Chancellor . . .'

The section came into force on September 24, 1996, but no rate has yet been prescribed. Lord Mackay of Clashfern, the previous Lord Chancellor, was said to be awaiting the decision of the Court of Appeal in the instant cases. It goes without saying that the sooner the Lord Chancellor sets the rate the better. The present uncertainty does not make the settling of claims any easier.

In the meantime it is for your Lordships to set guidelines to replace the old 4 to 5 per cent bracket. There is something to be said for a bracket, since it allows some flexibility in exceptional cases, as where, for example, the impact of higher-rate tax would result in substantial undercompensation. Thus on an award of £2m higher rate tax payable over the first half of a 20-year period would alone amount to nearly £75,000. But the majority of your Lordships prefer a single figure. I do not disagree provided it is subject to the same flexibility as is to be found in section 1(2) of the 1996 Act.

What then should the figure be? The average gross redemption yield on I.L.G.S. has fallen steadily over the last year. In May 1997 it was 3.68 per cent, by May 1998 it was only 2.8 per cent. Less tax at, say, 15 per cent, this would give a net return of 2.38 per cent. Logically, therefore, we should take 2.5 per cent as the guideline figure, since the assumption is that the plaintiff will purchase in the market at that price. The higher-yielding stock is no longer available. If therefore the calculation is done at 3 per cent instead of 2.5 per cent, he would be substantially under-compensated.

But since it is undesirable that the guidelines should be changed too often, it may be better that the average gross return should be ascertained over a period of months rather than on a particular day; and since, as I have said, the average return has been falling over the last year, one would expect the average return over that period to be higher than the current return. Such proves to be the case. Over the last six months and 12 months to March 1998 the average return has been 3.02 per cent and 3.28 per cent respectively. These figures justify a guideline rate of return of 3 per cent net rather than 2.5 per cent, and this is the rate which I would propose for general use until the Lord Chancellor has specified a new rate under section 1 of the Act of 1996.

I would not, however, accept that the average should be taken over as long a period as three years. For if the rate of return had been falling steadily over the whole period (in fact this has not been the case) it would work very unfavourably to the plaintiffs; and vice versa if it had been rising steadily over three years. A year would seem to be the best compromise period. Once the net return has been established to the nearest 0.5 per cent, it is a simple enough matter to find the correct multiplier from the Ogden Tables."

7.29 Their Lordships also dealt with another problem of general importance. They held that, as 3 per cent was now the "going rate" for discounting future loss, the same rate should be adopted in a *Roberts v. Johnstone* calculation. *Per* Lord Lloyd at pp. 347.F to 348.F.:

> "I can deal with the second of the two miscellaneous points in *Thomas v. Brighton Health Authority* quite shortly. In October 1990, 15 months after the plaintiff's birth, and five years before the trial, the plaintiff's parents moved into a larger house. They needed more space, because of his disability. The additional cost was some £60,000 which they raised by way of a mortgage. The question is how the additional cost should be reflected in the award of damages.
>
> Obviously the plaintiff is not entitled to the additional capital cost, since the larger house is a permanent addition to the family's assets. It will be there, and could be realised, at the end of the period covered by the award. How then should this head of damages be calculated? Should it be the interest on the mortgage? Or interest calculated in some other way?
>
> The answer to this question, described in *Kemp and Kemp, The Question of Damages*, vol 1, para. 5–044 as "a satisfactory and elegant solution" was provided by the Court of Appeal in *Roberts v. Johnstone* [1989] Q.B. 878. It is to be assumed that the plaintiff will pay for the additional accommodation out of his own capital. It is further to be assumed that the capital input will be risk-free over the period of the award, and protected against inflation, by a corresponding increase in the value of the house. What the plaintiff has therefore lost is the income which the capital would have earned over the period of the award after deduction of tax.
>
> But the lost income is not to be calculated by reference to a normal commercial rate of interest. For interest, as Lord Diplock explained in *Wright v. British Railways Board* [1983] 2 A.C. 773, 781, normally includes two elements, a reward for taking a risk of loss or reduction of capital, and "a reward for forgoing the use of the capital sum for the time being". Since the capital input in the new accommodation is free of risk, or virtually free of risk, it is only the second of the two elements of interest that the plaintiff has lost, namely the 'going rate' for forgoing the use of money. The Court of Appeal in *Roberts v. Johnstone* took 2 per cent as the "going rate". This was the figure originally chosen by Lord

Denning MR in *Birkett v. Hayes* [1982] 1 W.L.R. 816 and accepted by Lord Diplock in *Wright v. British Railways Board*. *Birkett v. Hayes* and *Wright v. British Railways Board* were both cases of non-pecuniary loss, but the point is the same.

Both sides accept that the correct approach is that adopted by the Court of Appeal in *Roberts v. Johnstone*. The only question is how that approach should be applied. Collins J. arrived at the "going rate" by taking the average return on I.L.G.S. as the best possible indicator of the real return on a risk-free investment over the period of the award. In other words, he took the same discount of 3 per cent net of tax as he had taken for the calculation of future loss. The Court of Appeal disagreed. They took the "conventional rate" of 2 per cent, pointing out the Stocker L.J. had not tied his 2 per cent to the return on any particular form of investment.

It is true that there is no reference to I.L.G.S. in *Roberts v. Johnstone*. But in *Wright v. British Railways Board* Lord Diplock chose the return on I.L.G.S. as the first (and in my view simpler) of the two routes by which courts can arrive at the appropriate or 'conventional' rate of interest for foregoing the use of capital. At that time the net return on 15-year and 25-year index-linked stocks was 2 per cent. I can see no reason for regarding 2 per cent as sacrosanct now that the average net return on I.L.G.S. has changed. The current rate is 3 per cent. This therefore is the rate which should now be taken for calculating the cost of additional accommodation. It has two advantages. In the first place it is the same as the rate for calculating future loss. Secondly it will be kept up to date by the Lord Chancellor when exercising his powers under section 1 of the Act of 1996. On this point I would restore the order of Collins J."

7.30 The *ratio decidendi* of the *Roberts v. Johnstone* issue has implications in respect of a more important issue, namely, the rate to be used when calculating interest on general damages for pain and suffering and loss of amenities. This question was not in issue before their Lordships, but their reasoning should surely result in this rate becoming three per cent rather than the hitherto conventional rate of two per cent, since three per cent is now the "going rate". At the date of revising th is Chapter, there has been no reported decision on this point.

7.31 Their Lordships also dealt with the so-called "Judicial

Discount". They held that, while there may be grounds for a discount when assessing damages for future loss of earning there is (apart from special cases) no ground for any discount when assessing life-long future cost of care. *per.* Lord Lloyd at pp. 345G to 347F.

"*Thomas v. Brighton Health Authority*
The agreed medical evidence was that the plaintiff has a life expectancy to the age of 60. Collins J. ([1996] P.I.Q.R. Q.44, 57) held, however, that he ought to reduce the arithmetical multiplier by about 20 per cent "to cater for the hazards of life in such cases". In the result he took a multiplier of 23. The Court of Appeal agreed with the judge's approach but started from a different starting point. With a 4.5 per cent discount rate the arithmetical multiplier came to 20. Reduced by 15 per cent, rather than 20 per cent, they arrived at a multiplier of 17.

Was it correct for the judge and the Court of Appeal to reduce the arithmetical multiplier, and therefore, in effect, override the expectation of life agreed by the doctors? Mr Owen submitted that there could be no rational basis for applying a further discount for "contingencies", since the doctors had already taken account of all the contingencies that might affect the plaintiff, such as the increased risk of accident, chest infection, and so on. The only reason given by the judge was that the courts had 'tended to reduce multipliers by about 20 per cent'. The Court of Appeal took the same line.

I can see no answer to Mr Owen's argument. The inevitable result of reducing the multiplier to 17, as Mr Havers pointed out, will be that the plaintiff's damages will run out when he is 39. He will have nothing to cover his needs for the remaining 21 years of his life.

Mr Havers conceded that there is room for a judicial discount when calculating the loss of future earnings, when contingencies may indeed affect the result. But there is no room for any discount in the case of a whole life multiplier with an agreed expectation of life. In the case of loss of earnings the contingencies can work in only one direction—in favour of the defendant. But in the case of life expectancy, the contingency can work in either direction. The plaintiff may exceed his normal expectation of life, or he may fall short of it.

There is no purpose in the courts making as accurate a

prediction as they can of the plaintiff's future needs if the resulting sum is arbitrarily reduced for no better reason than that the prediction might be wrong. A prediction remains a prediction. Contingencies should be taken into account where they work in one direction, but not where they cancel out. There is no more logic or justice in reducing the whole life multiplier by 15 per cent or 20 per cent on an agreed expectation of life than there would be in increasing it by the same amount.

It follows from what I have said that I do not agree with the discount which McCullough J. allowed in *Janardan v. East Berkshire Health Authority* [1990] 2 Med. L.R. 1. In that case the plaintiff, aged five at the time of trial, had a life expectancy to 55. This indicated a multiplier of just under 20 by reference to a 4.5 per cent discount rate (p. 8). McCullough J. held (at p. 7) that a discount was required to allow for the possibility that the plaintiff might not survive to 55. I do not accept this; and it may be that McCullough J. would not have accepted it either, if he had not felt constrained by previous authority. Left to himself, he said at p. 9, he would have taken a whole life multiplier of 17.5 to 18. But the multiplier chosen by the Court of Appeal in *Croke v. Wiseman* [1982] 1 W.L.R. 71 and by the House in *Lim Poh Choo v. Camden and Islington Area Health Authority* [1980] A.C. 174 required him to choose 17 instead. But this meant, as Mr Havers pointed out, that the plaintiff in *Janardan's* case would have run out of damages at the age of 33, although he was expected to live to 55.

In *Hunt v. Severs* [1994] 2 A.C. 350 the plaintiff had a life expectancy of 25 years. The appropriate multiplier by reference to a 4.5 per cent discount rate was 14.821. But the judge reduced this figure to 14 because 14 seemed more in line with the multiplier applied in other comparable cases. The Court of Appeal [1993] Q.B. 815, correctly in my view, substituted a multiplier of 15, as being the nearest round figure to 14.821. Sir Thomas Bingham M.R. observed, at p. 841, that an allowance for contingencies may sometimes be appropriate. But he continued: "Such an allowance is not appropriate in the present case, where the agreed life expectancy of the plaintiff is 25 years. That is a fact, or rather an agreed assumption, upon which the damages payable for future care must be based."

But the House disagreed. Lord Bridge of Harwich said at p. 365):

> "The passage I have cited from the judgment of the Court of Appeal appears to show the court as treating the circumstance that both doctors in evidence estimated the plaintiff's expectation of life at 25 years as establishing the "fact" or "assumption" that she would live for 25 years and thus converting the process of assessing future loss into "a simple arithmetical calculation". I cannot think that this was the correct approach to the evidence. A man or woman in normal health, at a given age, no doubt has an ascertainable statistical life expectancy. But in using such a figure as the basis for assessment of damages with respect to future losses, some discount in respect of life's manifold contingencies is invariably made."

I have some difficulty with this passage. The plaintiff's life expectancy was not derived from any tables. It was the agreed life expectancy of this particular plaintiff, taking her individual characteristics into account. I cannot for my part see what further room there was for "life's manifold contingencies". The whole point of agreeing a life expectancy, if it can be done, is to exclude any further speculation. With respect therefore I prefer the approach of Sir Thomas Bingham M.R. and the Court of Appeal.

The explanation for the different approach of the House in *Hunt v. Severs* may be a continuing hesitation to embrace the actuarial tables. I do not suggest that the judge should be a slave to the tables. There may well be special factors in particular cases. But the tables should now be regarded as the starting point, rather than a check. A judge should be slow to depart from the relevant actuarial multiplier on impressionistic grounds, or by reference to "a spread of multipliers in comparable cases" especially when the multipliers were fixed before actuarial tables were widely used. This may be the explanation for the relatively low multiplier chosen by the House in *Lim Poh Choo's* case.

For the reasons I have given, I consider that the Court of Appeal in the present case were wrong to substitute a multiplier of 17 for the judge's 23. But the judge himself was also too low. The appropriate multiplier derived from the tables on the agreed life expectancy was 26.58."

7.32 The decision in *Wells* will result in significantly higher damages for future loss, particularly where whole-life care is involved. Various aspects of the practical impact of *Wells* are considered in a special edition of "Quantum" published in September 1998.

THE COURT'S ATTITUDE TO ACTURIAL EVIDENCE

Initial reluctance to have regard to actuarial evidence

7.33 Judges have in the past shown reluctance to have regard to actuarial evidence. Any truly actuarial calculations will have taken mortality into account. There appears sometimes to have been a judicial misconception as to the way in which actuarial calculations take mortality into account.

We emphasise that they do not employ an annuity certain for the period of the expectation of life to represent the value of a life annuity. Instead, the actuary in his calculations allows for the chance that the individual in question will depart one way or the other from the average, *i.e.* will not live for the average period by which people of his age survive that age.

It follows that Sir Gordon Willmer was in error when he said in *Mitchell v. Mulholland*: [1972] 1 GB 65 at 85

> "The average man has an expectation of life of a certain number of years. This is a matter of probability, but *for purposes of actuarial calculation it has to be treated as a certainty.* Yet nobody can say whether an individual plaintiff is an average man, or that he will live for the expectation of life of an average man of his age. *Any actuarial calculation must, therefore, be discounted to allow for the chance that he may only live for a shorter period*" [emphasis added].

This statement was based upon a misapprehension of the nature of standard actuarial calculations. Unfortunately, this error has been repeated by all three members of the Court of Appeal in *Auty v. National Coal Board.* [1985] 1 WLR 784

Per Waller L.J..

> "The judge said that ... death before 65 ... was the major discount. It was submitted that the risk of death was already taken into consideration in the expectation of life. This is a

misunderstanding. *The expectation of life is an average and assumes everybody lives to that age and then dies, but in fact some die before and some after. Those who die before are the important ones.*" [Emphasis added].

Waller L.J. then cited the above mentioned passage from Sir Gordon Willmer's judgment and said that he agreed with it.

Per Oliver L.J.

> "The other specific criticisms which have been made are that the judge made, in effect, a double discount for contingencies, in that he based his figure largely on the possibility of death before 65, a possibility which, it is argued, is already taken into account in the average life expectancy. For the reasons which Waller L.J. has given, there is nothing in this point."

Per Purchas L.J.

> "Mr Mortimer also submitted that the result of calculating the periods of expectation of life from the age at trial and then discounting the overall figure for day-to-day contingencies was that there was a double discount for the period between ages 34 and 65 . . . This was based on the fact that life tables are averages anyway. As Waller L.J. has already explained, by reference to the judgment of Sir Gordon Willmer in *Mitchell v. Mulholland* (No. 2) [1972] 1 Q.B. 65, this argument was misconceived."

7.34 The evidence before the court in *Auty's case* was actuarial evidence. The concept of "expectation of life" has no place in actuarial calculations, and formed no part of the evidence before the court. It will have been noted, however, that all the members of the Court of Appeal made reference in the passages cited above from their judgments to "expectation of life" or to "life expectancy". If the plaintiff's argument in fact involved reference to expectation of life, it is understandable why the court was confused. Nevertheless, the statement of Sir Gordon Willmer that "any actuarial calculation must be discounted to allow for the chance that he may only live for a shorter period" is clearly misconceived. And the fact that all members of the Court of Appeal in *Auty's case* expressly approved and relied upon Sir Gordon Willmer's statement shows that they did not understand the principles on which actuarial calculations are made.

7.35 At least in the passages cited above the court has recognised that mortality had been taken into account to some extent and the misunderstanding was limited to the fact that the court did not appreciate that the possibility that the plaintiff might depart form the average in either direction had also been taken into account by the actuary. Occasionally, however, judges appear not to have realised that mortality had been taken into account at all!

Per Streatfield J. in *Pope v. Murphy & Son Ltd* [1961] 1 Q.B. 222 at 227:

> "I agree that it would be quite wrong to take any annuity basis as the final figure because . . . I would . . . have to discount it because of the ordinary changes and chances of life. [The plaintiff] might suffer some other accident or disaster . . . or *he might die*." [Emphasis added.]

Similarly, an Australian judge, having accepted the actuarial value of a particular sum on the joint lives of husband and wife, proceeded to reduce it, *inter alia*, for "the possibility of her death from natural causes or from unavoidable accident": Abbott J. in *Hine v. O'Connor* [1951] SASR 1, 13.

7.36 Misconceptions of this nature may partly explain the English courts' earlier dislike and distrust of actuarial evidence. Courts in other Commonwealth countries have found it hard to understand the attitude. Actuarial evidence is regularly adduced and accepted in the courts of Australia and Canada. Indeed, the Australian Judge, Blackburn J., said in *Charlion v. Public Trustee (NT)* (1967) 11 F.L.R. 42, that the absence of actuarial evidence is "always regrettable".

7.37 In previous editions of this work we set out in some detail successive recommendations by the Law Commission and other bodies in favour of actuarial evidence, but the decision of the House of Lords in *Wells* has revolutionised the court's attitude to such evidence. There is no point in repeating past history and past arguments. The court's previous misconceptions have been swept away. Lord Lloyd stated the position in clear and unequivocal terms: [1998] 3 W.L.R. at 347D:

"I do not suggest that the judge should be a slave to the [actuarial] tables. There may well be special factors in particular cases. *But the tables should now be regarded as the starting-point, rather than a check*. A judge should be slow to depart from the relevant actuarial multiplier on impressionistic grounds, or by reference to 'a spread of multipliers in comparable cases' especially where the multipliers were fixed before actuarial tables were widely used." [Emphasis added.]

7.38 No doubt the Chancellor will now bring into effect section 10 of the Civil Evidence Act 1996. This would make actuarial tables issued from time to time by the Government Actuary's Department admissible in evidence for the purpose of assessing, in an action for personal injury, the sum to be awarded as general damages for future pecuniary loss. This would merely recognise the present *de facto* position.

SOME PRACTICAL PROBLEMS

Loss of pension rights

7.39 There is no difference in principle between the assessment of damages for loss of pension rights and the assessment of damages for loss of earnings. The difficulty for the courts appears to be the deferment element that is involved: the fact that, in addition to the other uncertainties, the lost payments would not have commenced until a further date, and then only if the plaintiff had survived to that date. There are also other complications—for example, a pension benefit that is not a level payment. The pension might reduce at the time a state pension benefit becomes payable, or it might include guaranteed increases in respect of the cost of living, usually at a low compound rate.

7.40 The explanatory notes to the working party tables explain how to apply them in straightforward cases to the valuation of loss of pension. It may be difficult, however, for the courts to assess loss of pension rights without actuarial assistance. There is a tendency, because of these problems, to attempt the assessment, not by looking to the benefits lost, but by looking at the rates of contribution payable to a pension scheme by both the plaintiff and his employer. The loss is then estimated either by reference to the total of past contributions from both employee and employer or by reference to the annual future level of joint contributions.

7.41 These practices are, in the author's view, dangerous because in most schemes the level of the employer's contributions is assessed globally by an actuary in relation to the overall liabilities of the scheme and has no particular relevance to the level of benefits for an individual member. It is therefore important to value a loss of pension benefits positively by considering the benefits which the plaintiff would have received if the tort had not occurred and those to which he may still be entitled. In a large and complicated case actuarial assistance may be essential.

The child plaintiff

7.42 Particular problems arise in the assessment of damages for loss of future earnings when the injured plaintiff is a child. In most fatal accident or personal injury cases the actual earnings of the deceased or of the injured plaintiff as at the date of the accident are known. But in the case of a child plaintiff there is no such starting figure. Moreover, the future period over which all of the usual uncertainties familiar to the courts extend is considerably longer.

7.43 All that can be done is to have regard to the parental background as some guide to the child's likely educational and employment potential, and of course to consider the child's own educational attainment up to the date of the accident. In the thalidomide test cases, in which the author gave evidence to the court, the assessments submitted took account of IQ measurements. In the case of *Taylor v. Glass* 23 May 1979 (unreported), this was not possible as the injury had occurred when the plaintiff was only one year old. In this case the author submitted alternative assessments on the basis that the plaintiff would either have attained "national average earnings" or one and one half times this level. Smith J in his judgment remarked:

> "I agree that there is some uncertainty, but I must bear in mind that [the plaintiff] comes from an excellent home with caring, responsible parents in a comfortable position who, had this tragedy not occurred, would have seen that he was properly educated and trained in the requisite skills to enable him to be, in all probability, a higher than average wage-earner."

In these circumstances Smith J. assessed damages for lost earnings on the basis that the plaintiff would have earned one and a half times the average national wages.

7.44 A further example is provided by the Court of Appeal decision in *Cassel v. Riverside Health Authority* [1992] P.I.Q.R. Q. 1. The plaintiff was aged eight at the date of the trial. He would never be gainfully employed. His expectation of life was virtually unaffected by his injuries. The trial judge, Rose J., had reviewed the evidence as to the heredity and environment of the plaintiff and found the omens to be propitious. The family pattern on both sides was one of effort and success. There was a good prospect that, had he wished, he could have entered a profession, in particular the legal profession. There were also artistic and entrepreneurial genes within him. Rose J. held that the plaintiff would probably have started work at the age of 23 and would have continued working until the age of 65. Evidence, based on the earnings of a partner in a medium-sized firm of City Solicitors or Accountants was before the court in the form of projected earning starting at £16,000 a year at age 24 and reaching £100,000 a year at age 65, plus appropriate perquisites. On this basis Rose j. assessed the average net earnings at £35,000 a year. The Court of Appeal upheld this figure.

APPENDIX A

Cassel v. Hammersmith and Fulham Health Authority [1992] P.I.Q.R. Q.1 and Q.168

Note: The purpose of Appendix A is to illustrate the way in which the court deals with a case of severe personal injury.

General Damages: £110,000 (£145,000 in terms of the £1 in 1998); Total Award: £1,223,820; December 21, 1990; Rose J.; Severe brain damage—The plaintiff was a boy aged eight at the date of the trial. He was severely brain damaged. Judgment on liability had been entered for 90 per cent of his total damages. Rose J. gave a very careful judgment which cannot be adequately summarised in a headnote. The reader is referred to the full judgment below. In particular the assessment of future loss of earnings is enlightening. On the basis of full liability damages of £1,176,122 (excluding interest) were assessed plus Court of Protection fees of £47,000.

The levels of damages were as follows:

		(£)
1	Pain, suffering and loss of amenities	110,000
2	Net cost of past paid care	25,678
3	Past parental care: £8,500 × 6.2	53,125
4	Net past medical and other costs	16,948
5	Cost of future care, multiplier of 18 divided into two phases: 7½ and 10½ (Phase i): £32,098 × 7½ = £240,735 (less saved private school fees of £65,000)	175,735
	(Phase ii): £31,698 × 10½ 332,829	
6	Future accommodation costs	13,000
7	Cost of small swimming pool	32,500

8	Future cost of purchases for careers £723 × 18	13,014
9	Future cost of educational tour £350 × 7½	2,625
10	Miscellaneous future costs including holidays £2,387 × 18	42,960
11	Future cost of appliances and medical costs	7,762
12	Loss of future earnings £35,000 × 10	350,000
	TOTAL	1,176,122
	Court of Protection Fees	47,700

Note

In this case the defendants submitted to judgment for 90 per cent of the total assessment of damages. The Court of Appeal upheld Rose J's award on March 18, 1992 except on two issues. The court disallowed the cost of a swimming pool and held that the Court of Protection fees were part of the damages so that only 90 per cent of the total should be awarded. Rose J had regarded these fees as costs and had awarded them in full.

JUDGMENT OF ROSE J.

"Hugo Cassel was born on September 3, 1982. Shortly before and during his birth he was severely asphyxiated. He almost died. He suffered cerebral palsy; that is, in this case, grave and irreparable brain damage. In this action by his father he claims damages against the health authority in whose care he and his mother were at the time.

The defendants have admitted that they were negligent. With the court's approval, judgment on liability has previously been entered in the boy's favour for 90 per cent of damages to be assessed. My task is to assess the damages. I shall do so under seven heads.

It is first convenient to set out my findings as to the nature and extent of Hugo's present and likely future disabilities. Little dispute arises between the parties as to these. There are many reports before me, a number of witnesses have given evidence and I have also seen a long video film taken earlier this year.

I find as follows: apart from two operations, one for a divergent squint when Hugo was a few months old and one to insert grommets into his ears, pain has not been and is not a feature of this case. But there is an enormous loss of amenity and Hugo has suffered and will continue to suffer considerably, particularly in terms of frustration, for he has insight, albeit limited, into his predicament. He is a good looking boy, of normal build for his age. He is mobile. He can walk reasonably well, though not always in a straight line, and runs for a few somewhat ungainly steps with a floppy movement of the arms.

With help in mounting and dismounting he can ride a pony at the walk and, if led, at the trot. He loves water, can do a dog-paddle and will probably be able to swim in the near future. He enjoys a climbing frame. His hearing is reasonably good. The vision in his right eye is very poor indeed. Although the vision in his left eye is good, he appears to have serious difficulty in remembering and interpreting what he sees, though he has no real difficulty in getting about in familiar surroundings. There is a fifty-fifty chance he will need a second operation for squint and a one-in-three chance he will need a third.

Some activities, such as eating, he carries out more by touch and feel than vision, though he can use a fork and spoon once food has been cut up for him. He also has to be supervised at the table because otherwise clumsiness leads to him knocking over crockery and glasses.

The extent of his visual impairment is such as to require his hand to be held and moved by the teacher when he is being taught Makoton sign language. He has some impairment of fine movements in the fingers, but he can dress and undress himself with help and supervision. His speech is limited to a very small number of words and one or two short phrases. He is doubly incontinent and wears a nappy at night, though his condition in this respect is slowly improving.

His principal handicap is his mental condition, by reason of which he needs constant skilled supervision. His behaviour, educational skills and comprehension are, at best, those of a two to three-year-old. He is impulsive, hyperactive and easily distracted and he does not appreciate dangers: for example, from fire and traffic. He has tantrums which can sometimes, particularly at school, be anticipated and headed off, but are sometimes unpredictable. They vary in length. He may, for example, refuse to eat or to get into or out of the bath. Sometimes he lies on the floor. Sometimes he screams for a considerable period.

His six-year-old sister and two-and-a-half-year-old brother suffer both from Hugo's excessive demands for their mother's attention and from violence in the form of slaps, bites, pulling of hair and twisting of fingers at Hugo's hands, a consequence, no doubt, of his frustration and jealousy at being unable to act and speak as they can.

He has considerable awareness of what is happening around him. For example, it was noticeable on several occasions during the filming of the video that he appeared to be aware of the camera. He goes by taxi to a special school from about 8.30 in the morning to 3.30 in the afternoon. He goes to bed about 8.30 pm, but has to be taken to the lavatory between 11 and midnight. On three or four nights a week, usually between 3 and 4 am he disturbs not only his sister, whose bedroom he usually shares, but his parents and/or the carer, who helps to look after him, by hyperactivity. This takes the form of jumping up and down in bed, throwing toys around the room and wandering about the house upstairs and downstairs. Sometimes he will only settle down again if moved to his parents' bedroom.

As he grows bigger he is becoming increasingly difficult to control, divert and entertain and this has been compounded by the lack, until very recently, of adequate carers. In the words of Mrs Walker, Mrs Cassel's sister with whom he has stayed, "Looking after Hugo is totally exhausting".

There is a 3 to 5 per cent risk of epilepsy. Because of this risk his lack of recognition of dangers and the possible difficulty in indicating symptoms of illness, Professor Ross tentatively suggests, and Dr Rosenbloom does not dissent from this, that Hugo's life expectancy is reduced below normal: to 60 years or thereabouts. Professor Rose accepts, however, that this estimate is partly based on statistical information which is somewhat out of date. He agrees that a high degree of care, a controlled healthy diet and a lack of exposure to the risk of driving on the highway will tend to prolong Hugo's life beyond the normal.

Professor Corbett has access to recently published data involving research into 2,000 mentally handicapped people in the Birmingham area which shows rapidly increasing life expectancy, approaching that for normal people.

In the light of all this evidence it seems to me to be a proper inference that Hugo's life expectancy, bearing in mind his present fitness and the close care which he will receive, is reduced below normal to only a very slight extent. I find and approach the case on the basis that he is likely to live until 65 or more.

So far as the future is concerned, the doctors agree that any improvement in his skills is likely to be slight. He will never be able to live independently, marry or work. Dr Rosenbloom said, and I accept, that with optimum help he may be able, in time, to function as a four to five-year-old. As to hyperactivity and behavioural problems, all agree Hugo will not improve significantly in the short or medium term. Professor Ross hopes, without promising, that by his mid-teens Hugo's sleep patterns will improve and he will become more biddable. Dr Rosenbloom and Professor Corbett say that, provided he receives consistent help from now on, he will tend to improve in 10, 15 or 20 years' time and Dr Rosenbloom expects some improvement in the sleep patterns by about the age of 15.

Inattention is likely to continue, with little improvement. Progress with his serious language problem is likely to be slow, even with the best of help, and he is unlikely to be able to make use of Makoton signing except in a very limited way. Although he will never be able to read books, it is possible he may learn a sufficient degree of labelling to be able to distinguish, for example, between a ladies' and a men's lavatory. Continence should continue to improve, though there are always likely to be faecal accidents.

All three doctors stress separately and unanimously the importance of continuity and consistency in Hugo's care in relation to the acquisition of new skills and the retention of old ones.

I turn to the different heads of claim:

Pain, suffering and loss of amenity

Mr Whitfield, whose submissions for the defendants have been very helpful on all aspects of this case, referred me to a number of authorities. In *Housecroft v. Burnett* [1986] 1 All E.R. 332, the Court of Appeal said that in April 1985, £75,000 was the appropriate award for a typical case of tetraplegia when there is no physical pain and expectation of life is 25 years or more, powers of speech, sight and hearing are present, and help is needed with bodily functions.

In *Cunningham v. Camberwell Area Health Authority*, unreported, November 9, 1989, the Court of Appeal updated that figure to £90,000 because of inflation and awarded that sum in a case of serious brain damage.

In *Almond v. Leeds Western Health Authority* (1990) 1 M.L.R. 370, before Fennell J. it was accepted that, in April 1990 terms, the Cunningham figure should then be £97,500. Before me Mr Whitfield accepts that today the equivalent figure is £100,000 and I do not understand Mr Scrivener to disagree. Fennell J. in *Almond's* case awarded £105,000. Mr Whitfield submits that Hugo's condition is not as bad as, and Mr Scrivener that it is worse than, that of Nicholas Almond. Mr Whitfield suggests £95,000, Mr Scrivener an unspecified figure in excess of £105,000.

In my judgment no useful purpose is served by a point by point comparison between different cases. The question is what is fair compensation in the instant case, having regard to the general level of roughly comparable awards. I bear in mind the passage of O'Connor L.J. in *House-croft v. Burnett* at p.338C, cited by Farquharson L.J. in *Cunningham v. Camberwell* at p.4 of the transcript.

> "The factors which operate to make the case one for awarding more than average are physical pain and any diminution in the powers of speech, sight or hearing. The factors which operate to make the case one for awarding less than average are lack of awareness of the condition and a reduction in expectation of life. These factors often cancel each other to a greater or lesser extent, especially where there is severe brain damage."

Hugo's speech and sight are gravely impaired. He has some awareness of his condition. His life expectancy is long. In my judgment this is not a case of cancelling out. Hugo's condition is, it seems to me, significantly worse than average. I bear in mind that in *Housecroft v. Burnett*, at p. 340a, O'Connor L.J. said that he would not expect there to be many cases calling for much increase on what has to be a conventional sum. The present case, in my judgment, calls for some increase in the conventional sum. I award £110,000.

Past care and expenses

There are three sub-headings. Actual cost of care, parental care and miscellaneous expenditure.

(1) The cost actually incurred for help is agreed at £45,246. It is also agreed that an au pair would have been employed for Hugo in any event and Mr Whitfield suggests, and Mr Scrivener does not dissent from, a figure of £19,968 as credit for this. The net award for past cost of care is therefore £25,678.

(2) The award for parental care must take into account the presence of frequently changing paid carers. It must also reflect that, until very recently, financial constraints prior to the making of an interim payment have inhibited the hiring of suitably qualified or experienced carers so that the burden on the parents has been particularly marked. Hugo's mother, Mrs Cassel, who is now 39, has been marvellously determined and devoted and totally unstinting in the time, patience, affection and organisational skills which she has lavished on Hugo, both directly herself and indirectly in

obtaining the helpful services of others, as illustrated in schedule 2. For the last six-and-a-quarter years, since Hugo was two, he has dominated her life day and night for the reasons and in the circumstances set out at the beginning of this judgment.

Hugo's father, Mr Cassel, is now 40. His burden has been somewhat less than Mrs Cassel's, partly because of absence at work during week days, partly because during the last two years he has sometimes spent the night at the Grange Hotel in York, a new enterprise which, as managing director of the operating company, he has successfully launched; and partly because, sadly, he suffers from an eye condition which has prevented him from driving for the last four years. The family live half an hour's drive from York in a rented house in a rural area.

The claim presented by Mr Scrivener in schedule 1 is that compensation should be paid for parental care at commercial rates based on Mrs Sargent's evidence as to Hugo's requirements and to current rates of pay. That is at the rate of £24,215 a year. Mr Whitfield argues that compensation based on a mixture of nanny- and carer-type services, taking into account Miss Gough's evidence for the defendants (see vol. 6 at p. 14) would be adequate. He suggests that, after omitting from Mrs Sargent's calculation placement fees, food and National Insurance, one should take an average figure between Mrs Sargent and Miss Gough, including a sleeper, and dividing the resultant figure of £15,762 by half to produce £7,881 per annum. Such a figure, he submits, fairly reflects, first, that the starting point for Mrs Sargent and Miss Gough is 1990 figures, (whereas compensation is being assessed for earlier years) and secondly, that there are tax, travel and profit elements in the figure for carers' earnings.

It is convenient to say at this stage, though it is of more significance when I come to future care, that I accept the evidence of Mrs Sargent, confirmed, as to a large extent it is, by both Dr Rosenbloom and Professor Ross, as to the qualities of the carers whom Hugo needs. I also accept her evidence as to the cost of that care. A nanny-type figure would be wholly inadequate. The girls who Mrs Cassel has until recently employed have, generally speaking, not been up to the task. This is not surprising as an eight-year-old's body behaving like a two-year-old is likely to require special skills which, in most cases, they did not possess.

I accept that Hugo needs live-in attendance with experience of caring for children and adolescents with special needs who probably have a social services background and, therefore, command a higher than usual salary. At present, for example, a Mrs Richardson, who is suitably skilled, is being paid £4 an hour plus tax and National Insurance. I accept that to employ two carers, each working a ten hour day for three-and-a-half days a week and being paid £3.50 an hour plus £15 a night as a sleeper will be the most practicable course of care. This produces (see schedule 1) £18,250 which, in today's terms, is the basic annual commercial cost of the services which Mr and Mrs Cassel have provided. They have, of course, as I have said, had some assistance for which, until recently, they have paid approximately £4,000 to £5,000 a year. (See schedule 2.) I must make allowance for the fact that £18,250 is the figure for 1990 and not for the span of Hugo's life to date.

Taking all these factors into account, it seems to me that £8,500 a year is a fair figure for the value of the parental care which Hugo has received over and above that of a normal child. The suggested multiplier of 6.25 from age two is, in my view, appropriate because in the first two years of his life little, if any, additional care was called for. I therefore award £53,125 for this aspect.

(3) There are agreed medical expenses of £8,267 and agreed miscellaneous expenses of £21,700. Against these, credit is to be given for agreed allowances of £13,019. The net figure here is therefore £16,948. Accordingly, past care and expenses total £95,751 which will attract interest at the special damage rate calculated with due regard to interim payments.

Future care

After careful consideration, both Mr and Mrs Cassel have now rejected the possibility of Hugo going away to a special school. They are determined that, as child and adult, he will remain integrated as closely as possible within the family. The evidence has dealt with the consequential cost of caring for him in two stages. Stage one, until he is 19, and stage two for the rest of his life. It is agreed that the appropriate multiplier is 18, split as to 7.5 to phase one and 10.5 to phase two.

I have already indicated that I accept Mrs Sargent's assessment with regard to the quality of carers required. I also accept Mrs Cassel's evidence that it would not be reasonable for one carer to have responsibility for Hugo for more than five days a week and that the most satisfactory solution, if it is achievable, will be to have two carers each working for three-and-half days. This, taking into account food, National Insurance, holiday and sickness cover, Community Charge and placement fee produces, as itemised in schedule 3, £24,915 a year. Mr Scrivener claims that the cost of teaching assistance, or enablers, will add £4,536 a year and occupational and speech therapy £3,900 each a year, producing a total annual figure for phase one of £37,251.

Mr Whitfield attacks this proposed multiplicand on five grounds. First, he submits that improvement in Hugo's sleeping patterns justifies a reduction of £2,000 for part of the cost of sleepers, on the basis that it should, in time, be possible to negotiate a lower rate of pay because the sleepers will be disturbed less. I am unable to accept this. As I have indicated, there is in Professor Ross's and Dr Rosenbloom's evidence a tentative basis for hoping for an improvement in Hugo's sleeping pattern by his mid-teens. But even if this does occur, the nights when he is hyperactive, as it seems to me, cannot be other than unpredictable and I see no basis on which it can be reasonably anticipated that negotiating lower rates of pay will be a practical possibility. The risk of having to get up will, as it seems to me, have to be allowed for in the carers' wage rates. There is, indeed, no evidence before me to suggest otherwise.

Secondly, Mr Whitfield challenges the sum of £700 claimed for two Poll Tax payments on the basis, first, that this may not be payable at all for a carer who lives in the household for only three-and-a-half days a week. Secondly, that the life expectancy of the Poll Tax is so short that it should be disregarded. I note that Miss Gough, in her calculations for the defendants, includes Poll Tax as payable by the employer, albeit for an employee working five-and-a-half days. This seems to me to be clear confirmation, if any be needed, that employers are today expected to pay the Poll Tax for their employees. I take the view, however, that some discount from the £700 is called for to reflect both the uncertain future of that tax—though it is equally uncertain by what it will be replaced—and the possibility that, even if it persists in some form, it may not have to be paid, whether because of variations in the number of days worked or otherwise, in respect of both carers. I shall therefore allow £400 instead of £700 for this.

Thirdly, Mr Whitfield submits only £100 instead of £3,900 should be allowed for occupational therapy on the basis that Miss Grant—Hugo's school teacher—and Mrs Grindley—the occupational therapist called for the defendants—suggest that significantly less occupational therapy will be required; and that Mrs Porter, called for the plaintiff, is a speech therapist rather than an occupational therapist.

On the other hand, Dr Rosenbloom's prognosis that Hugo may come to function as a four- to five-year-old depends on optimum help being given. In his third report he suggested bursts of speech and occupational therapy three times a week for a period of weeks, followed by a gap. In evidence he stressed the importance of consistently applied patterns of care to enable socially useful routines to be learned by repetition. He said that during school holidays regular help from a therapist once a week or once a fortnight would be appropriate. I understand him to mean that, although therapy should be primarily based on the school model, there should be not only liaison between school and home but therapy during the holidays. Furthermore, Professor Ross, in evidence, said that carers at home should understand the principles of therapy and be supervised by therapists when necessary.

I should perhaps add that Mrs Grindley was not, in my view, a very compelling witness. In her report and in her evidence she understated the extent of Hugo's physical disabilities. She was in several instances unwilling to make reasonable concessions when her opinions were challenged.

Putting all these matters together, it seems to me that need is shown for about one-quarter of the sum claimed for occupational therapy. I shall therefore allow £1,000 a year, rather than the £3,900 claimed.

Fourthly, Mr Whitfield submits that only one-third of the sum claimed for speech therapy should be allowed. But Professor Ross, in his report, emphasised the need for particular attention to speech therapy during adolescence and Mrs Porter, the speech therapist called for the plaintiff, was a very impressive witness indeed. I accept her evidence, which is substantially confirmed by Dr Rosenbloom and Professor Ross, that Hugo will benefit from three sessions of speech therapy a week. The cost of this at £25 per session is £3,900 a year. I award this sum.

Fifthly, Mr Whitfield claims credit for attendance allowance. This is £1,953 for day and night supervision and £1,303 for day or night supervision. As I have already found that a carer will have to be paid at sleeper rates, the higher figure is appropriate and must be credited. Accordingly, I allow against the figure of £37,351, £300 in relation to Poll Tax, £2,900 in relation to occupational therapy and £1,953 for attendance allowance—a total of £5,153. The multiplicand is therefore £32,098. Applying the agreed multiplier of 7.5 produces a figure of £240,735.

There remains the question of the cost of private schooling for Hugo. He was put down for Eton at or before birth and it was expected that he would also go away to prep school at Aysgarth. It was agreed that the total cost of this would have been £65,000. Mr Scrivener contends that this figure should, to some extent, be discounted in case Hugo did not go to these schools. I am unable to accept this. The family background is such that, whether he went to these schools or not, it is inevitable that he would have been privately educated. There is no evidence before me to suggest that private education elsewhere would have been significantly cheaper.

It is possible that some allowance ought to be made for the cost of Hugo's keep embraced within the school fees. But I have heard no argument on this and it may be that it has already been taken into account in agreeing the sum of £65,000. Accordingly, it appears that the whole £65,000 falls to be deducted. The resultant figure of damages for future care until age 19 is therefore £175,735.

As to phase two there is claimed annually, in addition to the figure of £24,915 for two sleeping carers, £8,736 for an enabler or teaching assistant, (this higher figure being because Hugo will no longer be at school), £1,092 for additional domestic help, and £3,900 each—the same figure as for phase one—for occupational and speech therapy—a total annual sum of £42,543 (schedule 4).

Mr Whitfield challenges this on six grounds. First, he submits that payment for sleepers is not established. I am not able to accept this. The evidence suggests that, so far as any material improvement in sleeping patterns is concerned, this will occur, if at all, in the years of adolescence. As I indicated in relation to the phase one claim, the continuing unpredictability of sleeping patterns, even if there is an improvement, is in my view likely to require that wage rates for carers incorporate the night allowance.

Secondly, he challenges the figure of £700 for the Poll Tax. For the reasons given earlier, I find that some discounted allowance for this should be given and I see no reasons to alter the sum of £400 which I allowed in phase one.

Thirdly, he challenges all the sums claimed for occupational and speech therapy, save for one £25 session of occupational therapy which Mrs Grindley contemplates as being required. Dr Rosenbloom, in his first report said that, as an adult, Hugo was unlikely to need continuation of physiotherapy and speech therapy. In cross-examination he accepted that he had proceeded on the basis that specialist therapy would not be needed as an adult. But some adults, he said, need short bursts of therapy for special problems and it would be unwise to rule it out altogether.

Professor Corbett said there is evidence that the mentally handicapped go on learning skills for as long as anyone else does. Professor Ross thought that there was a possibility but no likelihood of a need for therapy in adulthood. In my judgment the picture which emerges from this evidence is that, from time to time in adulthood, Hugo may well benefit from a short burst of speech and or occupational therapy. Doing the best I can, I shall allow for 12 sessions a year, that is a total of £300 for therapy as against £7,800 claimed.

Fourthly, Mr Whitfield challenges half the claimed cost for enablers on the basis that Hugo is likely to attend a day centre for part of the week. The evidence shows that there are two day centres in York, though there is no evidence as to their quality, as to the facilities which they provide, or as to whether the demand for places is satisfied by or exceeds availability. The evidence shows that provision of day centres varies considerably in different parts of the country. Hugo may not always live near York. In any event, as I have mentioned earlier, the overwhelming message from the doctors is that consistency is the crucial element in Hugo's case. Even if he is able to attend a satisfactory day centre once or twice a week, I cannot envisage how the enablers whom he needs could be satisfactorily partially dispensed with. Accordingly, I allow the claim for enablers in full.

Fifthly, as to domestic help, Mr Whitfield submits that Hugo's family circumstances are such that he would have employed domestic help anyway. Mr Scrivener contends that £1,092 is a reasonable sum for extra domestic help. Having regard to the loss of amenity award, and to the sums already provided for carers and enablers, I am not persuaded that any further item for additional domestic help is reasonable. I make no award for this.

Sixthly, Mr Whitfield claims credit for the attendance allowance. In view of my finding as to continuing need for sleepers, this must be at the higher rate of £1,953 per annum.

Accordingly, the multiplicand for phase two is as follows: carers, less £300 Poll Tax, £24,615; enablers, £8,736; speech and occupational therapy, £300; total £33,651. Less attendance allowance, £1,953, leaves £31,698. Applying the multiplier of 10.5 produces a figure of £332,829 for care in phase two. The total award for future care is, therefore, £508,564. It is to be noted that this figure includes nothing for extra parental care in the future.

Future accommodation

There are four items to be considered. First, alterations to the present accommodation are agreed at £8,000.

Secondly, a discounted figure of £5,000 is agreed for necessary alterations to provide accommodation for Hugo and two carers if Hugo moves elsewhere on or after age 19. Mr Whitfield rightly points out that Mr and Mrs Cassel intend that Hugo will remain within the family unit and not move to a separate abode. On the other hand, it cannot be right to assume either that the family will always remain in the present house, or that Mr and Mrs Cassel's intentions for Hugo will necessarily be borne out. It has to be faced, for example, that they may die before him. Having regard to the requirements of the other two children, it does not seem to me to be possible to say that Hugo's present tenancy, if I may so describe it, in the present family home is permanently assured. The figure of £5,000 for future alterations is, as it seems to me, accordingly, properly recoverable.

Thirdly, it is agreed that a twelve foot by six foot swimming pool in a suitable locked building will cost £32,500. But two issues arise. First, is such an additional claim allowable at all, or is it catered for by the loss of amenity award? Secondly, will it enhance the value of the property so that the cost should be discounted in accordance with *Roberts v. Johnstone* [1988] 3 W.L.R. 1247. As to whether the item is separately recoverable, no case has been found in which a swiming pool has been allowed and one has been found, (Alliott J. at first instance in *Roberts v. Johnstone*, unreported), where, in roughly similar circumstances, it has not. The point did not arise in the Court of Appeal. In the relevant transcript with which I have been provided, Alliott J. at p. 21E quoted from the expert evidence before him as follows,

> "I am not certain that one could justify a medical prescription for a personal swimming pool, but there would be nothing lost in considering this possibility."

Alliott J. went on,

> "I ventured to endorse the medical view with a legal one when the matter was discussed in the hearing. I have no doubt that the installation of a pool would be a sensible application of the award for general damages in this case. But I have equally no doubt that this claim is not recoverable as a separate head of damages against the defendants. O'Connor J,. as he then was, had to consider the claim of a plaintiff who would also benefit from a pool in *Chambers v. Karia*, February 2, 1979, and said there, 'The plaintiff is entitled to fair compensation but not to the best that is available. I do not think it right to bring into play the pool'."

Alliott J. concluded: "I make no award under this head."
I have also been referred to the passage in the judgment of O'Connor L.J. in *Housecroft v. Burnett*, 337g:

> "The facts of an individual case may well justify the trial judge in leaving the award for loss of amenity to take care of items specifically claimed."

He referred to *Chambers v. Karia* as providing an example of this, in relation it should be noted, to driving expenses not the swimming pool. I do not understand Alliott J. to have been seeking to establish any general principle with regard to swimming pools. If he was, then I respectfully disagree. For it seems to me that the matter must turn on the evidence in each case. Indeed, it appears that O'Connor J. in *Chambers v. Karia* disallowed a pool not because it was covered by the loss of amenity award, but because it was claimed for purposes of therapy and the judge held that other forms of therapy, in particular the use of a chest expander, were available as reasonable alternatives in that case.

Furthermore, I see nothing in the judgment of O'Connor J. in *Housecroft* which stands in the way of a separate award for a pool in an appropriate case. On the contrary, the main thrust of that judgment involves recognition that, in recent years, awards for loss of amenity have been made "net of sums separately assessed which, in fact, compensate for loss of amenity in part". (See 338b).

The evidence before me is that, for Hugo, swimming is not merely an alternative form of therapy or a source of enjoyment, but his principal source of relaxation and pleasure. It is the one thing he is able to do himself. Bearing in mind the difficulties of supervision in a public pool, it is in my judgment reasonable that he should have a suitably modest private pool and that he should not have to bear the cost of this from his loss of amenity award.

As to the appropriate figure, Mr Whitfield contends that the agreed sum of £32,500 should be discounted in accordance with *Roberts v. Johnstone* by taking 2 per cent of the capital cost and applying the multiplier of 18 to produce £11,700, or, allowing for only a partial increase in the value of the property, £15,000. It seems to me that there is a fatal objection to this argument. I am wholly unsatisfied that a pool of the sort here contemplated will enhance the value of the property. There is no evidence before me one way or the other. But I think it reasonable to assume that not every prospective purchaser of property in Britain regards the presence of an ordinary swimming pool as an asset rather than a liability, and I see no basis for finding that a pool of the dimensions here contemplated should be regarded as enhancing property value. Accordingly, no *Roberts v. Johnstone* calculation falls to be made in my judgment and the sum £32,500 is recoverable in full.

Fourthly, a *Roberts v. Johnstone* claim is made for £4,000 a year, with an 18 year multiplier, representing the sum £200,000 said to be needed for future accommodation costs for Hugo. I see no evidential basis for this claim. Mr Jarvis, of course, has made some calculations, but the whole case for the plaintiff has been conducted on the basis that he is unlikely to require separate accommodation. Even if, one day, he does, that is something which he would have needed had he not been disabled. It is, in my view, inconceivable that £200,000 would need to be spent over and above his normal needs. This aspect, it seems to me, is properly catered for by the discounted figure of £5,000 already awarded for necessary alterations to any other property. The total award for future accommodation is, therefore, £45,500.

Future miscellaneous costs

There is a substantial measure of agreement as to many of these. First, there are one-off appliances: a wheel chair, a Cosimat toilet and safety rails, amounting to £2,702. Then there are medical expenses agreed at £5,000. The items listed in schedule 9 were eventually all agreed, save three—educational toys after age 19, extra use of the telephone by carers and extra household purchases for carers.

The argument for educational toys after age 19 cannot, in my view, be sustained. The claimed annual costs of £350 would, as it seems to me, be far outweighed by the cost of the sort of gifts which, had he not been disabled, Hugo would have received from his parents.

The claim for extra use of the telephone by carers was ultimately abandoned when Mr Scrivener accepted that, as a normal teenager, Hugo would no doubt have used the telephone to at least an equal extent.

As to extra household purchases for carers, I accept Mr Whitfield's contention that, as only one carer will be present at a time, half Mr Hellier's figure of £1,446, that is £723, is appropriate. With a multiplier of 18, that is £13,014.

Accordingly, to the item for educational toys must be applied only the multiplier of 7.5, producing £2,625. The other items listed in schedule 9, which include extra household purchases for Hugo and the extra cost of family holidays, amount in total to £2,387 to which the multiplier of 18 must be applied, producing £42,966.

The remaining claim under this head is transport until age 19. An 1800cc four wheel drive Subaru has been ordered. Including a car telephone, the capital cost is calculated in schedule 6 as £16,100, with extra annual running costs of £1,900. Mr Whitfield offered, but Mr Scrivener rejected, £7,500 for this. It is common ground that, leaving aside the telephone, the claim must succeed in full or fail entirely. The present position in the family is that there are two somewhat elderly motor cars: a Mercedes and a Volkswagen Golf. The Mercedes is used partly for the hotel. Mrs Cassel drives, Mr Cassel does not. Hugo's carer is provided with the Golf.

When in a car, even if in a seat belt, Hugo is, as his mother described him, "like an octopus" and throws missiles such as his shoes and, therefore, has to be accompanied by someone strong in addition to the driver. Mr Scrivener submits that Mrs Cassel and the other two children, for their varying needs, occupy one car, Hugo needs his own car and the carer will expect to take a car home. The telephone is vital if the car breaks down. It seems to me that this submission founders. So far as a telephone is concerned, Hugo's behaviour in the car means that there is always likely to be a responsible person, apart from the driver, with him in the event of breakdown. Accordingly, no need for a telephone is shown.

As to a third car, there would be no one to drive it. I quite understand that if car 1 is at the hotel in York and car 2 has been taken home by a carer, it would be useful for Mrs Cassel to have a third car. But this would be a convenience for all three children and is, in any case, a situation which results from the needs, not of Hugo, but of the hotel. The likelihood, having regard to the rural area in which the family lives, is that, whoever works as an enabler will have a car of her own which can be used if both the Cassel cars are missing. The occasional expense of this is, it seems to me, exactly the sort of item which is properly left out of the loss of amenity award. I accept Mr Whitfield's submission that what the evidence shows is a need for two reliable cars and a wish, but no reasonable need, for a third car. This head of claim, therefore, fails.

Accordingly, the total of future miscellaneous costs is £66,307.

Loss of future earnings

This, as it seems to me, is much the most difficult matter to resolve with fairness to both sides of the many imponderables. Mr Scrivener seeks an award on the basis that Hugo would have become a partner in a medium sized City firm of solicitors or accountants. Mr Jarvis, of Dixon Wilson, puts the loss, on this basis, as £323,000 in earnings and a further £78,000 in car benefits and pension rights. Mr Oliver, of Touche Ross, says the earnings figures on which these calculations are based are conservative. In this respect, Mr Whitfield relies on Stoy Hayward's figures in relation to dropping out from the accountancy profession. But his principal submission starts from a different standpoint, namely, the national average for non-manual males: £14,491. This Mr Whitfield increases by 50 per cent in accordance with the approach adopted by the late Smith J. in *Taylor v. Glass*, May 23, 1979, and followed by Fennell J. in *Almond v. Leeds Western Health Authority*, and suggests applying to the resultant figure of £19,671 a multiplier either of 10 on the basis that Hugo would not have obtained a degree or 8.5 on the basis that he would have gone on to university, polytechnic or some other form of education after leaving school. On the lower multiplier, this produces approximately £167,000 and a vast gulf between the parties.

In assessing the appropriate multiplicand, I start from what I hope is an uncontroversial proposition, namely, that heredity and environment each plays a part in a person's make-up and development. In these respects the omens for Hugo were propitious. He was born into a caring, close-knit and happy family whose financial circumstances are perhaps most aptly described in the old-fashioned expression "well-to-do". In addition to seeing in the witness box and on the video both his parents and his mother's sister, Mrs Walker, I have read agreed statements from all four grandparents. On his father's side, Hugo's uncle, grandfather and great grandfather all became Queen's Counsel.

On his mother's side, his forbears have included two who engaged in tea planting and other commercial activities in India, two who were distinguished artists in Victorian times, one who was a distinguished soldier, one who became a successful industrialist in Canada, several from a Huguenot glass-making family, and a grandfather who farmed and developed substantial estates in Scotland and England. On both sides, for very many years, the general pattern seems to have been that each generation, starting reasonably comfortably but without any great inherited wealth, has been soundly educated and has made its way successfully.

Hugo's parents have repeated that pattern. Mr Cassel obtained 11 "O" levels and two "A" levels at Eton and two diplomas at the Sorbonne. Thereafter, he trained and worked as a restaurant manager with the Savoy Group and elsewhere for about ten years. He then embarked with his wife on raising capital by property refurbishment. It appears that their joint starting capital was not more than £100,000 or so. By November 1988, after a succession of moves over nine years, the matrimonial home was sold for £750,000, of which £450,000 was available for investment in the Grange Hotel at York. Substantial further funds were raised by Mr Cassel for the Hotel which opened in March 1990. In the present embryonic state of that business, Mr Cassel is drawing a salary of £20,000.

Mrs Cassel obtained nine "O" levels and two "A" levels at school and thereafter went to Edinburgh Art School and the British Institute in Florence. For 12 years prior to Hugo's birth, she ran a picture framing business in London. She has played a major role in the new hotel's interior design and she draws a salary of £5,000.

As I have earlier indicated, Hugo was destined to Aysgarth and Eton. In the light of his parents' academic achievements, it seems reasonable to assume that he would have been able, if he wished, to gain entry to a university, polytechnic, or some other place of advanced education; and that there was a good prospect that, had he wished to do so, he could have entered a profession, in particular the legal profession. It also seems reasonable to assume that, as well as legal, there are artistic and entrepreneurial genes in Hugo. This is not to say, of course, that he would have entered and remained in a profession or become a starving or famous artist, or made a fortune or gone bankrupt as a businessman. But he would certainly have had as good an education as money can buy and, equally certainly, he would have had the chance to explore very many more avenues of opportunity than are open to most people.

It is at this point, as it seems to me, that the likely nature of Hugo's character and personality become material. The assessment of this is, of course, fraught with tremendous problems and there can be no certainty. But, having seen both his parents and one of his aunts, it seems to me that in addition to being, as he is, physically attractive, it is likely that he would have been highly intelligent, with a strong and determined but sensitive character, an open and engaging personality, and a well-developed sense of humour. It is not surprising that an anonymous social worker in one of the reports before me speaks of "a superb family".

If thus equipped, Hugo's chances of success in exploring the avenues of opportunity to which I have referred would, in my judgment, have been high. Whether that success would have been reflected in monetary terms is another matter. As I have already said, it is impossible to assume that he would necessarily have wanted or academically achieved entry into a profession, or that, if he entered a profession, he would have wished to practise it in the City of London. I cannot, therefore, make the assumptions which are a necessary pre-condition for acceptance of Mr Jarvis's figures. On the other hand, to find that Hugo's financial prospects would have been no better than 50 per cent higher than the national average, as Mr Whitfield contends, is, as it seems to me, seriously to understate the well above average advantages of family, education and character which Hugo would probably have enjoyed when the came to choose a career.

I bear in mind that, over the span of his working life, he may well have had periods of unemployment and may have changed jobs possibly several times. I also bear in mind the uncertainties about where he may have chosen to live. The richer financial diet of the City may have held less appeal than greener provincial pastures.

It seems to me that there is one further factor which can properly be taken into account, although it can only have a modest impact on the multiplicand. This is the possibility that, quite apart from employment in the traditional sense, Hugo may well have been able to increase his assets by investing in property or otherwise. I cannot assume that early in the next century it will be possible to achieve capital appreciation in property comparable to that which occurred during the 1980s and of which Hugo's parents took considerable advantage. But it seems to me to be reasonable to allow for the distinct possibility that someone of Hugo's background, with ready access to skilled advice, would, as his father and others of his family have done in the past, increase his assets by prudent investment as well as employment.

Taking all the various probabilities, possibilities and imponderables into account, a multiplicand fair to both sides in this case is, in my judgment, £35,000 net, which represents a gross income of about £55,000. The appropriateness of this figure can, it seems to me, be cross-checked in several ways. If Hugo had joined and remained with a medium-sized City firm he would have achieved this level of income in his 30s, rather less when younger and considerably more when older. From a different standpoint, £35,000 is a little less than two-and-a-half times the national average earnings figure, which seems to me to be a reasonable estimate of Hugo's potential. From another standpoint, although it is more than Hugo's father is presently earning at 40, in the special circumstances of the new hotel business, it appears to be in line with the average of £40,000 or so a year free of tax which Mr Cassel was making in his 30s from his property activities.

I turn to the multiplier. It is likely, almost to the point of certainty, that Hugo would have started earning between the ages of 18 and 23. I find it impossible to state precisely when within that bracket he would have done so, though I find that an age nearer the upper limit than the lower would have been a likelier starting point. He is now just over eight and, as I found earlier, his life expectancy is such that he will probably have a normal working life to the age of 65. Having regard to these matters, a multiplier of 10 is, in my view, appropriate. I therefore award as damages for future loss of earnings £350,000.

Accordingly, leaving aside for the moment the final head of claim which relates to Court of Protection costs, the total sum of damages which I award on a full liability basis, excluding interest, is £1,176,122. This, by English standards, is an enormous sum. But I am satisfied that it is consonant with the level of other awards in the last five years in cases of injuries of maximum severity. Hugo is entitled to 90 per cent of this sum. That is £1,058,510, plus the appropriate interest when this has been calculated.

I turn to the final head of claim, which will not be subject to a 10 per cent reduction.

Court of protection

It is common ground that administration of the available fund will be through the Court of Protection which levies annual administrative fees laid down by Parliament and calculated by reference to "the clear annual income" of the fund. It is agreed that, in the present case, the appropriate calculation can and should be made assuming an income of 4.5 per cent of the available funds after there has been stripped out from my total award the damage for compensating others, in particular Mr and Mrs Cassel.

This is a matter of mathematical calculation which is, no doubt, capable of agreement. But the scale of fees which is appropriate to a particular "clear annual income" depends on whether or not the public trustee is the receiver. The court has power under the Mental Health Act 1983, s. 99 to appoint a receiver and the Court of Protection Rules 1984 set out the procedure. Mr Whitfield submits that if the public trustee is not the receiver, the receiver's costs are not recoverable from the defendants but fall on the fund, if not in whole then at least in part. He accepts that there is no direct authority on the point, but refers me to *Francis v. Bostock* (1985) *The Times*, 9 November, a decision of Russell J., as he then was, which was followed by Otton J. in *Cunningham v. Camberwell Health Authority* and by Owen J. in *Blackwell v. Newcastle Area Health Authority*, August 1, 1988, unreported.

Russell J. held that a claim for the fees of stockbrokers, financial advisers, accountants and the like, involved in the management of the plaintiff's investment portfolio, failed on the ground of remoteness, such advice being a consequence of the award, not a consequence of the defendant's negligence. However, Russell J. distinguished the case of *Duller v. South East Lines Engineers* [1981] C.L.Y. 585 in which Mr Edwin Jowitt Q.C., as he then was, awarded damages for future expenses of the Court of Protection, the plaintiff being unable to manage his own affairs, and the judge having himself directed administration of the fund by the Court of Protection.

There is before me an agreed statement from Mr Hooper, the plaintiff's solicitor, indicating that his fee, if he were to be appointed as receiver, would be £2,650 a year, which is somewhat, though not greatly, higher than would be incurred if the public trustee were the receiver. The statement indicates the services which he would provide. These include regular meetings with the parents and child, distribution of income from the fund through a bank account, dealing with tax returns, commenting on investment advice obtained by the Court of Protection, and preparing an annual account and report for the Court of Protection. Mr Whitfield accepts that, if the public trustee were the receiver, the Court of Protection costs based on this would properly be recoverable from the defendants. That being so, it seems to me that the only question on this aspect is whether, in the circumstances of the present case, the appointment of a professional receiver other than the public trustee would be reasonable. In my judgment the answer is plainly yes. The exceptional size of the fund merits a professional receiver and the high level of parental involvement and responsibility which here exist would, it seems to me, be most satisfactorily catered for by personal liaison of this kind which Mr Hooper's statement contemplates.

The remaining question is whether, in relation to the Court of Protection's administration fees and the receiver's fees, the multiplier of 18 should be reduced to reflect the fund's diminution over the years. Mr Whitfield submits that each year, as capital is disposed of, leading ultimately to notional extinction of the fund, "clear annual income" will be reduced as will in consequence the Court of Protection's fees. Accordingly, he submits, the multiplier should be reduced to 12. This approach found favour with Alliott J. in *Roberts v. Johnstone* when 16 was reduced to about 11.9 and with Tucker J. in *Thames v. North West Surrey Health Authority*, January 11, 1990, unreported, when 17 was reduced to 12.75. Mr Scrivener, on the other hand, contends that a continuing level of contributions to Hugo's maintenance and care will only be achieved by an interesting number of capital disposals, so there is no reason to believe that the charges levied by the Court of Protection will diminish.

In my judgment, there is no basis for reducing the multiplier so far as a professional receiver's costs are concerned for they are not related to "clear annual income" and there is no reason to believe that the professional receiver's responsibilities and activities will become any less over the years. On this aspect, therefore, I award 18 times £2,650. That is £47,700.

With regard to the Court of Protection's fees, however, it seems to me that the matter turns on whether that Court levies its fees by reference to "clear annual income" as earned by the capital fund or coming from other sources, or "clear annual income" in terms of distribution to the patient. In the former case it is, in my judgment, appropriate to reduce the multiplier, in the latter case it is not. My enquiries of the Court of Protection indicate that the former interpretation, which is clearly preferable as a matter of construction, is, in fact, applied by the Court of Protection. Nothing in the letter from the Public Trust Office, dated December 17, 1990, produced by Mr Scrivener this morning, or in his submission based on that letter, persuades me otherwise. Accordingly, I shall reduce the multiplier from 18 to 14. This multiplier will be applied to the multiplicand, calculated as I have already indicated in order to ascertain the sum to be awarded for Court of Protection fees.

My total award is, therefore, £1,058,510 and appropriate interest, plus £47,700 for receiver's fees and plus such further sum in respect of Court of Protection fees as results from the calculation which I have indicated. It may be helpful to the parties if I hand down a summary of the figures which I have just indicated."

DA McIK

Appendix B

Statutory Material

Law Reform (Miscellaneous Provisions) Act 1934

(24 & 25 GEO 5 C. 41)

[July 25, 1934]

Effect of death on certain causes of action

1—(1) Subject to the provisions of this action, on the death of any person after the commencement of this Act all causes of action subsisting against or vested in him shall survive against, or, as the case may be, for the benefit of, his estate. Provided that this subsection shall not apply to causes of action for defamation. [...][1]

[(1A) The right of a person to claim under section 1A of the Fatal Accidents Act 1976 (bereavement) shall not survive for the benefit of his estate on his death.][2]

(2) Where a cause of action survives as aforesaid for the benefit of the estate of a deceased person, the damages recoverable for the benefit of the estate of that person:

[(a) shall not include—
  (i) any exemplary damages;
  (ii) any damages for loss of income in respect of any period after that person's death;][3]

(b) [...][4]

(c) where the death of that person has been caused by the act or omission which gives rise to the cause of action, shall be calculated without references to any loss or gain to his estate consequent on his death, except that a sum in respect of funeral expenses may be included.

(3) [...]

(4) Where damage has been suffered by reason of any act or omission in respect of which a cause of action would have subsisted against any person if that person had not died before or at the same time as the damage was suffered, there shall be deemed, for the purpose of this Act, to have been subsisting against him before his death such cause of action in respect of that act or omission as would have subsisted if he had died after the damage was suffered.

(5) The rights conferred by this Act for the benefit of the estates of deceased persons shall be in addition to and not in derogation of any rights conferred on the dependants of deceased persons by the Fatal Accidents Acts 1846 to 1908[...][5] and so much of this Act as relates to causes of action against the estates of deceased persons shall apply in relation to causes of action under the said Act as it applies in relation to other causes of action

not expressly excepted from the operation of subsection (1) of this section.

(6) In the event of the insolvency of an estate against which proceedings are maintainable by virtue of this section, any liability in respect of the cause of action in respect of which the proceedings are maintainable shall be deemed to be a debt provable in the administration of the estate, notwithstanding that it is a demand in the nature of unliquidated damages arising otherwise than by a contract, promise or breach of trust.

[1] *Omitted by Administration of Justice Act 1982 (c. 53), s. 75(1), Sched. 9, Part 1 and the Law Reform (Miscellaneous Provisions) Act 1970, s. 7(2), Sched.*

[2] *Inserted by Administration of Justice Act 1982, s. 4(1) and applies where the cause of action accrues on or after January 1, 1983.*

[3] *Substituted by Administration of Justice Act 1982, s. 4(2) and has effect where a person has died after January 1, 1983.*

[4] *Repealed by Law Reform (Miscellaneous Provisions) Act 1970, s. 7, Sched.*

[5] *Repealed by Carriage by Air Act 1961, s. 14(3), Sched. 2.*

[6] *Repealed by the Statute Law Revision Act 1950.*

Law Reform (Contributory Negligence) Act 1945

(8 & 9 GEO 6 C. 28)

Apportionment of liability in case of contributory negligence

1—(1) Where any person suffers damage as the result partly of his own fault and partly of the fault of any other person or persons, a claim in respect of that damage shall not be defeated by reason of the fault of the person suffering the damage, but the damages recoverable in respect thereof shall be reduced to such extent as the court thinks just and equitable having regard to the claimant's share in the responsibility for the damage;

Provided that—

(a) this subsection shall not operate to defeat any defence arising under a contract;

(b) where any contract or enactment providing for the limitation of liability is applicable to the claim, the amount of damages recoverable by the claimant by virtue of this subsection shall not exceed the maximum limit so applicable.

(2) Where damages are recoverable by any person by virtue of the foregoing subsection subject to such reduction as is therein mentioned, the court shall find and record the total damages which would have been recoverable if the claimant had not been at fault.

(3) [. . .][1]

(4) [. . .][2]

(5) Where, in any case to which subsection (1) of this section applies, one of the persons at fault avoids liability to any other such person or his personal representative by pleading the Limitation Act 1939, or any other enactment limiting the time within which proceedings may be taken, he shall not be entitled to recover any damages [. . .] from that other person or representative by virtue of the said subsection.

(6) Where any case to which subsection (1) of this section applies is tried with a jury, the jury shall determine the total damages which would have been recoverable if the claimant had not been at fault and the extent to which those damages are to be reduced.

(7) [. . .][3]

[1] *Repealed by Civil Liability (Contribution) Act 1978, s. 9(2), Sched. 2.*
[2] *Repealed by Fatal Accidents Act 1976, s. 6(2), Sched. 2.*
[3] *Repealed by Carriage by Air Act 1961, s. 14(3), Sched. 2.*

. . . . .

Interpretation

4—The following expressions have the meanings hereby respectively assigned to them, that is to say—

"court" means, in relation to any claim, the court or arbitrator by or before whom the claim falls to be determined;

"damage" includes loss of life and personal injury;

[. . .][1]

"fault" means negligence, breach of statutory duty or other act or omission which gives rise to a liability in tort or would, apart from this Act, give rise to the defence of contributory negligence.

[1] *Repealed by the National Insurance (Industrial Injuries) Act 1946, s. 89(1), Sched. 9 and by the Fatal Accidents Act 1976, s. 6(2), Sched. 2.*

Law Reform (Personal Injuries) Act 1948

(11 & 12 Geo 6 c. 41)

Measure of damages

2—(1) [...][1]

(1A) [...][1]

(2) [...][2]

(3) [...][1]

(4) In an action for damages for personal injuries (including any such action arising out of a contract), there shall be disregarded, in determining the reasonableness of any expenses, the possibility of avoiding those expenses or part of them by taking advantage of facilities available under the [National Health Service Act 1977][3] or the National Health Service (Scotland) Act 1978 or of any corresponding facilities in Northern Ireland.

(5) [...][4]

(6) [...].[1]

[1] *Repealed by Social Security (Recovery of Benefits) Act 1997 (c. 27) Scheds. 3 and 4.*

[2] *Repealed by Social Security Act 1989 (c. 24), s. 31(2), Sched. 9.*

[3] *Substituted by National Health Service Act 1977 (c. 49), s. 129, Sched. 15, para. 8.*

[4] *Repealed by Fatal Accidents Act 1959, s. 3(3), Sched.*

Civil Evidence Act 1968

(1968 C. 64)

ARRANGEMENT OF SECTIONS

Part I

[Repealed by Civil Evidence Act 1995 (c. 38), Sched. 2. Note: the text of the 1995 Act is reproduced on page 333 below]

Part II

PART II MISCELLANEOUS AND GENERAL

Convictions, etc as evidence in civil proceedings

Convictions as evidence in civil proceedings

11—(1) In any civil proceedings the fact that a person has been convicted of an offence by or before any court in the United Kingdom or by a court-martial there or elsewhere shall (subject to subsection (3) below) be admissible in evidence for the purpose of proving, where to do so is relevant to any issue in those proceedings, that he committed that offence, whether he was so convicted upon a plea of guilty or otherwise and whether or not he is a party to the civil proceedings; but no conviction other than a subsisting one shall be admissible in evidence by virtue of this section.

(2) In any civil proceedings in which by virtue of this section a person is proved to have been convicted of an offence by or before any court in the United Kingdom or by a court-martial there or elsewhere—

- (a) he shall be taken to have committed that offence unless the contrary is proved; and
- (b) without prejudice to the reception of any other admissible evidence for the purpose of identifying the facts on which the conviction was based, the contents of any document which is admissible as evidence of the conviction, and the contents of the information, complaint, indictment or charge-sheet on which the person in question was convicted, shall be admissible in evidence for that purpose.

(3) Nothing in this section shall prejudice the operation of section 13 of this Act or any other enactment whereby a conviction or a finding of fact in any criminal proceedings is for the purposes of any other proceedings made conclusive evidence of any fact.

(4) Where in any civil proceedings the contents of any document are admissible in evidence by virtue of subsection (2) above, a copy of that document, or of the material part thereof, purporting to be certified or otherwise authenticated by or on behalf of the court or authority having custody of that document shall be admissible in evidence and shall be taken to be a true copy of that document or part unless the contrary is shown.

(5) Nothing in any of the following enactments, that is to say—

(a) [[section (1C)][1] of the Powers of Criminal Courts Act 1973][2] (under which a conviction leading to [. . .][3] discharge is to be disregarded except as therein mentioned);

(b) [section 191 of the Criminal Procedure (Scotland) Act 1975][4] (which makes similar provision in respect of convictions on indictment in Scotland); and

(c) section 8 of the Probation Act (Northern Ireland) 1950 (which corresponds to the said section 12) or any corresponding enactment of the Parliament of Northern Ireland for the time being in force,

shall effect the operation of this section; and for the purposes of this section any order made by a court of summary jurisdiction in Scotland under section 383 or section 384 of the said Act of 1975 shall be treated as a conviction.

(6) In this section "court-martial" means a court-martial constituted under the Army Act 1955, the Air Force Act 1955 or the Naval Discipline Act 1957 or a disciplinary court constituted under section [52G][5] of the said Act of 1957, and in relation to a court-martial "conviction", as regards a court-martial constituted under either of the said Acts of 1955, means a finding of guilty which is, or falls to be treated as, a finding of the court duly confirmed and,[5] means a finding of guilty which is, or falls to be treated as, the finding of the court, and "convicted" shall be construed accordingly.

[1] *Substituted by the Criminal Justice Act 1991 (c. 53), s. 100, Sched. 11, para. 5.*
[2] *Substituted by the Powers of Criminal Courts Act 1973, ss. 56(1), 60(2), Sched. 5, para. 31.*
[3] *Repealed by the Criminal Justice Act 1991 (c. 53), s. 101(2), Sched. 13.*
[4] *Substituted by the Criminal Procedure (Scotland) Act 1975.*
[5] *Repealed by Armed Forces Act 1996 (c. 46), Sched. 1, para. 100.*

. . . . .

Civil Evidence Act 1972

(1972 c. 30)

Arrangement of Sections

[June 12, 1972]

Application of Part I of Civil Evidence Act 1968 to statements of opinion

1—[. . .][1]

[1] *Repealed by Civil Evidence Act 1995 (c. 38), s. 15(2) and Sched. 2.*

Rules of court with respect to expert reports and oral expert evidence

2—(1)[. . .][1]

(2) [. . .][1]

(3) Notwithstanding any enactment or rule of law by virtue of which documents prepared for the purpose of pending or contemplated civil proceedings or in connection with the obtaining or giving of legal advice are in certain circumstances privileged from disclosure, provision may be made by rules of court—

(a) for enabling the court in any civil proceedings to direct, with respect to medical matters or matters of any other class which may be specified in the direction, that the parties or some of them shall each by such date as may be so specified (or such later date as may be permitted or agreed in accordance with the rules) disclose to the other or others in the form of one or more expert reports the expert evidence on matters of that class which he proposed to adduce as part of his case at the trial; and

(b) for prohibiting a party who fails to comply with a direction given in any such proceedings under rules of court made [...][1] except with the leave of the court, any statement (whether of fact or opinion) contained in any expert report whatsoever in so far as that statement deals with matters of any class specified in the direction.

(4) Provision may be made by rules of court as to the conditions subject to which oral expert evidence may be given in civil proceedings.

(5) Without prejudice to the generality of subsection (4) above, rules of court made in pursuance of that subsection may make provision for prohibiting a party who fails to comply with a direction given as mentioned in subsection (3)(b) above from adducing, except with the leave of the court, any oral expert evidence whatsoever with respect to matters of any class specified in the direction.

(6) Any rules of court made in pursuance of this section may make different provision for different classes of cases, for expert reports dealing with matters of different classes, and for other different circumstances.

(7) References in this section to an expert report are references to a written report by a person dealing wholly or mainly with matters on which he is (or would if living be) qualified to give expert evidence.

(8) Nothing in the foregoing provisions of this section shall prejudice the generality of [...][2] [section 75 of the County Courts Act 1984],[3] [section 144 of the Magistrates' Court Act 1980][4] or any other enactment conferring power to make rules of court; and nothing in [...][2] [section 75(2) of the County Courts Act 1984][3] or any other enactment restricting the matters with respect to which rules of court may be made shall prejudice the making of rules of court in pursurance of this section or the operation of any rules of court so made.

[1] *Repealed by Civil Evidence Act 1995 (c. 38), s. 15(2), Sched. 2.*
[2] *Repealed by Supreme Court Act 1981 (c. 54), s. 152(4), Sched. 7.*
[3] *Substituted by County Courts Act 1984 (c. 28), s. 148(1), Sched. 2, para. 43.*
[4] *Substituted by Magistrates' Court 1980 (c. 43), s. 154, Sched. 7, para. 114.*

Admissibility of expert opinion and certain expressions of non-expert opinion

3—(1) Subject to any rules of court made in pursuance of [...][1] this Act, where a person is called as a witness in any civil proceedings, his opinion on any relevant matter on which he is qualified to give expert evidence shall be admissible in evidence.

(2) It is hereby declared that where a person is called as a witness in any civil proceedings, a statement of opinion by him on any relevant matter on which he is not qualified to give expert evidence, if made as a way of conveying relevant facts personally perceived by him, is admissible as evidence of what he perceived.

(3) In this section "relevant matter" includes an issue in the proceedings in question.

[1] *Wards repealed by Civil Evidence Act 1995 (c. 38), s. 15(2), and Sched. 2.*

. . . . .

Interpretation, application to arbitration, etc, and savings

5—(1) [In this Act "civil proceeding" means civil proceedings, before any tribunal, in relation to which the strict rules of evidence apply, whether as a matter of law or by agreement of the parties and references to "the court" shall be construed accordingly.[1]]

(2) [The rules of court made for the purpose of the applications of sections 2 and 4 of this Act, to proceedings in the High Court apply, except in so far as their application is excluded by agreement, to proceedings before tribunals other than the ordinary courts of law, subject to such modifications as may be appropriate . . .][1]

(3) Nothing in this Act shall prejudice—

(a) any power of a court, in any civil proceedings, to exclude evidence (whether by preventing questions from being put or otherwise) at its discretion; or

(b) the operation of any agreement (whenever made) between the parties to any civil proceedings as to the evidence which is to be admissible (whether generally or for any particular purpose) in those proceedings.

[1] *Substituted by Civil Evidence Act 1995 (c. 38), s. 15(1) and Sched. 1.*

. . . . .

Fatal Accidents Act 1976

(1976 c. 30)

ARRANGEMENT OF SECTIONS

An Act to consolidate the Fatal Accidents Acts.

[July 22, 1976]

[Right of action for wrongful act causing death

1[1]—(1) If death is caused by any wrongful act, neglect or default which is such as would (if death had not ensued) have entitled the person injured to maintain an action and recover damages in respect thereof, the person who would have been liable if death had not ensued shall be liable to an action for damages, notwithstanding the death of the person injured.

(2) Subject to section 1A(2) below, every such action shall be for the benefit of the dependents of the person ("the deceased") whose death has been so caused.

(3) In this Act "dependent" means—

- (a) the wife or husband or former wife or husband of the deceased;
- (b) any person who—
  - (i) was living with the deceased in the same household immediately before the date of the death; and
  - (ii) had been living with the deceased in the same household for at least two years before that date; and
  - (iii) was living during the whole of that period as the husband or wife of the deceased.
- (c) any parent or other ascendant of the deceased;
- (d) any person who was treated by the deceased as his parent;

(e) any child or other descendant of the deceased;
(f) any person (not being a child of the deceased) who, in the case of any marriage to which the deceased was at any time a party, was treated by the deceased as a child of the family in relation to that marriage;
(g) any person who is, or is the issue of, a brother, sister, uncle or aunt of the deceased.

(4) The reference to the former wife or husband of the deceased in subsection (3)(a) above includes a reference to a person whose marriage to the deceased has been annulled or declared void as well as a person whose marriage to the deceased has been dissolved.

(5) In deducing any relationship for the purposes of subsection (3) above—
(a) any relationship by affinity shall be treated as a relationship by consanguinity, any relationship of the half blood as a relationship of the whole blood, and the step-child of any person as his child, and
(b) an illegitimate person shall be treated as the legitimate child of his mother and reputed father.

(6) Any reference in this Act to injury includes any disease and any impairment of a person's physical or mental condition.]

[1] *Substituted by Administration of Justice Act 1982 (c. 53), s. 3(1).*

[Bereavement

1A[1]—(1) An action under this Act may consist of or include a claim for damages for bereavement.

(2) A claim for damages for bereavement shall only be for the benefit:
(a) of the wife or husband of the deceased; and
(b) where the deceased was a minor who was never married:
(i) of his parents, if he was legitimate; and
(ii) of his mother, if he was illegitimate.

(3) Subject to subsection (5) below, the sum to be awarded as damages under this section shall be [£7,500].[2]

(4) Where there is a claim for damages under this section for the benefit of both the parents of the deceased, the sum awarded shall be divided equally between them (subject to any deduction falling to be made in respect of costs not recovered from the defendant).

(5) The Lord Chancellor may by order made by statutory instrument, subject to annulment in pursuance of a resolution of either House of Parliament, amend this section by varying the sum for the time being specified in subsection (3) above.]

[1] *Inserted by Administration of Justice Act 1982 (c. 53) s. 3(1).*
[2] *Substituted by the Damages for Bereavement (Variation of sum) (England and Wales) Order 1990 (SI No 2575). The previous sum of £3,500 applies where the course of action arose before April 1, 1991.*

[Persons entitled to bring the action

2—(1) The action shall be brought by and in the name of the executor or administrator of the deceased.

(2)If—

(a) there is no executor or administrator of the deceased, or

(b) no action is brought within six months after the death by and in the name of an executor or administrator of the deceased,

the action may be brought by and in the name of all or any of the persons for whose benefit an executor or administrator could have brought it.

(3) Not more than one action shall lie for and in respect of the same subject matter of complaint.

(4) The plaintiff in the action shall be required to deliver to the defendant or his solicitor full particulars of the persons for whom and on whose behalf the action is brought and of the nature of the claim in respect of which damages are sought to be recovered.][1]

[1] *Substituted by Administration of Justice Act 1982 (c. 53), s. 3(1).*

[Assessment of damages

3—(1) In the action such damages, other than damages for bereavement, may be awarded as are proportioned to the injury resulting from the death to the dependants respectively.

(2) After deducting the costs not recovered from the defendant any amount recovered otherwise than as damages for bereavement shall be divided among the dependants in such shares as may be directed.

(3) In any action under this Act where there fall to be assessed damages payable to a widow in respect of the death of her husband there shall not be taken into account the remarriage of the widow or her prospects of remarriage.

(4) In an action under this Act where there fall to be assessed damages payable to a person who is a dependant by virtue of section 1(3)(b) above in respect of the death of the person with whom the dependant was living as husband or wife there shall be taken into account (together with any other matter that appears to the court to be relevant to the action) the fact that the dependant had no enforceable right to financial support by the deceased as a result of their living together.

(5) If the dependants have incurred funeral expenses in respect of the deceased, damages may be awarded in respect of those expenses.

(6) Money paid into court in satisfaction of a cause of action under this Act may be in one sum without specifying any person's share.][1]

[1] *Substituted by Administration of Justice Act 1982 (c. 53), s. 3(1).*

[Assessment of damages: disregard of benefits

4 In assessing damages in respect of a person's death in an action under this Act, benefits which have accrued or will or may accrue to any person from his estate or otherwise as a result of his death shall be disregarded.][1]

[1] *Substituted by Administration of Justice Act 1982 (c. 53), s. 3(1).*

Contributory negligence

5 Where any person is as the result partly of his own fault and partly of the fault of any other person or persons, and accordingly if an action were brought for the benefit of the estate under the Law Reform (Miscellaneous Provisions) Act 1934 the damages recoverable would be reduced under section 1(1) of the Law Reform (Contributory Negligence) Act 1945, any damages recoverable in an action [. . .][1] under this Act shall be reduced to a proportionate extent.

[1] *Repealed by Administration of Justice Act 1982 (c. 53), ss. 3(2), 75, and Sched. 9, Part 1.*

Consequential amendments and repeals

6—(1) Schedule 1 to this Act contains consequential amendments.

(2) The enactments in Schedule 2 to this Act are repealed to the extent specified in the third column of that Schedule.

Short title, etc

7—(1) This Act may be cited as the Fatal Accidents Act 1976.

(2) This Act shall come into force on 1 September 1976, but shall not apply to any cause of action arising on a death before it comes into force.

(3) This Act shall not extend to Scotland or Northern Ireland.

. . . . .

Civil Liability (Contribution) Act 1978

(1978 c. 47)

ARRANGEMENT OF SECTIONS

Proceedings for contribution

Proceedings for the same debt or damage

Supplemental

Proceedings for contribution

Entitlement to contribution

1—(1) Subject to the following provisions of this section, any person liable in respect of any damage suffered by another person may recover contribution from any other person liable in respect of the same damage (whether jointly with him or otherwise).

(2) A person shall be entitled to recover contribution by virtue of subsection (1) above notwithstanding that he has ceased to be liable in respect of the damage in question since the time when the damage occurred, provided that he was so liable immediately before he made or was ordered or agreed to make the payment in respect of which the contribution is sought.

(3) A person shall be liable to make contribution by virtue of subsection

(1) above notwithstanding that he has ceased to be liable in respect of the damage in question since the time when the damage occurred, unless he ceased to be liable by virtue of the expiry of a period of limitation or prescription which extinguished the right on which the claim against him in respect of the damage was based.

(4) A person who has made or agreed to make any payment in bona fide settlement or compromise of any claim made against him in respect of any damage (including a payment into court which has been accepted) shall be entitled to recover contribution in accordance with this section without regard to whether or not he himself is or ever was liable in respect of the damage, provided, however, that he would have been liable assuming that the factual basis of the claim against him could be established.

(5) A judgment given in any action brought in any part of the United Kingdom by or on behalf of the person who suffered the damage in question against any person from whom contribution is sought under this section shall be conclusive in the proceedings for contribution as to any issue determined by that judgment in favour of the person from whom the contribution is sought.

(6) References in this section to a person's liability in respect of any damage are references to any such liability which has been or could be established in an action brought against him in England and Wales by or on behalf of the person who suffered the damage; but it is immaterial whether any issue arising in any such action was or would be determined (in accordance with the rules of private international law) by reference to the law of a country outside England and Wales.

Assessment of contribution

2—(1) Subject to subsection (3) below, in any proceedings for contribution under section 1 above the amount of the contribution recoverable from any person shall be such as may be found by the court to be just and equitable having regard to the extent of that person's responsibility for the damage in question.

(2) Subject to subsection (3) below, the court shall have power in any such proceedings to exempt any person from liability to make contribution or to direct that the contribution to be recovered from any person shall amount to a complete indemnity.

(3) Where the amount of the damages which have or might have been awarded in respect of the damage in question in any action brought in England and Wales by or on behalf of the person who suffered it against the person from whom the contribution is sought was or would have been subject to—

- (a) any limit imposed by or under any enactment or by any agreement made before the damage occurred;
- (b) any reduction by virtue of section 1 of the Law Reform (Contributory Negligence) Act 1945 or section 5 of the Fatal Accidents Act 1976; or
- (c) any corresponding limit or reduction under the law of a country outside England and Wales;

the person from whom the contribution is sought shall not by virtue of any contribution awarded under section 1 above be required to pay in respect of the damage a greater amount than the amount of those damages as so limited or reduced.

Proceedings for the same debt or damage

Proceedings against persons jointly liable for the same debt or damage

3 Judgment recovered against any person liable in respect of any debt or damage shall not be a bar to an action, or to the continuance of an action, against any other person who is (apart from any such bar) jointly liable with him in respect of the same debt or damage.

Successive actions against persons liable (jointly or otherwise) for the same damage

4 If more than one action is brought in respect of any damage by or on behalf of the person by whom it was suffered against persons liable in respect of the damage (whether jointly or otherwise) the plaintiff shall not be entitled to costs in any of those actions, other than that in which judgment is first given, unless the court is of the opinion that there was reasonable ground for bringing the action.

Supplemental

Application to the Crown

5 Without prejudice to section 4(1) of the Crown Proceedings Act 1947 (indemnity and contribution), this Act shall bind the Crown, but nothing in this Act shall be construed as in any way affecting Her Majesty in Her private capacity (including in right of Her Duchy of Lancaster) or the Duchy of Cornwall.

Interpretation

6—(1) A person is liable in respect of any damage for the purposes of this Act if the person who suffered it (or anyone representing his estate or dependants) is entitled to recover compensation from him in respect of that damage (whatever the legal basis of his liability, whether tort, breach of contract, breach of trust or otherwise).

(2) References in this Act to any action brought by or on behalf of the person who suffered any damage include references to an action brought for the benefit of his estate or dependants.

(3) In this Act "dependants" has the same meaning as in the Fatal Accidents Act 1976.

(4) In this Act, except in section 1(5) above, "action" means an action brought in England and Wales.

Savings

7—(1) Nothing in this Act shall affect any case where the debt in question became due or (as the case may be) the damage in question occurred before the date on which it comes into force.

(2) A person shall not be entitled to recover contribution or liable to make contribution in accordance with section 1 above by reference to any liability based on breach of any obligation assumed by him before the date on which this Act comes into force.

(3) The right to recover contribution in accordance with section 1 above supersedes any right, other than an express contractual right, to recover contribution (as distinct from indemnity) otherwise than under this Act in corresponding circumstances; but nothing in this Act shall affect—

(a) any express or implied contractual or other right to indemnity; or

(b) any express contractual provision regulating or excluding contribution;

which would be enforceable apart from this Act (or render enforceable any agreement for indemnity or contribution which would not be enforceable apart from this Act).

. . . . .

Limitation Act 1980

(1980 c. 58)

Actions for sums recoverable by statute

Special time limit for claiming contribution

10—(1) Where under section 1 of the Civil Liability (Contribution) Act 1978 any person becomes entitled to a right to recover contribution in respect of any damage from any other person, no action to recover contribution by virtue of that right shall be brought after the expiration of two years from the date on which that right accrued.

(2) For the purposes of this section the date on which a right to recover contribution in respect of any damage accrues to any person (referred to below in this section as "the relevant date") shall be ascertained as provided in subsections (3) and (4) below.

(3) If the person in question is held liable in respect of that damage—

(a) by a judgment given in any civil proceedings; or

(b) by an award made on any arbitration;

the relevant date shall be the date on which the judgment is given, or the date of the award (as the case may be).

For the purposes of this subsection no account shall be taken of any judgment or award given or made on appeal in so far as it varies the amount of damages awarded against the person in question.

(4) If, in any case not within subsection (3) above, the person in question makes or agrees to make any payment to one or more persons in compensation for that damage (whether he admits any liability in respect of the damage or not), the relevant date shall be the earliest date on which the amount to be paid by him is agreed between him (or his representative) and the person (or each of the persons, as the case may be) to whom the payment is to be made.

(5) An action to recover contributions shall be one to which sections 28, 32 and 35 of this Act apply, but otherwise Parts II and III of this Act (except sections 34, 37 and 38) shall not apply for the purposes of this section.

Actions in respect of wrongs causing personal injuries or death

Special time limit for actions in respect of personal injuries

11—(1) This section applies to any action for damages for negligence, nuisance or breach of duty (whether the duty exists by virtue of a contract or of provision made by or under a statute or independently of any contract or any such provision) where the damages claimed by the plaintiff for the negligence, nuisance or breach of duty consist of or include damages in respect of personal injuries to the plaintiff or any other person.

[(1A) This section does not apply to any action brought for damages under section 3 of the Protection from Harassment Act 1997.][1]

(2) None of the time limits given in the preceding provisions of this Act shall apply to an action to which this section applies.

(3) An action to which this section applies shall not be brought after the expiration of the period applicable in accordance with subsection (4) or (5) below.

(4) Except where subsection (5) below applies, the period applicable is three years from—

(a) the date on which the cause of action accrued; or

(b) the date of knowledge (if later) of the person injured.

(5) If the person injured dies before the expiration of the period mentioned in subsection (4) above, the period applicable as respects the cause of action surviving for the benefit of his estate by virtue of section 1 of the Law Reform (Miscellaneous Provisions) Act 1934 shall be three years from—

(a) the date of death; or

(b) the date of the personal representative's knowledge;

whichever is the later.

(6) For the purposes of this section "personal representative" includes any person who is or has been a personal representative of the deceased, including an executor who has not proved the will (whether or not he has renounced probate) but not anyone appointed only as a special personal representative in relation to settled land; and regard shall be had to any knowledge acquired by any such person while a personal representative or previously.

(7) If there is more than one personal representative, and their dates of knowledge are different, subsection (5)(b) above shall be read as referring to the earliest of those dates.

[1] *Inserted by Protection from Harassment Act 1997 (c. 40), s. 6.*

[Actions in respect of defective products

11A—(1) This section shall apply to an action for damages by virtue of any provision of Part I of the Consumer Protection Act 1987.

(2) None of the time limits given in the preceding provisions of this Act shall apply to an action to which this section applies.

(3) An action to which this section applies shall not be brought after the expiration of the period of ten years from the relevant time, within the meaning of section 4 of the said Act of 1987; and this subsection shall operate to extinguish a right of action and shall do so whether or not that right of action had accrued, or time under the following provisions of this Act had begun to run, at the end of the said period of ten years.

(4) Subject to subsection (5) below, an action to which this section applies in which the damages claimed by the plaintiff consist of or include damages

in respect of personal injuries to the plaintiff or any other person or loss of or damage to any property, shall not be brought after the expiration of the period of three years from whichever is the later of—

(a) the date on which the cause of action accrued; and

(b) the date of knowledge of the injured person or, in the case of loss of or damage to property, the date of knowledge of the plaintiff or (if earlier) of any person in which his cause of action was previously vested.

(5) If in a case where the damages claimed by the plaintiff consist of or include damages in respect of personal injuries to the plaintiff or any other person the injured person died before the expiration of the period mentioned in subsection (4) above, that subsection shall have effect as respects the cause of action surviving for the benefit of his estate by virtue of section 1 of the Law Reform (Miscellaneous Provisions) Act 1934 as if for the reference to that period there were substituted a reference to the period of three years from whichever is the later of—

(a) the date of death; and

(b) the date of the personal representative's knowledge.

(6) For the purposes of this section "personal representative" includes any person who is or has been a personal representative of the deceased, including an executor who has not proved the will (whether or not he has renounced probate) but not anyone appointed only as a special personal representative in relation to settled land; and regard shall be had to any knowledge acquired by any such person while a personal representative or previously.

(7) If there is more than one personal representative and their dates of knowledge are different, subsection (5)(b) above shall be read as referring to the earliest of those dates.

(8) Expressions used in this section or section 14 of this Act and in Part 1 of the Consumer Protection Act 1987 have the same meanings in this section or that section as in that Part; and section 1(1) of that Act (Part I to be construed as enacted for the purpose of complying with the product liability Directive) shall apply for the purpose of construing this section and the following provisions of this Act so far as they relate to an action by virtue of any provision of that Part as it applies for the purpose of construing that Part.][1]

[1] *Inserted by Consumer Protection Act 1987 (c. 43), s. 6(6), Sched. 1, para. 1.*

Special time limit for actions under Fatal Accidents legislation

12—(1) An action under the Fatal Accidents Act 1976 shall not be brought if the death occurred when the person injured could no longer maintain an action and recover damages in respect of the injury (whether because of a time limit in this Act or in any other Act, or for any other reason).

Where any such action by the injured person would have been barred by the time limit in section 11 [or 11A][1] of this Act, no account shall be taken of the possibility of that time limit being overridden under section 33 of this Act.

(2) None of the time limits given in the preceding provisions of this Act shall apply to an action under the Fatal Accidents Act 1976, but no such action shall be brought after the expiration of three years from—

(a) the date of death; or
(b) the date of knowledge of the person for whose benefit the action is brought; whichever is the later.

(3) An action under the Fatal Accidents Act 1976 shall be one to which sections 28, 33 and 35 of this Act apply, and the application to any such action of the time limit under subs (2) above shall be subject to section 39; but otherwise Parts II and III of this Act shall not apply to any such action.

[1] *Inserted by Consumer Protection Act 1987 (c.), s. 6(6), Sched. 1, para. 2.*

Operation of time limit under section 12 in relation to different dependants

13—(1) Where there is more than one person for whose benefit an action under the Fatal Accidents Act 1976 is brought, section 12(2)(b) of this Act shall be applied separately to each of them.

(2) Subject to subsection (3) below, if by virtue of subsection (1) above the action would be outside the time limit given by section 12(2) as regards one or more, but not all, of the persons for whose benefit it is brought, the court shall direct that any person as regards whom the action would be outside that limit shall be excluded from those for whom the action is brought.

(3) The court shall not give such a direction if it is shown that if the action were brought exclusively for the benefit of the person in question it would not be defeated by a defence of limitation (whether in consequence of section 28 of this Act or an agreement between the parties not to raise the defence, or otherwise).

Definition of date of knowledge for purposes of sections 11 and 12

14—(1) [Subject to subsection (1A) below,][1] in sections 11 and 22 of this Act references to a person's date of knowledge are references to the date on which he first had knowledge of the following facts—

(a) that the injury in question was significant; and
(b) that the injury was attributable in whole or in part to the act or omission which is alleged to constitute negligence, nuisance or breach of duty; and
(c) the identity of the defendant; and
(d) if it is alleged that the act or omission was that of a person other than the defendant, the identity of that person and the additional

facts supporting the bringing of an action against the defendant;

and knowledge that any acts or omissions did or did not, as a matter of law, involve negligence, nuisance or breach of duty is irrelevant.

[(1A) In section 11A of this Act and in section 12 of this Act so far as that section applies to an action by virtue of section 6(1)(a) of the Consumer Protection Act 1987 (death caused by defective product) references to a person's date of knowledge are references to the date on which he first had knowledge of the following facts—

(a) such facts about the damage caused by the defect as would lead a reasonable person who had suffered such damage to consider it sufficiently serious to justify his instituting proceedings for damages against a defendant who did not dispute liability and was able to satisfy a judgment; and
(b) that the damage was wholly or partly attributable to the facts and circumstances alleged to constitute the defect; and
(c) the identity of the defendant;

but, in determining the date on which a person first had such knowledge there shall be disregarded both the extent (if any) of that person's knowledge on any date of whether particular facts or circumstances would or would not, as a matter of law, constitute a defect and, in a case relating to loss of or damage to property, any knowledge which that person had on a date on which he had no right of action by virtue of Part I of that Act in respect of the loss or damage.][1]

(2) For the purposes of this section an injury is significant if the person whose date of knowledge is in question would reasonably have considered it sufficiently serious to justify his instituting proceedings for damages against a defendant who did not dispute liability and was able to satisfy a judgment.

(3) For the purposes of this section a person's knowledge includes knowledge which he might reasonably have been expected to acquire:

(a) from facts observable or ascertainable by him; or
(b) from facts ascertainable by him with the help of medical or other appropriate expert advice which it is reasonable for him to seek;

but a person shall not be fixed under this subsection with knowledge of a fact ascertainable only with the help of expert advice so long as he has taken all reasonable steps to obtain (and, where appropriate, to act on) that advice.

[1] *Inserted by Consumer Protection Act 1987 (c. 43), s. 6(6), Sched. 1, para. 3.*

. . . . .

Part II

Extension or Exclusion of Ordinary Time Limits

Disability

Extension of limitation period in case of disability

28—(1) Subject to the following provisions of this section, if on the date when any right of action accrued for which a period of limitation is prescribed by this Act, the person to whom it accrued was under a disability, the action may be brought at any time before the expiration of six years from the date when he ceased to be under a disability or died (whichever first occurred) notwithstanding that the period of limitation has expired.

(2) This section shall not affect any case where the right of action first accrued to some person (not under a disability) through whom the person under a disability claims.

(3) When a right of action which has accrued to a person under a disability accrues, on the death of that person while still under a disability, to another person under a disability, no further extension of time shall be allowed by reason of the disability of the second person.

. . . . .

(5) If the action is one to which section 10 of this Act applies, subsection (1) above shall have effect as if for the words "six years" there were substituted the words "two years".

(6) If the action is one to which section 11 or 12(2) of this Act applies, subsection (1) above shall have effect as if for the words "six years" there were substituted the words "three years".

(7) If the action is one to which section 11A[2] of this Act applies or one by virtue of section 6(1)(a) of the Consumer Protection Act 1987 (death caused by defective product), subsection (1) above—

- (a) shall not apply to the time limit prescribed by subsection (3) of the said section 11A or to that time limit as applied by virtue of section 12(1) of this Act; and
- (b) in relation to any other time limit prescribed by this Act shall have effect as if for the words "six years" there were substituted the words "three years".]

[1] *Inserted by Administration of Justice Act 1985 (c. 61), s. 57(3); applies to causes of action which arose on or after December 30, 1985.*

[2] *Inserted by Consumer Protection Act 1987 (c. 43), s. 6(6), Sched. 1, para. 4.*

. . . . .

Fraud, concealment and mistake

Postponement of limitation period in case of fraud, concealment or mistake

32—(1) Subject to [subsections (3) and (4A)][1] below, where in the case of any action for which a period of limitation is prescribed by this Act, either—

(a) the action is based upon the fraud of the defendant; or

(b) any fact relevant to the plaintiff's right of action has been deliberately concealed from him by the defendant; or

(c) the action is for relief from the consequences of a mistake;

the period of limitation shall not begin to run until the plaintiff has discovered the fraud, concealment or mistake (as the case may be) or could with reasonable diligence have discovered it.

References in this subsection to the defendant include references to the defendant's agent and to any person through whom the defendant claims and his agent.

(2) For the purposes of subsection (1) above, deliberate commissions of a breach of duty in circumstances in which it is unlikely to be discovered for some time amounts to deliberate concealment of the facts involved in that breach of duty.

(3) Nothing in this section shall enable any action—

(a) to recover, or recover the value of, any property; or

(b) to enforce any charge against, or set aside any transaction affecting any property;

to be brought against the purchaser of the property or any person claiming through him in any case where the property has been purchased for valuable consideration by an innocent third party since the fraud or concealment or (as the case may be) the transaction in which the mistake was made took place.

(4) A purchaser is an innocent third party for the purposes of this section—

(a) in the case of fraud or concealment of any fact relevant to the plaintiff's right of action, if he was not a party to the fraud or (as the case may be) to the concealment of that fact and did not at the time of the purchase know or have reason to believe that the fraud or concealment had taken place; and

(b) in the case of mistake, if he did not at the time of the purchase know or have reason to believe that the mistake had been made.

[(4A) Subsection (1) above shall not apply in relation to the time limit prescribed by section 11A(3) of this Act or in relation to that time limit as applied by virtue of section 12(1) of this Act.][2]

[(5) Sections 14A and 14B of this Act shall not apply to any action to which subsection (1)(b) above applies (and accordingly the period of limitation referred to in that subsection, in any case to which either of those sections would otherwise apply, is the period applicable under section 2 of this Act).][3]

[1] *Substituted by the Consumer Protection Act 1987, s. 6(6), Sched. 1, para. 5.*
[2] *Inserted by the Consumer Protection Act 1987, s. 6(6), Sched. 1, para. 5.*
[3] *Added by the Latent Damage Act 1986, s2(2).*

Discretionary exclusion of time limit for actions for defamation or malicious falsehood

32A—(1) If it appears to the court that it would be equitable to allow an action to proceed having regard to the degree to which—
- (a) the operation of section 4A of this Act prejudices the plaintiff or any person whom he represents, and
- (b) any decision of the court under this subsection would prejudice the defendant or any person whom he represents,

the court may direct that that section shall not apply to the action or shall not apply to any specified cause of action to which the action relates.

(2) In acting under this section the court shall have regard to all the circumstances of the case and in particular to—
- (a) the length of, and the reasons for, the delay on the part of the plaintiff;
- (b) where the reason or one of the reasons for the delay was that all or any of the fact relevant to the cause of action did not become known to the plaintiff until after the end of the period mentioned in section 4A—
  - (i) the date on which any such facts did become known to him, and
  - (ii) the extent to which he acted promptly and reasonably once he knew whether or not the facts in question might be capable of giving rise to an action; and
- (c) the extent to which, having regard to the delay, relevant evidence is likely—
  - (i) to be unavailable, or
  - (ii) to be less cogent than if the action had been brought within the period mentioned in section 4A.

(3) In the case of an action for slander of title, slander of goods or other malicious falsehood brought by a personal representative—
- (a) the references in subsection (2) above to the plaintiff shall be construed as including the deceased person to whom the cause of action accrued and any previous personal representative of that person; and
- (b) nothing in section 28(3) of this Act shall be construed as affecting the court's discretion under this section.

(4) In this section "the court" means the court in which the action has been brought.

[1] *Inserted by Administration of Justice Act 1985 (c. 61) and substituted by Defamation Act 1996 (c. 31), s. 5.*

Discretionary exclusion of time limit for actions in respect of personal injuries or death

Discretionary exclusion of time limit for actions in respect of personal injuries or death

33—(1) If it appears to the court that it would be equitable to allow an action to proceed having regard to the degree to which—

(a) the provisions of section 11 [or 11A][1] or 12 of this Act prejudice the plaintiff or any person whom he represents; and

(b) any decision of the court under this subsection would prejudice the defendant or any person whom he represents;

the court may direct that those provisions shall not apply to the action, or shall not apply to any specified cause of action to which the action relates.

[(1A) The court shall not under this section disapply—

(a) subsection (3) of section 11A; or

(b) where the damages claimed by the plaintiff are confined to damages for loss or of damage to any property, any other provision in its application to an action by virtue of Part I of the Consumer Protection Act 1987.][1]

(2) The court shall not under this section disapply section 12(1) except where the reason why the person injured could no longer maintain an action was because of the time limit in section 11 [or subsection (4) of section 11A].[1]

If, for example, the person injured could at his death no longer maintain an action under the Fatal Accidents Act 1976 because of the time limit in Article 29 in Schedule 1 to the Carriage by Air Act 1961, the court has no power to direct that section 12(1) shall not apply.

(3) In acting under this section the court shall have regard to all the circumstances of the case and in particular to—

(a) the length of, and the reasons for, the delay on the part of the plaintiff;

(b) the extent to which, having regard to the delay, the evidence adduced or likely to be adduced by the plaintiff or the defendant is or is likely to be less cogent than if the action had been brought within the time allowed by section 11 [by section 11A][1] or (as the case may be) by section 12;

(c) the conduct of the defendant after the cause of action arose, including the extent (if any) to which he responded to requests reasonably made by the plaintiff for information or inspection for the purpose of ascertaining facts which were or might be relevant to the plaintiff's cause of action against the defendant;

(d) the duration of any disability of the plaintiff arising after the date of the accrual of the cause of action;

(e) the extent to which the plaintiff acted promptly and reasonably once he knew whether or not the act or omission of the defendant, to which the injury was attributable, might be capable at that time of giving rise to an action for damages;

(f) the steps, if any, taken by the plaintiff to obtain medical, legal or other expert advice and the nature of any such advice he may have received.

(4) In a case where the person injured died when, because of section 11, [or subsection (4) of section 11A][1] he could no longer maintain an action and recover damages in respect of the injury, the court shall have regard in particular to the length of, and the reasons for, the delay on the part of the deceased.

(5) In a case under subsection (4) above, or any other case where the time limit, or one of the time limits, depends on the date of knowledge of a person other than the plaintiff, subsection (3) above shall have effect with appropriate modifications, and shall have effect in particular as if references to the plaintiff included references to any person whose date of knowledge is or was relevant in determining a time limit.

(6) A direction by the court misapplying the provisions of section 12(1) shall operate to disapply the provisions to the same effect in section 1(1) of the Fatal Accidents Act 1976.

(7) In this section "the court" means the court in which the action has been brought.

(8) References in this section to section 11 [or 11A][1] include references to that section as extended by any of the preceding provisions of this Part of this Act or by any provision of Part III of this Act.

[1] *Inserted by Consumer Protection Act 1987 (c. 43), s. 6(6), Sched. 1, para. 6.*

Part III

Miscellaneous and General

34—[Repealed by Arbitration Act 1996 (c. 23), Sched. 4].

New claims in pending actions: rules of court

35—(1) For the purposes of this Act, any new claim made in the course of any action shall be deemed to be a separate action and to have been commenced—

(a) in the case of a new claim made in or by way of third party proceedings, on the date on which those proceedings were commenced; and

(b) in the case of any other new claim, on the same date as the original action.

(2) In this section a new claim means many claim by way of set-off or counterclaim, and any claim involving either—

(a) the addition or substitution of a new cause of action; or

(b) the addition or substitution of a new party;

and "third party proceedings" means any proceedings brought in the course of any action by any party to the action against a person not previously a party to the action, other than proceedings brought by joining any such person as defendant to any claim already made in the original action by the party bringing the proceedings.

(3) Except as provided by section 33 of this Act or by rules of court, neither the High Court nor any county court shall allow a new claim within subsection (1)(b) above, other than an original set-off or counterclaim, to be made in the course of any action after the expiry of any time limit under this Act which would affect a new action to enforce that claim.

For the purposes of this subsection, a claim is an original set-off or an original counterclaim if it is a claim made by way of set-off or (as the case may be) by way of counterclaim by a party who has not previously made any claim in the action.

(4) Rules of court may provide for allowing a new claim to which subsection (3) above applies to be made as there mentioned, but only if the conditions specified in subsection (5) below are satisfied, and subject to any further restrictions the rules may impose.

(5) The conditions referred to in subsection (4) above are the following—

- (a) in the case of a claim involving a new cause of action, if the new cause of action arises out of the same facts or substantially the same facts as are already in issue on any claim previously made in the original action; and
- (b) in the case of a claim involving a new party, if the addition or substitution of the new party is necessary for the determination of the original action.

(6) The addition or substitution of a new party shall not be regarded for the purposes of subsection (5)(b) above as necessary for the determination of the original action unless either—

- (a) the new party is substituted for a party whose name was given in any claim made in the original action in mistake for the new party's name; or
- (b) any claim already made in the original action cannot be maintained by or against any existing party unless the new party is joined or substituted as plaintiff or defendant in that action.

(7) Subject to subsection (4) above, rules of court may provide for allowing a party to any action to claim relief in a new capacity in respect of a new cause of action notwithstanding that he had no title to make that claim at the date of the commencement of the action.

This subsection shall not be taken as prejudicing the power of rules of court to provide for allowing a party to claim relief in a new capacity without adding or substituting a new cause of action.

(8) Subsections (3) to (7) above shall apply in relation to a new claim made in the course of third party proceedings as if those proceedings were the original action, and subject to such other modifications as may be prescribed by rules of court in any case or class of case.

(9) [. . .][1]

[1] *Repealed by the Supreme Court Act 1981 (c. 54), s. 152(4), Sched. 7.*

. . . . .

Interpretation

38—(1) In this Act, unless the context otherwise requires:

"action includes any proceeding in a court of law, including an ecclesiastical court;

"land" includes corporeal hereditaments, tithes and rentcharges and any legal or equitable estate or interest therein,[1] but except as provided above in this definition does not include any incorporeal hereditament;

"personal estate" and "personal property" do not include chattels real;

"personal injuries" includes any disease and any impairment of a person's physical or mental condition, and "injury" and cognate expressions shall be construed accordingly;

"rent" includes a rentcharge and a rentservice;

"rentcharge" means any annuity or periodical sum of money charged upon or payable out of land, except a rentservice or interest on a mortgage on land;

"settled land", "statutory owner" and "tenant for life" have the same meanings respectively as in the Settled Land Act 1925;

"trust" and "trustee" have the same meanings respectively as in the Trustee Act 1925; and[1]

(2) For the purposes of this Act a person shall be treated as under a disability while he is an infant, or of unsound mind.

(3) For the purposes of subsection (2) above a person is of unsound mind if he is a person who, by reason of mental disorder within the meaning of the [1983][2] Mental Health Act, is incapable of managing and administering his property and affairs.

(4) Without prejudice to the generality of subsection (3) above, a person shall be conclusively presumed for the purposes of subsection (2) above to be of unsound mind—

(a) while he is liable to be detained or subject to guardianship under the [1983 (otherwise than by virtue of section 35 or 89)][2] Mental Health Act; and

(b) [while he is receiving treatment as an in-patient in any hospital within the meaning of the Mental Health Act 1983 or mental nursing home within the meaning of the Nursing Homes Act 1975 without being liable to be detained under the said Act of 1983 (otherwise than by virtue of section 35 or 89), being treatment which follows without any interval a period during which he was liable to be detained or subject to guardianship under the Mental Health Act 1959, or the said Act of 1983 (otherwise than by virtue of section 35 or 89) or by virtue of any enactment repealed or excluded by the Mental Health Act 1959].[2]

(5) Subject to subsection (6) below, a person shall be treated as claiming through another person if he became entitled by, through, under, or by the act of that other person to the right claimed, and any person whose estate or interest might have been barred by a person entitled to an entailed interest in possession shall be treated as claiming through the person so entitled.

(6) A person becoming entitled to any estate by virtue of a special power of appointment shall not be treated as claiming through the appointer.

(7) References in this Act to a right of action to recover land shall include references to a right to enter into possession of the land or, in the case of rentcharges and tithes, to distrain for arrears of rent or tithe, and references to the bringing of such an action shall include references to the making of such an entry or distress.

(8) References in this Act to the possession of land shall, in the case of tithes and rentcharges, be construed as references to the receipt of the tithe or rent, and references to the date of dispossession or discontinuance of possession of land shall, in the case of rentcharges, be construed as references to the date of the last receipt of rent.

(9) References in Part II of this Act to a right of action shall include references to—

- (a) a cause of action;
- (b) a right to receive money secured by a mortgage or charge on any property;
- (c) a right to recover proceeds of the sale of land; and
- (d) a right to receive a share or interest in the personal estate of a deceased person.

(10) References in Part II to the date of the accrual of a right of action shall be construed—

- (a) in the case of an action upon a judgment, as references to the date on which the judgment became enforceable; and
- (b) in the case of an action to recover arrears of rent or interest, or damages in respect of arrears of rent or interest, as references to the date on which the rent or interest became due.

[1] *Words repealed by Trusts of Land and Appointment of Trustees Act 1996 (c. 47) Sched. 4.*

[2] *Substituted by Mental Health Act 1983 (c. 20), s. 148, Sched. 4, para. 55.*

. . . . .

Supreme Court Act 1981

(1981 c. 54)

. . . . .

Powers

Orders for interim payment

32—(1) As regarded proceedings pending in the High Court, provision may be made by rules of court for enabling the court, in such circumstances as may be prescribed, to make an order requiring a party to the proceedings to make an interim payment of such amount as may be specified in the order, with provision for the payment to be made to such other party to the proceedings as may be specified or, if the order so provides by paying it into court.

(2) Any rules of court which make provision in accordance with subs (1) may include provision for enabling a party to any proceedings who, in pursuance of such an order, has made an interim payment to recover the whole or part of the amount of the payment in such circumstances, and from such other party to the proceedings, as may be determined in accordance with the rules.

(3) Any rules made by virtue of this section may include such incidental, supplementary and consequential provisions as the rule-making authority may consider necessary or expedient.

(4) Nothing in this section shall be construed as affecting the exercise of any power relating to costs, including any power to make rules of court relating to costs.

(5) In this section "interim payment", in relation to a party to any proceedings, means a payment on account of any damages, debt or other sum (excluding any costs) which that party may be held liable to pay to or for the benefit of another party to the proceedings if a final judgment or order of the court in the proceedings is given or made in favour of that other party.

[Orders for provisional damages for personal injuries

32A—(1) This section applies to an action for damages for personal injuries in which there is proved or admitted to be a chance that at some definite or indefinite time in the future the injured person will, as a result of the act or omission which gave rise to the cause of action, develop some serious disease or suffer some serious deterioration in his physical or mental condition.

(2) Subject to subsection (4) below, as regards any action for damages to which this section applies in which a judgment is given in the High Court, provision may be made by rules of court for enabling the court, in such circumstances as may be prescribed, to award the injured person—

(a) damages assessed on the assumption that the injured person will not develop the disease or suffer the deterioration in his condition; and

(b) further damages at a future date if he develops the disease or suffers the deterioration.

(3) Any rules made by virtue of this section may include such incidental, supplementary and consequential provisions as the rule-making authority may consider necessary or expedient.

(4) Nothing in this section shall be construed—

(a) as affecting the exercise of any power relating to costs, including any power to make rules of court relating to costs; or

(b) as prejudicing any duty of the court under any enactment or rule of law to reduce or limit the total changes which would have been recoverable apart from any such duty.][1]

[1] *Inserted by Administration of Justice Act 1982 (c. 53), s. 6(1).*

Powers of High Court exercisable before commencement of action[1]

33—(1) On the application of any person in accordance with rules of court, the High Court shall, in such circumstances as may be specified in the rules, have power to make an order providing for any one or more of the following matters, that is to say—

(a) the inspection, photographing, preservation, custody and detention of property which appears to the court to be property which may become the subject-matter of subsequent proceedings in the High Court, or as to which any question may arise in any such proceedings; and

(b) the taking of samples and of any such property as is mentioned in paragraph (a), and the carrying out of any experiment on or with any such property.

(2) On the application, in accordance with rules of court, of a person who appears to the High Court to be likely to be a party to subsequent proceedings in that court in which a claim in respect of personal injuries to a person, or in respect of a person's death, is likely to be made, the High Court shall, in such circumstances as may be specified in the rules, have power to order a person who appears to the court to be likely to be a party to the proceedings and to be likely to have or to have had in his possession, custody or power any documents which are relevant to an issue arising or likely to arise out of that claim—

(a) to disclose whether those documents are in his possession, custody or power; and

(b) to produce such of those documents as are in his possession, custody or power to the applicant or, on such conditions as may be specified in the order—

(i) to the applicant's legal advisers; or

(ii) to the applicant's legal advisers and any medical or other professional adviser of the applicant; or

(iii) if the applicant has no legal adviser, to any medical or other professional adviser of the applicant.

[1] *Sections 33, 34 and 35 were repealed in so far as they relate to county courts by the County Courts Act 1984 (c. 28), s. 148(3), Sched. 4.*

Power of High Court to order disclosure of documents, inspection of property etc in proceedings for personal injuries or death[1]

34—(1) This section applies to any proceedings in the High Court in which a claim is made in respect of personal injuries to a person, or in respect of a person's death.

(2) On the application, in accordance with rules of court of a party to any proceedings to which this section applies, the High Court shall, in such circumstances as may be specified in the rules, have power to order a person who is not a party to the proceedings and who appears to the court to be likely to have in his possession, custody or power any documents which are relevant to an issue arising out of the said claim—

(a) to disclose whether those documents are in his possession, custody or power; and

(b) to produce such of those documents as are in his possession, custody or power to the applicant or, on such conditions as may be specified in the order—

(i) to the applicant's legal advisers; or

(ii) to the applicant's legal advisers and any medical or other professional adviser of the applicant; or

(iii) if the applicant has no legal adviser, to any medical or other professional adviser of the applicant.

(3) On the application, in accordance with rules of court, of a party to any proceedings to which this section applies, the High Court shall, in such circumstances as may be specified in the rules, have power to make an order providing for any one or more of the following matters, that is to say—

(a) the inspection, photographing, preservation, custody and detention of property which is not the property of, or in the possession of, any party to the proceedings but which is the subject-matter of the proceedings or as to which any question arises in the proceedings;

(b) the taking of samples of any such property as is mentioned in paragraph (a) and the carrying out of any experiment on or with any such property.

(4) The preceding provisions of this section are without prejudice to the exercise of the High Court of any power to make orders which is exercisable apart from those provisions.

[1] *Sections 33, 34 and 35 were repealed in so far as they relate to county courts by the County Courts Act 1984 (c.), s. 148(3), Sched. 4.*

Provisions supplementary to sections 33 and 34[1]

35—(1) The High Court shall not make an order under section 33 or 34 if it considers that compliance with the order, if made, would be likely to be injurious to the public interest.

(2) Rules of court may make provision as to the circumstances in which an order under section 33 or 34 can be made; and any rules making such provision may include such incidental, supplementary and consequential provisions as the rule-making authority may consider necessary or expedient.

(3) Without prejudice to the generality of subsection (2), rules of court shall be made for the purpose of ensuring that the costs of and incidental to proceedings for an order under section 33(2) or 34 incurred by the person against whom the order is sought shall be awarded to that person unless the court otherwise directs.

(4) Sections 33(2) and 34 and this section bind the Crown; and section 33(1) binds the Crown so far as it relates to property as to which it appears to the court that it may become the subject-matter of subsequent proceedings involving a claim in respect of personal injuries to a person or in respect of a person's death.

In this subsection references to the Crown do not include reference to Her Majesty in Her private capacity or to Her Majesty in right of Her Duchy of Lancaster, or to the Duke of Cornwall.

(5) In sections [32A],[2] 33 and 34 and this section:

"property" includes any land, chattel or other corporeal property of any description;

"personal injuries" includes any disease and any impairment of a person's physical or mental condition.

[1] *Sections 33, 34 and 35 were repealed in so far as they relate to county courts by the County Courts Act 1984 (c.), s. 148(3), Sched. 4.*
[2] *Inserted by the Administration of Justice Act 1982 (c. 53), s. 6(2).*

[Power of High Court to award interest on debts and damages

35A—(1) Subject to rules of court, in proceedings (whenever instituted) before the High Court for the recovery of a debt or damages there may be included in any sum for which judgment is given simple interest, at such rate as the court thinks fit or as rules of court may provide, on all or any part of the debt or damages in respect of which judgment is given, or payment is made before judgment, for all any part of the period between the date when the cause of action arose and—

(a) in the case of any sum paid before judgment, the date of the payment; and

(b) in the case of the sum for which judgment is given, the date of the judgment.

(2) In relation to a judgment given for damages for personal injuries or death which exceed £200 subsection (1) shall have effect—

(a) with the substitution of "shall be included" for "may be included"; and

(b) with the addition of "unless the court is satisfied that there are special reason to the contrary" after "given", where first occurring.

(3) Subject to rules of court, where—

(a) there are proceedings (whenever instituted) before the High Court for the recovery of a debt; and

(b) the defendant pays the whole debt to the plaintiff (otherwise than in pursuance of a judgment in the proceedings),

the defendant shall be liable to pay the plaintiff simple interest at such rate as the court thinks fit or as rules of court may provide on all or any part of the debt for all or any part of the period between the date when the cause of action arose and the date of the payment.

(4) Interest in respect of a debt shall not be awarded under this section for a period during which, for whatever reason, interest on the debt already runs.

(5) Without prejudice to the generality of section 84, rules of court may provide for a rate of interest by reference to the rate specified in section 17 of the Judgments Act 1838 as that section has effect from time to time or by reference to a rate for which any other enactment provides.

(6) Interest under this section may be calculated at different rates in respect of different periods.

(7) In this section "plaintiff" means the person seeking the debt or damages and "defendant" means the person from whom the plaintiff seeks the debt or damages and "personal injuries" includes any disease and any impairment of a person's physical or mental condition.

(8) Nothing in this section affects the damages recoverable for the dishonour of a bill of exchange.][1]

[1] *Inserted by Administration of Justice Act 1982 (c. 53), s. 15(1), Sched. 1, Pt I.*

Subpoena issued by High Court to run throughout United Kingdom.

36—(1) If in any case or matter in the High Court it appears to the court that it is proper to compel the personal attendance at any trial of a witness who may not be within the jurisdiction of the court, it shall be lawful for the court, if in the discretion of the court it seems fit so to do, to order that a writ of subpoena ad testificandum or writ of subpoena duces tecum shall issue in special form commanding the witness to attend the trial wherever he shall be within the United Kingdom; and the service of any such writ in any part of the United Kingdom shall be as valid and effectual for all purposes as if it had been served within the jurisdiction of the High Court.

(2) Every such writ shall have at its foot a statement to the effect that it is

issued by the special order of the High Court, and no such writ shall issue without such a special order.

(3) If any person served with a writ issued under this section does not appear as required by the writ, the High Court, on proof to the satisfaction of the court of the service of the writ and of the default, may transmit a certificate of the default under the seal of the court or under the hand of a judge of the court—

(a) if the service was in Scotland, to the Court of Session at Edinburgh; or

(b) if the service was in Northern Ireland, to the High Court of Justice in Northern Ireland at Belfast;

and the court to which the certificate is sent shall thereupon proceed against and punish the person in default in like manner as if that person had neglected or refused to appear in obedience to process issued out of that court.

(4) No court shall in any case proceed against or punish any person for having made such default as aforesaid unless it is shown to the court that a reasonable and sufficient sum of money defray [:—

(a) the expenses of coming and attending to give evidence and of returning from giving evidence; and

(b) any other reasonable expenses which he has asked to be defrayed in connection with his evidence,

was tendered to him at the time when the writ was served upon him.][1]

(5) Nothing in this section shall affect—

(a) the power of the High Court to issue a commission for the examination of witnesses out of the jurisdiction of the court in any case in which, notwithstanding this section, the court thinks fit to issue such a commission; or

(b) the admissibility at any trial of any evidence which, if this section had not been enacted, would have been admissible on the ground of a witness being outside the jurisdiction of the court.

(6) In this section references to attendance at a trial include references to attendance before an examiner or commissioner appointed by the High Court in any cause or matter in that court, including an examiner or commissioner appointed to take evidence outside the jurisdiction of the court.

[1] *Substituted by Courts and Legal Services Act 1990 (c. 41), s. 125(2), Sched. 17.*

. . . . .

Administration of Justice Act 1982

(1982 c. 53)

Abolition of claims for damages etc

Abolition of right to damages for loss of expectation of life

1—(1) In an action under the law of England and Wales or the law of Northern Ireland for damages for personal injuries—

(a) no damages shall be recoverable in respect of any loss of expectation of life caused to the injured person by the injuries; but

(b) if the injured person's expectation of life has been reduced by the injuries, the court, in assessing damages in respect of pain and suffering caused by the injuries, shall take account of any suffering caused or likely to be caused to him by awareness that his expectation of life has been so reduced.

(2) The reference in subsection (1)(a) above to damages in respect of loss of expectation of life does not include damages in respect of loss of income.

Abolition of actions for loss of services etc

2—No person shall be liable in tort under the law of England and Wales or the law of Northern Ireland—

(a) to a husband on the ground only of his having deprived him of the services or society of his wife;

(b) to a parent (or person standing in the place of a parent) on the ground only of his having deprived him of the services of a child; or

(c) on the ground only—

(i) of having deprived another of the services of his menial servant;

(ii) of having deprived another of the services of his female servant by raping or seducing her; or

(iii) of enticement of a servant or harbouring a servant.

. . . . .

Maintenance at public expense

Maintenance at public expense to be taken into account in assessment of damages

5—In an action under the law of England and Wales or the law of Northern Ireland for damages for personal injuries (including any such action arising out of a contract) any saving to the injured person which is attributable to his maintenance wholly or partly at public expense in a hospital, nursing home or other institution shall be set off against any income lost by him as a result of his injuries.

. . . . .

County Courts Act 1984

(1984 c. 28)

Transfer of proceedings

[Transfer of proceedings to county court

40—(1) Where the High Court is satisfied that any proceedings before it are required by an provision of a kind mentioned in subsection (8) to be in a county court it shall—

(a) order the transfer of the proceedings to a county court; or

(b) if the court is satisfied that the person bringing the proceedings knew, or ought to have known, of that requirement, order that they be struck out.

(2) Subject to any such provision, the High Court may order the transfer of any proceedings before it to a county court.

(3) An order under this section may be made either on the motion of the High Court itself or on the application of any party to the proceedings.

(4) Proceedings transferred under this section shall be transferred to such county court as the High Court considers appropriate, having taken into account the convenience of the parties and that of any other persons likely to be affected and the state of business in the courts concerned.

(5) The transfer of any proceedings under this section shall not affect any right of appeal from the order directing the transfer.

(8)The provisions referred to in subsection (1) are any made—

(a) under section 1 of the Courts and Legal Services Act 1990; or

(b) by or under any other enactment.][1]

. . . . .

[1] *Substituted by Courts and Legal Services Act 1990 (c. 41), s. 2(1).*

Transfer to High Court by order of High Court

41—(1) If at any stage in proceedings commenced in a county court or transferred to a county court under section 40, the High Court thinks it desirable that the proceedings, or any part of them, should be heard and determined in the High Court, it may order the transfer to the High Court of the proceedings or, as the case may be, of that part of them.

. . . . .

[(3) The power conferred by subsection (1) shall be exercised subject to any provision made—

(a) under section 1 of the Courts and Legal Services Act 1990; or

(b) by or under any other enactment.][1]

[1] *Inserted by Courts and Legal Services Act 1990 (c. 41), s. 2(2).*

[Transfer to High Court by order of county court

42—(1) Where a county court is satisfied that any proceedings before it are required by any provision of a kind mentioned in subsection (7) to be in the High Court, it shall—

(a) order the transfer of the proceedings to the High Court; or
(b) if the court is satisfied that the person bringing the proceedings knew, or ought to have known, of that requirement, order that they be struck out.

(2) Subject to any such provision, a county court may order the transfer of any proceedings before it to the High Court.

(3) An order under this section may be made either on the motion of the court itself or on the application of any party to the proceedings.

(4) The transfer of any proceedings under this section shall not affect any right of appeal from the order directing the transfer.

(7) The provisions referred to in subsection (1) are any made—

(a) under section 1 of the Courts and Legal Services Act 1990; or
(b) by or under any other enactment.][1]

[1] *Substituted by Courts and Legal Services Act 1990 (c. 41), s. 2(3).*

. . . . .

Interim payments in pending proceedings

Orders of interim payment

50—(1) Provision may be made by [rules of court][1] for enabling the court, in such circumstances as may be prescribed, to make an order requiring a party to the proceedings to make an interim payment of such amount as may be specified in the order, with provision for the payment to be made to such other party to the proceedings as may be so specified or, if the order so provides, by paying it into court.

(2) Any [rules of court][1] which make provision in accordance with subsection (1) may include provision for enabling a party to any proceedings who, in pursuance of such an order, has made an interim payment to recover the whole or part of the amount of the payment in such circumstances, and from such other party to the proceedings, as may be determined in accordance with the rules.

(3) Any rules made by virtue of this section may include such incidental, supplementary and consequential provisions as the [Civil Procedure Rule Committee][1] may consider necessary or expedient.

(4) Nothing in this section shall be construed as affecting the exercise of any power relating to costs, including any power to make [rule of court][1] relating to costs.

(5) In this section "interim payment", in relation to a party to any proceedings, means a payment on account of any damages, debt or other sum (excluding any costs) which that party may be held liable to pay to or for the benefit of another party to the proceedings if a final judgement or order of the court in the proceedings is given or made in favour of that other party; and any reference to a party to any proceedings includes a reference to any person who for the purposes of the proceedings acts as next friend or guardian of a party to the proceedings.

[1] *Substituted by Civil Procedure Act 1997 (c. 12), Sched. 2, para. 2.*

Provisional damages for personal injuries

Orders for provisional damages for personal injuries

51—(1) This section applies to an action for damages for personal injuries in which there is proved or admitted to be a chance that at some definite or indefinite time in the future the injured person will, as a result of the act or omission which gave rise to the cause of action, develop some serious disease or suffer some serious deterioration in his physical or mental condition.

(2) Subject to subsection (4), as regards any action for damages to which this section applies in which a judgment is given in the county court, provision may be made by [rules of court][1] for enabling the court, in such circumstances as may be prescribed, to award the injured person—

- (a) damages assessed on the assumption that the injured person will not develop the disease or suffer the deterioration in his condition; and
- (b) further damages at a future date if he develops the disease or suffers the deterioration.

(3) Any rules made by virtue of this section may include such incidental, supplementary and consequential provisions as the [Civil Procedure Rules Committee][1] may consider necessary or expedient.

(4) Nothing in this section shall be construed—

- (a) as affecting the exercise of any power relating to costs, including any power to make [rules of court][1] relating to costs; or
- (b) as prejudicing any duty of the court under any enactment or rule of law to reduce or limit the total damages which would have been recoverable apart from any such duty.

(5) In this section "personal injuries" includes any disease and any impairment of a person's physical or mental condition.

[1] *Substituted by Civil Procedure Act 1997 (c. 12), Sched. 2, para. 2.*

Discovery and related procedures

52. Powers of court exercisable before commencement of action

(1) On the application of any person in accordance with rules of court, a county court shall, in such circumstances as may be prescribed, have power to make an order providing for any one or more of the following matters, that is to say—

- (a) the inspection, photographing, preservation, custody and detention of property which appears to the court to be property which may become the subject-matter of subsequent proceedings in the court, or as to which any question may arise in any such proceedings; and
- (b) the taking of samples of any such property as is mentioned in paragraph (a), and the carrying out of any experiment on or with any such property.

(2) On the application, in accordance with rules of court, of a person who appears to a county court to be likely to be party to subsequent proceedings in that court in which a claim in respect of personal injuries to a person, or in respect of a person death, is likely to be made, the county court shall, in such circumstances as may be prescribed, have power to order a person who appears to the court to likely to be a party to the proceedings and to be likely to have or to have had in his possession, custody or power any documents which are relevant to an issue arising or likely to arise out of that claim—

- (a) to disclose whether those documents are in his possession, custody or power; and
- (b) to produce such of those documents as may be specified in the order.—the applicant or, on such conditions as may be specified in the order,—
  - (i) to the applicant's legal advisers; or
  - (ii) to the applicant's legal advisers and any medical or other professional adviser of the applicant; or
  - (iii) to the applicant has no legal adviser, to any medical or other professional adviser of the applicant.

(3) [This section is subject to any provision made under section 38.][1]

[1] *Inserted by Courts and Legal Services Act 1990 (c. 41), Sched. 18, para. 43.*
[2] *Substituted by Civil Procedure Act 1997 (c. 12), Sched. 2, para. 2.*

Power of court to order disclosure of documents, inspection of property etc in proceedings for personal injuries or death

53—(1) This section applies to any proceedings in a county court in which a claim is made in respect of personal injuries to a person, or in respect of a person's death.

(2) On the application, in accordance with [rules of court][1] of a party to any proceedings to which this section applies, a county court shall, in such

circumstances as may be prescribed, have power to order a person who is not a party to the proceedings and who appears to the court to be likely to have in his possession, custody or power any documents which are relevant to an issue arising out of the said claim—

(a) to disclose whether those documents are in his possession, custody or power; and

(b) to produce such of those documents as are in his possession, custody or power to the applicant or, on such conditions as may be specified in the order—

(i) to the applicant's legal advisers; or

(ii) to the applicant's legal advisers and any medical or other professional adviser of the applicant, or

(iii) if the applicant has no legal adviser, to any medical or other professional adviser of the applicant.

(3) On the application, in accordance with [rules of court][1] of a party to any proceedings to which this section applies, a county court shall, in such circumstances as may be prescribed, have power to make an order providing for any one or more of the following matters, that is to say—

(a) the inspection, photographing, preservation, custody and detention of property which is not the property of, or in the possession of, any party to the proceedings but which is the subject-matter of the proceedings or as to which any question arises in the proceedings;

(b) the taking of samples of any such property as is mentioned in paragraph (a) and the carrying out of any experiment on or with any such property.

(4) The preceding provisions of this section are without prejudice to the exercise by a county court of any power to make orders which is exercisable apart from those provisions.

[(5) This section is subject to any provision made under section 38.][2]

[1] *Substituted by Civil Procedure Act 1997 (c. 12), Sched. 2, para. 2.*

[2] *Inserted by Courts and Legal Services Act 1990 (c. 41), s. 125(3), Sched. 18, para. 44.*

Provisions supplementary to sections 52 and 53

54—(1) A county court shall not make an order under section 52 or 53 if it considers that compliance with the order, if made, would be likely to be injurious to the public interest.

(2) [Rules of court][1] may make provision as to the circumstances in which an order under section 52 or 53 can be made; and any rules making such provision may include such incidental, supplementary and consequential provisions as the rule committee may consider necessary or expedient.

(3) Without prejudice to the generality of subsection (2), [rules of court][1] shall be made for the purpose of ensuring that the costs of and incidental to proceedings for an order under section 52(2) or 53 incurred by the person against whom the order is sought shall be awarded to that person unless the court otherwise directs.

(4) Sections 52(2) and 53 and this section bind the Crown; and section 51(1) binds the Crown so far as it relates to property as to which it appears to the court that it may become the subject-matter of subsequent proceedings involving a claim in respect of personal injuries to a person or in respect of a person's death.

In this subsection references to the Crown do not include references to Her Majesty in Her private capacity or to Her Majesty in right of Her Duchy of Lancaster or to the Duke of Cornwall.

(5) In sections 52 and 53 and this section—

"property" includes any land, chattel or other corporeal property of any description;

"personal injuries" includes any disease and any impairment of a person's physical or mental condition.

[(6) This section is subject to any provision made under section 38.][2]

[1] *Substituted by Civil Procedure Act 1997 (c. 12), Sched. 2, para. 2.*

[2] *Inserted by Courts and Legal Services Act 1990 (c. 41), s. 125(3), Sched. 18, para. 45.*

. . . . .

Interest on debts and damages

Power to award interest on debts and damages

69—(1) Subject to [rules of court],[1] in proceedings (whenever instituted) before a county court for the recovery of a debt or damages there may be included in any sum for which judgment is given simple interest, at such rate as the court thinks fit or as may be prescribed, on all or any part of the debt or damages in respect of which judgment is given, or payment is made before judgment, for all or any part of the period between the date when the cause of action arose and—

(a) in the case of any sum paid before judgment, the date of the payment; and

(b) in the case of the sum for which judgment is given, the date of the judgment.

(2) In relation to a judgment given for damages for personal injuries or death which exceed £200 subsection (1) shall have effect—

(a) with the substitution of "shall be included" for "may be included"; and

(b) with the addition of "unless the court is satisfied that there are special reasons to the contrary" after "given", where first occurring.

. . . . .

(5) Interest under this section may be calculated at different rates in respect of different periods.

(6) In this section "plaintiff" means the person seeking the debt or damages and "defendant" means the person from whom the plaintiff seeks

the debt or damages and "personal injuries" includes any disease and any impairment of a person's physical or mental condition.

[1] *Substituted by Civil Procedure Act 1997 (c. 12), Sched. 2, para. 2.*

. . . . .

Application of practice of High Court

76—In any case not expressly provided for by or in pursuance of this Act, the general principles of practice in the High Court may be adopted and applied to proceedings in a county court.

High Court and County Courts Jurisdiction Order 1991

(1991 No. 724)

. . . . .

Commencement of proceedings

5—(1) Proceedings in which county courts have jurisdiction and which include a claim for damages in respect of personal injuries shall be commenced in a county court, unless the value of the action is £50,000 or more.

(2) In this article "personal injuries" means personal injuries to the plaintiff or any other person, and includes disease, impairment of physical or mental condition, and death.

. . . . .

Definition of value of action

9—(1) For the purposes of articles 5 and 7—

- (a) the value of an action for a sum of money, whether specified or not, is the amount which the plaintiff or applicant reasonably expects to recover;
- (b) an action for specified relief other than a sum of money—
  - (i) has a value equal to the amount of money which the plaintiff or applicant could reasonably state to be the financial worth of the claim to him, or
  - (ii) where there is no such amount, has no quantifiable value;
- (c) an action which includes more than one claim—
  - (i) if one or more of the claims is of a kind specified in paragraph (b) (ii), has no quantifiable value;
  - (ii) in any other case, has a value which is the aggregate of the values of the claims as determined in accordance with paragraphs (a) and (b)(i).

(2) In determining the value of an action under paragraph (1), claims for—

- (a) unspecified further or other relief,
- (b) interest, other than interest pursuant to a contract, and
- (c) costs,

shall be disregarded.

(3) In determining the value, under paragraph (1), of an action which is brought by more than one plaintiff or applicant regard shall be had to the aggregate of the expectations or interests of all the plaintiffs or applicants.

(4) In determining the value of an action under paragraph (1) (a)—

(a) the sum which the plaintiff or applicant reasonably expects to recover shall be reduced by the amount of any debt which he admits that he owes to a defendant in that action and which arises from the circumstances which give rise to the action;

(b) no account shall be taken of a possible finding of contributory negligence, except to the extent, if any, that such negligence is admitted;

(c) where the plaintiff seeks an award of provisional damages as described in section 32A(2)(a) of the Supreme Court Act 1981, no account shall be taken of the possibility of a future application for further damages;

(d) the value shall be taken to include sums which, by virtue of section 22 of the Social Security Act 1989, are required to be paid to the Secretary of State.

10 The value of an action shall be determined—

(a) for the purposes of article 5, as at the time when the action is commenced;

. . . . .

Civil Evidence Act 1995

(1995 c. 38)

ARRANGEMENT OF SECTIONS

[November 8, 1995]

Admissibility of hearsay evidence

Admissibility of hearsay evidence

1—(1) In civil proceedings evidence shall not be excluded on the ground that it is hearsay.

(2) In this Act—

(a) "hearsay" means a statement made otherwise than by a person while giving oral evidence in the proceedings which is tendered as evidence of the matters stated; and

(b) references to hearsay include hearsay of whatever degree.

(3) Nothing in this Act affects the admissibility of evidence admissible apart from this section.

(4) The provisions of sections 2 to 6 (safeguards and supplementary provisions relating to hearsay evidence) do not apply in relation to hearsay evidence admissible apart from this section, notwithstanding that it may also be admissible by virtue of this section.

Safeguards in relation to hearsay evidence

Notice of proposal to adduce hearsay evidence

2—(1) A party proposing to adduce hearsay evidence in civil proceedings shall, subject to the following provisions of this section, give to the other party or parties to the proceedings—

(a) such notice (if any) of that fact, and

(b) on request, such particulars of or relating to the evidence,

as is reasonable and practicable in the circumstances for the purpose of enabling him or them to deal with any matters arising from its being hearsay.

(2) Provision may be made by rules of court—

(a) specifying classes of proceedings or evidence in relation to which subsection (1) does not apply, and

(b) as to the manner in which (including the time within which) the duties imposed by that subsection are to be complied with in the cases where it does apply.

(3) Subsection (1) may also be excluded by agreement of the parties; and compliance with the duty to give notice may in any case be waived by the person to whom notice is required to be given.

(4) A failure to comply with subsection (1), or with rules under subsection (2)(b), does not affect the admissibility of the evidence but may be taken into account by the court—

(a) in considering the exercise of its powers with respect to the course of proceedings and costs, and

(b) as a matter adversely affecting the weight to be given to the evidence in accordance with section 4.

Power to call witness for cross-examination on hearsay statement

3—Rules of court may provide that where a party to civil proceedings adduces hearsay evidence of a statement made by a person and does not call that person as a witness, any other party to the proceedings may, with the leave of the court, call that person as a witness and cross-examine him on the statement as if he had been called by the first-mentioned party and as if the hearsay statement were his evidence in chief.

Considerations relevant to weighing of hearsay evidence

4—(1) In estimating the weight (if any) to be given to hearsay evidence in civil proceedings the court shall have regard to any circumstances from which any inference can reasonably be drawn as to the reliability or otherwise of the evidence.

(2) Regard may be had, in particular, to the following—

(a) whether it would have been reasonable and practicable for the party by whom the evidence was adduced to have produced the maker of the original statement as a witness;

(b) whether the original statement was made contemporaneously with the occurrence or existence of the matters stated;

(c) whether the evidence involves multiple hearsay;

(d) whether any person involved had any motive to conceal or misrepresent matters;

(e) whether the original statement was an edited account, or was made in collaboration with another or for a particular purpose;

(f) whether the circumstances in which the evidence is adduced as hear-say are such as to suggest an attempt to prevent proper evaluation of its weight.

Supplementary provisions as to hearsay evidence

Competence and credibility

5—(1) Hearsay evidence shall not be admitted in civil proceedings if or to the extent that it is shown to consist of, or to be proved by means of, a statement made by a person who at the time he made the statement was not competent as a witness.

For this purpose "not competent as a witness" means suffering from such mental or physical infirmity, or lack of understanding, as would render a person incompetent as a witness in civil proceedings; but a child shall be treated as competent as a witness if he satisfied the requirements of section

96(2)(a) and (b) of the Children Act 1989 (conditions for reception of unsworn evidence of child).

(2) Where in civil proceedings hearsay evidence is adduced and the maker of the original statement, or of any statement relied upon to prove another statement, is not called as a witness—

(a) evidence which if he had been so called would be admissible for the purpose of attacking or supporting his credibility as a witness is admissible for that purpose in the proceedings; and

(b) evidence tending to prove that, whether before or after he made the statement, he made any other statement inconsistent with it is admissible for the purpose of showing that he had contradicted himself.

Provided that evidence may not be given of any matter of which, if he had been called as a witness and had denied that matter in cross-examination, evidence could not have been adduced by the cross-examining party.

Previous statements of witnesses

6—(1) Subject as follows, the provisions of this Act as to hearsay evidence in civil proceedings apply equally (but with any necessary modifications) in relation to a previous statement made by a person called as a witness in the proceedings.

(2) A party who has called or intends to call a person as a witness in civil proceedings may not in those proceedings adduce evidence of a previous statement made by that person, except—

(a) with the leave of the court, or

(b) for the purpose of rebutting a suggestion that his evidence has been fabricated.

This shall not be construed as preventing a witness statement (that is, a written statement of oral evidence which a party to the proceedings intends to lead) from being adopted by a witness in giving evidence or treated as his evidence.

(3) Where in the case of civil proceedings section 3, 4 or 5 of the Criminal Procedure Act 1865 applies, which make provision as to—

(a) how far a witness may be discredited by the party producing him,

(b) the proof of contradictory statements made by a witness, and

(c) cross-examination as to previous statements in writing,

this Act does not authorise the adducing of evidence of a previous inconsistent or contradictory statement otherwise than in accordance with those sections.

This is without prejudice to any provision made by rules of court under section 3 above (power to call witness for cross-examination on hearsay statement).

(4) Nothing in this Act affects any of the rules of law as to the circumstances in which, where a person called as a witness in civil proceedings is cross-examined on a document used by him to refresh his memory, that document may be made evidence in the proceedings.

(5) Nothing in this section shall be construed as preventing a statement of

any description referred to above from being admissible by virtue of section 1 as evidence of the matters stated.

Evidence formerly admissible at common law

7—(1) The common law rule effectively preserved by section 9(1) and (2)(a) of the Civil Evidence Act 1968 (admissibility of admissions adverse to a party) is superseded by the provisions of this Act.

(2) The common law rules effectively preserved by section 9(1) and (2)(b) to (d) of the Civil Evidence Act 1968, that is, any rule of law whereby in civil proceedings—

- (a) published works dealing with matters of a public nature (for example, histories, scientific works, dictionaries and maps) are admissible as evidence of facts of a public nature stated in them,
- (b) public documents (for example, public registers, and returns made under public authority with respect to matters of public interest) are admissible as evidence of facts stated in them, or
- (c) records (for example, the records of certain courts, treaties, Crown grants, pardons and commissions) are admissible as evidence of facts stated in them,

shall continue to have effect.

(3) The common law rules effectively preserved by section 9(3) and (4) of the Civil Evidence Act 1968, that is, any rule of law whereby in civil proceedings—

- (a) evidence of a person's reputation is admissible for the purpose of proving his good or bad character, or
- (b) evidence of reputation or family tradition is admissible—
  - (i) for the purpose of proving or disproving pedigree or the existence of a marriage, or
  - (ii) for the purpose of proving of disproving the existence of any public or general right or of identifying any person or thing,

shall continue to have effect in so far as they authorise the court to treat such evidence as proving or disproving that matter.

Where any such rule applies, reputation or family tradition shall be treated for the purposes of this Act as a fact and not as a statement or multiplicity of statements about the matter in question.

(4) The words in which a rule of law mentioned in this section is described are intended only to identify the rule and shall not be construed as altering it in any way.

Other matters

Proof of statements contained in documents

8—(1) Where a statement contained in a document is admissible as evidence in civil proceedings, it may be proved—

(a) by the production of that document, or
(b) whether or not that document is still in existence, by the production of a copy of that document or of the material part of it,

authenticated in such manner as the court may approve.

(2) It is immaterial for this purpose how many removes there are between a copy and the original.

Proof of records of business or public authority

9—(1) A document which is shown to form part of the records of a business or public authority may be received in evidence in civil proceedings without further proof.

(2) A document shall be taken to form part of the records of a business or public authority if there is produced to the court a certificate to that effect signed by an officer of the business or authority to which the records belong.

For this purpose—

(a) a document purporting to be a certificate signed by an officer of a business or public authority shall be deemed to have been duly given by such an officer and signed by him; and
(b) a certificate shall be treated as signed by a person if it purports to bear a facsimile of his signature.

(3) The absence of an entry in the records of a business or public authority may be proved in civil proceedings by affidavit of an officer of the business or authority to which the records belong.

(4) In this section—

"records" means records in whatever form:

"business" includes any activity regularly carried on over a period of time, whether for profit or not, by any body (whether corporate or not) or by an individual;

"officer" includes any person occupying a responsible position in relation to the relevant activities of the business or public authority or in relation to its records; and

"public authority" includes any public or statutory undertaking, any government department and any person holding office under Her Majesty.

(5) The court may, having regard to the circumstances of the case, direct that all or any of the above provisions of this section do not apply in relation to a particular document or record, or description of documents or records.

Admissibility and proof of Ogden Tables*

10—(1) The actuarial tables (together with explanatory notes) for use in personal injury and fatal accident cases issued from time to time by the Government Actuary's Department are admissible in evidence for the purpose of assessing, in an action for personal injury, the sum to be awarded as general damages for future pecuniary loss.

(2) They may be proved by the production of a copy published by Her Majesty's Stationery Office.

(3) For the purposes of this section—

(a) "personal injury" includes any disease and any impairment of a person's physical or mental condition; and

(b) "action for personal injury" includes an action brought by virtue of the Law Reform (Miscellaneous Provisions) Act 1934 or the Fatal Accidents Act 1976.

*[At the date when this edition went to the printers, this section had not yet been brought into force. By the date of publication it may well be in force.]

General

Meaning of "civil proceedings"

11—In this Act "civil proceedings" means civil proceedings, before any tribunal, in relation to which the strict rules of evidence apply, whether as a matter of law or by agreement of the parties. References to "the court" and "rules of court" shall be construed accordingly.

Provisions as to rules of court

12—(1) Any power to make rules of court regulating the practice or procedure of the court in relation to civil proceedings includes power to make such provision as may be necessary or expedient for carrying into effect the provisions of this Act.

(2) Any rules of court made for the purposes of this Act as it applies in relation to proceedings in the High Court apply, except in so far as their operation is excluded by agreement, to arbitration proceedings to which this Act applies, subject to such modifications as may be appropriate.

Any question arising as to what modifications are appropriate shall be determined, in default of agreement, by the arbitrator or umpire, as the case may be.

Interpretation

13—In this Act—

"civil proceedings" has the meaning given by section 11 and "court" and "rules of court" shall be construed in accordance with that section;

"document" means anything in which information of any description is recorded, and "copy", in relation to a document, means anything onto which information recorded in the document has been copied, by whatever means and whether directly or indirectly;

"hearsay" shall be construed in accordance with section 1(2);

"oral evidence" includes evidence which, by reason of a defect of speech or hearing, a person called as a witness gives in writing or by signs;

"the original statement", in relation to hearsay evidence, means the underlying statement (if any) by—
- (a) in the case of evidence of fact, a person having personal knowledge of that fact, or
- (b) in the case of evidence of opinion, the person whose opinion it is; and

"statement" means any representation of fact or opinion, however made

Savings

14—(1) Nothing in this Act affects the exclusion of evidence on grounds other than that it is hearsay.

This applies whether the evidence falls to be excluded in pursuance of any enactment or rule of law, for failure to comply with rules of court or an order of the court, or otherwise.

(2) Nothing in this Act affects the proof of documents by means other than those specified in section 8 or 9.

(3) Nothing in this Act affects the operation of the following enactments—
- (a) section 2 of the Documentary Evidence Act 1868 (mode of proving certain official documents);
- (b) section 2 of the Documentary Evidence Act 1882 (documents printed under the superintendence of Stationery Office);
- (c) section 1 of the Evidence (Colonial Statutes) Act 1907 (proof of statutes of certain legislatures);
- (d) section 1 of the Evidence (Foreign, Dominion and Colonial Documents) Act 1933 (proof and effect of registers and official certificates of certain countries);
- (e) section 5 of the Oaths and Evidence (Overseas Authorities and Countries) Act 1963 (provision in respect of public registers of other countries).

Consequential amendments and repeals

15—(1) The enactments specified in Schedule 1 are amended in accordance with that Schedule, the amendments being consequential on the provisions of this Act.

(2) The enactments specified in Schedule 2 are repealed to the extent specified.

Short title, commencement and extent

16—(1) This Act may be cited as the Civil Evidence Act 1995.

(2) The provisions of this Act come into force on such day as the Lord Chancellor may appoint by order made by statutory instrument, and different days may be appointed for different provisions and for different purposes.

(3) An order under subsection (2) may contain such transitional provi-

sions as appear to the Lord Chancellor to be appropriate; and subject to any such provision, the provisions of this Act shall not apply in relation to proceedings begun before commencement.

(4) This Act extends to England and Wales.

(5) Section 10 (admissibility and proof of Ogden Tables) also extends to Northern Ireland.

As it extends to Northern Ireland, the following shall be substituted for subsection (3)(b)—

> "(b) 'action for personal injury' includes an action brought by virtue of the Law Reform (Miscellaneous Provisions) (Northern Ireland) Act 1937 or the Fatal Accidents (Northern Ireland) Order 1977."

(6) The provisions of Schedules 1 and 2 (consequential amendments and repeals) have the same extent as the enactments respectively amended or repealed.

. . . . . .

Damages Act 1996

(1996 C. 48)

An Act to make new provision in relation to damages for personal injury, including injury resulting in death.

[July 24, 1996]

Assumed rate of return on investment of damages

1—(1) In determining the return to be expected from the investment of a sum awarded as damages for future pecuniary loss in an action for personal injury the court shall, subject to and in accordance with rules of court made for the purposes of this section, take into account such rate of return (if any) as may from time to time be prescribed by an order made by the Lord Chancellor.

(2) Subsection (1) above shall not however prevent the court taking a different rate of return into account if any party to the proceedings shows that it is more appropriate in the case in question.

(3) An order under subsection (1) above may prescribe different rates of return for different classes of case.

(4) Before making an order under subsection (1) above the Lord Chancellor shall consult the Government Actuary and the Treasury; and any order under that subsection shall be made by statutory instrument subject to annulment in pursuance of a resolution of either House of Parliament.

(5) In the application of this section to Scotland for references to the Lord Chancellor there shall be substituted references to the Secretary of State.

Consent orders for periodical payments

2—(1) A court awarding damages in an action for personal injury may, with the consent of the parties, make an order under which the damages are wholly or partly to take the form of periodical payments.

(2) In this section "damages" includes an interim payment which the court, by virtue of rules of court in that behalf, orders the defendant to make to the plaintiff (or, in the application of this section to Scotland, the defender to make to the pursuer).

(3) This section is without prejudice to any powers exercisable apart from this section.

Provisional damages and fatal accident claims

3—(1) This section applies where a person—

(a) is awarded provisional damages; and

(b) subsequently dies as a result of the act or omission which gave rise to the cause of action for which the damages were awarded.

(2) The award of the provisional damages shall not operate as a bar to an action in respect of that person's death under the Fatal Accidents Act 1976.

(3) Such part (if any) of—

(a) the provisional damages; and

(b) any further damages awarded to the person in question before his death,

as was intended to compensate him for pecuniary loss in a period which in the event falls after his death shall be taken into account in assessing the amount of any loss of support suffered by the person or persons for whose benefit the action under the Fatal Accidents Act 1976 is brought.

(4) No award of further damages made in respect of that person after his death shall include any amount for loss of income in respect of any period after his death.

(5) In this section "provisional damages" means damages awarded by virtue of subsection (2)(a) of section 32A of the Supreme Court Act 1981 or section 51 of the Country Courts Act 1984 and "further damages" means damages awarded by virtue of subsection (2)(b) of either of those sections.

(6) Subsection (2) above applies whether the award of provisional damages was before or after the coming into force of that subsection; and subsections (3) and (4) apply to any award of damages under the 1976 Act or, as the case may be, further damages after the coming into force of those subsections.

(7) In the application of this section to Northern Ireland—

(a) for references to the Fatal Accidents Act 1976 there shall be substituted references to the Fatal Accidents (Northern Ireland) Order 1977;

(b) for the reference to subsection (2)(a) and (b) of section 32A of the Supreme Court Act 1981 and section 51 of the County Courts Act 1984 there shall be substituted a reference to paragraph 10(2)(a) and (b) of Schedule 6 to the Administration of Justice Act 1982.

Enhanced protection for structured settlement annuitants

4—(1) In relation to an annuity purchased for a person pursuant to a structured settlement from an authorised insurance company within the meaning of the Policyholders Protection Act 1975 (and in respect of which that person as annuitant is accordingly the policyholder for the purposes of that Act) sections 10 and 11 of that Act (protection in the event of liquidation of the insurer) shall have effect as if any reference to ninety per cent of the amount of the liability, of any future benefit or of the value attributed to the policy were a reference to the full amount of the liability, benefit or value.

(2) Those sections shall also have effect as mentioned in subsection (1)

above in relation to an annuity purchased from an authorised insurance company within the meaning of the 1975 Act pursuant to any order incorporating terms corresponding to those of a structured settlement which a court makes when awarding damages for personal injury.

(3) Those section shall also have effect as mentioned in subsection (1) above in relation to an annuity purchased from or otherwise provided by an authorised insurance company within the meaning of the 1975 Act pursuant to terms corresponding to those of a structured settlement contained in an agreement made by—

(a) the Motor Insurers' Bureau; or

(b) a Domestic Regulations Insurer,

in respect of damages for personal injury which the Bureau or Insurer undertakes to pay in satisfaction of a claim or action against an uninsured driver.

(4) In subsection (3) above "the Motor Insurers' Bureau" means the company of that name incorporated on 14th June 1946 under the Companies Act 1929 and "a Domestic Regulations Insurer" has the meaning given in the Bureau's Domestic Regulations.

(5) This section applies if the liquidation of the authorised insurance company begins (within the meaning of the 1975 Act) after the coming into force of this section irrespective of when the annuity was purchased or provided.

Meaning of structured settlement

5—(1) In section 4 above a "structured settlement" means an agreement settling a claim or action for damages for personal injury on terms whereby—

(a) the damages are to consist wholly or partly of periodical payments; and

(b) the person to whom the payments are to be made is to receive them as the annuitant under one or more annuities purchased for him by the person against whom the claim or action is brought or, if he is insured against the claim, by his insurer.

(2) The periodical payments may be for the life of the claimant, for a specified period or of a specified number or minimum number or include payments of more than one of those descriptions.

(3) The amounts of the periodical payments (which need not be at a uniform rate or payable at uniform intervals) may be—

(a) specified in the agreement, with or without provision for increases of specified amounts or percentages; or

(b) subject to adjustment in a specified manner so as to preserve their real value; or

(c) partly specified as mentioned in paragraph (a) above and partly subject to adjustment as mentioned in paragraph (b) above.

(4) The annuity or annuities must be such as to provide the annuitant with sums which as to amount and time of payment correspond to the periodical payments described in the agreement.

(5) Payments in respect of the annuity or annuities may be received on

behalf of the annuitant by another person or received and held on trust for his benefit under a trust of which he is, during his lifetime, the sole beneficiary.

(6) The Lord Chancellor may by an order made by statutory instrument provide that there shall for the purposes of this section be treated as an insurer any body specified in the order, being a body which, though not an insurer, appears to him to fulfil corresponding functions in relation to damages for personal injury claimed or awarded against persons of any class or description, and the reference in subsection (1)(b) above to a person being insured against the claim and his insurer shall be construed accordingly.

(7) In the application of subsection (6) above to Scotland for the reference to the Lord Chancellor there shall be substituted a reference to the Secretary of State.

(8) Where—

(a) an agreement is made settling a claim or action for damages for personal injury on terms whereby the damages are to consist wholly or partly of periodical payments;

(b) the person against whom the claim or action is brought (or, if he is insured against the claim, his insurer) purchases one or more annuities; and

(c) a subsequent agreement is made under which the annuity is, or the annuities are, assigned in favour of the person entitled to the payments (so as to secure that from a future date he receives the payments as the annuitant under the annuity or annuities),

then, for the purposes of section 4 above, the agreement settling the claim or action shall be treated as a structured settlement and any such annuity assigned in favour of that person shall be treated as an annuity purchased for him pursuant to the settlement.

(9) Subsections (2) to (7) above shall apply to an agreement to which subsection (8) above applies as they apply to a structured settlement as defined in subsection (1) above (the reference in subsection (6) to subsection (1)(b) being read as a reference to subsection (8)(b)).

Guarantees for public sector settlements

6—(1) This section applies where—

(a) a claim or action for damages for personal injury is settled on terms corresponding to those of a structured settlement as defined in section 5 above except that the person to whom the payments are to be made is not to receive them as mentioned in subsection (1)(b) of that section; or

(b) a court awarding damages for personal injury makes an order incorporating such terms.

(2) If it appears to a Minister of the Crown that the payments are to be made by a body in relation to which he has, by virtue of this section, power to do so, he may guarantee the payments to be made under the agreement or order.

(3) The bodies in relation to which a Minister may give such a guarantee

shall, subject to subsection (4) below, be such bodies as are designated in relation to the relevant government department by guidelines agreed upon between that department and the Treasury.

(4) A guarantee purporting to be given by a Minister under this section shall not be invalidated by any failure on his part to act in accordance with such guidelines as are mentioned in subsection (3) above.

(5) A guarantee under this section shall be given on such terms as the Minister concerned may determine but those terms shall in every case require the body in question to reimburse the Minister, with interest, for any sums paid by him in fulfilment of the guarantee.

(6) Any sums required by a Minister for fulfilling a guarantee under this section shall be defrayed out of money provided by Parliament and any sums received by him by way of reimbursement or interest shall be paid into the Consolidated Fund.

(7) A Minister who has given one or more guarantees under this section shall, as soon as possible after the end of each financial year, lay before each House of Parliament a statement showing what liabilities are outstanding in respect of the guarantees in that year, what sums have been paid in that year in fulfilment of the guarantees and what sums (including interest) have been recovered in that year in respect of the guarantees or are still owing.

(8) In this section "government department" means any department of Her Majesty's government in the United Kingdom and for the purposes of this section a government department is a relevant department in relation to a Minister if he has responsibilities in respect of that department.

(9) The Schedule to this Act has effect for conferring corresponding powers on Northern Ireland departments.

Interpretation

7—(1) Subject to subsection (2) below, in this Act "personal injury" includes any disease and any impairment of a person's physical or mental condition and references to a claim or action for personal injury include references to such a claim or action brought by virtue of the Law Reform (Miscellaneous Provisions) Act 1934 and to a claim or action brought by virtue of the Fatal Accidents Act 1976.

(2) In the application of this Act to Scotland "personal injury" has the meaning given by section 10(1) of the Damages (Scotland) Act 1976.

(3) In the application of subsection (1) above to Northern Ireland for the references to the Law Reform (Miscellaneous Provisions) Act 1934 and to the Fatal Accidents Act 1976 there shall be substituted respectively references to the Law Reform (Miscellaneous Provisions) Act (Northern Ireland) 1937 and the Fatal Accidents (Northern Ireland) Order 1977.

Short title, extent and commencement

8—This Act may be cited as the Damages Act 1996.

(2) Section 3 does not extend to Scotland but, subject to that, this Act extends to the whole of the United Kingdom.

(3) This Act comes into force at the end of the period of two months beginning with the day on which it is passed.

SCHEDULE

GUARANTEES BY NORTHERN IRELAND DEPARTMENTS FOR PUBLIC SECTOR SETTLEMENTS

1. This Schedule applies where—
   (a) a claim or action for damages for personal injury is settled on terms corresponding to those of a structured settlement as defined in section 5 of this Act except that the person to whom the payments are to be made is not to receive them as mentioned in subsection (1)(b) of that section; or
   (b) a court awarding damages for personal injury makes an order incorporating such terms.

2. If it appears to a Northern Ireland department that the payments are to be made by a body in relation to which that department has, by virtue of this Schedule, power to do so, that department may guarantee the payments to be made under the agreement or order.

3. The bodies in relation to which a Northern Ireland department may give such a guarantee shall, subject to paragraph 4 below, be such bodies as are designated in relation to that department by guidelines agreed upon between that department and the Department of Finance and Personnel in Northern Ireland.

4. A guarantee purporting to be given by a Northern Ireland department under this Schedule shall not be invalidated by any failure on the part of that department to act in accordance with such guidelines as are mentioned in paragraph 3 above.

5. A guarantee under this Schedule shall be given on such terms as the Northern Ireland department concerned may determine but those terms shall in every case require the body in question to reimburse that department, with interest, for any sums paid by that department in fulfilment of the guarantee.

6. A Northern Ireland department which has given one or more guarantees under this Schedule shall, as soon as possible after the end of each financial year, lay before the Northern Ireland Assembly a statement showing what liabilities are outstanding in respect of the guarantees in that year, what sums have been paid in that year in fulfilment of the guarantees and what sums (including interest) have been recovered in that year in respect of the guarantees or are still owing.

Social Security (Recovery of Benefits) Act 1997

(1997 c. 27)

ARRANGEMENT OF SECTIONS

Introductory

SECT.
1. Cases in which this Act applies.
2. Compensation payments to which this Act applies.
3. "The relevant period".

Certificates of recoverable benefits

4. Applications for certificates of recoverable benefits.
5. Information contained in certificates.

Liability of person paying compensation

6. Liability to pay Secretary of State amount of benefits.
7. Recovery of payments due under section 6.

Reduction of compensation payment

8. Reduction of compensation payment.
9. Section 8: supplementary.

Reviews and appeals

10. Review of certificates of recoverable benefits.
11. Appeals against certificates of recoverable benefits.
12. Reference of questions to medical appeal tribunal.
13. Appeal to Social Security Commissioner.

Courts

Reduction of compensation: complex cases

Miscellaneous

Provisions relating to Northern Ireland

General

An Act to re-state, with amendments, Part IV of the Social Security Administration Act 1992.

[March 19, 1997]

Introductory

Cases in which this Act applies

1—(1) This Act applies in cases where—

(a) a person makes a payment (whether on his own behalf or not) to or in respect of any other person in consequence of any accident, injury or disease suffered by the other, and

(b) any listed benefits have been, or are likely to be, paid to or for the other during the relevant period in respect of the accident, injury or disease.

(2) The reference above to a payment in consequence of any accident, injury or disease is to a payment made—

(a) by or on behalf of a person who is, or is alleged to be, liable to any extent in respect of the accident, injury or disease, or

(b) in pursuance of a compensation scheme for motor accidents; but does not include a payment mentioned in Part I of Schedule 1.

(3) Subsection (1)(a) applies to a payment made—

(a) voluntarily, or in pursuance of a court order or an agreement, or otherwise, and

(b) in the United Kingdom or elsewhere.

(4) In a case where this Act applies—

(a) the "injured person" is the person who suffered the accident, injury or disease,

(b) the "compensation payment" is the payment within subsection (1)(a), and

(c) "recoverable benefit" is any listed benefit which has been or is likely to be paid as mentioned in subsection (1)(b).

Compensation payments to which this Act applies

2 This Act applies in relation to compensation payments made on or after the day on which this section comes into force, unless they are made in pursuance of a court order or agreement made before that day.

"The relevant period"

3—(1) In relation to a person ("the claimant") who has suffered any accident, injury or disease, "the relevant period" has the meaning given by the following subsections.

(2) Subject to subsection (4), if it is a case of accident or injury, the

relevant period is the period of five years immediately following the day on which the accident or injury in question occurred.

(3) Subject to subsection (4), if it is a case of disease, the relevant period is the period of five years beginning with the date on which the claimant first claims a listed benefit in consequence of the disease.

(4) If at any time before the end of the period referred to in subsection (2) or (3)—

(a) a person makes a compensation payment in final discharge of any claim made by or in respect of the claimant and arising out of the accident, injury or disease, or

(b) an agreement is made under which an earlier compensation payment is treated as having been made in final discharge of any such claim,

the relevant period ends at that time.

Certificates of recoverable benefits

Applications for certificates of recoverable benefits

4—(1) Before a person ("the compensator") makes a compensation payment he must apply to the Secretary of State for a certificate of recoverable benefits.

(2) Where the compensator applies for a certificate of recoverable benefits, the Secretary of State must—

(a) send to him a written acknowledgement of receipt of his application, and

(b) subject to subsection (7), issue the certificate before the end of the following period.

(3) The period is—

(a) the prescribed period, or

(b) if there is no prescribed period, the period of four weeks,

which begins with the day following the day on which the application is received.

(4) The certificate is to remain in force until the date specified in it for that purpose.

(5) The compensator may apply for fresh certificates from time to time.

(6) Where a certificate of recoverable benefits ceases to be in force, the Secretary of State may issue a fresh certificate without an application for one being made.

(7) Where the compensator applies for a fresh certificate while a certificate ("the existing certificate") remains in force, the Secretary of State must issue the fresh certificate before the end of the following period.

(8) The period is—

(a) the prescribed period, or

(b) if there is no prescribed period, the period of four weeks,

which begins with the day following the day on which the existing certificate ceases to be in force.

(9) For the purposes of this Act, regulations may provide for the day on

which an application for a certificate of recoverable benefits is to be treated as received.

Information contained in certificates

5—(1) A certificate of recoverable benefits must specify, for each recoverable benefit—

(a) the amount which has been or is likely to have been paid on or before a specified date, and

(b) if the benefit is paid or likely to be paid after the specified date, the rate and period for which, and the intervals at which, it is or is likely to be so paid.

(2) In a case where the relevant period has ended before the day on which the Secretary of State receives the application for the certificate, the date specified in the certificate for the purposes of subsection (1) must be the day on which the relevant period ended.

(3) In any other case, the date specified for those purposes must not be earlier than the day on which the Secretary of State received the application.

(4) The Secretary of State may estimate, in such manner as he thinks fit, any of the amounts, rates or periods specified in the certificate.

(5) Where the Secretary of State issues a certificate of recoverable benefits, he must provide the information contained in the certificate to—

(a) the person who appears to him to be the injured person, or

(b) any person who he thinks will receive a compensation payment in respect of the injured person.

(6) A person to whom a certificate of recoverable benefits is issued or who is provided with information under subsection (5) is entitled to particulars of the manner in which any amount, rate or period specified in the certificate has been determined, if he applies to the Secretary of State for those particulars.

Liability of person paying compensation

Liability to pay Secretary of State amount of benefits

6—(1) A person who makes a compensation payment in any case is liable to pay to the Secretary of State an amount equal to the total amount of the recoverable benefits.

(2) The liability referred to in subsection (1) arises immediately before the compensation payment or, if there is more than one, the first of them is made.

(3) No amount becomes payable under this section before the end of the period of 14 days following the day on which the liability arises.

(4) Subject to subsection (3), an amount becomes payable under this section at the end of the period of 14 days beginning with the day on which a certificate of recoverable benefits is first issued showing that the amount of

recoverable benefit to which it relates has been or is likely to have been paid before a specified date.

Recovery of payments due under section 6

7—(1) This section applies where a person has made a compensation payment but—

(a) has not applied for a certificate of recoverable benefits, or

(b) has not made a payment to the Secretary of State under section 6 before the end of the period allowed under that section.

(2) The Secretary of State may—

(a) issue the person who made the compensation payment with a certificate of recoverable benefits, if none has been issued, or

(b) issue him with a copy of the certificate of recoverable benefits or (if more than one has been issued) the most recent one,

and (in either case) issue him with a demand that payment of any amount due under section 6 be made immediately.

(3) The Secretary of State may, in accordance with subsections (4) and (5), recover the amount for which a demand for payment is made under subsection (2) from the person who made the compensation payment.

(4) If the person who made the compensation payment resides or carries on business in England and Wales and a county court so orders, any amount recoverable under subsection (3) is recoverable by execution issued from the county court or otherwise as if it were payable under an order of that court.

(5) If the person who made the payment resides or carries on business in Scotland, any amount recoverable under subsection (3) may be enforced in like manner as an extract registered decree arbitral bearing a warrant for execution issued by the sheriff court of any sheriffdom in Scotland.

(6) A document bearing a certificate which—

(a) is signed by a person authorised to do so by the Secretary of State, and

(b) states that the document, apart from the certificate, is a record of the amount recoverable under subsection (3),

is conclusive evidence that that amount is so recoverable.

(7) A certificate under subsection (6) purporting to be signed by a person authorised to do so by the Secretary of State is to be treated as so signed unless the contrary is proved.

Reduction of compensation payment

Reduction of compensation payment

8—(1) This section applies in a case where, in relation to any head of compensation listed in column 1 of Schedule 2—

(a) any of the compensation payment is attributable to that head, and

(b) any recoverable benefit is shown against that head in column 2 of the Schedule.

(2) In such a case, any claim of a person to receive the compensation payment is to be treated for all purposes as discharged if—

(a) he is paid the amount (if any) of the compensation payment calculated in accordance with this section, and

(b) if the amount of the compensation payment so calculated is nil, he is given a statement saying so by the person who (apart from this section) would have paid the gross amount of the compensation payment.

(3) For each head of compensation listed in column 1 of the Schedule for which paragraphs (a) and (b) of subsection (1) are met, so much of the gross amount of the compensation payment as is attributable to that head is to be reduced (to nil, if necessary) by deducting the amount of the recoverable benefit or, as the case may be, the aggregate amount of the recoverable benefits shown against it.

(4) Subsection (3) is to have effect as if a requirement to reduce a payment by deducting an amount which exceeds that payment were a requirement to reduce that payment to nil.

(5) The amount of the compensation payment calculated in accordance with this section is—

(a) the gross amount of the compensation payment, less

(b) the sum of the reductions made under subsection (3),

(and, accordingly, the amount may be nil).

Section 8: supplementary

9—(1) A person who makes a compensation payment calculated in accordance with section 8 must inform the person to whom the payment is made—

(a) that the payment has been so calculated, and

(b) of the date for payment by reference to which the calculation has been made.

(2) If the amount of a compensation payment calculated in accordance with section 8 is nil, a person giving a statement saying so is to be treated for the purposes of this Act as making a payment within section 1(1)(a) on the day on which he gives the statement.

(3) Where a person—

(a) makes a compensation payment calculated in accordance with section 8, and

(b) if the amount of the compensation payment so calculated is nil, gives a statement saying so,

he is to be treated, for the purpose of determining any rights and liabilities in respect of contribution or indemnity, as having paid the gross amount of the compensation payment.

(4) For the purposes of this Act—

(a) the gross amount of the compensation payment is the amount of the compensation payment apart from section 8, and

(b) the amount of any recoverable benefit is the amount determined in accordance with the certificate of recoverable benefits.

Reviews and appeals

Review of certificates of recoverable benefits

10—[(1) Any certificate of recoverable benefits may be reviewed by the Secretary of State—

(a) either within the prescribed period or in prescribed cases or circumstances; and

(b) either on an application made for the purpose or on his own initiative].[1]

(a) that it was issued in ignorance of, or was based on a mistake as to, a material fact, or

(b) that a mistake (whether in computation or otherwise) has occurred in its preparation.

(2) On a review under this section the Secretary of State may either—

(a) confirm the certificate, or

(b) (subject to subsection (3)) issue a fresh certificate containing such variations as he considers appropriate [, or

(c) revoke the certificate].[2]

(3) The Secretary of State may not vary the certificate so as to increase the total amount of the recoverable benefits unless it appears to him that the variation is required as a result of the person who applied for the certificate supplying him with incorrect or insufficient information.

[1] *Substituted by Social Security Act 1998 (c. 14), s. 86, Sched. 7, para. 149.*
[2] *Inserted by* ibid.

Appeals against certificates of recoverable benefits

11—(1) An appeal against a certificate of recoverable benefits may be made on the ground—

(a) that any amount, rate or period specified in the certificate is incorrect, or

(b) that listed benefits which have been, or are likely to be, paid otherwise than in respect of the accident, injury or disease in question have been brought into account, or

(c) that listed benefits which have not been, and are not likely to be, paid to the injured person during the relevant period have been brought into account, or

(d) that the payment on the basis of which the certificate was issued is not a payment within section 1(1)(a).][1]

(2) An appeal under this section may be made by—

(a) the person who applied for the certificate of recoverable benefits, or [(a)(a) (in a case where that certificate was issued under section 7(2)(a)) the person to whom it was so issued, or][1]

(b) (in a case where the amount of the compensation payment has been calculated under section 8) the injured person or other person to whom the payment is made.

(3) No appeal may be made under this section until—

(a) the claim giving rise to the compensation payment has been finally disposed of, and

(b) the liability under section 6 has been discharged.

(4) For the purposes of subsection (3)(a), if an award of damages in respect of a claim has been made under or by virtue of—

(a) section 32A(2)(a) of the Supreme Court Act 1981,

(b) section 12(2)(a) of the Administration of Justice Act 1982, or

(c) section 51(2)(a) of the County Courts Act 1984,

(orders for provisional damages in personal injury cases), the claim is to be treated as having been finally disposed of.

(5) Regulations may make provision—

(a) as to the manner in which, and the time within which, appeals under this section may be made,

(b) as to the procedure to be followed where such an appeal is made, and

(c) for the purpose of enabling any such appeal to be treated as an application for review under section 10.

(6) [. . .][2]

[1] *Inserted by Social Security Act 1998 (c. 14), s. 86, Sched. 7, para. 150.*
[2] *Repeated by* ibid., *and Sched. 8.*

Reference of questions to medical appeal tribunal

12—(1) [The Secretary of State must refer an appeal under section 11 to an appeal tribunal][1]

(2) [. . .][4]

(3) In determining [any appeal under section 11],[1] the tribunal must take into account any decision of a court relating to the same, or any similar, issue arising in connection with the accident, injury or disease in question.

(4) On [an appeal under section 11 an appeal tribunal][1] may either—

(a) confirm the amounts, rates and periods specified in the certificate of recoverable benefits, or

(b) specify any variations which are to be made on the issue of a fresh certificate under subsection (5) [or

(c) declare that the certificate of recoverable benefits is to be revoked.][2]

(5) When the Secretary of State has received [the decision of the tribunal on the appeal under section 11, he must in accordance with that decision][1]

(a) confirm the certificate against which the appeal was brought, or

(b) issue a fresh certificate. [or]

(c) revoke the certificate.][2]

(6) [. . .][3]

(7) Regulations [...][3] may (among other things) provide for the non-disclosure of medical advice or medical evidence given or submitted following a reference under subsection (1).

(8) [...][3]

[1] *Substituted by Social Security Act 1998 (c. 14), s. 86, Sched. 7, para. 151.*
[2] *Inserted by* ibid.
[3] *Repeated by* ibid., *and Sched. 8.*
[4] *By substituting for subss. (1) and (2) and new subs. (1) only, para. 151 of Sched. 7 to the Social Security Act 1998 (c. 14) and s. 86 are presumably impliedly repealing s. 12(2).*

Appeal to Social Security Commissioner

13—(1) An appeal may be made to a Commissioner against any decision of [an appeal tribunal][1] under section 12 on the ground that the decision was erroneous in point of law.

(2) An appeal under this section may be made by—

(a) the Secretary of State,

(b) the person who applied for the certificate of recoverable benefits, [...][2]

[(bb)(in a case where that certificate was issued under section 7(2)(a)) the person to whom it was so issued, or][3]

(c) (in a case where the amount of the compensation payment has been calculated in accordance with section 8) the injured person or other person to whom the payment is made.

(3) [Subsections (7) to (12) of section 14 of the Social Security Act 1998][1] apply to appeals under this section as they apply to appeals under that section.

(4) [...][2]

[1] *Substituted by Social Security Act 1998 (c. 14), s. 86, Sched. 7, para. 152.*
[2] *Repeated by* ibid., *and Sched. 8.*
[3] *Inserted by* ibid.

Reviews and appeals: supplementary

14—(1) This section applies in cases where a fresh certificate of recoverable benefits is issued as a result of a review under section 10 or an appeal under section 11.

(2) If—

(a) a person has made one or more payments to the Secretary of State under section 6, and

(b) in consequence of the review or appeal, it appears that the total amount paid is more than the amount that ought to have been paid,

regulations may provide for the Secretary of State to pay the difference to that person, or to the person to whom the compensation payment is made, or partly to one and partly to the other.

(3) If—

(a) a person has made one or more payments to the Secretary of State under section 6, and

(b) in consequence of the review or appeal, it appears that the total amount paid is less than the amount that ought to have been paid.

regulations may provide for that person to pay the difference to the Secretary of State.

(4) Regulations under this section may provide—

(a) for the re-calculation in accordance with section 8 of the amount of any compensation payment,

(b) for giving credit for amounts already paid, and

(c) for the payment by any person of any balance or the recovery from any person of any excess.

and may provide for any matter by modifying this Act.

Courts

Court orders

15—(1) This section applies where a court makes an order for a compensation payment to be made in any case, unless the order is made with the consent of the injured person and the person by whom the payment is to be made.

(2) The court must, in the case of each head of compensation listed in column 1 of Schedule 2 to which any of the compensation payment is attributable, specify in the order the amount of the compensation payment which is attributable to that head.

Payments into court

16—(1) Regulations may make provision (including provision modifying this Act) for any case in which a payment into court is made.

(2) The regulations may (among other things) provide—

(a) for the making of a payment into court to be treated in prescribed circumstances as the making of a compensation payment,

(b) for application for, and issue of, certificates of recoverable benefits, and

(c) for the relevant period to be treated as ending on a date determined in accordance with the regulations.

(3) Rules of court may make provision governing practice and procedure in such cases.

(4) This section does not extend to Scotland.

Benefits irrelevant to assessment of damages

17—In assessing damages in respect of any accident, injury or disease, the amount of any listed benefits paid or likely to be paid is to be disregarded.

Reduction of compensation: complex cases

Lump sum and periodical payments

18—(1) Regulations may make provision (including provision modifying this Act) for any case in which two or more compensation payments in the form of lump sums are made by the same person to or in respect of the injured person in consequence of the same accident, injury or disease.

(2) The regulations may (among other things) provide—

(a) for the re-calculation in accordance with section 8 of the amount of any compensation payment,

(b) for giving credit for amounts already paid, and

(c) for the payment by any person of any balance or the recovery from any person of any excess.

(3) For the purposes of subsection (2), the regulations may provide for the gross amounts of the compensation payments to be aggregated and for—

(a) the aggregate amount to be taken to be the gross amount of the compensation payment for the purposes of section 8,

(b) so much of the aggregate amount as is attributable to a head of compensation listed in column 1 of Schedule 2 to be taken to be the part of the gross amount which is attributable to that head;

and for the amount of any recoverable benefit shown against any head in column 2 of that Schedule to be taken to be the amount determined in accordance with the most recent certificate of recoverable benefits.

(4) Regulations may make provision (including provision modifying this Act) for any case in which, in final settlement of the injured person's claim, an agreement is entered into for the making of—

(a) periodical compensation payments (whether of an income or capital nature), or

(b) periodical compensation payments and lump sum compensation payments.

(5) Regulations made by virtue of subsection (4) may (among other things) provide—

(a) for the relevant period to be treated as ending at a prescribed time,

(b) for the person who is to make the payments under the agreement to be treated for the purposes of this Act as if he had made a single compensation payment on a prescribed date.

(6) A periodical payment may be a compensation payment for the purposes of this section even though it is a small payment (as defined in Part II of Schedule 1).

Payments by more than one person

19—(1) Regulations may make provision (including provision modifying this Act) for any case in which two or more persons ("the compensators") make compensation payments to or in respect of the same injured person in consequence of the same accident, injury or disease.

(2) In such a case, the sum of the liabilities of the compensators under section 6 is not to exceed the total amount of the recoverable benefits, and the regulations may provide for determining the respective liabilities under that section of each of the compensators.

(3) The regulations may (among other things) provide in the case of each compensator—

- (a) for determining or re-determining the part of the recoverable benefits which may be taken into account in his case,
- (b) for calculating or re-calculating in accordance with section 8 the amount of any compensation payment,
- (c) for giving credit for amounts already paid, and
- (d) for the payment by any person of any balance or the recovery from any person of any excess.

Miscellaneous

Amounts overpaid under section 6

20—(1) Regulations may make provision (including provision modifying this Act) for cases where a person has paid to the Secretary of State under section 6 any amount ("the amount of the overpayment") which he was not liable to pay.

(2) The regulations may provide—

- (a) for the Secretary of State to pay the amount of the overpayment to that person, or to the person to whom the compensation payment is made, or partly to one and partly to the other, or
- (b) for the receipt by the Secretary of State of the amount of the overpayment to be treated as the recovery of that amount.

(3) Regulations made by virtue of subsection (2)(b) are to have effect in spite of anything in section 71 of the Social Security Administration Act 1992 (overpayments—general).

(4) The regulations may also (among other things) provide—

- (a) for the re-calculation in accordance with section 8 of the amount of any compensation payment.
- (b) for giving credit for amounts already paid, and
- (c) for the payment by any person of any balance or the recovery from any person of any excess.

(5) This section does not apply in a case where section 14 applies.

Compensation payments to be disregarded

21—(1) If, when a compensation payment is made, the first and second conditions are met, the payment is to be disregarded for the purposes of sections 6 and 8.

(2) The first condition is that the person making the payment—

- (a) has made an application for a certificate of recoverable benefits which complies with subsection (3), and

(b) has in his possession a written acknowledgment of the receipt of his application.

(3) An application complies with this subsection if it—

(a) accurately states the prescribed particulars relating to the injured person and the accident, injury or disease in question, and

(b) specifies the name and address of the person to whom the certificate is to be sent.

(4) The second condition is that the Secretary of State has not sent the certificate to the person, at the address, specified in the application, before the end of the period allowed under section 4.

(5) In any case where—

(a) by virtue of subsection (1), a compensation payment is disregarded for the purposes of sections 6 and 8, but

(b) the person who made the compensation payment nevertheless makes a payment to the Secretary of State for which (but for subsection (1)) he would be liable under section 6,

subsection (1) is to cease to apply in relation to the compensation payment.

(6) If, in the opinion of the Secretary of State, circumstances have arisen which adversely affect normal methods of communication—

(a) he may by order provide that subsection (1) is not to apply during a specified period not exceeding three months, and

(b) he may continue any such order in force for further periods not exceeding three months at a time.

Liability of insurers

22—(1) If a compensation payment is made in a case where—

(a) a person is liable to any extent in respect of the accident, injury or disease, and

(b) the liability is covered to any extent by a policy of insurance,

the policy is also to be treated as covering any liability of that person under section 6.

(2) Liability imposed on the insurer by subsection (1) cannot be excluded or restricted.

(3) For that purpose excluding or restricting liability includes—

(a) making the liability or its enforcement subject to restrictive or onerous conditions,

(b) excluding or restricting any right or remedy in respect of the liability, or subjecting a person to any prejudice in consequence of his pursuing any such right or remedy, or

(c) excluding or restricting rules of evidence or procedure.

(4) Regulations may in prescribed cases limit the amount of the liability imposed on the insurer by subsection (1).

(5) This section applies to policies of insurance issued before (as well as those issued after) its coming into force.

(6) References in this section to policies of insurance and their issue include references to contracts of insurance and their making.

Provision of information

23—(1) Where compensation is sought in respect of any accident, injury or disease suffered by any person ("the injured person"), the following persons must give the Secretary of State the prescribed information about the injured person—

(a) anyone who is, or is alleged to be, liable in respect of the accident, injury or disease, and
(b) anyone acting on behalf of such a person.

(2) A person who receives or claims a listed benefit which is or is likely to be paid in respect of an accident, injury or disease suffered by him, must give the Secretary of State the prescribed information about the accident, injury or disease.

(3) Where a person who has received a listed benefit dies, the duty in subsection (2) is imposed on his personal representative.

(4) Any person who makes a payment (whether on his own behalf or not)—

(a) in consequence of, or
(b) which is referable to any costs (in Scotland, expenses) incurred by reason of,

any accident, injury or disease, or any damage to property, must, if the Secretary of State requests him in writing to do so, give the Secretary of State such particulars relating to the size and composition of the payment as are specified in the request.

(5) The employer of a person who suffers or has suffered an accident, injury or disease, and anyone who has been the employer of such a person at any time during the relevant period, must give the Secretary of State the prescribed information about the payment of statutory sick pay in respect of that person.

(6) In subsection (5) "employer" has the same meaning as it has in Part XI of the Social Security Contributions and Benefits Act 1992.

(7) A person who is required to give information under this section must do so in the prescribed manner, at the prescribed place and within the prescribed time.

(8) Section 1 does not apply in relation to this section.

Power to amend Schedule 2

24—(1) The Secretary of State may be regulations amend Schedule 2.

(2) A statutory instrument which contains such regulations shall not be made unless a draft of the instrument has been laid before and approved by resolution of each House of Parliament.

Provisions relating to Northern Ireland

Corresponding provision for Northern Ireland

25— An Order in Council made under paragraph 1(1)(b) of Schedule 1 to the Northern Ireland Act 1974 which contains a statement that it is made only for purposes corresponding to those of the provisions of this Act—

(a) shall not be subject to sub-paragraphs (4) and (5) of paragraph 1 of that Schedule (affirmative resolution of both Houses of Parliament), but

(b) shall be subject to annulment in pursuance of a resolution of either House of Parliament.

Residence of the injured person

26—(1) In a case where this Act applies, if the injured person's address is in Northern Ireland—

(a) the person making the compensation payment must apply for a certificate under the Northern Ireland provisions, and may not make any separate application for a certificate of recoverable benefits.

(b) any certificate issued as a result under the Northern Ireland provisions—

  (i) is to be treated as including a certificate of recoverable benefits,

  (ii) must state that it is to be so treated, and

  (iii) must state that any payment required to be made to the Secretary of State under this Act is to be made to the Northern Ireland Department as his agent, and

(c) any payment made pursuant to a certificate so issued is to be applied—

  (i) first towards discharging the liability of the person making the compensation payment under the Northern Ireland provisions, and

  (ii) then, as respects any remaining balance, towards discharging his liability under section 6.

(2) In a case where the Northern Ireland provisions apply, if the injured person's address is in any part of Great Britain—

(a) the person making the compensation payment must apply for a certificate of recoverable benefits, and may not make any separate application for a certificate under the Northern Ireland provisions,

(b) any certificate of recoverable benefits issued as a result—

  (i) is to be treated as including a certificate under the Northern Ireland provisions,

  (ii) must state that it is to be so treated, and

  (iii) must state that any payment required to be made to the Northern Ireland Department under the Northern Ireland provisions is to be made to the Secretary of State as its agent, and

(c) any payment made pursuant to a certificate of recoverable benefits so issued is to be applied—
   (i) first towards discharging the liability of the person making the compensation payment under section 6, and
   (ii) then, as respects any remaining balance, towards discharging his liability under the Northern Ireland provisions.

(3) In this section—

(a) "the injured person's address" is the address first notified in writing to the person making the payment by or on behalf of the injured person as his residence (or, if he has died, by or on behalf of the person entitled to receive the compensation payment as the injured person's last residence),

(b) "Northern Ireland Department" means the Department of Health and Social Services for Northern Ireland,

(c) "the Northern Ireland provisions" means—
   (i) any legislation corresponding to this Act (other than this section and section 27) and having effect in Northern Ireland, and
   (ii) this section and section 27,

and

(d) any reference in relation to the Northern Ireland provisions to—
   (i) the injured person, means the injured person within the meaning of those provisions,
   (ii) a certificate, means a certificate under those provisions corresponding to the certificate of recoverable benefits, and
   (iii) a compensation payment, means a compensation payment within the meaning of those provisions.

Jurisdiction of courts

27—(1) In a case where this Act applies, if immediately before making a compensation payment a person—

(a) is not resident and does not have a place of business in Great Britain, but

(b) is resident or has a place of business in Northern Ireland,

subsections (4) and (5) of section 7 apply in relation to him as if at that time he were resident or had a place of business in the relevant part of Great Britain.

(2) In a case where the Northern Ireland provisions apply, if immediately before making a compensation payment a person—

(a) is not resident and does not have a place of business in Northern Ireland, but

(b) is resident or has a place of business in any part of Great Britain,

any provision of the Northern Ireland provisions corresponding to subsection (4) or (5) of section 7 applies in relation to him as if at that time he were resident or had a place of business in Northern Ireland.

(3) In this section—

(a) "the relevant part of Great Britain" means—

(i) the part of Great Britain in which the injured person is or was most recently resident (as determined by any written statement given to the person making the payment by or on behalf of the injured person or, if he has died, by or on behalf of the person entitled to receive the compensation payment), or

(ii) if no such statement has been given, such part of Great Britain as may be prescribed, and

(b) "the Northern Ireland provisions" and references to compensation payments in relation to such provisions have the same meaning as in section 26.

General

The Crown

28—This Act applies to the Crown.

General interpretation

29—In this Act—

["appeal tribunal" means an appeal tribunal constituted under Chapter I of Part I of the Social Security Act 1998];[1]

"benefit" means any benefit under the Social Security Contributions and Benefits Act 1992, a jobseeker's allowance or mobility allowance,

"[Commissioner" has the same meaning as in Chapter II of Part I of the Social Security Act 1998 (see section 39);][1]

"compensation scheme for motor accidents" means any scheme or arrangement under which funds are available for the payment of compensation in respect of motor accidents caused, or alleged to have been caused, by uninsured or unidentified persons,

"listed benefit" means a benefit listed in column 2 of Schedule 2,

"payment" means payment in money or money's worth, and related expressions are to be interpreted accordingly,

"prescribed" means prescribed by regulations, and

"regulations" means regulations made by the Secretary of State.

[1] *"Inserted by Social Security Act 1998, (c. 14), s. 86, Sched. 7, para. 153.*

Regulations and orders

30—(1) Any power under this Act to make regulations or an order is exercisable by statutory instrument.

(2) A statutory instrument containing regulations or an order under this Act (other than regulations under section 24 or an order under section 34)

shall be subject to annulment in pursuance of a resolution of either House of Parliament.

(3) Regulations under section 20, under section 24 amending the list of benefits in column 2 of Schedule 2 or under paragraph 9 of Schedule 1 may not be made without the consent of the Treasury.

(4) Subsections (4), (5), (6) and (9) of section 189 of the Social Security Administration Act 1992 (regulations and orders—general) apply for the purposes of this Act as they apply for the purposes of that.

Financial arrangements

31—(1) There are to be paid out of the National Insurance Fund any expenses of the Secretary of State in making payments under section 14 or 20 to the extent that he estimates that those payments relate to sums paid out of that Fund.

(2) There are to be paid out of money provided by Parliament—

(a) any expenses of the Secretary of State in making payments under section 14 or 20 to the extent that the estimates that those payments relate to sums paid out of the Consolidated Fund, and

(b) (subject to subsection (1)) any other expenses of the Secretary of State incurred in consequence of this Act.

(3) Any sums paid to the Secretary of State under section 6 or 14 are to be paid—

(a) into the Consolidated Fund, to the extent that the Secretary of State estimates that the sums relate to payments out of money provided by Parliament, and

(b) into the National Insurance Fund, to the extent that he estimates that they relate to payments out of that Fund.

Power to make transitional, consequential etc. provisions

32—(1) Regulations may make such transitional and consequential provisions, and such savings, as the Secretary of State considers necessary or expedient in preparation for, in connection with, or in consequence of—

(a) the coming into force of any provision of this Act, or

(b) the operation of any enactment repealed or amended by a provision of this Act during any period when the repeal or amendment is not wholly in force.

(2) Regulations under this section may (among other things) provide—

(a) for compensation payments in relation to which, by virtue of section 2, this Act does not apply to be treated as payments in relation to which this Act applies,

(b) for compensation payments in relation to which, by virtue of section 2, this Act applies to be treated as payments in relation to which this Act does not apply, and

(c) for the modification of any enactment contained in this Act or referred to in subsection (1)(b) in its application to any compensation payment.

Consequential amendments and repeals

33—(1) Schedule 3 (which makes consequential amendments) is to have effect.

(2) The enactments shown in Schedule 4 are repealed to the extent specified in the third column.

Short title, commencement and extent

34—(1) This Act may be cited as the Social Security (Recovery of Benefits) Act 1997.

(2) Sections 1 to 24, 26 to 28 and 33 are to come into force on such day as the Secretary of State may by order appoint, and different days may be appointed for different purposes.

(3) Apart from sections 25 to 27, section 33 so far as it relates to any enactment which extends to Northern Ireland, and this section this Act does not extend to Northern Ireland.

SCHEDULES

SCHEDULE 1

COMPENSATION PAYMENTS

PART I

EXEMPTED PAYMENTS

1. Any small payment (defined in Part II of this Schedule).

2. Any payment made to or for the injured person under section 35 of the Powers of Criminal Courts Act 1973 or section 249 of the Criminal Procedure (Scotland) Act 1995 (compensation orders against convicted persons).

3. Any payment made in the exercise of a discretion out of property held subject to a trust in a case where no more than 50 per cent, by value of the capital contributed to the trust was directly or indirectly provided by persons who are, or are alleged to be, liable in respect of—

(a) the accident, injury or disease suffered by the injured person, or

(b) the same or any connected accident, injury or disease suffered by another.

4. Any payment made out of property held for the purposes of any prescribed trust (whether the payment also falls within paragraph 3 or not).

5. Any payment made to the injured person by an insurance company within the meaning of the Insurance Companies Act 1982 under the terms of any contract of insurance entered into between the injured person and the company before—

(a) the date on which the injured person first claims a listed benefit in consequence of the disease in question, or

(b) the occurrence of the accident or injury in question.

6. Any redundancy payment falling to be taken into account in the assessment of damages in respect of an accident, injury or disease.

7. So much of any payment as is referable to costs.

8. Any prescribed payment.

Part II

Power to Disregard Small Payments

9—(1) Regulations may make provision for compensation payments to be disregarded for the purposes of sections 6 and 8 in prescribed cases where the amount of the compensation payment, or the aggregate amount of two or more connected compensation payments, does not exceed the prescribed sum.

(2) A compensation payment disregarded by virtue of this paragraph is referred to in paragraph 1 as a "small payment".

(3) For the purposes of this paragraph—

(a) two or more compensation payments are "connected" if each is made to or in respect of the same injured person and in respect of the same accident, injury or disease, and

(b) any reference to a compensation payment is a reference to a payment which would be such a payment apart from paragraph 1.

SCHEDULE 2

CALCULATION OF COMPENSATION PAYMENT

(1) *Head of compensation*	(2) *Benefit*
1. Compensation for earnings lost during the relevant period	Disability working allowance Disablement pension payable under section 103 of the 1992 Act Incapacity benefit Income support Invalidity pension and allowance Jobseeker's allowance Reduced earnings allowance Severe disablement allowance Sickness benefit Statutory sick pay Unemployability supplement Unemployment benefit
2. Compensation for cost of care incurred during the relevant period	Attendance allowance Care component of disability living allowance Disablement pension increase payable under section 104 or 105 of the 1992 Act
3. Compensation for loss of mobility during the relevant period	Mobility allowance Mobility component of disability living allowance

NOTES

1—(1) References to incapacity benefit, invalidity pension and allowance, severe disablement allowance, sickness benefit and unemployment benefit also include any income support paid with each of those benefits on the same instrument of payment or paid concurrently with each of those benefits by means of an instrument for benefit payment.

(2) For the purpose of this Note, income support includes personal expenses addition, special transitional additions and transitional addition as defined in the Income Support (Transitional) Regulations 1987.

2. Any reference to statutory sick pay—

(a) includes only 80 per cent. of payments made between 6th April 1991 and 5th April 1994, and

(b) does not include payments made on or after 6th April 1994.

3. In this Schedule "the 1992 Act" means the Social Security Contributions and Benefits Act 1992.

. . . . .

The Social Security (Recovery of Benefits) Regulations 1997

(S.I. 1997 No. 2205)

Citation, commencement and interpretation

1—(1) These Regulations may be cited as the Social Security (Recovery of Benefits) Regulations 1997 and shall come into force on October 6, 1997.

(2) In these Regulations—

"the 1992 Act" means the Social Security Administration Act 1992;

"the 1997 Act" means the Social Security (Recovery of Benefits) Act 1997;

"commencement day" means the day these Regulations come into force;

"compensator" means a person making a compensation payment;

"Compensation Recovery Unit" means the Compensation Recovery Unit of the Department of Social Security at Reyrolle Building, Hebburn, Tyne and Wear NE31 1XB.

(3) A reference in these Regulations to a numbered section or Schedule is a reference, unless the context otherwise requires, to that section of or Schedule to the 1997 Act.

Exempted trusts and payments

2—(1) The following trusts are prescribed for the purposes of paragraph 4 of Schedule 1:

(a) the Macfarlane Trust established on March 10, 1988 partly out of funds provided by the Secretary of State to the Haemophilia Society for the relief of poverty or distress among those suffering from haemophilia;

(b) the Macfarlane (Special Payments) Trust established on January 29, 1990 partly out of funds provided by the Secretary of State, for the benefit of certain persons suffering from haemophilia;

(c) the Macfarlane (Special Payments) (No. 2) Trust established on May 3, 1991 partly out of funds provided by the Secretary of State for the benefit of certain persons suffering from haemophilia and other beneficiaries;

(d) the Eileen Trust established on March 29, 1993 out of funds provided by the Secretary of State for the benefit of persons eligible for payment in accordance with its provisions.

(2) The following payments are prescribed for the purposes of paragraph 8 of Schedule 1:

(a) any payment to the extent that it is made—
   (i) inconsequence of an action under the Fatal Accidents Act 1976;[1] or
   (ii) in circumstances where, had an action been brought, it would have been brought under that Act;

(b) any payment to the extent that it is made in respect of a liability arising by virtue of section 1 of the Damages (Scotland) Act 1976;[2]

(c) any payment made under the Vaccine Damage Payments Act 1979[3] to or in respect of the injured person;

(d) any award of compensation made to or in respect of the injured person under the Criminal Injuries Compensation Act 1995[4] or by the Criminal Injuries Compensation Board under the Criminal Injuries Compensation Scheme 1990 or any earlier scheme;

(e) any compensation payment made by British Coal in accordance with the NCB Pneumoconiosis Compensation Scheme set out in the Schedule to an agreement made on September 13, 1974 between the National Coal Board, the National Union of Mine Workers, the National Association of Colliery Overman Deputies and Shot-firers and the British Association of Colliery Management;

(f) any payment made to the injured person in respect of sensorineural hearing loss where the loss is less than 50 dB in one or both ears;

(g) any contractual amount paid to an employee by an employer of his in respect of a period of incapacity for work;

(h) any payment made under the National Health Service (Injury Benefits) Regulations 1995[5] or the National Health Service (Scotland) (Injury Benefits) Regulations 1974;[6]

(i) any payment made by or on behalf of the Secretary of State for the benefit of persons eligible for payment in accordance with the provisions of a scheme established by him on April 24, 1992 or, in Scotland, on April 10, 1992.

Information to be provided by the compensator

3. The following information is prescribed for the purposes of section 23(1):

(a) the full name and address of the injured person;

(b) where known, the date of birth or national insurance number of that person, or both if both are known;

(c) where the liability arises, or is alleged to arise, in respect of an accident or injury, the date of the accident or injury;

(d) the nature of the accident, injury or disease; and

(e) where known, and where the relevant period[1] may include a period prior to April 6, 1994, whether, at the time of the accident or injury or diagnosis of the disease, the person was employed under a contract of service, and, if he was, the name and address of his employer at that time and the person's payroll number.

Information to be provided by the injured person

4—The following information is prescribed for the purposes of section 23(2):

(a) whether the accident, injury or disease resulted from any action taken by another person, or from any failure of another person to act, and, if so, the full name and address of that other person;
(b) whether the injured person has claimed or may claim a compensation payment, and, if so, the full name and address of the person against whom the claim was or may be made;
(c) the amount of any compensation payment and the date on which it was made;
(d) the listed benefits claimed, and for each benefit the date from which it was first claimed and the amount received in the period beginning with that date and ending with the date the information is sent;
(e) in the case of a person who has received statutory sick pay during the relevant period and prior to April 6, 1994, the name and address of any employer who made those payments to him during the relevant period and the dates the employment with that employer began and ended; and
(f) any changes in the medical diagnosis relating to the condition arising from the accident, injury or disease.

Information to be provided by the employer

5—The following information is prescribed for the purposes of section 23(5):

(a) the amount of any statutory sick pay the employer has paid to the injured person since the first day of the relevant period and before April 6, 1994;
(b) the date the liability to pay such statutory sick pay first arose and the rate at which it was payable;
(c) the date on which such liability terminated; and
(d) the causes of incapacity for work during any period of entitlement to statutory sick pay during the relevant period and prior to April 6, 1994.

Provision of information

6.—A person required to give information to the Secretary of State under regulations 3 to 5 shall do so by sending it to the Compensation Recovery Unit not later than 14 days after—

(a) where he is a person to whom regulation 3 applies, the date on which he receives a claim for compensation from the injured person in respect of the accident, injury or disease;
(b) where he is a person to whom regulation 4 or 5 applies, the date

on which the Secretary of State requests the information from him.

Application for a certificate of recoverable benefits

7—(1) The following particulars are prescribed for the purposes of section 21(3)(a) (particulars to be included in an application for a certificate of recoverable benefits):

(a) the full name and address of the injured person;
(b) the date of birth and, where known, the national insurance number of that person;
(c) where the liability arises or is alleged to arise in respect of an accident or injury, the date of the accident or injury;
(d) the nature of the accident, injury or disease;
(e) where the person liable, or alleged to be liable, in respect of the accident, injury or disease, is the employer of the injured person, or has been such an employer, the information prescribed by regulation 5.

(2) An application for a certificate of recoverable benefits is to be treated for the purposes of the 1997 Act as received by the Secretary of State on the day on which it is received by the Compensation Recovery Unit, or if the application is received after normal business hours, or on a day which is not a normal business day at that office, on the next such day.

Payments into court

8—(1) Subject to the provisions of this regulation, where a party to an action makes a payment into court which, had it been paid directly to another party to the action ("the relevant party"), would have constituted a compensation payment—

(a) the making of that payment shall be treated for the purposes of the 1997 Act as the making of a compensation payment;
(b) a current certificate of recoverable benefits shall be lodged with the payment; and
(c) where the payment is calculated under section 8, the compensator must give the relevant party the information specified in section 9(1), instead of the person to whom the payment is made.

(2) The liability under section 6(1) to pay an amount equal to the total amount of the recoverable benefits shall not arise until the person making the payment into court has been notified that the whole or any part of the payment into court has been paid out of court to or for the relevant party.

(3) Where a payment into court in satisfaction of his claim is accepted by the relevant party in the initial period, then as respects the compensator in question, the relevant period shall be taken to have ended, if it has not done so already, on the day on which the payment into court (or if there were two or more such payments, the last of them) was made.

(4) Where, after the expiry of the initial period, the payment into court is accepted in satisfaction of the relevant party's claim by consent between the

parties, the relevant period shall end, if it has not done so already, on the date on which application to the court for the payment is made.

(5) Where, after the expiry of the initial period, payment out of court is made wholly or partly to or for the relevant party in accordance with an order of the court and in satisfaction of his claim, the relevant period shall end, if it has not done so already, on the date of that order.

(6) In paragraphs (3), (4) and (5), "the initial period" means the period of 21 days after the receipt by the relevant party to the action of notice of the payment into court having been made.

(7) Where a payment into court is paid out wholly to or for the party who made the payment (otherwise than to or for the relevant party to the action) the making of the payment into court shall cease to be regarded as the making of a compensation payment.

(8) A current certificate of recoverable benefits in paragraph (1) means one that is in force as described in section 4(4).

Reduction of compensation: complex cases

9—(1) This regulation applies where—

(a) a compensation payment in the form of a lump sum (an "earlier payment") has been made to or in respect of the injured person; and

(b) subsequently another such payment (a "later payment") is made to or in respect of the same injured person in consequence of the same accident, injury or disease.

(2) In determining the liability under section 6(1) arising in connection with the making of the later payment, the amount referred to in that subsection shall be reduced by any amount paid in satisfaction of the liability as it arose in connection with the earlier payment.

(3) Where—

(a) a payment made in satisfaction of the liability under section 6(1) arising in connection with an earlier payment is not reflected in the certificate of recoverable benefits in force at the time of a later payment, and

(b) in consequence, the aggregate of payments made in satisfaction of the liability exceeds what it would have been had that payment been so reflected,

the Secretary of State shall pay the compensator who made the later payment an amount equal to the excess.

(4) Where—

(a) a compensator receives a payment under paragraph (3), and

(b) the amount of the compensation payment made by him was calculated under section 8,

then the compensation payment shall be recalculated under section 8, and the compensator shall pay the amount of the increase (if any) to the person to whom the compensation payment was made.

(5) Where both the earlier payment and the later payment are made by the same compensator, he may—

(a) aggregate the gross amounts of the payments made by him;

(b) calculate what would have been the reduction made under section 8(3) if that aggregate amount had been paid at the date of the last payment on the basis that—
  (i) so much of the aggregate amount as is attributable to a head of compensation listed in column (1) of Schedule 2 shall be taken to be the part of the gross amount which is attributable to that head, and
  (ii) the amount of any recoverable benefits shown against any head in column (2) of that Schedule shall be taken to be the amount determined in accordance with the most recent certificate of recoverable benefits;

(c) deduct from that reduction calculated under sub-paragraph (b) the amount of the reduction under section 8(3) from any earlier payment; and

(d) deduct from the latest gross payment the net reduction calculated under sub-paragraph (c) (and accordingly the latest payment may be nil).

(6) Where the Secretary of State is making a refund under paragraph (3), he shall send to the compensator (with the refund) and to the person to whom the compensation payment was made a statement showing—

(a) the total amount that has already been paid by that compensator to the Secretary of State;

(b) the amount that ought to have been paid by that compensator; and

(c) the amount to be repaid to that compensator by the Secretary of State.

(7) Where the reduction of a compensation payment is recalculated by virtue of paragraph (4) or (5) the compensator shall give notice of the calculation to the injured person.

Structured settlements

10—(1) This regulation applies where—

(a) in final settlement of an injured person's claim, an agreement is entered into—
  (i) for the making of periodical payments (whether of an income or capital nature); or
  (ii) for the making of such payments and lump sum payments; and

(b) apart from the provisions of this regulation, those payments would fall to be treated for the purposes of the 1997 Act as compensation payments.

(2) Where this regulation applies, the provisions of the 1997 Act and these Regulations shall be modified in the following way—

(a) the compensator in question shall be taken to have made on that day a single compensation payment;

(b) the relevant period in the case of the compensator in question shall be taken to end (if it has not done so already) on the day of settlement;

(c) payments under the agreement referred to in paragraph (1)(a) shall be taken not to be compensation payments;

(d) paragraphs (5) and (7) of regulations 11 shall not apply.

(3) Where any further payment falls to be made to or in respect of the injured person otherwise then under the agreement in question, paragraph (2) shall be disregarded for the purpose of determining the end of the relevant period in relation to that further payment.

(4) In any case where—

(a) the person making the periodical payments ("the secondary party") does so in pursuance of arrangements entered into with another ("the primary party") (as in a case where the primary party purchases an annuity for the injured person from the secondary party), and

(b) apart from those arrangements, the primary party would have been regarded as the compensator,

then for the purposes of the 1997 Act, the primary party shall be regarded as the compensator and the secondary party shall not be so regarded.

(5) In this regulation "the day of settlement" means—

(a) if the agreement referred to in paragraph (1)(a) is approved by a court, the day on which that approval is given; and

(b) in any other case, the day on which the agreement is entered into.

Adjustments

11—(1) Where the conditions specified in subsection (1) and paragraphs (a) and (b) of subsection (2) of section 14 are satisfied, the Secretary of State shall pay the difference between the amount that has been paid and the amount that ought to have been paid to the compensator.

(2) Where the conditions specified in subsection (1) and paragraphs (a) and (b) of subsection (3) of section 14 are satisfied, the compensator shall pay the difference between the total amounts paid and the amount that ought to have been paid to the Secretary of State.

(3) Where the Secretary of State is making a refund under paragraph (1), or demanding payment of a further amount under paragraph (2), he shall send to the compensator (with the refund or demand) and to the person to whom the compensation payment was made a statement showing—

(a) the total amount that has already been paid to the Secretary of State;

(b) the amount that ought to have been paid; and

(c) the difference, and whether a repayment by the Secretary of State or a further payment to him is required.

(4) This paragraph applies where—

(a) the amount of the compensation payment made by the compensator was calculated under section 8; and

(b) the Secretary of State has made a payment under paragraph (1).

(5) Where paragraph (4) applies, the amount of the compensation payment shall be recalculated under section 8 to take account of the fresh

certificate of recoverable benefits and the compensator shall pay the amount of the increase (if any) to the person to whom the compensation payment was made.

(6) This paragraph applies where—

(a) the amount of the compensation payment made by the compensator was calculated under section 8;

(b) the compensator has made a payment under paragraph (2); and

(c) the fresh certificate of recoverable benefits issued after the review or appeal was required as a result of the injured person or other person to whom the compensation payment was made supplying to the compensator information knowing it to be incorrect or insufficient with the intent of enhancing the compensation payment calculated under section 8, and the compensator supplying that information to the Secretary of State without knowing it to be incorrect or insufficient.

(7) Where paragraph (6) applies, the compensator may recalculate the compensation payment under section 8 to take account of the fresh certificate of recoverable benefits and may require the repayment to him by the person to whom he made the compensation payment of the difference (if any) between the payment made and the payment as so recalculated.

Transitional provisions

12—(1) In relation to a compensation payment to which by virtue of section 2 the 1997 Act applies and subject to paragraph (2), a certificate of total benefit issued under Part IV of the 1992 Act shall be treated on or after the commencement date as a certificate of recoverable benefits issued under the 1997 Act and the amount of total benefit treated as that of recoverable benefits.

(2) Paragraph (1) shall not apply to a certificate of total benefit which specifies an amount in respect of disability living allowance without specifying whether that amount was, or is likely to be, paid wholly by way of the care component or the mobility component or (if not wholly one of them) specifying the relevant amount for each component.

(3) Any appeal under section 98 of the 1992 Act made on or after the commencement date shall be referred to and determined by a medical appeal tribunal notwithstanding that it would otherwise have been referred by the Secretary of State to a social security appeal tribunal.

(4) Paragraph (5) applies where—

(a) an amount has been paid to the Secretary of State under section 82(1)(b) of the 1992 Act,

(b) liability arises on or after the commencement day to make a payment under section 6(1), and

(c) the compensation payments which give rise to the liability to make both payments are to or in respect of the same injured person in consequence of the same accident, injury or disease.

(5) Where this paragraph applies, the liability under section 6 shall be

reduced by the payment (or aggregate of the payments, if more than one) described in paragraph (4)(a).

(6) Where—

(a) a payment into court has been made on a date prior to the commencement day but the initial period, as defined in section 93(6) of the 1992 Act, in relation to that payment, expires on or after the commencement day; and

(b) the payment into court is accepted by the other party to the action in the initial period,

that payment into court shall be treated as a compensation payment to which the 1992 Act, and not the 1997 Act, applies.

(7) Where a payment into court has been made prior to the commencement day, remains in court on that day and paragraph (6) does not apply, that payment into court shall be treated as a payment to which the 1997 Act applies, but paragraph (1)(b) and (c) of regulation 8 shall not apply.

The Social Security (Recovery of Benefits) (Appeals) Regulations 1997

(S.I. 1997 No. 2237)

Citation, commencement and interpretation

1—(1) These Regulations may be cited as the Social Security (Recovery of Benefits) (Appeals) Regulations 1997 and shall come into force on October 6, 1997.

(2) In these Regulations—

"the 1997 Act" means the Social Security (Recovery of Benefits) Act 1997;

"clerk to the tribunal" means a clerk to a medical appeal tribunal appointed in accordance with section 50 of, and paragraph 3 of Schedule 2 to, the Social Security Administration Act 1992;

"Commissioner" has the meaning given in section 191 of the Social Security Administration Act 1992;

"Compensation Recovery Unit" means the Compensation Recovery Unit of the Department of Social Security at Reyrolle Building, Hebburn, Tyne and Wear NE31 1XB;

"compensator" means a person making a compensation payment;

"full-time chairman" means a regional or other full-time chairman of medical appeal tribunals appointed under section 51(1) of the Social Security Administration Act 1992;

"President" means the President of social security appeal tribunals, medical appeal tribunals and disability appeal tribunals appointed under section 51(1) of the Social Security Administration Act 1992.

(3) A reference to these Regulations to the parties to the proceedings is a reference to the Secretary of State and any person entitled under section 11(2) of the 1997 Act to make an appeal.

(4) Where, by any provision of these Regulations—

(a) any notice or other document is required to be given or sent to the Compensation Recovery Unit, or the clerk to or a chairman of a tribunal, that notice or document shall be treated as having been so given or sent on the day that it is received in the office of the Compensation Recovery Unit or of the clerk to the relevant tribunal, as appropriate; and

(b) any notice or other document is required to be given or sent to any other person, that notice or document shall, if sent by post to that person's last known or notified address, be treated as having been given or sent on the day that it was posted.

(5) Subject to regulation 13(3), where by these Regulations any power is conferred on a chairman of a tribunal then—

- (a) if the power is to be exercised at the hearing of an appeal or application, it shall be exercised by the chairman of the tribunal hearing the appeal or application; and
- (b) otherwise, it shall be exercised by a person who is eligible to be nominated to act as a chairman of a medical appeal tribunal under section 50(4) of the Social Security Administration Act 1992.

Manner of making appeals and time limits

2—(1) Any appeal against a certificate of recoverable benefits shall, subject to paragraph (11), be in writing on a form approved by the Secretary of State and shall be given or sent to the Compensation Recovery Unit—

- (a) not later than 3 months after the date the compensator discharged the liability under section 6 of the 1997 Act;
- (b) where the certificate is reviewed by the Secretary of State in accordance with regulations made under section 11(5)(c) of the 1997 Act, not later than 3 months after the date the certificate is confirmed, or, as the case may be, a fresh certificate is issued; or
- (c) where an agreement is made under which an earlier compensation payment is treated as having been made in final discharge of a claim made by or in respect of an injured person and arising out of the accident, injury or disease, not later than 3 months after the date of that agreement.

(2) The time specified by this regulation for the making of any appeal may be extended, even though the time so specified may already have expired, provided the conditions set out in paragraphs (3) to (7) are satisfied; and any application for an extension of time under this paragraph shall be made to the Compensation Recovery Unit and shall be determined by a chairman of a medical appeal tribunal.

(3) Where the time specified for the making of an appeal has already expired, an application for an extension of time for making an appeal shall not be granted unless the applicant has satisfied the chairman considering the application that—

- (a) if the application is granted there are reasonable prospects that such an appeal will be successful; and
- (b) it is in the interest of justice that the application be granted.

(4) For the purposes of paragraph (3) it shall not be considered to be in the interests of justice to grant an application unless the chairman considering the application is satisfied that—

- (a) special reasons exist, which are wholly exceptional and which relate to the history or facts of the case; and
- (b) such special reasons have existed throughout the period beginning with the day following the expiry of the time specified by paragraph (1) for the making of an appeal and ending with the day on which the application for an extension of time is made; and

(c) such special reasons manifestly constitute a reasonable excuse of compelling weight for the applicant's failure to make an appeal within the time specified.

(5) In determining whether there are special reasons for granting an application for an extension of time for making an appeal under paragraph (2) the chairman considering the application shall have regard to the principle that the greater the amount of time that has elapsed between the expiry of the time specified for the making of the appeal and the making of the application for an extension of time, the more cogent should be the special reasons on which the application is based.

(6) In determining whether facts constitute special reasons for granting an application for an extension of time for making an appeal under paragraph (2) no account shall be taken of the following—

(a) that the applicant or anyone acting for him or advising him was unaware of or misunderstood the law applicable to his case (including ignorance or misunderstanding of any time limits imposed by paragraph (1));

(b) that a Commissioner or a court has taken a different view of the law from that previously understood and applied.

(7) Notwithstanding paragraph (2), no appeal may in any even be brought later than 6 years after the beginning of the period specified in paragraph (1) or if more than one such period is relevant, the one beginning later or latest.

(8) An application under paragraph (2) for an extension of time which has been refused may not be renewed.

(9) Any appeal or application under these Regulations shall contain the following particulars—

(a) in the case of an appeal, the date of the certificate of recoverable benefits or review decision of the Secretary of State against which the appeal is made, the question under section 11 of the 1997 Act to which the appeal relates, and a summary of the arguments relied on by the person making the appeal to support his contention that the certificate is wrong;

(b) in the case of an application under paragraph (2) for an extension of time in which to appeal, in relation to the appeal which it is proposed to being, the particulars required under sub-paragraph (a) together with particulars of the special reasons on which the application is based.

(10) Where the appeal or application under paragraph (2) for an extension of time is made by the injured person or other person to whom a compensation payment has been made, there shall be sent with that appeal or application a copy of the statement given to that person under section 9 of the 1997 Act or if that statement was not in writing, a written summary of it.

(11) Where an appeal is not made on the form approved for the time being, but is made in writing, contains all the particulars required under paragraph (9) and, where applicable, is accompanied by the document required under paragraph (10), the Secretary of State may treat that appeal as duly made.

(12) Where it appears to the Secretary of State that an appeal or application does not contain the particulars required under paragraph (9) or is not accompanied by the document required under paragraph (10) he may direct the person making the appeal or application to provide such particulars or such document.

(13) Where paragraph (12) applies, the Secretary of State may extend the time specified by this regulation for making the appeal or application by a period of not more than 14 days.

(14) Where further particulars or a document are required under paragraph (12) they shall be sent or delivered to the Compensation Recovery Unit within such period as the Secretary of State may direct.

(15) The date of an appeal shall be the date on which all the particulars required under paragraph (9) and, where applicable, the document required under paragraph (10) are received by the Compensation Recovery Unit.

(16) In the case of an application under paragraph (2) for an extension of time for making an appeal, the chairman who determines that application shall record his decision in writing together with a statement of the reasons for the decision.

(17) As soon as practicable after the decision has been made, it shall be communicated to the applicant and to the Secretary of State and if within 3 months of such communication being sent the applicant or the Secretary of State so requests in writing, a copy of the record referred to in paragraph (16) shall be supplied to the person making that request.

(18) The Secretary of State may treat any appeal as an application for review under section 10 of the 1997 Act, notwithstanding that a condition specified in paragraph (a) or (b) of section 10(1) is not satisfied.

General provisions relating to the procedure of tribunals

3—(1) Subject to the provisions of the 1997 Act and of these Regulations—

- (a) the procedure in connection with the consideration and determination of any reference to a medical appeal tribunal under section 12 of the 1997 Act shall be such as the chairman of the tribunal shall determine;
- (b) the chairman of a tribunal may give directions requiring any party to the proceedings to comply with any provision of these Regulations and may further at any stage of the proceedings either of his own motion or on a written application made to the clerk to the tribunal by any such party give such directions as he may consider necessary or desirable for the just, effective and efficient conduct of the proceedings any may direct any party to provide such further particulars or to produce such documents as may reasonably be required;
- (c) where under these Regulations the clerk to the tribunal is authorised to take steps in relation to the procedure of the tribunal, he may give directions requiring any party to the proceedings to comply with any provisions of these Regulations;
- (d) any person who by virtue of the provisions of these Regulations

has the right to be heard at a hearing may be accompanied and may be represented by another person whether having professional qualifications or not and, for the purposes of the proceedings at any such hearing, any such representative shall have all the rights and powers to which the person whom he represents is entitled under the 1997 Act and these Regulations.

(2) For the purpose of arriving at its decision a tribunal shall, and for the purpose of discussing any question of procedure may, notwithstanding anything contained in these Regulations, order all persons not being members of the tribunal, other than the person acting as clerk to the tribunal, to withdraw from the sitting of the tribunal, except that—

(a) a member of the Council on Tribunals or of the Scottish Committee of the Council and the President and any full-time chairman; and

(b) with the leave of the chairman of the tribunal,

(i) any person undergoing training as a chairman or other member of a medical appeal tribunal or as a clerk to such a tribunal, and

(ii) any other person to whose presence every party to the proceedings actually present consents,

may remain present at any such sitting.

(3) Nothing in these Regulations shall prevent a member of the Council on Tribunals or of the Scottish Committee of the Council from being present at a hearing before a tribunal, in his capacity as such, notwithstanding that the hearing is not in public.

(4) Where a reference is made to a tribunal by the Secretary of State, the clerk to the tribunal shall give notice of it to the other parties to the proceedings.

Requirement for oral hearings

4—(1) Where a reference is made to a tribunal, the clerk to the tribunal shall direct every party to the proceedings to notify him if that party wishes an oral hearing of that reference to be held.

(2) A notification under paragraph (1) shall be in writing and shall be made within 10 days of receipt of the direction from the clerk to the tribunal or within such other period as the clerk to the tribunal or the chairman of the tribunal may direct.

(3) Where the clerk to the tribunal receives a notification in accordance with paragraph (2) the tribunal shall hold an oral hearing.

(4) The chairman of a tribunal may of his own motion require an oral hearing to be held if he is satisfied that such a hearing is necessary to enable the tribunal to reach a decision.

Procedure at oral hearings

5—(1) Except where paragraphs (4) applies, not less than 7 days notice, beginning with the day on which the notice is given and ending on the day before the hearing, of the time and place of any oral hearing before a tribunal shall be given to every party to the proceedings, and if such notice has not been given to a person to whom it should have been given under the provisions of this paragraph the hearing may proceed only with the consent of that person.

(2) The chairman of a tribunal may given notice before or during an oral hearing for the determination at that hearing by the tribunal, in accordance with the provisions of these Regulations, of any question referred under section 12 of the 1997 Act notwithstanding that a party to the proceedings has failed to indicate his availability for a hearing or to provide all the information which may have been requested, if the chairman is satisfied that such party—

(a) has failed to comply with a direction regarding his availability or requiring information under regulation 3(1)(b) or (c); and

(b) has not given any explanation for his failure to comply with such a direction;

provided that the chairman is satisfied that the tribunal has sufficient particulars in order for the question to be determined.

(3) The chairman of a tribunal may give notice before or during, an oral hearing for the determination at that hearing by the tribunal, in accordance with the provisions of these Regulations, of any question where he believes the appeal on that ground has no reasonable prospect of success.

(4) Any party to the proceedings may waive his right to receive not less than 7 days notice of the time and place of any oral hearing as specified in paragraph (1).

(5) If a party to the proceedings to whom notice has been given under paragraph (1) fails to appear at the hearing the tribunal may, having regard to all the circumstances including any explanation offered for the absence and, where applicable, the circumstances set out in paragraph (2)(a) and (b), proceed with the hearing notwithstanding his absence, or give such directions with a view to the determination of any question referred to it as it may think proper.

(6) If a party to the proceedings has waived his right to be given notice under paragraph (4), the tribunal may proceed with the hearing notwithstanding his absence.

(7) Any oral hearing before a tribunal shall be in public except where the person making the appeal requests a private hearing or the chairman is satisfied that intimate personal or financial circumstances may have to be disclosed or that considerations of public security are involved, in which case the hearing shall be in private.

(8) At any oral hearing any party to the proceedings shall be entitled to be present and be heard.

(9) The following persons shall also be entitled to be present at an oral hearing (whether or not it is otherwise in private) but shall take no part in the proceedings—

(a) the President and any full-time chairman;

(b) any person undergoing training as a chairman or other member of a medical appeal tribunal or as a clerk to such a tribunal;

(c) any person acting on behalf of the President or the Secretary of

State in the training or supervision of clerks to medical appeal tribunals or of officers of the Secretary of State;

(d) any person undergoing training as an officer of the Secretary of State; and

(e) with the leave of the chairman of the tribunal and the consent of every party to the proceedings actually present, any other person.

(10) Nothing in paragraph (9) affects the rights of any person mentioned in sub-paragraph (a) and (b) of that paragraph at any oral hearing where he is sitting as a member of the tribunal or acting as its clerk, and nothing in his regulation prevents the presence at an oral hearing of any witness.

(11) Any person entitled to be heard at an oral hearing may address the tribunal, may give evidence, may call witnesses and may put questions directly to any other person called as a witness.

Postponement and adjournment

6—(1) Where a person to whom notice of an oral hearing by a tribunal has been given wishes to apply for that hearing to be postponed, he shall do so in writing to the clerk to the tribunal stating his reasons for the application, and the clerk may grant or refuse the request as he thinks fit or may pass the request to the chairman, who may grant or refuse the request as he thinks fit.

(2) The chairman or the clerk to the tribunal may of his own motion at any time before the beginning of an oral hearing postpone that hearing.

(3) An oral hearing may be adjourned by the tribunal at any time on the application of any party to the proceedings or of its own motion.

(4) Where an oral hearing is adjourned and at the hearing after the adjournment the tribunal is differently constituted, the proceedings at that hearing shall be by way of a complete rehearing of the case.

Withdrawal of appeals

7—Any appeal may be withdrawn by the person who made the appeal—

(a) before a question has been referred to a tribunal under section 12 of the 1997 Act, by written notice in writing to the Compensation Recovery Unit and with the consent of the Secretary of State;

(b) after the reference has been made and before the hearing begins, by written notice to the chairman of the tribunal to which a question was referred and with the written consent of the Secretary of State;

(c) after the hearing has begun, at any time before the determination is made with the leave of the chairman of the tribunal and the consent of the Secretary of State.

Non-disclosure of medical evidence

8—(1) Where, in connection with the consideration of any question, there is before a tribunal medical advice or medical evidence relating to a person which has not been disclosed to him, and in the opinion of the chairman of the tribunal the disclosure to that person of that advice or evidence would be harmful to his health, such advice or evidence shall not be required to be disclosed.

(2) Evidence such as is mentioned in paragraph (1) shall not be disclosed to any person acting for or representing the person to whom it relates unless the chairman is satisfied that it is in the interests of the person to whom the evidence relates to do so.

(3) A tribunal shall not be precluded from taking into account for the purposes of the determination evidence which has not been disclosed to a person under the provisions of paragraph (1) or (2).

Decisions of tribunals

9—(1) The decision of the majority of the tribunal shall be the decision of the tribunal.

(2) Every decision of a tribunal shall be recorded in summary by the chairman is such written form of decision notice as shall have been approved by the President, and such decision notice shall be signed by the chairman.

(3) As soon as may be practicable after a case has been decided by a tribunal, a copy of the decision notice made in accordance with paragraph (2) shall be sent or given to every party to the proceedings who shall also be informed of—

(a) his right under paragraph (6); and

(b) the conditions governing appeals to a Commissioner.

(4) A statement of the reasons for the tribunal's decision and of its findings on questions of fact material thereto may be given—

(a) orally at the hearing; or

(b) in writing at such later date as the chairman may determine.

(5) Where the statement referred to in paragraph (4) is given orally, it shall be recorded in such medium as the chairman may determine.

(6) A copy of the statement referred to in paragraph (4) shall be supplied to the parties to the proceedings if requested by any of them within 21 days after the decision notice has been sent or given, and if the statement was given orally at the hearing, that copy shall be supplied in such medium as the chairman may direct.

(7) If a decision is not unanimous, the statement referred to in paragraph (4) shall record that one of the members dissented and the reasons given by him for dissenting.

(8) A record of the proceedings at the hearing shall be made by the chairman is such medium as he may direct and preserved by the clerk to the tribunal for 18 months, and a copy of such record shall be supplied to the parties if requested by any of them within that period.

Correction of accidental errors in decisions

10—(1) Subject to regulation 12 (provisions common to regulations 10 and 11) accidental errors in any decision or record of a decision may at any time be corrected by the tribunal which gave the decision or by another medical appeal tribunal.

(2) A correction made to, or to the record of, a decision shall be deemed to be part of the decision or of that record and written notice of it shall be given as soon as practicable to every party to the proceedings.

Setting aside decisions on certain grounds

11—(1) Subject to regulation 12 (provisions common to regulations 10 and 11), on an application made by a party to the proceedings, a decision may be set aside by the tribunal which gave the decision or by another medical appeal tribunal in a case where it appears just to set the decision aside on the ground that—

(a) a document relating to the proceedings in which decision was given was not sent to, or was not received at an appropriate time by, a party to the proceedings or the party's representative or was not received at an appropriate time by the tribunal which gave the decision; or

(b) a party to the proceedings in which the decision was given or the party's representative was not present at a hearing relating to the proceedings; or

(c) the interests of justice so require.

(2) In determining whether it is just to set aside a decision on the ground set out in paragraph (1)(b), the tribunal shall determine whether the party making the application gave a notification to the clerk of the tribunal that he wished an oral hearing to be held, and if that party did not give such a notification the tribunal shall not set the decision aside unless it is satisfied that the interests of justice manifestly so require.

(3) An application under this regulation shall—

(a) be made in writing;

(b) be given or sent to the office of the clerk to the tribunal which made the relevant decision not later than three months after the date when notice of the tribunal's decision was sent or given to the applicant;

(c) contain particulars of the grounds on which it is made.

(4) The time specified in paragraph (3) for the making of an application may be extended for special reasons, even though the time so specified may already have expired, by the chairman of the tribunal; and regulation 2(16) and (17) (recording reasons for a decision and providing a copy of the record) shall apply in relation to any determination by a chairman.

(5) Where an application to set aside a decision is entertained under paragraph (1), every party to the proceedings shall be sent a copy of the application and shall be afforded a reasonable opportunity of making representations on it before the application is determined.

(6) Notice in writing of a determination on an application to set aside a decision shall be given to every party to the proceedings as soon as may be practicable and the notice shall contain a statement giving the reasons for the determination.

(7) For the purposes of determining under these Regulations an applica-

tion to set aside a decision there shall be disregarded regulation 1(4) and any provision in any enactment or instrument to the effect that any notice or other document required or authorised to be given or sent to any person shall be deemed to have been given or sent if it was sent by post to that person's last known or notified address.

Provisions common to regulations 10 and 11

12—(1) In calculating any time specified in regulation 11 or 13, there shall be disregarded any day falling before the day on which notice was given of a correction of a decision or the record thereof pursuant to regulation 10 or on which notice is given of a determination that a decision shall not be set aside following an application made under regulation 11, as the case may be.

(2) Without prejudice to provisions for appeals to Commissioners, there shall be no other appeal against a correction made under regulation 10 or a refusal to make such a correction or against a determination given under regulation 11.

(3) Nothing in regulation 10 or 11 shall be construed as derogating from any power to correct errors or set aside decisions which is exercisable apart from these Regulations.

Application to a chairman for leave to appeal to a Commissioner

13—(1) Subject to the following provisions of this regulation, an application to the chairman of a tribunal for leave to appeal to a Commissioner from a decision of a tribunal shall—

- (a) be made in writing;
- (b) be given or sent to the office of the clerk to the tribunal which made the relevant decision not later than 3 months after the date when a notice of the tribunal's decision was sent or given to the applicant;
- (c) contain particulars of the grounds on which it is made;
- (d) have annexed thereto a copy of the statement of the reasons for the tribunal's decision referred to in regulation 9(4).

(2) Where an application for leave to appeal is made by the Secretary of State, the clerk to the tribunal shall, as soon as may be practicable, send a copy of the application to every other party to the proceedings.

(3) The decision if the chairman on an application for leave to appeal shall be recorded in writing and copies shall be given or sent to every party to the proceedings.

(4) Where in any case it is impracticable, or it will be likely to cause undue delay, for an application for leave to appeal against the decision of a tribunal to be determined by the person who was the chairman of that tribunal, that application shall be determined by any other person eligible to be nominated to act as a chairman of a medical appeal tribunal under section 50(4) of the Social Security Administration Act 1992.

(5) A person who has made an application to the chairman of the tribunal for leave to appeal to a Commissioner against a decision of a tribunal may withdraw his application at any time before it is determined by giving written notice of intention to withdraw to the chairman.

Appendix C

Rules of the Supreme Court 1965

Order 38 Evidence

I General Rules

II Writs of Subpoena

III Hearsay Evidence

IV Expert Evidence

. . . . .

[1] *Substituted by Rules of The Supreme Court (Amendment) Order 1996, (s. 1 1996 No. 3219).*

Order 18

Pleadings

. . . . .

[Conviction, etc to be adduced in evidence: matters to be pleaded

7A—(1) If in any action which is to be tried with pleadings any party intends, in reliance on section 11 of the Civil Evidence Act 1968 (convictions as evidence in civil proceedings), to adduce evidence that a person was convicted of an offence by or before a court in the United Kingdom or by a court-martial there or elsewhere, he must include in his pleading a statement of his intention with particulars of—

(a) the conviction and the date thereof,
(b) the court or court-martial which made the conviction, and
(c) the issue in the proceedings to which the conviction is relevant.

. . . . .

(3) Where a party's pleading includes such a statement as is mentioned in para. (1) or (2) then if the opposite party—

(a) denies the conviction, finding of authority or adjudication of paternity to which the statement relates, or
(b) alleges that the conviction, finding or adjudication was erroneous, or
(c) denies that the conviction, finding or adjudication is relevant to any issue in the proceedings,

he must make the denial or allegation in his pleading.][1]

[1] *Inserted by Rules of the Supreme Court (Amendment) 1969 (S.I. No. 1105).*

. . . . .

Particulars of pleading

[12—(1) Subject to paragraph (2), every pleading must contain the necessary particulars of any claim, defence or other matter pleaded including, without prejudice to the generality of the foregoing—

(a) Particulars of any misrepresentation, fraud, breach of trust, wilful default or undue influence on which the party pleading relies;
(b) where a party pleading alleges any condition of the mind of any person, whether any disorder or disability of mind or any malice, fraudulent intention or other condition of mind except knowledge, particulars of the facts on which the party relies; and
(c) where a claim for damages is made against a party pleading, particulars of any facts on which the party relies in mitigation of, or otherwise in relation to, the amount of damages.][1]

[(1A) Subject to paragraph (1B), a plaintiff in an action for personal injuries shall serve with his statement of claim—

(a) a medical report, and

(b) a statement of the special damages claimed.

(1B) Where the documents to which paragraph (1A) applies are not served with the statement of claim, the Court may—

(a) specify the period of time within which they are to be provided, or

(b) make such other order as it thinks fit (including an order dispensing with the requirement of paragraph (1A) or staying the proceedings).

(1C) For the purposes of this rule—

"medical report" means a report substantiating all the personal injuries alleged in the statement of claim which the plaintiff proposes to adduce in evidence as part of his case at the trial;

"a statement of the special damages claimed" means a statement giving full particulars of the special damages claimed for expenses and losses already incurred and an estimate of any future expenses and losses (including loss of earnings and of pension rights).][2]

[1] *Substituted by Rules of the Supreme Court (Amendment No. 4) 1989 (S.I. No. 2427).*

[2] *Inserted by Rules of the Supreme Court (Amendment No. 4) 1989 (S.I. No. 2427).*

. . . . .

Order 25

Summons for directions

. . . . .

Automatic directions in personal injury actions

8—(1) When the pleadings in any action to which this rule applies are deemed to be closed the following directions shall take effect automatically—

(a) there shall be discovery of documents within 14 days in accordance with Order 24, rule 2, and inspection within 7 days thereafter, save that where liability is admitted, or where the action arises out of a road accident, discovery shall be limited to disclosure by the plaintiff of any documents relating to special damages;

[(b) subject to paragraph (2), where any party intends to place reliance at the trial on—

(i) expert evidence, he shall, within 14 weeks, disclose the substance of that evidence to the other parties in the form of a written report, which shall be agreed if possible; and

(ii) any other oral evidence, he shall, within 14 weeks, serve on the other parties written statements of all such oral evidence which he intends to adduce][1];

(c) unless such reports are agreed, the parties shall be at liberty to call as expert witnesses those witnesses the substance of whose evidence has been disclosed in accordance with the preceding sub-paragraph, except that the number of expert witnesses shall be limited in any case to two medical experts and one expert of any other kind;

(d) photographs, a sketch plan and the contents of any police accident report book shall be receivable in evidence at the trial, and shall be agreed if possible;

(e) subject to Order 77, rule 13, the action shall be tried [at the trial centre for the place in which the action is proceeding or at such other trial centre as the parties may in writing agree][2];

(f) the action shall be tried by judge alone, as a case of substance or difficulty (Category B), and shall be set down within six months;

(g) the court shall be notified, on setting down, of the estimated length of the trial.

[(1A) Nothing in paragraph (1) shall require a party to produce a further medical report if he proposes to rely at the trial only on the report provided pursuant to Order 18, rule 12(1A) or (1B) but, where a party claiming damages for personal injuries discloses a further report, that report shall be accompanied by a statement of the special damages claimed and, in this paragraph, "statement of the special damages claimed" has the same meaning as in Order 18, rule 12(1C).][3]

[(2) Paragraphs (4) to (16) of Order 38, rule 2A shall apply with respect to statements and reports served under sub-paragraph (1)(b) as they apply with respect to statements served under that rule.][1]

(3) Nothing in paragraph (1) shall prevent any party to an action to which this rule applies from applying to court for such further or different directions or orders as may, in the circumstances, be appropriate [or prevent the making of an order for the transfer of the proceedings to a county court][4].

(4) For the purposes of this rule—

"a road accident" means an accident on land due to a collision or apprehended collision involving a vehicle; and "documents relating to special damages" include—

(a) documents relating to any industrial injury, industrial disablement or [incapacity][6] benefit rights, and

(b) where the claim is made under the Fatal Accidents Act 1976, documents relating to any claim for dependency on the deceased.

(5) This rule applies to any action for personal injuries except—

(a) any Admiralty action; and

(b) any action where the pleadings contain an allegation of a negligent act or omission in the course of medical treatment][5].

[1] *Substituted by Rules of the Supreme Court (Amendment No. 2) 1992 (S.I. No. 1907).*
[2] *Substituted by Rules of the Supreme Court (Amendment No. 3) 1982 (S.I. No. 1786).*
[3] *Inserted by Rules of the Supreme Court (Amendment No. 4) 1989 (S.I. No. 2427).*
[4] *Inserted by Rules of the Supreme Court (Amendment No. 3) 1982 (S.I. No. 1786).*
[5] *Inserted by Rules of the Supreme Court (Amendment No. 2) 1980 (S.I. No. 1010).*
[6] *Substituted by Rules of the Supreme Court (Amendment) 1995 (S.I. No. 2206).*

Order 29

Interlocutory injunctions, interim preservation of property, interim payments etc

. . . . .

I Interlocutory injunctions, interim preservation of property etc

Inspection etc of property under [section 33(1) of the Act][1] or [section 34(3) of the Act][1]

[**7A**—(1) An application for an order under [section 33(1) of the Act][1] in respect of property which may become the subject-matter of subsequent proceedings in the High Court or as to which any question may arise in any such proceedings shall be made by originating summons and the person against whom the order is sought shall be made defendant to the summons.][2]

(2) An application after the commencement of proceedings for an order under [section 34(3) of the Act] in respect of property which is not the property of or in the possession of any party to the proceedings shall be made by summons, which must be served on the person against whom the order is sought personally and on every party to the proceedings other than the applicant.

[(3) A summons under paragraph (1) or (2) shall be supported by affidavit which must specify or describe the property in respect of which the order is sought and show, if practicable by reference to any pleading served or intended to be served in the proceedings or subsequent proceedings, that it is property which is or may become the subject-matter of the proceedings or as to which any question arises or may arise in the proceedings.][2]

(4) A copy of the supporting affidavit shall be served with the summons on every person on whom the summons is required to be served.

(5) An order made under the said [section 33(1) or 34(3)][1] may be made conditional on the applicant's giving security for the costs of the person against whom it is made or on such other terms, if any, as the court thinks just.

(6) No such order shall be made if it appears to the court—

(a) that compliance with the order, if made, would result in the disclosure of information relating to a secret process, discovery or invention not in issue in the proceedings, and

(b) that the application would have been refused on that ground if—

(i) in the case of a summons under paragraph (1), the subsequent proceedings had already been begun, or

(ii) in the case of a summons under paragraph (2), the person against whom the order is sought were a party to the proceedings.][3]

[1] *Substituted by Rules of the Supreme Court (Amendment No. 2) 1982 (S.I. No. 1111).*

[2] *Substituted by Rules of the Supreme Court (Amendment No. 5) 1971 (S.I. No. 1955).*

[3] *Inserted by Rules of the Supreme Court (Amendment No. 4) 1971 (S.I. No. 1269).*

II Interim payments

[Interpretation of part II

9—In this part of this Order—

"interim payments", in relation to a defendant, means a payment on account of any damages, debt or other sum (excluding costs) which he may be held liable to pay to or for the benefit of the plaintiff; and any reference to the plaintiff or defendant includes a reference to any person who, for the purpose of the proceedings, acts as next friend of the plaintiff or guardian of the defendant.][1]

[1] *Substituted by Rules of the Supreme Court (Amendment No. 2) 1980 (S.I. No. 1010).*

[Application for interim payment

10—(1) The plaintiff may, at any time after the writ has been served on a defendant and the time limited for him to acknowledge service has expired, apply to the court for an order requiring that defendant to make an interim payment.

(2) An application under this rule shall be made by summons but may be included in a summons for summary judgment under Order 14 or Order 86.

(3) An application under this rule shall be supported by an affidavit which shall—

(a) verify the amount of the damages, debt or other sum to which the application relates and the grounds of the application;
(b) exhibit any documentary evidence relied on by the plaintiff in support of the application; and
(c) if the plaintiff's claim is made under the Fatal Accidents Act 1976, contain the particulars mentioned in section 2(4) of that Act.

(4) The summons and a copy of the affidavit in support and any documents exhibited thereto shall be served on the defendant against whom the order is sought not less than 10 clear days before the return day.

(5) Notwithstanding the making or refusal of the order for an interim payment, a second or subsequent application may be made upon cause shown.][1]

[1] *Substituted by Rules of the Supreme Court (Amendment No. 2) 1980 (S.I. No. 1010).*

[Order for interim payment in respect of damages

11—(1) If, on the hearing of an application under rule 10 in an action for damages, the court is satisfied—
(a) that the defendant against whom the order is sought (in this paragraph referred to as "the respondent") has admitted liability for the plaintiff's damages, or
(b) that the plaintiff has obtained judgment against the respondent for damages to be assessed; or
(c) that, if the action proceeded to trial, the plaintiff would obtain judgment for substantial damages against the respondent or, where there are two or more defendants, against any of them,

the court may, if it thinks fit and subject to paragraph (2), order the respondent to make an interim payment of such amount as it thinks just, not exceeding a reasonable proportion of the damages which in the opinion of the court are likely to be recovered by the plaintiff after taking into account any relevant contributory negligence and any set-off, cross-claim or counterclaim on which the respondent may be entitled to rely.

(2) No order shall be made under paragraph (1) in an action for personal injuries if it appears to the court that the defendant is not a person falling within one of the following categories, namely—
[(a) a person who is insured in respect of the plaintiff's claim or whose liability will be met by an insurer under section 151 of the Road Traffic Act 1988 or an insurer concerned under the Motor Insurers' Bureau Agreement][2];
(b) a public authority; or
(c) a person whose means and resources are such as to enable him to make the interim payment.][1]

[1] *Substituted by Rules of the Supreme Court (Amendment No. 2) 1980 (S.I. No. 1010).*

[2] *Substituted by S.I. 1996 No. 2892 and amended by S.I. 1996 No. 3219*

[Order for interim payment in respect of sums other than damages

12—If, on the hearing of an application under rule 10, the court is satisfied—

(a) that the plaintiff has obtained an order for an account to be taken as between himself and the defendant and for any amount certified due on taking the account to be paid; or

(b) that the plaintiff's action includes a claim for possession of and and, if the action proceeded to trial, the defendant would be held liable to pay to the plaintiff a sum of money in respect of the defendant's use and occupation of the land during the pendency of the action, even if a final judgment or order were given or made in favour of the defendant; or

(c) that, if the action proceeded to trial the plaintiff would obtain judgment against the defendant for a substantial sum of money apart from any damages or costs,

the court may, if it thinks fit, and without prejudice to any contentions of the parties as to the nature or character of the sum to be paid by the defendant, order the defendant to make an interim payment of such amount as it thinks just, after taking into account any set-off, cross-claim or counterclaim on which the [defendant][1] may be entitled to rely.][2]

[1] *Substituted by Rules of the Supreme Court (Amendment No. 3) 1980 (S.I. 1980 No. 1908).*
[2] *Substituted by Rules of the Supreme Court (Amendment No. 2) 1980 (S.I. 1980 No. 1010).*

[Manner of payment

13—(1) Subject to Order 80, rule 12, the amount of any interim payment ordered to be made shall be paid to the plaintiff unless the order provides for it to be paid into court, and where the amount is paid into court, the court may, on the application of the plaintiff, order the whole or any part of it to be paid out to him at such time or times as the court thinks fit.

(2) An application under the preceding paragraph for money in court to be paid out may be made *ex parte*, but the court hearing the application may direct a summons to be issued.

(3) An interim payment may be ordered to be made in one sum or by such instalments as the court thinks fit.

(4) Where a payment is ordered in respect of the defendant's use and occupation of land the order may provide for periodical payments to be made during the pendency of the action.][1]

[1] *Substituted by Rules of the Supreme Court (Amendment No. 2) 1980 (S.I. 1980 No. 1010).*

[Directions on applications under rule 10

14—Where an application is made under rule 10, the court may give directions as to the further conduct of the action, and, so far as may be applicable, Order 25, rules 2 to 7, shall, with the omission of so much of rule 7(1) as requires the parties to serve a notice specifying the orders and directions which they require and with any other necessary modifications, apply as if the application were a summons for directions, and, in particular, the court may order an early trial of the action.][1]

[1] *Substituted by Rules of the Supreme Court (Amendment No. 2) 1980 (S.I. No. 1010).*

[Non-disclosure of interim payment

15—The fact that an order has been made under rule 11 or 12 shall not be pleaded and, unless the defendant consents or the court so directs, no communication of that fact or of the fact that an interim payment has been made, whether voluntarily or pursuant to an order, shall be made to the court at the trial, or hearing, of any question or issue as to liability or damages until all questions of liability and amount have been determined.][1]

[1] *Substituted by Rules of the Supreme Court (Amendment No. 2) 1980 (S.I. No. 1010).*

[Payment into court in satisfaction

16—Where, after making an interim payment, whether voluntarily or pursuant to an order, a defendant pays a sum of money into court under Order 22, rule 1, the notice of payment must state that the defendant has taken into account the interim payment.][1]

[1] *Substituted by Rules of the Supreme Court (Amendment No. 2) 1980 (S.I. No. 1010).*

[Adjustment on final judgment or order or on discontinuance

17—Where a defendant has been ordered to make an interim payment or has in fact made an interim payment, whether voluntarily or pursuant to an order, the court may, in giving or making a final judgment or order, or granting the plaintiff leave to discontinue his action or to withdraw the claim in respect of which the interim payment has been made, or at any other stage of the proceedings on the application of any party, make such order with respect to the interim payment as may be just, and in particular—

(a) an order for the repayment by the plaintiff of all or part of the interim payment, or

(b) an order for the payment to be varied or discharged, or

(c) an order for the payment by any other defendant of any part of the interim payment which the defendant who made it is entitled to recover from him by way of contribution or indemnity or in respect of any remedy or relief relating to or connected with the plaintiff's claim.][1]

[1] *Substituted by Rules of the Supreme Court (Amendment No. 2) 1980 (S.I. No. 1010).*

[Counterclaims and other proceedings

18—The preceding rules in this Part of this Order shall apply, with the necessary modifications, to any counterclaim or proceeding commenced otherwise than by writ, where one party seeks an order for an interim payment to be made by another.][1]

[1] *Substituted by Rules of the Supreme Court (Amendment No. 2) 1980 (S.I. No. 1010).*

. . . . .

Order 37

Damages: assessment after judgment and orders for provisional damages

. . . . .

II Orders for provisional damages for personal injuries

[Application and interpretation

7—(1) This Part of this Order applies to actions to which section 32A of the Act (in this Part of this Order referred to an "section 32A") applies.

(2) In this Part of the Order "award of provisional damages" means an award of damages for personal injuries under which—

(a) damages are assessed on the assumption that the injured person will not develop the disease or suffer the deterioration referred to in section 32A; and

(b) the injured person is entitled to apply for further damages at a future date if he develops the disease or suffers the deterioration.][1]

[1] *Added by Rules of Supreme Court (Amendment No. 2) 1985 (S.I. 1985 No. 846).*

[Order for provisional damages

8—(1) The court may on such terms as it thinks just and subject to the provisions of this rule make an award of provisional damages if—

(a) the plaintiff has pleaded a claim for provisional damages, and

(b) The court is satisfied that the action is one to which section 32A applies.

(2) An order for an award of provisional damages shall specify the disease or type of deterioration in respect of which an application may be made at a future date, and shall also, unless the court otherwise determines, specify the period within which such application may be made.

(3) The court may, on the application of the plaintiff made within the period, if any, specified in paragraph (2), by order extend that period if it thinks it just to do so, and the plaintiff may make more than one such application.

(4) An order for an award of provisional damages may be made in respect of more than one disease or type of deterioration and may in respect of each disease or deterioration specify a different period within which an application may be made at a future date.

(5) Orders 13 and 19 shall not apply in relation to an action in which the plaintiff claims provisional damages.][1]

[1] *Inserted by Rules of the Supreme Court (Amendment No. 2) 1985 (S.I. 1985 No. 846).*

[Offer to submit to an award

9—(1) Where an application is made for an award of provisional damages, any defendant may at any time (whether or not he makes a payment into court) make a written offer to the plaintiff—

(a) to tender a sum of money (which may include an amount, to be specified, in respect of interest) in satisfaction of the plaintiff's claim for damages assessed on the assumption that the injured person will not develop the disease or suffer the deterioration referred to in section 32A [and identifying the disease or deterioration in question][1]; and

(b) to agree to the making of an award of provisional damages.

(2) Any offer made under paragraph (1) shall not be brought to the attention of the court until after the court has determined the claim for an award of provisional damages.

(3) Where an offer is made under paragraph (1), the plaintiff may, within 21 days after receipt of the offer, give written notice to the defendant of his acceptance of the offer and shall on such acceptance make an application to the court for an order in accordance with the provisions of rule 8(2).][2]

[1] *Inserted by Rules of the Supreme Court (Amendment No. 4) 1989 (S.I. No. 2427).*

[2] *Added by Rules of the Supreme Court (Amendment No. 2) 1985 (S.I. No. 846).*

[Application for award of further damages

10—(1) This rule applies where the plaintiff, pursuant to an award of provisional damages, claims further damages.

(2) No application for further damages may be made after the expiration of the period, if any, specified under rule 8(2), or of such period as extended under rule 8(3).

(3) The plaintiff shall give not less than three months' written notice to the defendant of his intention to apply for further damages and, if the defendant is to the plaintiff's knowledge insured in respect of the plaintiff's claim, to the insurers.

(4) The plaintiff must take out a summons for directions as to the future conduct of the action within 21 days after the expiry of the period of notice referred to in paragraph (3).

(5) On the hearing of the summons for directions the court shall give such directions as may be appropriate for the future conduct of the action including, but not limited to, the disclosure of medical reports and the place, mode and date of the hearing of the application for further damages.

(6) Only one application for further damages may be made in respect of each disease or type of deterioration specified in the order for the award of provisional damages.

(7) The provision of Order 29 with regard to the making of interim payments shall, with the necessary modifications, apply where an application is made under this rule.

(8) The court may include in an award of further damages simple interest at such rate as it thinks fit on all or any part thereof for all or any part of the period between the date of notification of the plaintiff's intention to apply for further damages and the date of the award.][1]

[1] *Added by Rules of the Supreme Court (Amendment No. 2) 1985 (S.I. 1985 No. 846).*

Order 38

Evidence

I General Rules

General rule: witnesses to be examined orally

1—Subject to the provisions of these rules and of the [Civil Evidence Act 1968][1] and the [Civil Evidence Act 1972][2], and any other enactment relating to evidence, any fact required to be proved at the trial of any action begun by writ by the evidence of witnesses shall be proved by the examination of witnesses orally and in open court.

[1] *Substituted by Rules of the Supreme Court (Amendment) 1969 (S.I. No. 1105).*
[2] *Inserted by Rules of the Supreme Court (Amendment No. 4) 1979 (S.I. No. 1542).*

Evidence by affidavit

2—(1) The court may, at or before the trial of an action begun by writ, order that the affidavit of any witness may be read at the trial if in the circumstances of the case it thinks it reasonable so to order.

(2) An order under paragraph (1) may be made on such terms as to the filing and giving of copies of the affidavits and as to the production of the deponents for cross-examination as the court thinks fit but, subject to any such terms and to any subsequent order of the court, the deponents shall not be subject to cross-examination and need not attend the trial for the purpose.

(3) In any cause or matter begun by originating summons, originating motion or petition, and on any application made by summons or motion, evidence may be given by affidavit unless in the case of any such cause, matter or application any provision of these rules otherwise provides or the court otherwise directs, but the court may, on the application of any party, order the attendance for cross-examination of the person making any such affidavit, and where, after such an order has been made, the person in question does not attend, his affidavit shall not be used as evidence without the leave of the court.

[Exchange of witness statements

2A— . . .

(4) Statements served under this rule shall—

- (a) be dated and, except for good reason (which should be specified by letter accompanying the statement), be signed by the intended witness and shall include a statement by him that the contents are true to the best of his knowledge and belief;
- (b) sufficiently identify any documents referred to therein; and
- (c) where they are to be served by more than one party, be exchanged simultaneously.

(5) Where a party is unable to obtain a written statement from an intended witness in accordance with paragraph (4)(a), the court may direct the party wishing to adduce that witness's evidence to provide the other party with the name of the witness and (unless the court otherwise orders) a statement of the nature of the evidence intended to be adduced.

(6) Subject to paragraph (9), where the party serving a statement under this rule does not call the witness to whose evidence it relates, no other party may put the statement in evidence at the trial.

(7) Subject to paragraph (9), where the party serving the statement does call such a witness at the trial—

- (a) except where the trial is with a jury, the court may, on such terms as it thinks fit, direct that the statement served, or part of it, shall stand as the evidence in chief of the witness or part of such evidence;
- (b) the party may not without the consent of the other parties or the leave of the court adduce evidence from that witness the substance of which is not included in the statement served, except—

(i) where the court's directions under paragraph (2) or (17) specify that statements should be exchanged in relation to only some issues of fact, in relation to any other issues;
(ii) in relation to new matters which have arisen since the statement was served on the other party;

(c) whether or not the statement or any part of it is referred to during the evidence in chief of the witness, any party may put the statement or any part of it in cross-examination of that witness.

(8) Nothing in this rule shall make admissible evidence which is otherwise inadmissible.

(9) Where any statement served is one to which the Civil Evidence Acts 1968 and 1972 apply, paragraphs (6) and (7) shall take effect subject to the provisions of those Acts and Parts III and IV of this Order.

The service of a witness statement under this rule shall not, unless expressly so stated by the party serving the same, be treated as a notice under the said Acts of 1968 and 1972; and where a statement or any part thereof would be admissible in evidence by virtue only of the said Act of 1968 or 1972 the appropriate notice under Part III or Part IV of this Order shall be served with the statement notwithstanding any provision of those Parts as to the time for serving such a notice. Where such a notice is served a counter-notice shall be deemed to have been served under Order 38, rule 26(1).

(10) Where a party fails to comply with a direction for the exchange of witness statements he shall not be entitled to adduce evidence to which the direction related without the leave of the court.

(11) Where a party serves a witness statement under this rule, no other person may make use of that statement for any purpose other than the purpose of the proceedings in which it was served—

(a) unless and to the extent that the party serving it gives his consent in writing or the court gives leave; or
(b) unless and to the extent that it has been put in evidence (whether pursuant to a direction under paragraph (7)(a) or otherwise).

(12) Subject to paragraph (13), the judge shall, if any person so requests during the course of the trial, direct the associate to certify as open to inspection any witness statement which was ordered to stand as evidence in chief under paragraph (7)(a).

A request under this paragraph may be made orally or in writing.

(13) The judge may refuse to give a direction under paragraph (12) in relation to a witness statement, or may exclude from such a direction any words or passages in a statement, if he considers that inspection should not be available—

(a) in the interests of justice or national security,
(b) because of the nature of any expert medical evidence in the statement, or
(c) for any other sufficient reason.

(14) Where the associate is directed under paragraph (12) to certify a witness statement as open to inspection he shall—

(a) prepare a certificate which shall be attached to a copy ("the certified copy") of that witness statement; and
(b) make the certified copy available for inspection.

(15) Subject to any conditions which the court may be special or general direction impose, any person may inspect and (subject to payment of the prescribed fee) take a copy of the certified copy of a witness statement from the time when the certificate is given until the end of 7 days after the conclusion of the trial.

(16) In this rule—
(a) any reference in paragraphs (12) to (15) to a witness statement shall, in relation to a witness statement of which only part has been ordered to stand as evidence in chief under paragraph (7)(a), be construed as a reference to that part;
(b) any reference to inspecting or copying the certified copy of a witness statement shall be construed as including a reference to inspecting or copying a copy of that certified copy.][1]

[1] *Substituted by Rules of the Supreme Court (Amendment No. 2) Order 1992 (S.I. 1992 No. 1907).*

Evidence of particular facts

3—(1) Without prejudice to rule 2, the court may, at or before the trial of any action, order that evidence of any particular fact shall be given at the trial in such manner as may be specified by the order.

(2) The power conferred by paragraph (1) extends in particular to ordering that evidence of any particular fact may be given at the trial—
(a) by statement on oath of information or belief, or
(b) by the production of documents or entries in books, or
(c) by copies of documents or entries in books, or
(d) in the case of a fact which is or was a matter of common knowledge either generally or in a particular district, by the production of a specified newspaper which contains a statement of that fact.

Limitation of expert evidence

4 The court may, at or before the trial of any action, order that the number of medical or other expert witnesses who may be called at the trial shall be limited as specified by the order.

Limitation of plans etc in evidence

5 Unless, at or before the trial, the court for special reasons otherwise orders, no plan, photograph or model shall be receivable in evidence at the trial of an action unless at least 10 days before the commencement of the trial the parties, other than the party producing it, have been given an opportunity to inspect it and to agree to the admission thereof without further proof.

[Revocation or variation of orders under rules 2 to 5

6 Any order under rules 2 to 5 (including an order made on appeal) may, on sufficient cause being shown, be revoked or varied by a subsequent order of the court made at or before the trial.][1]

[1] *Substituted by Rules of the Supreme Court (Amendment) 1974 (S.I. 1974 No. 295).*

Application to trials of issues, references, etc

8—The foregoing rules of this Order [(other than rule 2A)][1] shall apply to trials of issues or questions of fact or law, references, inquiries and assessments of damages as they apply to the trial of actions.

[1] *Inserted by Rules of the Supreme Court (Amendment No. 2) 1986 (S.I. 1986 No. 1187).*

Depositions: when receivable in evidence at trial

9—(1) No deposition taken in any cause or matter shall be received in evidence at the trial of the cause or matter unless—

(a) the deposition was taken in pursuance of an order under Order 39, rule 1, and

(b) either the party against whom the evidence is offered consents or it is proved to the satisfaction of the court that the deponent is dead, or beyond the jurisdiction of the court or unable from sickness or other infirmity to attend the trial.

(2) A party intending to use any deposition in evidence at the trial of a cause or matter must, a reasonable time before the trial, give notice of his intention to do so to the other party.

(3) A deposition purporting to be signed by the person before whom it was taken shall be receivable in evidence without proof of the signature being the signature of that person.

Court documents admissible or receivable in evidence

10—(1) Office copies of writs, records, pleadings and documents filed in the High Court shall be admissible in evidence in any cause or matter and between all parties to the same extent as the original would be admissible.

(2) Without prejudice to the provisions of any enactment, every document purporting to be sealed with the seal of any office or department of the Supreme Court shall be received in evidence without further proof, and any document purporting to be so sealed and to be a copy of a document filed in, or issued out of, that office or department shall be deemed to be an office copy of that document without further proof unless the contrary is shown.

Evidence at trial may be used in subsequent proceedings

12—Any evidence taken at the trial of any cause or matter may be used in any subsequent proceedings in that cause or matter.

Order to produce document at proceeding other than trial

13—(1) At any stage in a cause or matter the court may order any person to attend any proceeding in the cause or matter and produce any document, to be specified or described in the order, the production of which appears to the court to be necessary for the purpose of that proceeding.

(2) No person shall be compelled by an order under paragraph (1) to produce any document at a proceeding in a cause or matter which he could not be compelled to produce at the trial of that cause or matter.

II Writs of subpoena

Form and issue of writ of subpoena

14—(1) A writ of subpoena must be in Form 28, 29 or 30 in Appendix A, whichever is appropriate.

(2) Issue of a writ of subpoena takes place upon its being sealed by an officer of the office out of which it is issued.

(3) Where a writ of subpoena is to be issued in a cause or matter which is not proceeding in a district registry, the appropriate office for the issue of the writ is the Central Office or, if the cause or matter has been set down for trial [outside the Royal Courts of Justice][1], either the Central Office or the registry for the district comprising the city or town at which the cause or matter has been set down for trial.

(4) Where a writ of subpoena is to be issued in a cause or matter which is proceeding in a district registry, the appropriate office for the issue of the writ is—

- (a) that registry, or
- (b) if the cause or matter has been set down for trial at a city or town not comprised in the district of that registry, either that registry or the registry for the district comprising that city or town, or
- (c) if the cause or matter has been set down for trial at the Royal Courts of Justice, either the Central Office or the registry in which the cause or matter is proceeding.

(5) Before a writ of subpoena is issued a praecipe for the issue of the writ must be filed in the office out of which the writ is to issue; and the praecipe must contain the name and address of the party issuing the writ, if he is acting in person, or the name or firm and business address of that party's solicitor and also (if the solicitor is the agent of another) the name or firm and business address of his principal.

[1] *Substituted by Rules of the Supreme Court (Amendment No. 5) 1971 (S.I. 1971 No. 1955).*

More than one name may be included in one writ of subpoena

15 The names of two or more persons may be included in one writ of subpoena ad testificandum.

Amendment of writ of subpoena

16 Where there is a mistake in any person's name or address in a writ of subpoena, then, if the writ has not been served, the party by whom the writ was issued may have the writ resealed in correct form by filing a second praecipe under rule 14(5) endorsed with the words "Amended and resealed".

Service of writ of subpoena

17 A writ of subpoena must be served personally and, subject to rule 19, the service shall not be valid unless effected within twelve weeks after the date of issue of the writ [and not less than 4 days or such other period as the court may fix, before the day on which attendance before the court is required.][1]

[1] *Added by Rules of the Supreme Court (Amendment No. 2) 1980 (S.I. 1980 No. 1010).*

Duration of writ of subpoena

18 Subject to rule 19, a writ of subpoena continues to have effect until the conclusion of the trial at which the attendance of the witness is required.

Writ of subpoena in aid of inferior court or tribunal

19—(1) The office of the Supreme Court out of which a writ of subpoena ad testificandum or a writ of subpoena duces tecum in aid of an inferior court or tribunal may be issued is the Crown Office, and no order of the court for the issue of such a writ is necessary.

(2) A writ of subpoena in aid of an inferior court or tribunal continues to have effect until the disposal of the proceedings before that court or tribunal at which the attendance of the witness is required.

(3) A writ of subpoena issued in aid of an inferior court or tribunal must be served personally.

(4) Unless a writ of subpoena issued in aid of an inferior court or tribunal is duly served on the person to whom it is directed not less than 4 days, or such other period as the court may fix, before the day on which the attendance of that person before the court or tribunal is required by the writ, that person shall not be liable to any penalty or process for failing to obey the writ.

(5) An application to set aside a writ of subpoena issued in aid of an

inferior court or tribunal may be heard by a master of the Queen's Bench Division.

III Hearsay evidence

[Application and interpretation

20.—(1) In this Part of this Order the "1995 Act" means the Civil Evidence Act 1995 and any expressions used in this Part of this Order and in the 1995 Act have the same meanings in this Part of this Order as they have in the Act.

(2) In this Part of this Order:

"hearsay evidence" means evidence consisting of hearsay within the meaning of section 1(2) of the 1995 Act;

"hearsay notice" means a notice under section 2 of the 1995 Act.

(3) This Part of this Order applies in relation to the trial or hearing of an issue or question arising in a cause or matter and to a reference, inquiry and assessment of damages, as it applies to the trial or hearing of a cause or matter.][1]

[1] *Inserted by Rules of the Supreme Court (Amendment) (S.I. 1996 No. 3219).*

Hearsay notices

21.—(1) A hearsay notice must

(a) state that it is a hearsay notice;

(b) identify the hearsay evidence;

(c) identify the person who made the statement which is to be given in evidence; and

(d) state why that person will (or may) not be called to give oral evidence; and

(e) if the hearsay evidence is contained in a witness statement, refer to the part of the witness statement where it is set out.

(2) A single hearsay notice may deal with the hearsay evidence of more than one witness.

(3) The requirement to give a hearsay notice does not apply to

(a) evidence which is authorised to be given by or in an affidavit; or

(b) a statement which a party to a probate action desires to give in evidence and which is alleged to have been made by the person whose estate is the subject of the action.

(4) Subject to paragraph (5), a party who desires to give in evidence at the trial or hearing of a cause or matter hearsay evidence shall

(a) in the case of a cause or matter which is required to be set down for trial or hearing or adjourned into Court, within 28 days after it is set down or so adjourned or within such other period as the Court may specify, and

(b) in any other case, within 28 days after the date on which an appointment for the first hearing of the cause or matter is obtained, or within such other period as the Court may specify,

serve a hearsay notice on every party to the cause or matter.

(5) Where witness statements are served under rule 2A of this Order, any hearsay notice served under this rule shall be served at the same time as the witness statements.][1]

[1] *Substituted by Rules of the Supreme Court (Amendment) order 1996 (S.I. 1996 No.3219).*

[Power to call witness for cross-examination on hearsay evidence

22.—(1) Where a party tenders as hearsay evidence a statement made by a person but does not propose to call the person who made the statement to give evidence, the court may, on application, allow another party to call and cross-examine the person who made the statement on its contents.

(2) An application under paragraph (1) shall be made on notice to all other parties not later than 28 days after service of the hearsay notice.

(3) Where the court allows another party to call and cross-examine the person who made the statement, it may give such directions as it thinks fit to secure the attendance of that person and as to the procedure to be followed.][1]

[1] *Substituted by Rules of the Supreme Court (Amendment) Order 1996 (S.I. 1996 No. 3219).*

[Credibility

23.—(1) If

(a) a party tenders as hearsay evidence a statement made by a person but does not call the person who made the statement to give oral evidence, and

(b) another party wishes to attack the credibility of the person who made the statement:

that other party shall notify the party tendering the hearsay evidence of his intention.

(2) A notice under paragraph (1) shall be given not later than 28 days after service of the hearsay notice.][1]

[1] *Substituted by Rules of the Supreme Court (Amendment) Order 1996 (S.I. 1996 No. 3219).*

[Powers exercisable in chambers

24. The jurisdiction of the Court under rules 20 to 23 may be exercised in chambers.][1]

[1] *Substituted by Rules of the Supreme Court (Amendment) Order 1996 (S.I. 1996 No. 3219).*

IV Expert evidence

[Interpretation

35—In this Part of this Order a reference to a summons for directions includes a reference to any summons or application to which, under any of these rules, Order 25, rules 2 to 7, apply and expressions used in this Part of this Order which are used in the Civil Evidence Act 1972 have the same meanings in this Part of this Order as in that Act.][1]

[1] *Inserted by Rules of the Supreme Court (Amendment) 1974 (S.I. 1974 No. 295).*

[Restrictions on adducing expert evidence

36—(1) Except with the leave of the court or where all parties agree, no expert evidence may be adduced at the trial or hearing of any cause or matter unless the party seeking to adduce the evidence—

[(a)][1] has applied to the court to determine whether a direction should be given under rule 37 or 41 (whichever is appropriate) and has complied with any direction given on the application, [or

(b) has complied with automatic directions taking effect under Order 25, rule 8(1)(b).][2]

(2) Nothing in paragraph (1) shall apply to evidence which is permitted to be given by affidavit or shall affect the enforcement under any other provision of these rules (except Order 45, rule 5) of a direction given under this Part of this Order.][3]

[1] *Inserted by Rules of the Supreme Court (Amendment No. 2) 1980 (S.I. 1980 No. 1010).*
[2] *Inserted by Rules of the Supreme Court (Amendment) 1974 (S.I. 1974 No. 295).*

[Direction that expert report be disclosed

[37—(1) Subject to paragraph (2), where in any cause or matter an application is made under rule 36(1) in respect of oral expert evidence, then, unless the court considers that there are special reasons for not doing so, it shall direct that the substance of the evidence be disclosed in the form of a written report or reports to such other parties and within such period as the court may specify.

(2) Nothing in paragraph (1) shall require a party to disclose a further medical report if he proposes to rely at the trial only on the report provided pursuant to Order 18, rule 12(1A) or (1B) but, where a party claiming damages for personal injuries discloses a further report, that report shall be accompanied by a statement of the special damages claimed and, in this paragraph, "statement of the special damages claimed" has the same meaning as in Order 18, rule 12(1C).][1]

[1] *Substituted by Rules of the Supreme Court (Amendment No. 4) 1989 (S.I. 1989 No. 2427). Applies to proceedings commenced by a writ issued on or after June 4, 1990.*

[Meeting of experts

38—In any cause or matter the court may, if it thinks fit, direct that there be a meeting "without prejudice" of such experts within such periods before or after the disclosure of their reports as the court may specify, for the purpose of identifying those parts of their evidence which are in issue. Where such a meeting takes place the experts may prepare a joint statement indicating those parts of their evidence on which they are, and those on which they are not, in agreement.][1]

[1] *Substituted by Rules of the Supreme Court (Amendment) 1987 (S.I. 1987 No. 1423).*

[Disclosure of part of expert evidence

39—Where the court considers that any circumstances rendering it undesirable to give a direction under rule 37 relate to part only of the evidence sought to be adduced, the court may, if it thinks fit, direct disclosure of the remainder.][2]

[2] *Inserted by Rules of the Supreme Court (Amendment) 1974 (S.I. 1974 No. 295).*

. . . . .

[Expert evidence contained in statement

41—Where an application is made under rule 36 in respect of expert evidence contained in a statement and the applicant alleges that the maker of the statement cannot or should not be called as a witness, the court may direct that the provisions of rules 20 to 23 and 25 to 33 shall apply with such modifications as the court thinks fit.][1]

[1] *Inserted by Rules of the Supreme Court (Amendment) 1974 (S.I. 1974 No. 295).*

[Putting in evidence expert report disclosed by another party

42—A party to any cause or matter may put in evidence any expert report disclosed to him by any other party in accordance with this Part of this Order.][1]

[1] *Inserted by Rules of the Supreme Court (Amendment) 1974 (S.I. No. 295).*

[Time for putting expert report in evidence

43—Where a party to any cause or matter calls as a witness the maker of a report which has been disclosed in accordance with a direction given under rule 37, the report may be put in evidence at the commencement of its maker's examination in chief or at such other time as the court may direct.][1]

[1] *Inserted by Rules of the Supreme Court (Amendment) 1974 (S.I. No. 295).*

[Revocation and variation of directions

44—Any direction given under this Part of this Order may on sufficient cause being shown be revoked or varied by a subsequent direction given at or before the trial of the cause or matter.][1]

[1] *Inserted by Rules of the Supreme Court (Amendment) 1974 (S.I. No. 295).*

Appendix D

County Court Rules 1981

28 Application of RSC 426

. . . . .

[1] *Substituted by County Court (Amendment) (No. 3) Rules 1996 (S.I. 1996 No. 3218).*

Order 6

Particulars of claim

General requirements

1—(1) Subject to the provisions of this rule, a plaintiff shall, at the time of commencing an action, file particulars of his claim specifying his cause of action and the relief or remedy which he seeks and stating briefly the material facts on which he relies.

. . . . .

[(5) Subject to paragraph (6), a plaintiff in an action for personal injuries shall file with particulars of claim—

(a) a medical report, and

(b) a statement of the special damages claimed, together with a copy of those documents for each defendant.

(6) Where the documents to which paragraph (5) applies are not filed with the particulars of claim, the court—

(a) may specify the period of time within which they are to be provided, in which case the plaintiff shall within the time so specified file a copy of them and serve further copies on each defendant; or

(b) may make such other order as it thinks fit (including an order dispensing with the requirements of paragraph (5) or staying the proceedings).

(7) For the purposes of this rule—

"medical report" means a report substantiating all the personal injuries alleged in the particulars of claim which the plaintiff proposes to adduce in evidence as part of his case at the trial;

"a statement of the special damages claimed" means a statement giving full particulars of the special damages claimed for expenses and losses already incurred and an estimate of any future expenses and losses (including loss of earnings and of pension rights).][1]

[1] *Inserted by County Court (Amendment No. 4) Rules 1989 (S.I. No. 2426).*

[Claim for interest

1A Where the plaintiff claims interest under [section 69][1] of the Act or otherwise his particulars of claim shall contain a statement to that effect.][2]

[1] *Substituted by County Court (Amendment No. 2) Rules 1984 (S.I. No. 878).*
[2] *Inserted by County Court (Amendment) Rules 1983 (S.I. No. 275).*

Order 13

Applications and orders in the course of proceedings

Application of RSC relating to other interlocutory matters

7—(1) Subject to the following paragraphs of this rule, the provisions of the RSC with regard to—

. . . . .

(g) the exercise of the powers conferred by [sections 33 to 35 of the Supreme Court Act 1981][1];

shall apply in relation to proceedings or, as the case may be, subsequent proceedings in a county court as they apply in relation to proceedings or subsequent proceedings in the High Court.

[(2A) The provisions of the RSC mentioned in sub-paragraph (g) of paragraph (1) shall apply as if for any reference therein to section 33 or section 34 of the Supreme Court Act 1981 there were substituted a reference to section 52 or section 53 respectively of the County Courts Act 1984.][2]

(3) An application for the exercise of the powers conferred by [section 52(1) or 52(2) of the Act][3] shall be made by originating application and the affidavit in support of the application shall show that the subsequent proceedings are such as the court to which the application is made has jurisdiction to hear and determine.

(4) An application for any other relief mentioned in paragraph (1) shall be made by notice and, in the case of an application for the exercise of the powers conferred by [section 53 of the Act][3], the notice shall be served on the person against whom the order is sought.

[1] *Substituted by County Court (Amendment No. 2) Rules 1982 (S.I. No. 1140).*
[2] *Inserted by County Court (Amendment No. 2) Rules 1984 (S.I. No. 878).*
[3] *Substituted by County Court (Amendment No. 2) Rules 1984 (S.I. No. 878).*

. . . . .

[Interim payments

12—(1) Subject to the following paragraphs of this rule, the provisions of RSC Order 29 Part II shall apply in relation to proceedings in a county court [except where those proceedings stand referred for arbitration under][1] [Order 19, rule 3][2].

(2) RSC Order 29, rule 10 shall apply with the substitution in rule 10(4), for the words "not less than 10 clear days before the return day", of the words "not less than 7 days before the day fixed for the hearing of the application".

(3) RSC Order 29, rule 13(1) shall apply with the substitution, for the

reference to RSC Order 80, rule 12, of a reference to Order 10, rule 11 of these Rules.

(4) RSC Order 29, rule 14 shall not apply but where an application is made for an order requiring the defendant to make an interim payment the court may treat the hearing of the application as a pre-trial review and Order 17 with the necessary modifications shall apply accordingly.][3]

[1] *Substituted by County Court (Amendment No. 4) Rules 1991 (S.I. No. 1882).*
[2] *Substituted by County Court (Amendment No. 2) Rules 1992 (S.I. No. 1965).*
[3] *Inserted by County Court (Amendment No. 3) Rules 1982 (S.I. No. 1794).*

Order 17

Pre-trial review

. . . . .

[Automatic directions

11—(1) This rule applies to any default or fixed date action except—

(a) an action for the administration of the estate of a deceased person;
(b) an Admiralty action;
(c) proceedings which are referred for arbitration under Order 19;
(d) an action arising out of a regulated consumer credit agreement within the meaning of the Consumer Credit Act 1974;
(e) an action for the delivery of goods;
(f) an action for the recovery of income tax;
(g) interpleader proceedings or an action in which an application is made for relief by way of interpleader;
(h) an action of a kind mentioned in section 66(3) of the Act (trial by jury);
(i) an action for the recovery of land;
(j) a partnership action;
(k) an action to which Order 48A applies (patent actions);
(l) a contentious probate action;
(m) [. . .][1]
(n) an action to which Order 5, rule 5 applies (representative proceedings);
(o) an action to which [Order 9, rule 3(6)][2] applies (admission of part of plaintiff's claim);
(p) an action on a third party notice or similar proceedings under Order 12;
(q) an action to which Order 47, rule 3 applies (actions in tort between husband and wife).
(r) an action to which Order 48C applies (the Central London County Court Business List).][3]

[(1A) This rule applies to actions transferred from the High Court as it applies to actions commenced in a county court but (without prejudice to paragraph (2)) where directions have been given by the High Court, directions taking effect automatically under this rule shall have effect subject to any directions given by the High Court.][4]

(2) In an action to which this rule applies—

(a) except where a pre-trial review is ordered pursuant to a direction given under paragraph 4(a), the foregoing provisions of this Order shall not apply and directions shall take effect automatically in accordance with the following paragraphs of this rule;

(b) where the court gives directions with regard to any matter arising in the course of proceedings, directions taking effect automatically under this rule shall have effect subject to any directions given by the court.][2]

(3) When the pleadings are deemed to be closed, the following directions shall take effect—

(a) there shall be discovery of documents within 28 days, and inspection within 7 days thereafter, in accordance with paragraph (5);

[(b) except with the leave of the court or where all parties agree—

(i) no expert evidence may be adduced at the trial unless the substance of that evidence has been disclosed to the other parties in the form of a written report within 10 weeks;

(ii) subject to paragraph (7), the number of expert witnesses of any kind shall be limited to two; and

(iii) any party who intends to place reliance at the trial on any other oral evidence shall, within 10 weeks, serve on the other parties written statements of all such oral evidence which he intends to adduce;][5]

(c) photographs and sketch plans and, in an action for personal injuries, the contents of any police accident report book shall be receivable in evidence at the trial and shall be agreed if possible;

(d) unless a day has already been fixed, the plaintiff shall within 6 months request the proper officer to fix a day for the hearing and rule 12 shall apply where such request is made.

[(3A) Paragraphs (4) to (16) of Order 20, rule 12A shall apply with respect to statements and reports served under sub-paragraph (3)(b) as they apply with respect to statements served under that rule.][6]

[(4) Nothing in paragraph (3) shall—

(a) prevent the court from giving, of its own motion or on the application of any party, such further or different directions or orders as may in the circumstances be appropriate (including an order that a pre-trial review be held or fixing a date for the hearing or dismissing the proceedings or striking out any claim made therein); or

(b) prevent the making of an order for the transfer of the proceedings to the High Court or another county court;

and rule 3 shall apply where an application is made under this paragraph as it applies to applications made on a pre-trial review.][2]

(5) Subject to paragraph (6), the parties must make discovery by serving lists of documents and—

(a) subject to sub-paragraph (c), each party must make and serve on every other party a list of documents which are or have been in his possession, custody or power relating to any matter in question between them in the action;

(b) the court may, on application—

(i) order that discovery under this paragraph shall be limited to such documents or classes of documents only, or as to such only of the matters in question, as may be specified in the Order, or

(ii) if satisfied that discovery by all or any of the parties is not necessary, order that there shall be no discovery of documents by any or all of the parties; and the court shall make such an order if and only so far as it is of opinion that discovery is not necessary either for disposing fairly of the action or for saving costs;

(c) where liability is admitted or in an action for personal injuries arising out of a road accident, discovery shall be limited to disclosure of any documents relating to the amount of damages;

(d) the provisions of Order 14 of these rules relating to inspection of documents shall apply where discovery is made under this paragraph as it applies where discovery is made under that Order.

(6) Discovery under paragraph (5) shall not apply in proceedings to which the Crown is a party.

(7) In an action for personal injuries—

(a) the number of expert witnesses shall be limited in any case to two medical experts and one expert of any other kind;

(b) nothing in paragraph (3) shall require a party to produce a further medical report if he proposes to rely at the trial only on the report provided pursuant to Order 6, rule 1(5) or (6) but, where a further report is disclosed, that report shall be accompanied by an amended statement of the special damages claimed, if appropriate.

(8) Where the plaintiff makes a request pursuant to paragraph (3)(a) for the proper officer to fix a day for the hearing, he shall file a note which shall if possible be agreed by the parties giving—

(a) an estimate of the length of the trial, and

(b) the number of witnesses to be called.

(9) If no request is made pursuant to paragraph (3)(d) within 15 months of the day on which pleadings are deemed to be closed (or within 9 months after the expiry of any period fixed by the court for making such a request), the action shall be automatically struck out.

(10) Where the proper officer fixes a day for the hearing, he shall give not less than 21 days' notice thereof to every party.

(11) For the purposes of this rule—

(a) pleadings shall be deemed to be closed 14 days after the delivery of a defence in accordance with Order 9, rule 2 or, where a counterclaim is served with the defence, 28 days after the delivery of the defence;

(b) "a road accident" means an accident on land due to a collision or apprehended collision involving a vehicle;

(c) "a statement of the special damages claimed" has the same meaning as in Order 6, rule 1(7).

(12) Unless the context otherwise requires, references in these rules to the return day in relation to a fixed date action to which this rule applies shall be construed as references to the date on which directions take effect under this rule.][7]

[1] *Repealed by County Court (Amendment No. 3) Rules 1993 (S.I. 1993 No. 2175).*
[2] *Substituted by County Court (Amendment No. 2) Rules 1991 (S.I. 1991 No. 1126).*
[3] *Inserted by County Court (Amendment No. 2) Rules 1994 (S.I. 1994 No. 1288).*
[4] *Inserted by County Court (Amendment No. 3) Rules 1991 (S.I. 1991 No. 1328).*
[5] *Substituted by County Court (Amendment No. 2) Rules 1992 (S.I. 1992 No. 1965).*
[6] *Inserted by County Court (Amendment No. 2) Rules 1992 (S.I. 1992 No. 1965).*
[7] *Substituted by County Court (Amendment No. 3) Rules 1990 (S.I. 1990 No. 1764).*

. . . . .

Order 20

Evidence

. . . . .

Part II Evidence generally

Evidence generally to be given orally and in open court

4—Subject to any provision made by or under any Act or rule and to any rule of law, any fact required to be proved at the hearing of an action or matter by the evidence of witnesses shall be proved by the examination of the witnesses orally and in open court.

. . . . .

Evidence of particular facts

8—The court may, at or before the trial or hearing of any action or matter and on or before any application in the course of proceedings or any pre-trial review, order that evidence of any particular fact shall be given at the hearing of the action or matter or, as the case may be, on the application or pre-trial review in such manner as may be specified in the order, and in particular—

(a) by the production of documents or entries in books, or

(b) by copies of documents or entries in books, or

(c) in the case of a fact which is or was a matter of common knowledge either generally or in a particular district, by the production of a specified newspaper which contains a statement of that fact.

. . . . .

Part III Summoning and examination of witnesses

Witness summons

12—(1) Where a party to an action or matter desires a person to be summoned as a witness to give oral evidence or to produce a document in his possession, custody or power, the proper officer shall, on an application made by the party in accordance with paragraph (2), issue a witness summons, together with a copy.

(2) The applicant shall file a request for the issue of the summons and, if the summons is to be served by an officer of the court, deposit in the court office the money to be paid or tendered under paragraph (7).

(3) The summons shall contain the name of one witness only but may, as regards such name, be issued in blank.

[(4) (a) The summons shall not be issued less than seven days before the date upon which attendance before the court is required unless the judge or registrar [district judge] otherwise directs and shall be served on the witness not less than four days before the date upon which attendance before the court is required unless the judge or registrar otherwise directs.

(b) Service under this paragraph shall, subject to paragraph (5), be effected by delivering the summons to the witness personally.][1]

(5) Where the applicant or his solicitor gives a certificate for postal service, the summons shall, unless the registrar [district judge] otherwise directs, be served on the witness by an officer of the court sending it to him by first-class post at the address stated in the request for the summons and, unless the contrary is shown, the date of service shall be deemed to be the seventh day after the date on which the summons was sent to the witness.

(6) Where the summons has been served by post, the witness shall not be fined for failing to appear on the return day unless the judge is satisfied that—

(a) the summons came to his knowledge in sufficient time for him to appear on that day, and

(b) the money to be paid or tendered under paragraph (7) was sent to him with the summons.

(7) At the time of service of the summons there shall be paid or tendered to the witness the sum of £6 for a police officer and £8.50 for any other person and, in addition, a sum reasonably sufficient to cover his expenses in travelling to and from the court.

(8) No summons shall be issued to require a witness to give evidence at a hearing in chambers for directions without leave of the judge or registrar [district judge], the application for which shall be made ex parte.][2]

[1] *Substituted by County Court (Amendment) Rules 1989 (S.I. No. 236).*
[2] *Inserted by County Court (Amendment) Rules 1989 (S.I. No. 236).*

[Exchange of witness statements

12A

. . . . .

(4) Statements served under this rule shall—

(a) be dated and, except for good reason (which should be specified by letter accompanying the statement), be signed by the intended witness and shall include a statement by him that the contents are true to the best of his knowledge and belief;

(b) sufficiently identify and documents referred to therein; and

(c) where they are to be served by more than one party, be exchanged simultaneously.

(5) Where a party is unable to obtain a written statement from an intended witness in accordance with paragraph (4)(a), the court may direct the party wishing to adduce that witness's evidence to provide the other party with the name of the witness and (unless the court otherwise orders) a statement of the nature of the evidence intended to be adduced.

(6) Subject to paragraph (9), where the party serving a statement does call such a witness at the trial—

(a) except where the trial is with a jury, the trial judge may, on such terms as he thinks fit, direct that the statement served, or part of it, shall stand as the evidence in chief of the witness or part of such evidence;

(b) the party may not without the consent of the other parties or the leave of the trial judge adduce evidence from that witness the substance of which is not included in the statement served, except—

(i) where the court's directions under paragraph (2) or (17) specify that statements should be exchanged in relation to only some issues of fact, in relation to any other issues;

(ii) in relation to new matters which have arisen since the statement was served on the other party;

(c) whether or not the statement or any part of it is referred to during the evidence in chief of the witness, any party may put the statement or any part of it in cross-examination of that witness.

(8) Nothing in this rule shall make admissible evidence which is otherwise inadmissible.

(9) Where any statement served is one to which the Civil Evidence Acts 1968 and 1972 apply, paragraphs (6) and (7) shall take effect subject to the provisions of those Acts and Parts III and IV of this Order.

The service of a witness statement under this rule shall not, unless expressly so stated by the party serving the same, be treated as a notice under the said Acts of 1968 and 1972; and where a statement or any part thereof would be admissible in evidence by virtue only of the said Act of

1968 or 1972 the appropriate notice under Part IV of this Order shall be served with the statement notwithstanding any provision of that Part as to the time for serving such a notice. Where such a notice is served a counter-notice shall be deemed to have been served under Order 20, rule 17(1).

(10) Where a party fails to comply with a direction for the exchange of witness statements he shall not be entitled to adduce evidence to which the direction related without the leave of the court.

(11) Where a party serves a witness statement under this rule, no other person may make use of that statement for any purpose other than the purpose of the proceedings in which it was served—

(a) unless and to the extent that the party serving it gives his consent in writing or the court gives leave; or

(b) unless and to the extent that it has been put in evidence (whether pursuant to a direction under paragraph (7)(a) or otherwise).

(12) Subject to paragraph (13), the judge shall, if any person so requests during the course of the trial, direct that any witness statement which was ordered to stand as evidence in chief under paragraph (7)(a) shall be certified as open to inspection.

A request under this paragraph may be made orally or in writing.

(13) The judge may refuse to give a direction under paragraph (12) in relation to a witness statement, or may exclude from such a direction any words or passages in a statement, if he considers that inspection should not be available—

(a) in the interests of justice or national security,

(b) because of the nature of any expert medical evidence in the statement, or

(c) for any other sufficient reason.

(14) Where a direction is given under paragraph (12) that a witness statement shall be certified as open to inspection—

(a) a certificate shall be attached by the proper office to a copy ("the certified copy") of that witness statement; and

(b) the certified copy shall be made available for inspection.

(15) Subject to any directions issued by the Lord Chancellor under Order 50, rule 1 and to any conditions which the court may by special direction impose, any person may inspect and (subject to payment of the prescribed fee) take a copy of the certified copy of a witness statement during office hours from the time when the certificate is given until the end of 7 days after the conclusion of the trial.

(16) In this rule—

(a) any reference in paragraphs (12) to (15) to a witness statement shall, in relation to a witness statement of which only part has been ordered to stand as evidence in chief under paragraph (7)(a), be construed as a reference to that part;

(b) any reference to inspecting or copying the certified copy of a witness statement shall be construed as including a reference to inspecting or copying a copy of that certified copy.

(17) The court shall have power to vary or override any of the provisions of this rule (except paragraphs (1), (8) and (12) to 16)) and to give such alternative directions as it thinks fit.][1]

[1] *Substituted by County Court (Amendment No. 2) Rules 1992 (S.I. No. 1965).*

. . . . .

Part IV Hearsay evidence

[Application and interpretation

14—(1) In this Part of this Order the "1995 Act" means the Civil Evidence Act 1995 and any expressions used in this Part of this Order and in the 1995 Act have the same meanings in this Part of this Order as they have in the Act.

(2) In this Part of this Order:

"hearsay evidence" means evidence consisting of hearsay within the meaning of section 1(2) of the 1995 Act;

"hearsay notice" means a notice under section 2 of the 1995 Act.

(3) This Part of this Order applies in relation to the trial or hearing of an issue arising in an action or matter and to a reference under section 65 of the Act (Power of judge to refer to district judge or referee) as it applies to the hearing of an action or matter.

(4) Nothing in this Part of this Order shall apply in relation to proceedings which have been referred to arbitration under section 64 of the Act.][1]

[1] *Substituted by County Court (Amendment No. 3) Rules 1996 S.I. 1996 No. 3218).*

Hearsay notices

15—(1) A hearsay notice must

(a) state that it is a hearsay notice:

(b) identify the hearsay evidence:

(c) identify the person who made the statement which is to be given in evidence;

(d) state why that person will (or may) not be called to give oral evidence, and

(e) if the hearsay evidence is contained in a witness statement, refer to the part of the witness statement where it is set out.

(2) A single hearsay notice may deal with the hearsay evidence of more than one witness.

(3) The requirement to give a hearsay notice does not apply to

(a) evidence which is authorised to be given by or in an affidavit; or

(b) a statement which a party to a probate action desires to give in evidence and which is alleged to have been made by the person whose estate is the subject of the action.

(4) Subject to paragraphs (5) and (6), a party who desires to give in evidence at the trial or hearing of an action or matter hearsay evidence shall, not less than 28 days before the day fixed for the trial or hearing, serve a hearsay notice on every party and file a copy in the court.

(5) Unless the court otherwise directs, paragraph (4) shall not apply to an

action or matter in which no defence or answer has been filed and, where a defence or answer is filed less than 28 days before the day fixed for the trial or hearing, any party who is required to give a hearsay notice shall apply to the court for an adjournment or for such other directions as may be appropriate.

(6) Where witness statements are served under rule 12A of this Order (or under that rule as it is applied by Order 17, rule 11), any hearsay notice served under this rule shall be served at the same time as the witness statements.][1]

[1] *Substituted by County Court (Amendment) (No. 3) Rules 1996 (S.I. 1996 No. 3218).*

[Power to call witness for cross-examination on hearsay evidence

16—(1) Where a party tenders as hearsay evidence a statement made by a person but does not propose to call the person who made the statement to give evidence, the court may, on application, allow another party to call and cross-examine the person who made the statement on its contents.

(2) An application under paragraph (1) shall be made on notice to all other parties not later than 28 days after service of the hearsay notice.

(3) Where the court allows another party to call and cross-examine the person who made the statement, it may give such directions as it thinks fit to secure the attendance of that person and as to the procedure to be followed.][1]

[1] *Substituted by County Court (Amendment) (No. 3) Rules 1996 (S.I. 1996 No. 3218).*

[Credibility

17.—(1) If

(a) a party tenders as hearsay evidence a statement made by a person but does not call the person who made the statement to give oral evidence, and

(b) another party wishes to attack the credibility of the person who made the statement; that other party shall notify the party tendering the hearsay evidence of his intention.

(2) A notice under paragraph (1) shall be given not later than 28 days after service of the hearsay notice.][1]

[1] *Substituted by County Court (Amendment) (No. 3) Rules 1996 (S.I. 1996 No.3218).*

[Evidence of findings on foreign law

25.—(1) Subject to the provisions of this rule, a party who intends to adduce in evidence a finding or decision on a question of foreign law by virtue of section 4 (2) of the Civil Evidence Act 1972 shall, not less than 14 days before the day fixed for the trial or hearing or within such other period as the court may specify, serve notice of his intention on every other party to the proceedings.

(2) The notice shall specify the question on which the finding or decision was given or made and specify the document in which it is reported or recorded in citable form.

(3) In any action or matter in which evidence may be given by affidavit, an affidavit specifying the matters contained in paragraph (2) shall constitute notice under paragraph (1) if served within the period mentioned in that paragraph.

(4) Unless in any particular case the court otherwise directs, paragraph (1) shall not apply to an action or matter in which no defence or answer has been filed.][1]

[1] *Substituted by County Court (Amendment) (No. 3) Rules 1996 (S.I. 1996 No. 3218).*

Part V Expert evidence

Restrictions on adducing expert evidence

27—(1) [Except—

(a) with the leave of the court,

(b) in accordance with the provisions of Order 17, rule 11, or

(c) where all parties agree,][1]

no expert evidence may be adduced at the trial or hearing of an action or matter, unless the party seeking to adduce the evidence has applied to the court to determine whether a direction should be given under rule 37, 38 or 41 (whichever is appropriate) of RSC Order 38, as applied by rule 28 of this Order, and has complied with any direction given on the application.

(2) Nothing in paragraph (1) shall apply to expert evidence which is permitted to be given by affidavit or which is to be adduced in an action or matter in which no defence or answer has been filed or in proceedings referred to arbitration under [section 64][2] of the Act.

(3) Nothing in paragraph (1) shall affect the enforcement under any other provision of these rules (except Order 29, rule 1) of a direction given under this Part of this Order.

[1] *Substituted by County Court (Amendment No. 3) Rules 1990 (S.I. No. 1764).*
[2] *Substituted by County Court (Amendment No. 2) Rules 1984 (S.I. No. 878).*

Application of RSC

28 RSC Order 38, rules 37 to 44 shall apply in relation to an application under rule 27 of this Order as they apply in relation to an application under rule 36(1) of the said Order 38.

. . . . .

Appendix E
Updating Awards

The Inflation Table

By applying the multiplier shown in the Inflation Table practitioners will be able to convert, with relative simplicity, an earlier award into "money of the day", to use Lord Diplock's phrase. The result will be sufficiently accurate for most purposes, even though the earlier award may have been made in some month other than January or the month in which the calculation is to be made may itself not be January.

This table was referred to by Megaw L.J. in *Gammell v. Wilson* [1982] A.C. 27 at p. 421B as "the helpful table in *Kemp & Kemp's Quantum of Damages*".

In *Walker v. John McLean & Sons Ltd* [1979] 1 W.L.R. 760 Cumming-Bruce LJ, giving the judgment of the court, said: "Counsel for both parties before us accepted for the purpose of argument the accuracy of the table [in] *Kemp & Kemp* showing the value of the £ at various dates".

In this context the following passage from Lord Diplock's speech in *Wright v. British Railways Board* [1983] A.C. 773 at p. 782C should be noted:

> "If judges carry out their duty of assessing damages for non-economic loss in the money of the day at the date of the trial—*and this is a rule of practice that judges are required to follow, not a guide line from which they have a discretion to depart* if there are special circumstances that justify their doing so—there are two routes by which the judge's task of arriving at the appropriate conventional rate of interest to be applied to the damages so assessed can be approached. *The starting point for each of them is to ascertain from the appropriate table of retail price indices covering the period between service of the writ and trial what would have been the equivalent of those damages in the money of the day at the date of service reckoned in pounds sterling at the higher value that then stood at the very beginning of the period for which simple interest is to be given.* That figure represents both the real, and what was then the nominal value also, of the sum of money for the loss of which the plaintiff is to be compensated by interest. Such interest, *like the damages*

> *on which it is to be given*, is to be calculated in the money of the day at the date of trial, the real value of which has been depreciated by the full amount of inflation that has taken place since the date of service of the writ. [Emphasis added.]

The logic of this passage from Lord Diplock's speech clearly requires that judges, when having regard to previous comparable awards, should ascertain from the appropriate table of retail indices what has been the decrease in the value of money since the date of a particular comparable award in order that their award "in the money of the day" may be truly comparable in real terms with the earlier award.

THE RETAIL PRICES INDEX

For the most accurate calculations, the Retail Price Index should be used. A simple formula can then be used to determine the value of the damages award at today's date. The formula used is:

$$\text{damages at today's date} = \frac{A}{B} \times \text{damages at date of judgment,}$$

where A = the RPI at today's date
and B = the RPI at the date of judgment

As an example, say a judgment was given in February 1992 for £65,000. To determine what this judgment is worth at January 1995, using the formula, gives:

$$\text{damages at January 1995} = \frac{146.00}{136.30} \times £65{,}000$$

$$= £69{,}625$$

Using the inflation table, the multiplier to use would be the one for 1992, ie 1.06. This means that the rough figure would be

$$= 1.06 \times £65{,}000$$

$$= £68{,}900$$

Inflation table showing the value of £ at various dates

In the left-hand column of this table is the year and in the right-hand column the multiplier which should be applied to the £ in January of that year to show its value in terms of the £ in January 1995.

Year	*Multiplier*	*Year*	*Multiplier*
1948	21.05	1974	6.34
1949	20.13	1975	5.29
1950	19.42	1976	4.29
1951	18.70	1977	3.68
1952	16.56	1978	3.35
1953	15.86	1979	3.06
1954	15.64	1980	2.59
1955	15.03	1981	2.29
1956	14.29	1982	2.04
1957	13.70	1983	1.95
1958	13.22	1984	1.85
1959	12.95	1985	1.76
1960	13.01	1986	1.67
1961	12.73	1987	1.61
1962	12.16	1988	1.56
1963	11.85	1989	1.45
1964	11.62	1990	1.35
1965	11.11	1991	1.24
1966	10.64	1992	1.19
1967	10.27	1993	1.17
1968	10.01	1994	1.14
1969	9.43	1995	1.10
1970	8.98	1996	1.07
1971	8.28	1997	1.04
1972	7.65	1998	1.01
1973	7.10		

This table has been calculated from the official Retail Prices Index, the value of the £ being taken from the figures published in January of each year, ending with January 1995. It was kindly prepared by J Prevett, OBE, FIA. The table is regularly updated in *Kemp & Kemp*, Vol I, p. 131.

	Jan	Feb	Mar	Apr	May	June	July	Aug	Sep	Oct	Nov	Dec
1998	159.50	160.30	160.80	162.60	163.50	163.40	163.00	163.70	164.40			
1997	154.40	155.00	155.40	156.30	156.90	157.50	157.50	158.50	159.30	159.30	159.60	160.00
1996	150.20	150.90	151.50	152.60	152.90	153.00	152.40	153.10	153.80	153.80	153.90	154.40
1995	146.00	146.90	147.50	149.00	149.60	149.80	149.10	149.90	150.60	149.80	149.80	150.70
1994	141.30	142.10	142.50	144.20	144.70	144.70	144.00	144.70	145.00	145.20	145.30	146.00
1993	137.90	138.80	139.30	140.60	141.10	141.00	140.70	141.30	141.90	141.80	141.60	141.90
1992	135.60	136.30	136.70	138.80	139.30	139.30	138.80	138.90	139.40	139.90	139.70	139.20
1991	130.20	130.90	131.40	133.10	133.50	134.10	133.80	134.10	134.60	135.10	135.60	135.70
1990	119.50	120.20	121.40	125.10	126.20	126.70	126.80	128.10	129.30	130.30	130.00	120.90
1989	111.00	111.80	112.30	114.30	115.00	115.40	115.50	115.80	116.60	117.50	118.50	118.80
1988	103.30	103.70	104.10	105.80	106.20	106.60	106.70	107.90	108.40	109.50	110.00	110.30
1987	100.00	100.40	100.60	101.80	101.90	101.90	101.80	102.10	102.40	102.90	103.40	103.30
1986	96.25	96.60	96.73	97.67	97.85	97.79	97.52	97.82	98.30	98.45	99.29	99.62
1985	91.20	91.94	92.80	94.78	95.21	95.41	95.23	95.49	95.44	95.59	95.92	96.05
1984	86.84	87.20	87.48	88.64	88.97	89.20	89.10	89.94	90.11	90.67	90.95	90.87
1983	82.61	82.97	83.12	84.28	84.64	84.84	85.30	85.68	86.06	86.36	86.67	86.89
1982	78.73	78.76	79.44	81.04	81.62	81.85	81.88	81.90	81.85	82.26	82.66	82.51
1981	70.29	70.93	71.99	74.07	74.55	74.98	75.31	75.87	76.30	76.98	77.79	78.28
1980	62.18	63.07	63.93	66.11	66.72	67.35	67.91	68.06	68.49	68.92	69.48	69.86
1979	52.52	52.95	53.38	54.30	54.73	55.67	58.07	58.53	59.11	59.72	60.25	60.68
1978	48.04	48.31	48.62	49.33	49.61	49.99	50.22	50.54	50.75	50.98	51.33	51.76
1977	43.70	44.13	44.56	45.70	46.06	46.54	46.59	46.82	47.07	47.28	47.50	47.76
1976	37.49	37.97	38.17	38.91	39.34	39.54	39.62	40.18	40.71	41.44	42.03	42.59
1975	30.39	30.90	31.51	32.72	34.09	34.75	35.11	35.31	35.61	36.12	36.55	37.01
1974	25.35	25.78	26.01	26.89	27.28	27.55	27.81	27.83	28.14	28.69	29.20	29.63
1973	22.64	22.78	22.92	23.35	23.52	23.64	23.75	23.82	24.03	24.50	24.69	24.87
1972	21.01	21.12	21.19	21.38	21.49	21.63	21.70	21.87	21.99	22.30	22.37	22.49
1971	19.43	19.53	19.69	20.11	20.25	20.39	20.51	20.52	20.55	20.67	20.79	20.89
1970	17.91	18.00	18.11	18.38	18.44	18.49	18.62	18.61	18.70	18.90	19.03	19.16

	Jan	*Feb*	*Mar*	*Apr*	*May*	*June*	*July*	*Aug*	*Sep*	*Oct*	*Nov*	*Dec*
1969	17.06	17.15	17.22	17.41	17.38	17.46	17.46	17.42	17.47	17.60	17.64	17.76
1968	16.07	16.15	16.20	16.49	16.51	16.57	16.59	16.61	16.63	16.71	16.74	16.97
1967	15.66	15.67	15.67	15.79	15.78	15.85	15.75	15.71	15.70	15.82	15.91	16.02
1966	15.11	15.12	15.15	15.33	15.44	15.48	15.41	15.50	15.48	15.52	15.61	15.63
1965	14.47	14.47	14.52	14.80	14.85	14.89	14.89	14.92	14.93	14.95	15.01	15.08
1964	13.84	13.85	13.90	14.02	14.14	14.19	14.19	14.25	14.25	14.26	14.38	14.43
1963	13.57	13.69	13.71	13.74	13.73	13.73	13.65	13.61	13.65	13.71	13.74	13.77
1962	13.22	13.23	13.28	13.47	13.51	13.60	13.55	13.43	13.41	13.40	13.45	13.52
1961	12.63	12.63	12.68	12.74	12.78	12.89	12.89	13.01	12.99	13.01	13.15	13.17
1960	12.36	12.36	12.34	12.41	12.41	12.47	12.50	12.42	12.43	12.53	12.59	12.62
1959	12.42	12.41	12.41	12.32	12.27	12.29	12.26	12.29	12.23	12.28	12.37	12.40
1958	12.16	12.10	12.19	12.33	12.28	12.40	12.20	12.18	12.19	12.31	12.35	12.40
1957	11.74	11.73	11.71	11.75	11.77	11.89	11.99	11.97	11.93	12.05	12.11	12.17
1956	11.25	11.25	11.39	11.55	11.53	11.52	11.47	11.51	11.48	11.55	11.60	11.63
1955	10.70	10.70	10.70	10.76	10.74	10.97	11.00	10.93	11.00	11.11	11.29	11.29
1954	10.28	10.26	10.35	10.39	10.36	10.42	10.60	10.53	10.51	10.56	10.61	10.66
1953	10.14	10.17	10.24	10.33	10.30	10.35	10.35	10.29	10.27	10.27	10.30	10.26
1952	9.71	9.72	9.77	9.93	9.93	10.09	10.08	10.02	10.00	10.09	10.08	10.15
1951	8.60	8.68	8.74	8.88	9.10	9.13	9.27	9.31	9.38	9.44	9.48	9.54
1950	8.28	8.30	8.32	8.35	8.37	8.33	8.33	8.30	8.35	8.44	8.47	8.52
1949	7.99	8.01	7.98	7.96	8.11	8.14	8.15	8.16	8.19	8.23	8.23	8.25
1948	7.64	7.78	7.80	7.91	7.90	8.04	7.92	7.92	7.93	7.95	7.97	7.98
1947	–	–	–	–	–	7.33	7.38	7.34	7.37	7.43	7.58	7.60

Index

All references are to paragraph number